Lecture Notes in Artificial Intelligence   10630

Subseries of Lecture Notes in Computer Science

LNAI Series Editors

Randy Goebel
   University of Alberta, Edmonton, Canada
Yuzuru Tanaka
   Hokkaido University, Sapporo, Japan
Wolfgang Wahlster
   DFKI and Saarland University, Saarbrücken, Germany

LNAI Founding Series Editor

Joerg Siekmann
   DFKI and Saarland University, Saarbrücken, Germany

More information about this series at http://www.springer.com/series/1244

Max Bramer · Miltos Petridis (Eds.)

Artificial Intelligence XXXIV

37th SGAI International Conference
on Artificial Intelligence, AI 2017
Cambridge, UK, December 12–14, 2017
Proceedings

 Springer

Editors
Max Bramer
University of Portsmouth
Portsmouth
UK

Miltos Petridis
Middlesex University
London
UK

ISSN 0302-9743   ISSN 1611-3349 (electronic)
Lecture Notes in Artificial Intelligence
ISBN 978-3-319-71077-8   ISBN 978-3-319-71078-5 (eBook)
https://doi.org/10.1007/978-3-319-71078-5

Library of Congress Control Number: 2017958571

LNCS Sublibrary: SL7 – Artificial Intelligence

© Springer International Publishing AG 2017
This work is subject to copyright. All rights are reserved by the Publisher, whether the whole or part of the material is concerned, specifically the rights of translation, reprinting, reuse of illustrations, recitation, broadcasting, reproduction on microfilms or in any other physical way, and transmission or information storage and retrieval, electronic adaptation, computer software, or by similar or dissimilar methodology now known or hereafter developed.
The use of general descriptive names, registered names, trademarks, service marks, etc. in this publication does not imply, even in the absence of a specific statement, that such names are exempt from the relevant protective laws and regulations and therefore free for general use.
The publisher, the authors and the editors are safe to assume that the advice and information in this book are believed to be true and accurate at the date of publication. Neither the publisher nor the authors or the editors give a warranty, express or implied, with respect to the material contained herein or for any errors or omissions that may have been made. The publisher remains neutral with regard to jurisdictional claims in published maps and institutional affiliations.

Printed on acid-free paper

This Springer imprint is published by Springer Nature
The registered company is Springer International Publishing AG
The registered company address is: Gewerbestrasse 11, 6330 Cham, Switzerland

Preface

This volume, entitled *Artificial Intelligence XXXIV*, comprises the refereed papers presented at AI-2017, the 37th SGAI International Conference on Innovative Techniques and Applications of Artificial Intelligence, held in Cambridge in December 2017 in both the technical and the application streams. The conference was organized by SGAI, the British Computer Society Specialist Group on Artificial Intelligence.

The volume is the successor to *Research and Development in Intelligent Systems XXXIII* and *Applications and Innovations in Intelligent Systems XXIV*, which comprised the proceedings of AI-2016, and brings the two series together.

The technical papers included present new and innovative developments in the field, divided into sections on "Machine Learning and Neural Networks" and "Machine Learning, Speech and Vision, and Fuzzy Logic." This year's Donald Michie Memorial Award for the best refereed technical paper was won by the paper entitled "Using Constraint Satisfaction Problem Solving to Enable Workflow Flexibility by Deviation" by L. Grumbach and R. Bergmann (University of Trier, Germany).

The application papers included present innovative applications of AI techniques in a number of subject domains. This year, the papers are divided into sections on "AI for Healthcare", "Applications of Machine Learning", "Applications of Neural Networks and Fuzzy Logic", "Case-Based Reasoning", and "AI Techniques". This year's Rob Milne Memorial Award for the best refereed application paper was won by the paper entitled "Cable Belief Networks" by A. Ferguson and S. Thompson (BT Labs, UK).

The volume also includes the text of short papers in both streams presented as posters at the conference.

On behalf of the conference Organizing Committee we would like to thank all those who contributed to the organization of this year's programme, in particular the Programme Committee members, the Executive Programme Committees, and our administrators Mandy Bauer and Bryony Bramer.

October 2017
Max Bramer
Miltos Petridis

Organization

AI-2017 Conference Committee

Conference Chair

Max Bramer   University of Portsmouth, UK

Technical Programme Chair

Max Bramer   University of Portsmouth, UK

Application Programme Chair

Miltos Petridis   Middlesex University, UK

Deputy Application Programme Chair

Jixin Ma   University of Greenwich, UK

Workshop Organizer

Adrian Hopgood   University of Portsmouth, UK

Treasurer

Rosemary Gilligan

Poster Session Organizer

Nirmalie Wiratunga   Robert Gordon University, Aberdeen, UK

AI Open Mic and Panel Session Organizer

Andrew Lea   Amplifying Life, UK

Publicity Organizer

Frederic Stahl   University of Reading, UK

FAIRS 2017

Giovanna Martinez   University of Nottingham, UK

UK CBR Organizer

Miltos Petridis   Middlesex University, UK

Conference Administrator

Mandy Bauer   BCS

Paper Administrator

Bryony Bramer

Technical Executive Programme Committee

Max Bramer	University of Portsmouth, UK (Chair)
Frans Coenen	University of Liverpool, UK
John Kingston	University of Brighton, UK

Applications Executive Programme Committee

Miltos Petridis	Middlesex University, UK (Chair)
Rosemary Gilligan	University of Hertfordshire, UK
Stelios Kapetanakis	University of Brighton, UK
Andrew Lea	Amplifying Life, UK
Richard Wheeler	University of Edinburgh, UK

Technical Programme Committee

Andreas Albrecht	Middlesex University, UK
Abdallah Arioua	IATE INRA, France
Raed Batbooti	University of Swansea, UK; University of Basra, Iraq
Yaxin Bi	Ulster University, UK
Mirko Boettcher	University of Magdeburg, Germany
Max Bramer	University of Portsmouth, UK
Krysia Broda	Imperial College, University of London, UK
Ken Brown	University College Cork, Ireland
Marcos Bueno	Radboud University Nijmegen, The Netherlands
Frans Coenen	University of Liverpool, UK
Ireneusz Czarnowski	Gdynia Maritime University, Poland
Frank Eichinger	DATEV eG, Nuremberg, Germany
Mohamed Gaber	Robert Gordon University Aberdeen, UK
Hossein Ghodrati Noushahr	De Montfort University, Leicester, UK
Adriana Giret	Universidad Politecnica de Valencia, Spain
Wael Hamdan	MIMOS Berhad., Kuala Lumpur, Malaysia
Peter Hampton	Ulster University, UK
Chris Headleand	University of Lincoln, UK
Adrian Hopgood	University of Portsmouth, UK
Zina Ibrahim	Kings College, London, UK
Navneet Kesher	Facebook, Seattle WA, USA
John Kingston	University of Brighton, UK
Konstantinos Kotis	University of Piraeus, Greece
Ivan Koychev	University of Sofia, Bulgaria
Nicole Lee	University of Hong Kong, SAR China

Anne Liret	British Telecom France
Fernando Lopes	LNEG-National Research Institute, Portugal
Jixin Ma	University of Greenwich, UK
Stephen Matthews	Newcastle University, UK
Silja Meyer-Nieberg	Universität der Bundeswehr München, Germany
Roberto Micalizio	Università di Torino, Italy
Daniel Neagu	University of Bradford, UK
Lars Nolle	Jade University of Applied Sciences, Germany
Joanna Isabelle Olszewska	University of Gloucestershire, UK
Dan O'Leary	University of Southern California, USA
Juan Jose Rodriguez	University of Burgos, Spain
Fernando Saenz-Perez	Universidad Complutense de Madrid, Spain
Miguel A. Salido	Universidad Politecnica de Valencia, Spain
Rainer Schmidt	University Medicine of Rostock, Germany
Sid Shakya	BT TSO – Research & Technology, UK
Frederic Stahl	University of Reading, UK
Simon Thompson	BT Innovate, UK
M.R.C. van Dongen	University College Cork, Ireland
Martin Wheatman	Yagadi Ltd., UK
Graham Winstanley	University of Brighton, UK
Nirmalie Wiratunga	Robert Gordon University, UK

Application Programme Committee

Hatem Ahriz	Robert Gordon University, UK
Tony Allen	Nottingham Trent University, UK
Ines Arana	Robert Gordon University, UK
Mercedes Arguello Casteleiro	University of Manchester, UK
Juan Carlos Augusto	Middlesex University London, UK
Ken Brown	University College Cork, Ireland
Nikolay Burlutskiy	ContextVision AB, UK
Xiaochun Cheng	Middlesex University London, UK
Sarah Jane Delany	Dublin Institute of Technology, Ireland
Richard Ellis	Helyx SIS Ltd., UK
Roger Evans	University of Brighton, UK
Andrew Fish	University of Brighton, UK
Yvonne Fryer	University of Greenwich, UK
Rosemary Gilligan	University of Hertfordshire, UK
John Gordon	AKRI Ltd., UK
Chris Hinde	Loughborough University, UK
Adrian Hopgood	University of Portsmouth, UK
Chris Huyck	Middlesex University, UK
Carl James-Reynolds	Middlesex University, UK
Stelios Kapetanakis	University of Brighton, UK
Jixin Ma	University of Greenwich, UK

Lars Nolle   Jade University of Applied Sciences, Germany
Sanjib Raj Pandey   International Study Center, University of Sussex, UK
Miltos Petridis   Middlesex University, UK
Elena Irena Popa   University of Greenwich, UK
Miguel A. Salido   Universidad Politecnica de Valencia, Spain
Roger Tait   Birmingham City University, UK
Richard Wheeler   Edinburgh Scientific, UK
Markus Wolf   University of Greenwich, UK
Patrick Wong   Open University, UK

Contents

Short Technical Papers

Application Stream Papers

AI for Healthcare

Short Application Papers

Technical Stream Papers

Papers Included in the Technical Stream of AI-2017

The following four sections comprise refereed papers accepted for the technical stream of AI-2017 divided into the following categories:

- Best Technical Paper
- Machine Learning and Neural Networks
- Machine Learning, Speech and Vision, and Fuzzy Logic
- Short Technical Papers

The winner of the Donald Michie Memorial Award for the best refereed technical paper in the conference was the paper "Using Constraint Satisfaction Problem Solving to Enable Workflow Flexibility by Deviation" by L. Grumbach and R. Bergmann (University of Trier, Germany).

The final section comprises the text of short technical papers which were presented as posters at the conference.

Using Constraint Satisfaction Problem Solving to Enable Workflow Flexibility by Deviation (Best Technical Paper)

Lisa Grumbach(✉) and Ralph Bergmann

University of Trier, Trier, Germany
{grumbach,bergmann}@uni-trier.de

Abstract. This paper introduces a novel approach for flexible workflow management by applying constraint satisfaction problem solving. This enables us to support workflow deviations at runtime, react to upcoming events or unpredictable circumstances, but still support the user through worklist suggestions. The developed workflow engine is completely based on declarative workflow representations, whereas procedural languages are used for workflow modeling. The described approach is fully implemented and our experiments demonstrate sufficient runtime performance for practical use.

Keywords: Workflow management · Flexibility by Deviation · Declarative workflow · Constraint satisfaction problem solving

1 Introduction

In small and medium-sized enterprises (SMEs) there is a strong demand for support concerning management of documents, business data, and processes as well as a need for supervision and control of all running and completed transactions [15]. Especially for employees who are unaware of common processes, a Process-Aware Information System (PAIS, [1]) would be of advantage, as they may profit from guidance concerning ideal workflow execution and task suggestion. Additionally, compliance concerning standards and guidelines would be facilitated, as benefit for the enterprises. However, the use of PAISs has not yet been broadly established in SMEs. A reason for this is that current PAISs control process execution by traditional workflow engines in which workflows are prescribed without providing any flexibility to deviate, if necessary [5,16]. This is a particular problem in SMEs as their processes are only slightly standardized and weakly structured and may vary significantly from case to case [9,18].

Artificial Intelligence (AI) is a key technology for various support strategies in Business Process Management (BPM), as it allows for automated decision making and thus, facilitates the users work. Allowing flexibility requires such intelligent technologies, as the user should only be guided executing a workflow and not be burdened with taking difficult decisions that could be automated.

© Springer International Publishing AG 2017
M. Bramer and M. Petridis (Eds.): SGAI-AI 2017, LNAI 10630, pp. 3–17, 2017.
https://doi.org/10.1007/978-3-319-71078-5_1

Declarative workflows are a means of implicitly offering flexibility but therefore require technologies from the field of AI for workflow control. DECLARE [2] is a tool suite for declarative workflow modeling and enactment. Declarative models consist of constraints which define undesired behaviour. Constraints are then transformed to finite-state automata which allow for reasoning about workflow states. A drawback of this approach is that this transformation process is inefficient for more than about 50 constraints [10] and thus runtime support for changing circumstances is not provided. With an approach based on constraint satisfaction problem (CSP) solving we aim at achieving model changes at runtime efficiently, as constraints can simply be added or retracted without the need of a transformation. Furthermore with a combination of imperative and declarative paradigms the presented approach leads to an increased flexibility.

In this paper we present an approach for flexible workflow execution utilizing CSP solving to handle occurring deviations and to control worklist suggestions. First, the foundations concerning flexible workflow management are sketched, followed by the introduction of our new concept for combining imperative and declarative paradigms for flexible workflow execution. This approach is further described by algorithms which are based on CSP solving. Furthermore, our experimental results as well as a brief outlook on future work are described.

2 Foundations and Related Work

A workflow is "the automation of a business process, in whole or part, during which documents, information or tasks are passed from one participant to another for action, according to a set of procedural rules" [22]. A Workflow Management System (WfMS) supports the execution of workflows by a workflow engine that interprets the process definitions and interacts with a worklist handler, which is in charge of assigning work items to users.

Workflow Flexibility. Traditional WfMS are rigid and do not allow any deviations from modeled workflows. Users feel restricted and such systems are rapidly considered as a burden. Thus, users bypass the systems, which is counterproductive for attaining the expected benefits [5]. Consequently, PAISs that allow a workflow to flexibly deviate are essential for efficiency in SMEs. Schonenberg et al. [17] distinguish between four kinds of workflow flexibility: Flexibility by Design, Change, Underspecification, and Deviation. The first three types require either complete knowledge about all possible workflow executions at design-time or demand a remodeling at run-time. Hence, a flexible reaction to sudden changing circumstances during run-time is prevented, or actions are required to manually change the process instance, which is impossible for inexperienced users. "Flexibility by Deviation is the ability for a process instance to deviate at runtime from the execution path prescribed by the original process without altering its process model" [17]. Although this approach eliminates the previously mentioned disadvantages, little research exists on how to implement this approach.

Only the system FLOWer [3] implements this idea to a limited extent by allowing the user to skip, undo, or redo a task or to insert a new task, but still the user has to intervene manually to obtain flexibility.

Workflow Modeling Paradigms. Workflow modeling paradigms range from imperative (procedural) to declarative [6]. Imperatively modeled workflows explicitly specify all possible allowed execution paths, for example using a flow-based modeling language such as BPEL [4]. Here, the control flow of tasks as well as the related flow of data items is modeled, which results in a high complexity and a huge modeling effort. Declarative workflows, however, define forbidden behavior and states of the workflow. Imperative workflows only describe a subset of valid procedures, while declarative constructs describe specific undesired states, leading to the acceptance of every other state [11] and thus, implicitly providing flexibility concerning workflow execution.

Current declarative workflow approaches such as DECLARE [2], formally base on Linear Temporal Logic formulae representing constraints, which are further transformed into finite-state automata, used for constraint validation and thus as workflow engine and for worklist handling. Though there is a differentiation between mandatory and optional constraints, and optional constraints may be violated, a possibility to retract constraints is not specified and therefore no unforeseen situation can be handled with flexibility. The concept of DCR graphs [8] is described as offering more flexibility, but also has no possibility to restore consistency after deviations. In later work Maggi et al. [10] developed an approach, called Mobucon, based on colored automata, with the ability to detect deviations and in addition to support continuously through various strategies. A drawback of this approach is that these strategies need to be determined beforehand, and cannot be changed during runtime, as the construction of a new automaton would take too long (for 30–50 constraints 5–10 s) [10]. Algorithms developed by Westergaard [21] also solve this issue with efficient runtime modifications, e.g. models with up to 50 constraints are handled in less seconds.

Our approach also aims at achieving efficient automated runtime modifications and thus requires the ability to react adequately to deviations, even to undesired situations. A main difference between related work and our approach is that our workflow control bases on the interpretation of incoming documents and their semantic information. The identification of semantic information has a significant impact on workflow control and can be easily defined as logical constraints. Furthermore constraints can be added or retracted ad-hoc, without the need of a time-consuming recompilation of the model. Therefore we regard the identification of executable tasks as constraint satisfaction problem.

3 Concept of the Workflow Engine

With the presented concept we aim to increase the acceptance of users, as the presented concept does not prescribe, but still guides, if needed. Additionally, transactions are logged for monitoring purposes. The implementation of Flexibility by Deviation as presented in this paper is embedded in the SEMAFLEX[1]-architecture [7], which semantically integrates flexible workflow management with knowledge-based document management and will be developed further in the SEMANAS[2] project. An important characteristic is that the information about task enactment can either result from a user interaction, e.g. a manual selection of a task being performed, or due to upcoming documents, which are analyzed automatically and mapped to a certain task, whose enactment is derived subsequently. These logged task enactments construct the actually conducted workflow as a sequence of activities that have been performed. While the workflow engine proposes tasks which should be done next, the user is not forced to follow these suggestions. In principle, the user is able to do what s/he wants and in which order s/he wants. S/he can either follow the tasks in the worklist, suggesting the standard course of action, or do something else and upload documents created as a result of what s/he did. Through both, explicitly completing a task and uploading documents, the actual workflow is identified and recorded. Progress in turn affects the worklist handling, including detected deviations.

3.1 Combination of Imperative and Declarative Paradigms

For a suitable representation of the workflows concerning this concept, we explicitly differentiate between modeled workflow, *de jure workflow*, and executed workflow, *de facto workflow* [1]. The de facto workflow is an actually enacted instance derived from a de jure workflow. Thus, it stores the actually conducted transactions and might deviate from the de jure workflow.

In our approach de jure workflows are modeled procedurally, as it is more intuitive and comprehensible than declarative modeling [12]. The workflow engine, however, is completely based on a declarative representation, as this paradigm implicitly offers flexibility concerning execution. To reach a maximum of flexibility, we transform the de jure workflow into declarative constraints, which are used to control the suggested execution order of tasks, but which are not regarded as mandatory and consequently might be violated. Hence, the de jure workflow is only considered as guidance, but deviations are tolerated. Nevertheless, some deviations are critical and should never occur, considering e.g. compliance or safety aspects. For this reason, additional mandatory constraints can be modeled manually, to explicitly specify invalid workflow states. Those are possibly connected with a severity specification, a warning message or even a proposed corrective measure, in case the constraint is violated. Such mandatory constraints can refer to the execution order of the tasks within a de jure workflow or they could be global constraints specifying order constraints across classes of workflows. Of course those mandatory constraints might actually be violated by the user, as the workflow engine never prescribes an activity and thus is not

[1] SEMAFLEX is funded by Stiftung Rheinland-Pfalz für Innovation, grant no. 1158.
[2] SEMANAS is funded by the Federal Ministry of Education and Research (BMBF), grant no. 13FH013IX6.

able to actively prevent violations. Nevertheless, the violation of constraints can be detected. Depending on the kind of constraint violation the workflow engine shall be able to react adequately. If a non-mandatory constraint is violated, the deviation is not critical, but the workflow engine must reason about the next task to propose. If a mandatory constraint is violated, a warning is issued or a corrective measure is performed according to what is specified for the constraint.

3.2   Declarative Workflow Representation

For the declarative workflow representation, we utilize five different constraint types of the DECLARE language [2], which countervail possible deviations:

- Precedence(t_a, t_b): Task t_b can only be executed after t_a.
- Response(t_a, t_b): Task t_a requires the enactment of t_b.
- Existence(t_a): Task t_a is mandatory.
- Not Co-Existence(t_a, t_b): Task t_a and t_b exclude each other.
- Absence(t_a, x): Task t_a can only be executed x times.

Precedence and Response prevent undesirable skipping, concerning previous or subsequent tasks. Existence contradicts the undoing of a task. Redoing and creating additional instances of a task are intercepted by the constraint Absence. Not Co-Existence avoid invoking undesired task enactments.

Preventing the user from constraint violations in our case can only be achieved, if the user manually chooses tasks from the worklist, as only such tasks are proposed that lead to a valid workflow state. As non-mandatory constraints might be violated, the worklist could consider tasks that contradict these constraints but with lower priority. Mandatory constraints should never be disregarded. Worklist handling is easy for procedurally modeled workflows, if no deviations are possible. However, if a deviation occurs, one would not be able to suggest an appropriate further proceeding. Constraints suit this situation perfectly, as even if one is violated, it might be retracted, and still valid suggestions can be computed with the help of remaining constraints. How valid task suggestions are identified, will be explained in the following section.

A prerequisite for the presented enactment approach is that each construct of the de jure workflow, modeled imperatively, is automatically transformed into corresponding declarative expressions.

3.3   Transformation into Declarative Constructs

We consider the essential structures of imperative modeling languages on the basis of Weske [20]. The transformation rules, as described in Table 1, are defined analogously to [19], who in contrast uses Relation Algebra as formal specification language. The resulting constraints are used for validating upcoming enactment states of the workflow and for proposing tasks enabled for execution. The following section describes the algorithm that computes possible task suggestions on the basis of these declarative constraints.

Table 1. Mapping imperative workflow patterns to declarative constructs

Pattern	Example	Corresponding Constraints
Sequence	A → B	Precedence(A,B)
Xor-Split	A → X → B, C	Precedence(A,B) and Precedence(A,C)
Xor-Join	B, C → X → D	Precedence(B,D) or Precedence(C,D)
Xor-Sequences	X → A → B → X, X → C → D → X	Not Co-Existence(A,C) and Not Co-Existence(B,C) and Not Co-Existence(A,D) and Not Co-Existence(B,D)
And-Split	A → + → B, C	Precedence(A,B) and Precedence(A,C)
And-Join	B, C → + → D	Precedence(B,D) and Precedence(C,D)

4   Worklist Handling by Means of Constraint Satisfaction Problem Solving

According to Russell and Norvig [14] a constraint satisfaction problem (CSP) is defined by a set of *decision variables* $X = \{X_1, X_2, ..., X_n\}$ and a set of *constraints* $C = \{C_1, C_2, ..., C_m\}$. Each decision variable has a *domain* D_i, which is a nonempty set of possible values for X_i. A constraint C_j is a relation over a subset of the variables $\{X_k, ..., X_l\}$, specifying the set of combination of allowed values. An assignment of values to some or all of the variables is called *state* of the problem, which is denoted as *consistent*, if it does not violate any constraint. If values are assigned to every variable, the assignment is named *complete*. A consistent and simultaneously complete assignment is called *solution*. In the following we formulate the problem of selecting the next tasks for execution in case of deviation from the de jure workflow as a constraint satisfaction problem.

4.1   Application of CSP Solving

The CSP solving algorithm is applied during workflow execution at the start of each workflow and after each task enactment. The initial state for the algorithm is a partially completed workflow, the de facto workflow, and its corresponding ideal course of events, the de jure workflow. The desired output is the set of tasks, called worklist, that can be enacted next without violating constraints.

To utilize CSP solving for worklist handling, we regard the workflow tasks as decision variables $X = T$. For each task $j_i \in J = \{j_0, \ldots, j_{n-1}\}$ of the de jure workflow, a variable t_{j_i} is created and added to T. Subsequently, T is supplemented with one single variable t_{end}, to be able to determine whether the workflow has completed. To simplify the explanation of the algorithm we regard only single executions of tasks until now, but in Sect. 4.4 extend the CSP to be able to handle loop patterns and repeated task executions.

The assignment of values to tasks represents a sequential order of all tasks, including not only already executed tasks, but also possible future executions of tasks. Thus, a valid order, determined by ascending integer values, of tasks is calculated. As the only thing of interest is, which task may be executed next at a specific point in time, it does not matter if any other tasks might be or have been executed in parallel. Consequently, the domain for each decision variable is a set of integer values $D_i = \{0, 1, \ldots, n\}$, with n as the number of tasks extracted from the de jure workflow including the additional variable t_{cnd}.

As the assignment represents a sequential execution order of all tasks, the first given constraint (see (1)) states that each assigned value of a decision variable is different from all others. Thus, only a bijective mapping of domain values to decision variables is a *solution* to the CSP.

$$C = \{alldifferent\,(T)\,, \tag{1}$$
$$t_i = c_i, \ldots \qquad \text{(for de facto)} \tag{2}$$
$$t_a < t_b, \qquad Precedence(t_a, t_b) \tag{3}$$
$$(t_{end} < t_a) \vee (t_a < t_b \wedge t_b < t_{end}), \qquad Response(t_a, t_b) \tag{4}$$
$$t_a < t_{end}, \qquad Existence(t_a) \tag{5}$$
$$(t_{end} < t_b) \vee (t_{end} < t_a), \qquad Not\ Co\text{-}Existence(t_a, t_b) \tag{6}$$
$$(s_i = a_1) \Rightarrow (t_{end} < t_2), \tag{7}$$
$$\wedge\, (s_i = a_2) \Rightarrow (t_{end} < t_1)\} \tag{8}$$

Second, as we apply the CSP at a specific point in time during execution of the workflow, some tasks are already enacted and therefore the respective variables have a fixed assignment c_i, which is a constant value specifying the sequential execution position in the de facto workflow (see (2)). All additional constraints either result from the transformation of imperatively modeled workflow to declarative language constructs or originate from manually modeled mandatory constraints. Each type of constraint has a corresponding formal definition to be used in the CSP solving algorithm (see (3) to (6), $Absence(t_a, x)$ will be defined in Sect. 4.4). As some constraint violation explicitly depends upon workflow completion, t_{end} is used to determine the termination of a workflow. This is necessary to assert a mandatory enactment of a task, a required execution of a task after a certain one, or even to assure that some tasks have not been conducted. Considering the solution of the CSP every task with a higher integer assigned than t_{end} is regarded as not enacted.

Due to the construction of the CSP, we are also able to influence the control of the workflow on the basis of semantic information. Control-flow nodes are additionally considered as constraints to further automate the control process. On this basis tasks are excluded from enactment proposals. For each xor or loop construct (cf. Fig. 1) two constraints are included (see (7, 8)). With s_i representing a decision variable, which either takes a_1 or a_2 as value, we are able to derive which path in the workflow should be followed. For workflow control the execution of the oppositional path is prevented, e.g. if the information of s_i is known to be a_1, task t_2 should not be enacted ($t_{end} < t_2$).

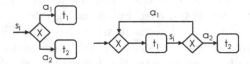

Fig. 1. Xor and loop construct including semantic information concerning control flow

Furthermore, considering the importance of data nodes for the presented approach, additional constraints are generated on the basis of data dependencies. For example, if data node d_1 is output of task t_1 and input of t_2, a constraint $Precedence(t_1, t_2)$ is inserted in the set of constraints, as it is necessary to enact task t_1 to subsequently process d_1 with t_2.

Table 2 shows an example transformation from procedurally modeled workflow to constraints to logical formulae, which are then used by the algorithm.

Table 2. Example workflow and corresponding constraints

Example workflow	Declarative constraints	Logical formulae for the CSP
	Precedence(A,B),	$A < B \wedge A < C \wedge$
	Precedence(A,C),	$(B < D \vee C < D) \wedge$
	Precedence(B,D) or	$(End < B \vee End < C) \wedge$
	Precedence(C,D),	$(XY = yes) \Rightarrow (End < C) \wedge$
	Not Co-Existence(B,C)	$(XY = no) \Rightarrow (End < B)$

4.2 Worklist Handling Algorithm

To identify all tasks that might be enacted next, a *solution* to the presented CSP, on the basis of the previously explained generated constraints, is searched for (cf. Algorithm 1). The algorithm takes the sets T and C as input for CSP Solving, whereas the domains D_i are derived from the size of T. The set F, also used as input, represents the de facto workflow and contains the variables from T, whose referenced tasks have been enacted. As output the variable *result* is introduced, which represents the set of tasks that might be enacted next. The value of the expected tasks, denoted here as *current*, is determined by the size of F, as this is the position which will be occupied by a task executed next.

```
Input   : T, C, F
Output: result: Tasks that might be executed next
1  result = ∅;
2  foreach D_i ∈ D do D_i = {0, ..., |T| − 1};
3  current = |F|;
4  foreach x ∈ T \ F do
5  |    if solveCSP(T, D, C ∪ {x = current}) ≠ ∅ then
6  |    |    result = result ∪ {x}
7  |    end
8  end
9  return result;
```

Algorithm 1. Determination of tasks which might be executed next

If every solution to the CSP would be computed, this would result in redundant computations. To accelerate proceedings, we apply the CSP solving algorithm only once for each decision variable that has not been assigned a value yet, thus, has not been executed. If the CSP solving algorithm finds a solution, this task might be executed next and therefore is appended to *result*. If no solution is found, the user must not execute the task next and thus, it is not proposed.

4.3   Deviation Detection

If a task enactment occurs, variable assignments are updated and constraints are validated to analyze the state of the workflow and possibly restore consistency. Algorithm 2 illustrates this procedure. As input, the enacted task j_n of the de jure workflow is received. First, the length of the de facto workflow needs to be determined, which identifies the assigned value to the variable of the currently enacted task within the CSP. The corresponding variable t_{j_n} is included in the de facto workflow F, and constraints are extended with the value assignment of *current* to t_{j_n}. As this task enactment might result in a constraint violation, and consequently in an inconsistent workflow state, all constraints need to be evaluated. If no solution is found, the violated constraint or even a set of constraints needs to be identified and retracted from C to restore consistency. In case a mandatory constraint is violated, the respective warnings and corrective actions are triggered.

After each task enactment the constraint set is simplified in order to prevent unnecessary computations. Based on the value assignments due to the de facto workflow, which will never change for a workflow instance, some constraints will always resolve to true, while other parts always resolve to false, even without constraint violations, e.g. disjunctive associated propositions. Assuming that the constraint set is available in conjunctive normal form $C = c_1 \wedge \ldots \wedge c_n$, clauses c_i are linked conjunctively and each clause represents a disjunction of literals $c_i = l_1 \vee \ldots \vee l_n$. The literals mostly result from the transformation of declarative workflow constructs to logical representations and thus, relate two tasks with the ordering "<". Other literals may be equations, such as $t_1 = 0$, depicting the de

---

Input : Task j_n, F, C

1 $current = |F|$;
2 $F = F \cup \{t_{j_n}\}$;
3 $C = C \cup \{t_{j_n} = current\}$;
4 **if** *!validateConstraints(C)* **then**
5 | retractViolated();
6 **end**
7 simplifyConstraints(t_{j_n});

Algorithm 2. Deviation Detection

facto workflow, or *alldifferent(T)* due to the construction of the CSP. The literals of interest for CSP simplification are the first ones. If a task enactment of task t_i occurs, all clauses with t_i on the left side (e.g. $t_i < t_j$) in one of the literals are withdrawn, as this clause will resolve to true in any case. Furthermore single literals, which contain t_i on the right side, e.g. $t_j < t_i$, can be retracted. Those will never be fulfilled, but the remaining literals in the clause have to be.

One impact of this simplification strategy after each task enactment is that violated constraints can be easily determined. A clause consisting of a single literal, e.g. $t_i < t_j$, where the currently enacted task t_j is on the right side, is violated, as t_i has not yet been enacted, as otherwise the clause would have been withdrawn from the constraint set previously.

4.4   Extension of the CSP for Loop Patterns

Until now the approach is limited to a singular execution of tasks and not incorporating loop constructs or considering deviations like redoing a task. Prerequisites as well as an algorithm to be able to handle the previously mentioned scenarios are explained in the following.

To differentiate between individual task instances in case of a repeated enactment, the decision variables in T are extended with a second index variable l, e.g. $t_{(j_n, l)}$, denoting the numbering of task instances referencing one single task, here j_n, of the de jure workflow. This second index also simplifies the validation of the constraint $Absence(j_n, i)$, because i might be compared to the second index l of the tasks that have already been executed. Thus, for each such constraint $Absence(j_n, i)$ the following formula needs to be checked during constraint validation: $\forall t_{(j_n, l)} \in F : l \leq i$. If this evaluates to false, the corresponding *Absence* constraint is violated and needs to be retracted.

For including recurring tasks in the CSP algorithm, another algorithm is needed which alters the input sets for Algorithm 1. The trigger for this processing (cf. Algorithm 3) is an enactment of task j_n of the de jure workflow. At first, the variable $t_{(k, l)}$ corresponding to task j_n has to be found. If such a variable does not exist, it is an unexpected repetition of a task, thus a deviation. As Algorithm 1 also has to cope with such enactments, a new variable has to be created and added to T. Domains have to be extended with one additional value for the new variable. On the other hand the following condition checks whether

```
Input  : Task jₙ
Output: T, D, C
```

1 find $t_{(k,l)}$ such that $k = j_n$ and $t_{(k,l)} \in T \setminus F$;
2 if $t_{(k,l)}$ *not exists* then
3   find $t_{(k,l)}$ such that $k = j_n$ and $t_{(k,l)} \in F$;
4      $T = T \cup \{t_{(k,l+1)}\}$;
5   foreach $D_i \in D$ do $D_i = D_i \cup \{|T| - 1\}$;
6 end
7 else if $isFirstTaskInLoop(j_n)$ then
8   foreach $j_m \in loop$ do
9          $T = T \cup \{t_{(j_m,l+1)}\}$;
10   foreach $D_i \in D$ do $D_i = D_i \cup \{|T| - 1\}$;
11   addConstraints;
12   end
13 end

Algorithm 3. CSP extension for loop patterns and task repetitions

the enacted task was the first of a loop construct. If so, the CSP is extended considering a possible further execution within the loop. Thus, a new decision variable $t_{(j_m,l+1)}$, for each task j_m in the loop, is included with an increased numbering variable $(l+1)$. Domains have to be expanded and constraints considering the new loop tasks have to be incorporated (cf. Table 3). The first line shows constraints representing sequential information without a repetition of the loop. Lines 2–4 represent the additional constraints which are added for a potential repetition at every entry of the loop, exemplarily depicted for the execution of B_1. Sequential constraints for the return to the loop beginning and a possible second run need to be incorporated (see line 2). Additionally the tasks after the loop need to be linked to those in the loop, but only in case of a repetition (cf. $B_2 < End$ and $C_2 < End$).

Table 3. Mapping loop pattern to declarative construct

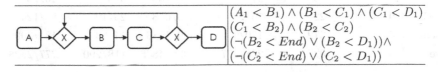

	$(A_1 < B_1) \wedge (B_1 < C_1) \wedge (C_1 < D_1)$
	$(C_1 < B_2) \wedge (B_2 < C_2)$
	$(\neg(B_2 < End) \vee (B_2 < D_1)) \wedge$
	$(\neg(C_2 < End) \vee (C_2 < D_1))$

5   Experiment

With the experiment we aim at validating two hypotheses concerning performance of the presented algorithm for practically relevant workflows. **H1**: The computation of the constructed CSPs and thus the worklist completes in less than a few seconds. **H2**: The restoration of consistency is achieved in less than a few seconds. The presented approach has been implemented with the use of Choco [13], an open-source constraint programming library. Different experiments have been conducted to validate the performance. Table 4 shows the results of the different experiments. We constructed several workflows manually. The first workflow, reflecting a real world example from deficiency management in construction, serves as base workflow (*base*). This workflow origins from a cooperation enterprise and is actually used in practice. It is used as reference workflow in SEMAFLEX to validate practicability and consists of 15 tasks, which are transformed to 51 constraints. The second workflow (*base3*) additionally repeats some parts of the base workflow three times, the third workflow (*base5*) links the same parts five times. In the last workflow (*base**) several tasks were inserted into parallel control flow (xor) sequences to increase the amount of generated constraints, as for each pair of tasks of the different paths a *Not Co-Existence* constraint is created, resulting in a number of 1027 constraints for 65 tasks. We ran two experiments *a* and *b* on each of the workflows. In experiment *a* we simulated the user going through the workflow, choosing one task for enactment out of the proposals of the worklist. In experiment *b* the simulated user randomly chooses tasks to be enacted, completely ignoring the worklist. In this experiment the algorithm is confronted with violated constraints and first has to restore consistency, until worklist proposals can be identified. We logged the CPU time for computing the worklist including construction of the constraints, simplification and restoration of the constraint set (*Total*). Furthermore, the CPU time only for the plain CSP runs (*CSP*) checking tasks for worklist compatibility was monitored. For each workflow both experiments are run five times, while the average and maximum time is shown in Table 4.

Table 4. Experimental results. Computation times in milliseconds are indicated for both experiments in the form a/b.

Workflow	Number of tasks	Number of constraints	Average time total in ms	Max time total in ms	Average time CSP in ms	Max time CSP in ms
Base	15	52	31/9	226/156	6/3	20/20
Base3	39	220	75/22	500/648	25/12	83/124
Base5	55	372	170/91	839/1683	54/63	184/390
Base*	65	1027	238/377	2322/4848	118/290	777/2328

Hypothesis **H1** is verified, as worklists were computed in the worst case in about two seconds (*Max CSP*). The overall algorithm needed at most roughly two seconds supplementary for restoring consistency and simplifying the constraint set (*Max total*), also confirming hypothesis **H2**. Average runtimes for calculating only the worklist with constraint solving as well as the overall algorithm yield encouraging results in less than a second and show, that from a practical point of view the algorithm is applicable.

Results of single runs of the experiment, as shown exemplarily in Fig. 2, also confirm the made assumptions. Runtimes decrease during the workflow execution, as constraints are simplified and a smaller number of tasks are possible candidates for the worklist, and thus less CSPs have to be solved.

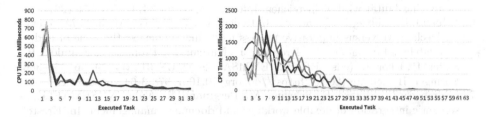

Fig. 2. Computation times in milliseconds of single runs of the workflow *base**. Results from experiment *a* on the left and experiment *b* on the right side.

6   Conclusion and Future Work

In this paper we presented a novel concept for workflow flexibility by deviation that combines procedural and declarative workflow paradigms. Upcoming documents and extracted semantic information are used to determine the current state of the workflow and for control purposes. In order to react to deviations and still propose the best way of proceeding with the workflow, constraint satisfaction problem solving is applied. First experiments on the implemented algorithm show promising results. Future work will focus on a more detailed elaboration of the single algorithms and possible improvements to achieve better results. As the algorithm used for this evaluation is a first prototypical implementation we expect improved results in further iterations and enhancements of the presented algorithm. Subsequently, the implementation will be evaluated against related approaches. Additionally, the concept will be developed further, as the workflow designer should be granted more freedom to choose how strict or flexible the constraints should be treated for worklist handling and, furthermore, which and how countermeasures could be specified.

References

1. van der Aalst, W.M.P.: Business process management - a comprehensive survey. ISRN Softw. Eng. **2013**, 1–37 (2013)
2. van der Aalst, W.M.P., Pesic, M., Schonenberg, H.: Declarative workflows balancing between flexibility and support. Comput. Sci. R&D **23**(2), 99–113 (2009)
3. van der Aalst, W.M.P., Weske, M., Grünbauer, D.: Case handling: a new paradigm for business process support. Data Knowl. Eng. **53**(2), 129–162 (2005)

4. Andrews, T., Curbera, F., Dholakia, H., Goland, Y., Klein, J., Leymann, F., Liu, K., Roller, D., Smith, D., Thatte, S., Trickovic, I., Weerawarana, S.: Business process execution language for web services, version 1.1. Technical report, BEA Systems, International Business Machines Corporation, Microsoft Corporation (2003)
5. Dadam, P., Reichert, M., Rinderle-Ma, S.: Prozessmanagementsysteme - nur ein wenig Flexibilität wird nicht reichen. Inform. Spektrum **34**(4), 364–376 (2011)
6. Fahland, D., Lübke, D., Mendling, J., Reijers, H., Weber, B., Weidlich, M., Zugal, S.: Declarative versus imperative process modeling languages: the issue of understandability. In: Halpin, T., Krogstie, J., Nurcan, S., Proper, E., Schmidt, R., Soffer, P., Ukor, R. (eds.) BPMDS/EMMSAD-2009. LNBIP, vol. 29, pp. 353–366. Springer, Heidelberg (2009). https://doi.org/10.1007/978-3-642-01862-6_29
7. Grumbach, L., Rietzke, E., Schwinn, M., Bergmann, R., Kuhn, N.: SEMAFLEX - semantic integration of flexible workflow and document management. In: Krestel, R., Mottin, D., Müller, E. (eds.) Proceedings of the Conference "Lernen, Wissen, Daten, Analysen", CEUR Workshop Proceedings, Potsdam, Germany, 12–14 September 2016, vol. 1670, pp. 43–50 (2016). CEUR-WS.org
8. Hildebrandt, T.T., Mukkamala, R.R.: Declarative event-based workflow as distributed dynamic condition response graphs. In: Proceedings Third Workshop on Programming Language Approaches to Concurrency and communication-cEntric Software, PLACES 2010, Paphos, Cyprus, 21 March 2010, pp. 59–73 (2010)
9. Hoffmann, D.: Schlanke Formen des Geschäftsprozessmanagements Das richtige BPM-Rezept, February 2013. http://www.it-zoom.de/it-mittelstand/e/das-richtige-bpm-rezept-5287/
10. Maggi, F.M., Montali, M., Westergaard, M., van der Aalst, W.M.P.: Monitoring business constraints with linear temporal logic: an approach based on colored automata. In: Rinderle-Ma, S., Toumani, F., Wolf, K. (eds.) BPM 2011. LNCS, vol. 6896, pp. 132–147. Springer, Heidelberg (2011). https://doi.org/10.1007/978-3-642-23059-2_13
11. Pesic, M.: Constraint-based workflow management systems: shifting control to users. Ph.D. thesis, Technische Universiteit Eindhoven (2008)
12. Pichler, P., Weber, B., Zugal, S., Pinggera, J., Mendling, J., Reijers, H.A.: Imperative versus declarative process modeling languages: an empirical investigation. In: Daniel, F., Barkaoui, K., Dustdar, S. (eds.) BPM 2011. LNBIP, vol. 99, pp. 383–394. Springer, Heidelberg (2012). https://doi.org/10.1007/978-3-642-28108-2_37
13. Prud'homme, C., Fages, J.G., Lorca, X.: Choco Documentation. TASC, INRIA Rennes, LINA CNRS UMR 6241, COSLING S.A.S. (2016). http://www.choco-solver.org
14. Russell, S.J., Norvig, P.: Artificial Intelligence - A Modern Approach, 3rd edn. Pearson Education, London (2010)
15. Saam, M., Viete, S., Schiel, S.: Digitalisierung im Mittelstand: Status Quo, aktuelle Entwicklungen und Herausforderungen, August 2016
16. Schlecht, M.: Prozessmanagement in der Cloud. ERP Management 4/2013: Betriebsformen moderner Systeme, vol. 3, pp. 33–36 (2013)
17. Schonenberg, H., Mans, R., Russell, N., Mulyar, N., van der Aalst, W.M.P.: Process flexibility: a survey of contemporary approaches. In: Dietz, J.L.G., Albani, A., Barjis, J. (eds.) CIAO!/EOMAS -2008. LNBIP, vol. 10, pp. 16–30. Springer, Heidelberg (2008). https://doi.org/10.1007/978-3-540-68644-6_2
18. Supyuenyong, V., Islam, N., Kulkarni, U.R.: Influence of SME characteristics on knowledge management processes: the case study of enterprise resource planning service providers. J. Enterp. Inf. Manag. **22**(1/2), 63–80 (2009)

19. Wedemeijer, L.: Transformation of imperative workflows to declarative business rules. In: Shishkov, B. (ed.) BMSD 2013. LNBIP, vol. 173, pp. 106–127. Springer, Cham (2014). https://doi.org/10.1007/978-3-319-06671-4_6

20. Weske, M.: Business Process Management: Concepts, Languages, Architectures. Springer, Heidelberg (2007). https://doi.org/10.1007/978-3-642-28616-2

21. Westergaard, M.: Better algorithms for analyzing and enacting declarative workflow languages using LTL. In: Rinderle-Ma, S., Toumani, F., Wolf, K. (eds.) BPM 2011. LNCS, vol. 6896, pp. 83–98. Springer, Heidelberg (2011). https://doi.org/10.1007/978-3-642-23059-2_10

22. Workflow Management Coalition: Workflow Management Coalition Terminology & Glossary, February 1999

Machine Learning and Neural Networks

Masked Conditional Neural Networks
for Environmental Sound Classification

Fady Medhat$^{(\boxtimes)}$, David Chesmore, and John Robinson

Department of Electronic Engineering, University of York, York, UK
{fady.medhat,david.chesmore,john.robinson}@york.ac.uk

Abstract. The ConditionaL Neural Network (CLNN) exploits the nature of the temporal sequencing of the sound signal represented in a spectrogram, and its variant the Masked ConditionaL Neural Network (MCLNN) induces the network to learn in frequency bands by embedding a filterbank-like sparseness over the network's links using a binary mask. Additionally, the masking automates the exploration of different feature combinations concurrently analogous to handcrafting the optimum combination of features for a recognition task. We have evaluated the MCLNN performance using the Urbansound8k dataset of environmental sounds. Additionally, we present a collection of manually recorded sounds for rail and road traffic, YorNoise, to investigate the confusion rates among machine generated sounds possessing low-frequency components. MCLNN has achieved competitive results without augmentation and using 12% of the trainable parameters utilized by an equivalent model based on state-of-the-art Convolutional Neural Networks on the Urbansound8k. We extended the Urbansound8k dataset with YorNoise, where experiments have shown that common tonal properties affect the classification performance.

Keywords: Conditional Neural Networks · CLNN · Masked Conditional Neural Networks · MCLNN · Restricted Boltzmann Machine, RBM · Conditional Restricted Boltzmann Machine · CRBM · Deep Belief Nets · Environmental Sound Recognition · ESR · YorNoise.

1 Introduction

Automatic feature extraction for signals either image or sound is gaining a wide interest from the research community aiming to eliminate the efforts invested in handcrafting the optimum features for a recognition task. Inspired by the generative Deep Belief Nets (DBN) introduced by Hinton and Salakhutdinov [1], the deep architectural structure got adapted to other models such as the Convolutional Neural Networks (CNN) [2]. These deep architectures are used to extract an abstract representation of the features that can be further classified using a conventional classifier, e.g. SVM [3]. An attempt to use a neural network based architecture over the raw sound signal has been considered by

This work is funded by the European Union's Seventh Framework Programme for research, technological development and demonstration under grant agreement no. 608014 (CAPACITIE).

© Springer International Publishing AG 2017
M. Bramer and M. Petridis (Eds.): SGAI-AI 2017, LNAI 10630, pp. 21–33, 2017.
https://doi.org/10.1007/978-3-319-71078-5_2

Dieleman and Schrauwen in [4]. Their work endeavored to bypass the need for spectrograms as an intermediate signal representation, but their findings showed that spectrograms prevail. An attempt to use stacked Restricted Boltzmann Machines [5] forming a DBN for the task of music genre classification was in the work of Hamel and Eck [6], where the extracted features were classified using an SVM. Despite the successful attempts in using the DBN as a feature extractor for sound, it treats each spectrogram frame as an isolated entity. This ignores the temporal relation across the frames.

To capture the successional relationship in sequential data, extending from an RBM structure, Taylor et al. proposed the Conditional RBM (CRBM) [7]. Taylor used the CRBM for modeling the human motion through tracking the joints position of the human body as features across time. The CRBM was applied for sound signals such as drum pattern analysis in [8]. The CRBM as shown in Fig. 1 accounts for the inter-frames relation of a temporal signal by including conditional links from the previous visible nodes $(\hat{v}_{-n}, \ldots, \hat{v}_{-2}, \hat{v}_{-1})$ to both the hidden layer $\hat{h}$ and the current visible input $\hat{v}_0$. The Interpolating CRBM (ICRBM) [9], a variant of the CRBM, enhanced the speech phoneme recognition accuracy compared to the CRBM by considering future frames in addition to the past ones.

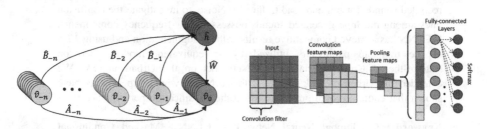

Fig. 1. The conditional RBM structure   **Fig. 2.** Convolutional neural network

The Convolutional Neural Network (CNN) [2], shown in Fig. 2, is another very successful model that achieved breakthrough results in image recognition [10]. The CNN operates using two consecutive layers of convolution and pooling operations. In the convolutional layer, the input is scanned with an array of filters to generate a number of feature maps matching the number of filters. Then a pooling layer is used to compress the resolution of the convolutional layer's output either through mean or max pooling. Several of these two layers can be stacked on top of each other in a deep architectural structure, where the output of the last convolutional or pooling layer can be fed into a dense layer for the final classification decision. The CNN depends on weight sharing, which does not preserve the spatial locality of the learned feature. The locality of the features detected in a spectrogram is crucial for distinguishing between sounds, which induced attempts [11, 12] to tailor the CNN filters for sound recognition to capture both the temporal and spectral properties in addition to tackling the translation invariance property of the CNN.

Long Short-Term Memory (LSTM) [13] is a Recurrent Neural Network (RNN) architecture that allows considering a past sequence of temporal frames using internal memory. Choi et al. [14] exploited the use of a hybrid model in the

Convolutional RNN, where they used a CNN to extract the local features and an LSTM to capture the long-term dependencies of a temporal signal for music.

The Convolutional DBN (ConvDBN) [15] was an extension to the generative models based on the RBM. The ConvDBN investigated the use of the unsupervised training of an RBM for images by adapting the convolutional behavior of a CNN and through introducing a probabilistic pooling layer. ConvDBN was adopted in [16] for music and speech tasks.

We have highlighted the most relevant architectures to this work. Models were developed for other applications, primarily image recognition, and then adapted to the nature of the sound signal. This may not optimally harness the multidimensional representation of an audio signal as a spectrogram. For example, the DBN ignores the inter-frame relations of a temporal signal, where it treats the frames as isolated entities in a Bag-of-Frames classification. Also, models based on the convolution operation like the CNN depends on weight sharing, which permits CNNs to scale well for images of large dimensions without having a dedicated weight for each pixel in the input. Weight sharing makes the CNN translation invariant, which does not preserve the spatial locality of the learned features. The ConditionaL Neural Networks (CLNN) [17] and its variant the Masked ConditionaL Neural Network (MCLNN) [17] are developed from the ground up exploiting the nature of the sound signal. The CLNN considers the inter-frames relation in a temporal signal and the MCLNN embeds a filterbank-like behavior that enables individual bands and suppresses others through an enforced systematic sparseness. Additionally, the mask in the MCLNN automates the exploration of different feature combinations concurrently, which is usually a handcrafted operation of finding the optimum feature combinations through exhaustive trials. Meanwhile, the MCLNN preserves the spatial locality of the learned features. In this work, we extend the evaluation of the MCLNN in [18] to the Urbansound8k dataset. Additionally, we investigate the confusion across machine generated sounds possessing common low tonal components through YorNoise, a dataset we are presenting in this work focusing on rail and road traffic sounds.

2 Conditional Neural Networks

Sound frames can be classified one frame at a time, but higher accuracy is achieved by exploiting the relationship between the frames across time, as in the CRBM discussed earlier. A CRBM is a generative model possessing directed links between the previous frames and both the current visible and hidden layers as shown in Fig. 1. These links hold the conditional relation of observing a particular pattern of neurons' activations at either of the hidden or visible layer conditioned on the previous n visible vectors. These directed links convert an RBM into the Conditional RBM.

A CLNN captures the temporal nature of a spectrogram and allows end-to-end discriminative training by extending from the CRBM using the past n visible-to-hidden links in addition to the future ones as proposed in the ICRBM. This allows the network to learn from the temporal data and acts as the main skeleton for the MCLNN.

For notation purposes, matrices are represented with uppercase symbols with the hat operator $\widehat{W}$ and vectors with lowercase symbols $\hat{x}$. $\widehat{W}_u$ is the matrix at index u in the tensor $\widehat{W}$. $W_{i,j,u}$ is the element at location $[i, j]$ of a matrix $\widehat{W}_u$, similarly x_i is the ith element of the vector $\hat{x}$. The dot operator $(\cdot)$ refers to vector-matrix multiplication. Element-wise multiplication between vectors or matrices of the same sizes uses $(\circ)$. The absence of any operators or the use $(\times)$ refers to normal elements multiplication $\left(l \times e \text{ or } x_i\, W_{i,j}\right)$.

The CLNN hidden layer is formed of vector-shaped neurons and accepts an input of size $[l, d]$, where l is the length of the feature vector and d is the number of frames in a window following (1)

$$d = 2n + 1, \quad n \geq 1 \tag{1}$$

where the order n controls the number of frames in a single temporal direction, $2n$ is for the frames on either side of the window's central frame, and 1 is for the middle frame itself. Accordingly, at any temporal instance, the CLNN hidden layer activations are conditioned on the window's central frame and the $2n$ neighboring frames. A single input vector within the window is fully connected with the hidden layer having e-neurons. The dense connections between each vector and the hidden layer are captured in a dedicated weight matrix $\widehat{W}_u$, where u is the index of the weight matrix residing in the weight tensor. The index u ranges within $[-n, n]$ matching the number of frames d. The activation of hidden neuron follows (2)

$$y_{j,t} = f\left(b_j + \sum_{u=-n}^{n} \sum_{i=1}^{l} x_{i,u+t} W_{i,j,u} \right) \tag{2}$$

where $y_{j,t}$ is the activation of the jth neuron, f is the activation function, b_j is the bias at the jth neuron, $x_{i,u+t}$ is the ith feature in the feature vector at index $u + t$, where u is the index of the vector in the window, and $W_{i,j,u}$ is the weight between the ith feature of the feature vector at index u in the window and the jth neuron of the hidden layer, where each frame at index u has a corresponding weight matrix of the same index in the weight tensor. The t index in the equation refers to the index of the frame in a sequence of frames, which we will refer to as the segment (discussed later in detail). Accordingly, the frame at index t within the segment is the window's central frame $\hat{x}_{u+t}$ at $u = 0$. The vector formulation of (2) is given in (3)

$$\hat{y}_t = f\left(\hat{b} + \sum_{u=-n}^{n} \hat{x}_{u+t} \cdot \widehat{W}_u \right) \tag{3}$$

where $\hat{y}_t$ is the predicted activations of the window's middle frame $\hat{x}_t$ ($u = 0$) conditioned on $2n$ off-central frames within $[-n + t, n + t]$, f is the transfer function, $\hat{b}$ is the bias vector at the hidden layer, $\hat{x}_{u+t}$ is the feature vector (having length l) within the window at index u, where $\hat{x}_t$ is the frame at index t of the segment and also the window's central frame at $u = 0$, and $\widehat{W}_u$ is the weight matrix (having a size [feature vector l, hidden layer length e]) at index u corresponding to the vector at index $u + t$. The generated d vectors from the vector-matrix multiplication are summed per dimension to generate a single vector to apply the transfer function on. The generated vector is a representative frame for the input window of frames. The conditional distribution of the frames can be captured using a sigmoid function at the hidden layer or through the final output softmax through $p(\hat{y}_t|\hat{x}_{-n+t}, \ldots, \hat{x}_{-1+t}, \hat{x}_t, \hat{x}_{1+t}, \ldots, \hat{x}_{n+t}) = \sigma(\ldots)$, where σ is the transfer function used.

According to (3), the output of a CLNN step over a window of d frames is a single vector $\hat{y}$. This highlights the consumption of the frames in a CLNN layer, where the output is $2n$ frames fewer than the input. To account for such reduction of frames in a deep CLNN architecture, a segment of frames is fed to the deep architecture following (4)

$$q = (2n)m + k, \quad n, m \text{ and } k \geq 1 \tag{4}$$

where q is the width of the segment, n is the order (multiplied by 2 to account for past and future frames) controlling the width of the window at a single CLNN layer, m is for the number of layers and k is for the extra frames. k specifies the number of frames that should remain beyond the CLNN layers to be flattened to a single vector or globally pooled [19] across the temporal dimension. This behaves as an aggregation over a texture window that was studied in [20] for music classification. Finally, the generated vector is introduced to a densely connected neural network for the final classification.

Figure 3 shows a deep CLNN structure composed of two layers, $m = 2$, and having an order $n = 1$. In this setting, each frame is conditioned on one previous and one

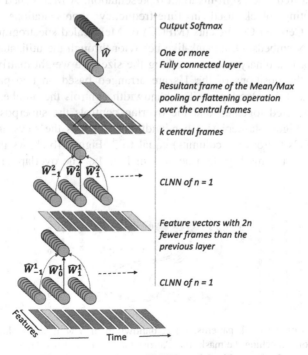

Output Softmax

One or more
Fully connected layer

Resultant frame of the Mean/Max
pooling or flattening operation
over the central frames

k central frames

CLNN of n = 1

Feature vectors with 2n
fewer frames than the
previous layer

CLNN of n = 1

Fig. 3. A two layer CLNN model with $n = 1$

succeeding frame. Each CLNN layer is composed of a weight tensor $\widehat{W}^b$, where b is layer index ($b = 1, 2, \ldots, m$). The center weight matrix $\widehat{W}_0^b$ processes the main frame at time $u + t$ at $u = 0$ and an additional $2n$ weight matrices, where at $n = 1$ there are $\widehat{W}_{-1}^b$ to handle one previous frame and $\widehat{W}_1^b$ to handle for the future one. The figure also depicts the remaining k frames to be flattened or pooled across before the densely-connected layers.

3 Masked Conditional Neural Networks

The Masked ConditionaL Neural Networks (MCLNN) [17] use the same structure and behavior as the CLNN and additionally enforces a systematic sparseness over the network's connections through a masking operation.

Spectrograms have been used widely as an intermediate signal representation. They allow an in-depth analysis of the signal structure and the frequency components forming the signal. They describe the change in the energy assigned to each frequency bin as the signal progresses through time. However, they have some shortcomings for sound recognition. The energy of the different frequencies of a sound signal is affected by environmental acoustic factors during the signal propagation. These factors may cause the energy to be shifted from one frequency bin to a nearby frequency bin for the same sound signal, resulting in a different feature vector to a recognition system. Filterbanks are used in this regard to subdivide the frequency spectrum into bands, which provide a frequency shift-invariant representation. A Mel-Scaled filterbank is a principle operating block used in time-frequency representations of sound in Mel-Frequency Cepstral Coefficients (MFCC) or Mel-Scaled spectrograms.

The MCLNN embeds a filterbank-like behavior through the utilization of a binary mask. The mask is a binary matrix matching the size of a weight matrix as shown in Fig. 4a, where the positions of the 1's are arranged based on two parameters: the Bandwidth bw and the Overlap ov. The bandwidth controls the number of frequency bins to be considered together, and the overlap controls the superposition distance between bands. Figure 4a depicts a bandwidth of 5 across the rows and an overlap between the bands (across the columns) equal to 3. Figure 4b shows the active connections matching the mask pattern defined in Fig. 4a. The overlap can be assigned

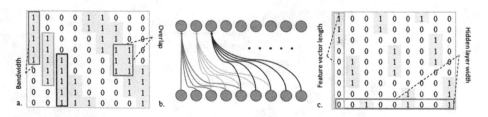

Fig. 4. Examples of the mask patterns. (a) A bandwidth of 5 with an overlap of 3, (b) The allowed connections matching the mask in a. Across the neurons of two layers, (c) A bandwidth of 3 and an overlap of −1.

negative values, which refer to the non-overlapping distance between the successive bands as shown in Fig. 4c. The mask design is based on a linear spacing that follows (5)

$$lx = a + (g - 1)(l + (bw - ov))$$ (5)

where the linear index lx of a position of a binary value 1 is given by the bandwidth bw and the overlap ov. The values of a are within the interval $[0, bw - 1]$ and the values of g are in the interval $[1, \lceil (l \times e)/(l + (bw - ov)) \rceil]$.

The mask suppresses the weights in the 0's locations by elementwise multiplication, enforcing a systematic sparseness over the network's connections between the input to any layer and the scope of the interest of each hidden node as formulated in (6).

$$\hat{Z}_u = \hat{W}_u \circ \hat{M}$$ (6)

where $\hat{W}_u$ is the original weight matrix and $\hat{M}$ is the mask pattern. $\hat{Z}_u$ is the masked weight matrix to substitute $\hat{W}_u$ in (3).

Another important role of the mask is the process of automating the exploration of a range of feature combinations concurrently similar to the manual hand-crafting of different feature combinations. This is implemented in the mask through the presence of several shifted versions of the filterbank-like binary pattern. For example, in Fig. 4c (columns map to the hidden layer neurons), the 1st neuron will learn about the first three features in the input feature vector (ignoring the temporal dimension for simplicity) matching the positions of the three 1's present in the mask. The 4th neuron will learn about the first two features, and the 7th neuron will learn about the first feature

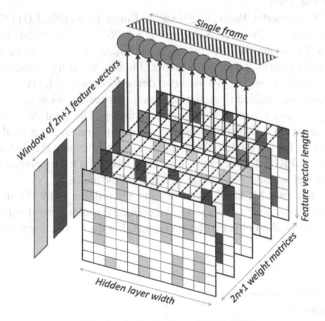

Fig. 5. A single step of MCLNN

only. This behavior allows different neurons to observe a focused region of features in the feature vector while preserving the spatial locality of the learned features.

Figure 5 shows a single step of the MCLNN, where $2n + 1$ frames have a matching number of $2n + 1$ matrices. The highlighted regions represent the active connections following the mask design. The output of a single MCLNN step processing the $2n + 1$ input frames is a single representative frame.

4 Experiments

We performed the experiments using the Urbansound8k [21] and the YorNoise (presented in this work) datasets of environmental sounds. The Urbansound8k dataset is composed of 8732 audio sample of 10 categories of urban sounds: air conditioner, car horns, children playing, dog bark, drilling, engine idling, gunshot, jackhammers, siren and street music. The maximum duration of each file is 4 s. The dataset is released into 10-folds. We used the same arrangement of folds to unify the benchmarking and eliminate the data split influence on the reported accuracies.

All files were re-sampled to a monaural channel of 22050 Hz sampling rate and 16-bit word depth wav format. The files were transformed to a logarithmic Mel-scaled spectrogram of 60 bins using an FFT window of 1024 and a 50% overlap and with their delta (first derivative of the spectrogram along the temporal dimension). The spectrogram and the delta were concatenated to generate a spectrogram of 120 bin. Following the time-frequency transformation, segments were extracted following (4). All training files are standardized feature-wise using z-scoring, and the standardization parameters (mean and standard deviation) of the training folds were applied on both the validation and test folds.

For the MCLNN model, Parametric Rectifier Linear Units (PReLU) [22] were used as activation functions. The MCLNN layers are followed by a global mean pooling layer [19], but for a temporal signal such as sound, it is a feature-wise single-dimensional pooling across the k extra frames. Finally, the fully-connected layers are used before the softmax output. We used two densely connected layers of 100 neurons each. The network was trained to minimize the categorical cross-entropy using ADAM [23], and Dropout [24] was used to prevent overfitting. The final decision of a clip's category was based on a probability voting across the frames. We used Keras[1] and Theano[2] on a GPU for the model's implementation, and the signal transformation was carried out using LibROSA[3] and FFmpeg[4]. Table 1 lists the hyper-parameters used for the MCLNN model we adopted for the Urbansound8k dataset.

The model has two MCLNN layers having an order $n = 15$ (Future work will consider different order across the layers). We noticed through several experiments that having a wider bandwidth in the first layer compared to the second layer provides better

---

[1] https://keras.io.

[2] http://deeplearning.net/software/theano.

[3] https://librosa.github.io/.

[4] http://ffmpeg.org/.

Table 1. MCLNN model parameters for Urbansound8k

Layer	Type	Nodes	Mask bandwidth	Mask overlap	Order n
1	MCLNN	300	20	−5	15
2	MCLNN	200	5	3	15

performance. The role of the mask in the first layer is to process sub-bands within the spectrogram and the narrower bandwidth in the second layer's mask focuses on distinctive features over a small region of bins. The same applies for the overlap, where more sparseness is required in the first layer, through the negative overlap, to eliminate the noisy effect of smearing bins in proximity to each other. The single dimensional global mean pooling was used to pool across $k = 5$ extra frames and finally the fully connected layers for classification.

Table 2 lists the mean accuracy achieved by the MCLNN across the 10-fold cross validation, in addition to other methods applied on the Urbansound8k dataset. The MCLNN achieved an accuracy of 73.3%, which is the highest neural based accuracy for the Urbansound8k dataset. The highest non-neural accuracy is 73.7%, reported in the work of Salamon [25], used the random forest as a classifier applied over a dictionary established using Spherical K-Means [28]. As an intermediate representation, they used a Mel-scaled spectrogram dimensionally reduced by PCA.

Table 2. Accuracies reported on the Urbansound8k

Classifiers and features	Acc.%
Random Forest + Spherical K-Means + PCA + Mel-Spectrogram [25]	73.7
MCLNN + Mel-Spectrogram (This Work)	**73.3**
Piczak-CNN + Mel-Spectrogram [26]	73.1
S&B-CNN + Mel-Spectrogram [27]	73.0
RBF-SVM + MFCC [21][1]	68.0

To be able to benchmark the MCLNN compared to other proposed CNN models having a similar depth, we adopted the same spectrogram transformation used for the CNN proposed by Piczak in [26] (60 bin mel-scaled spectrogram with its Delta). Piczak used a separate channel for each of the spectrogram and the Delta to train a CNN. To fit this to the MCLNN, we concatenated both transformations column-wise, resulting in a frame size of 120 features. Piczak experimented with two segment sizes extracted from the spectrogram to train a CNN, where a short segment is composed of 41 frames, and a long segment comprises 101 frames. The highest accuracy reported in [26] was 73.1% using a long segment variant to train the Piczak-CNN. The CNN proposed by Piczak in [26] is composed of two convolution layers of 80 filters each, two pooling layers followed by two fully-connected layers of 5000 neurons each and finally the output Softmax. The number of trainable weights in Piczak-CNN exceed 25 million parameters, on the other hand, the two MCLNN layers we used for this work required approximately 3 million parameters trained over segments of 65 frames. The deeper

CNN architecture proposed by Salamon in [27] used fewer parameters. Accordingly, we will consider deeper MCLNN architectures for future work. MCLNN achieved comparable results to state-of-the-art attempts using 12% of the network parameters of a CNN having a similar depth. The work of Salamon in [27] proposed the use of an augmentation stage by applying different modification, e.g. pitch shifting, time stretching, to the input signal to increase the dataset and consequently enhance the model generalization. Piczak [26] reported the absence of a performance gain when applying augmentation on the Urbansound8k dataset. We did not consider augmentation as it is not relevant to benchmarking the MCLNN performance against other proposed models.

Figure 6 shows the confusion matrix for the Urbansound8k using the MCLNN. The highest confusion is between the Air Conditioner, Drilling, Engine Idling and Jackhammer. This is related to the presence of common low tones across the four classes. Similar confusion was reported in [27].

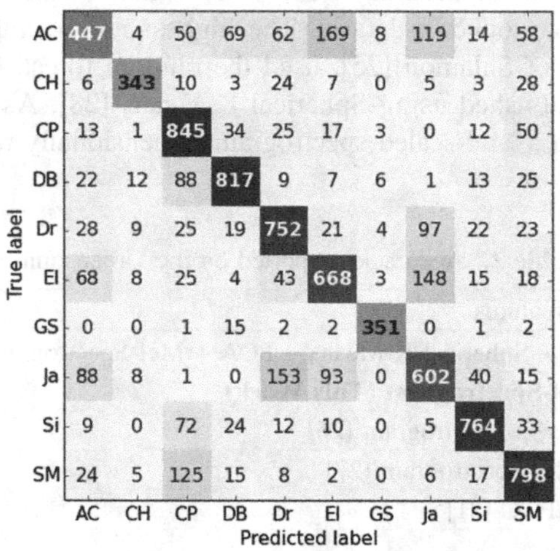

Classes: Air Conditioner(AC), Car Horns(CH), Children Playing(CP), Dog Bark(DB), Drilling(Dr), Engine Idling(EI), Gun Shot(GS), Jackhammers(Ja), Siren(Si) and Street Music(SM)

Fig. 6. Confusion matrix for the Urbansound8k using the MCLNN

We wanted to further analyze the effect of the common low tonal components across the machine generated sounds. For this analysis, we introduce YorNoise[5], a dataset focusing on urban generated sounds especially road vehicles and trains. We collected the sound samples from different locations within the city of York in the United Kingdom. The sound files were recorded using a professional recorder fixed at an altitude of one meter above the ground. The captured mono files were recorded at a 44100 Hz sampling rate, with 5 minutes for each recording on average. Each

---

[5] https://github.com/fadymedhat/YorNoise.

5 minutes file is split into multiple samples of 4 s each matching the setting of the Urbansound8k. We examined every 4 s file and cleared disrupted samples and silent ones. The files for both categories are distributed across 10-folds while making sure that the 4 s samples belonging to the same 5 min file are residing in the same fold. The total number of files is 907 of road traffic sounds and 620 for rail.

We applied the same preprocessing used for the Urbansound8k to YorNoise. We appended the 10-folds of YorNoise to the Urbansound8k, which generated a dataset of 12 categories totaling to 10259 sound files (Urbansound8k categories in addition to YorNoise: Rail and Traffic). We applied the same model used for the Urbansound8k to the 12 sound categories. MCLNN achieved a mean accuracy of 75.13% for a 10-folds cross-validation with the confusion shown in Fig. 7. Despite the high recognition accuracy of 95.6% and 97.5% for rail and traffic, respectively, it is clear that Yor-Noise's categories are either confused among themselves (due to the similarity between the train engine and road vehicles) or with the low tonal classes of the Urbansound8k (the Air Conditioner, Drilling, Engine Idling and Jackhammer). This further validates the noticeable confusion rates among the low tonal classes of the Urbansound8k.

True label	AC	CH	CP	DB	Dr	EI	GS	Ja	Si	SM	Ra	Tr
AC	376	3	45	83	145	138	1	63	7	55	64	20
CH	10	341	5	3	21	11	0	7	1	27	2	1
CP	17	3	821	35	27	12	2	1	12	53	11	6
DB	24	12	97	793	12	7	5	1	13	28	3	5
Dr	36	3	17	20	757	22	7	13	27	18	5	15
EI	75	3	22	11	27	654	2	112	9	18	42	25
GS	0	0	1	16	1	6	346	0	1	1	2	0
Ja	100	0	1	0	121	110	1	601	3	16	44	3
Si	12	0	55	31	3	18	0	5	748	43	1	13
SM	14	10	115	15	7	8	0	9	19	790	12	1
Ra	4	0	0	0	0	5	0	2	1	0	593	15
Tr	3	0	0	0	1	0	0	0	1	0	18	884

Predicted label

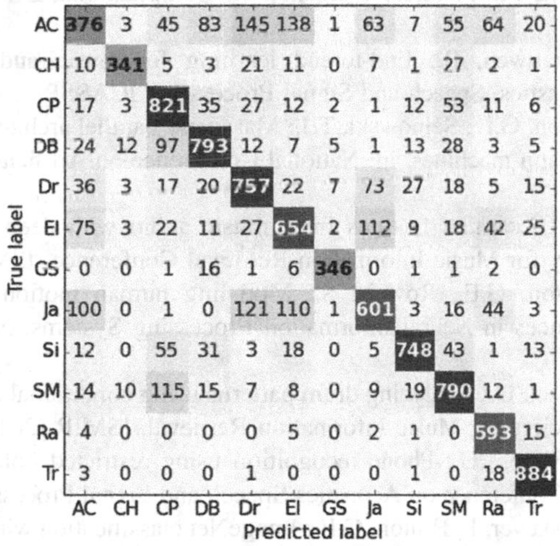

Classes: Air Conditioner(AC), Car Horns(CH), Children Playing(CP), Dog Bark(DB), Drilling(Dr), Engine Idling(EI), Gun Shot(GS), Jackhammers(Ja), Siren(Si), Street Music(SM), Rail (Ra) and Traffic (Tr)

Fig. 7. Confusion matrix for the Urbansound8k and YorNoise using the MCLNN

5 Conclusions and Future Work

The ConditionaL Neural Network (CLNN) and its extension the Masked ConditionaL Neural Network (MCLNN) are designed for multi-dimensional temporal signals representations. The CLNN considers the inter-frames relation across a temporal signal, and the MCLNN embeds a filterbank-like behavior within the network through an enforced systematic sparseness over the network's links allowing the network to learn in bands rather than bins. Additionally, the presence of several shifted versions of the filterbank-like pattern automates handcrafting the optimum combination of features. MCLNN has shown competitive results compared to state-of-the-art Convolutional Neural Networks on the Urbansound8k environmental sounds dataset. We investigated the confusion across sounds of low tonal component mainly machine generated sounds, through the YorNoise dataset, we introduce in this work, focusing on rail and road traffic. Future work will consider further optimization to the MCLNN architecture and the hyperparameters used. We will also consider multi-channel temporal signals other than sound.

References

1. Hinton, G.E., Salakhutdinov, R.R.: Reducing the dimensionality of data with neural networks. Science **313**, 504–507 (2006)
2. LeCun, Y., Bottou, L., Bengio, Y., Haffner, P.: Gradient-based learning applied to document recognition. Proc. IEEE **86**, 2278–2324 (1998)
3. Boser, B.E., Guyon, I.M., Vapnik, V.N.: A training algorithm for optimal margin classifiers. In: Proceedings of the Fifth Annual Workshop on Computational Learning Theory, COLT (1992)
4. Dieleman, S., Schrauwen, B.: End-to-end learning for music audio. In: International Conference on Acoustics, Speech and Signal Processing, ICASSP (2014)
5. Fahlman, S.E., Hinton, G.E., Sejnowski, T.J.: Massively parallel architectures for AI: NETL, Thistle, and Boltzmann machines. In: National Conference on Artificial Intelligence, AAAI (1983)
6. Hamel, P., Eck, D.: Learning features from music audio with deep belief networks. In: International Society for Music Information Retrieval Conference, ISMIR (2010)
7. Taylor, G.W., Hinton, G.E., Roweis, S.: Modeling human motion using binary latent variables. In: Advances in Neural Information Processing Systems, NIPS, pp. 1345–1352 (2006)
8. Battenberg, E., Wessel, D.: Analyzing drum patterns using conditional deep belief networks. In: International Society for Music Information Retrieval, ISMIR (2012)
9. Mohamed, A.-R., Hinton, G.: Phone recognition using restricted boltzmann machines In: IEEE International Conference on Acoustics Speech and Signal Processing, ICASSP (2010)
10. Krizhevsky, A., Sutskever, I., Hinton, G.E.: ImageNet classification with deep convolutional neural networks. In: Neural Information Processing Systems, NIPS (2012)
11. Abdel-Hamid, O., Mohamed, A.-R., Jiang, H., Deng, L., Penn, G., Yu, D.: Convolutional neural networks for speech recognition. IEEE/ACM Trans. Audio Speech Lang. Process. **22**, 1533–1545 (2014)
12. Pons, J., Lidy, T., Serra, X.: Experimenting with musically motivated convolutional neural networks. In: International Workshop on Content-based Multimedia Indexing, CBMI (2016)
13. Hochreiter, S., Schmidhuber, J.: Long short-term memory. Neural Comput. **9**, 1735–1780 (1997)
14. Choi, K., Fazekas, G., Sandler, M., Cho, K.: Convolutional recurrent neural networks for music classification. In: arXiv preprint arXiv:1609.04243 (2016)
15. Lee, H., Grosse, R. Ranganath, R., Ng, A.Y.: Convolutional deep belief networks for scalable unsupervised learning of hierarchical representations. In: Proceedings of the 26th Annual International Conference on Machine Learning, ICML, pp. 1–8 (2009)

16. Lee, H., Largman, Y., Pham, P., Ng, A.Y.: Unsupervised feature learning for audio classification using convolutional deep belief networks. In: Neural Information Processing Systems (NIPS) (2009)
17. Medhat, F., Chesmore, D., Robinson, J.: Masked conditional neural networks for audio classification. In: Lintas, A., Rovetta, S., Verschure, P., Villa, A. (eds.) Artificial Neural Networks and Machine Learning – ICANN 2017. LNCS, vol. 10614, pp. 349–358. Springer, Cham (2017). https://doi.org/10.1007/978-3-319-68612-7_40
18. Medhat, F., Chesmore, D., Robinson, J.: Masked conditional neural networks for automatic sound events recognition. In: IEEE International Conference on Data Science and Advanced Analytics (DSAA) (2017)
19. Lin, M., Chen, Q., Yan, S.: Network in network. In: International Conference on Learning Representations, ICLR (2014)
20. Bergstra, J., Casagrande, N., Erhan, D., Eck, D., Kégl, B.: Aggregate features and AdaBoost for music classification. Mach. Learn. **65**, 473–484 (2006)
21. Salamon, J., Jacoby, C., Bello, J.P.: A dataset and taxonomy for urban sound research. In: Proceedings of the 22nd ACM International Conference on Multimedia, pp. 1041–1044 (2014)
22. He, K., Zhang, X., Ren, S., Sun, J.: Delving deep into rectifiers: surpassing human-level performance on imagenet classification. In: IEEE International Conference on Computer Vision, ICCV (2015)
23. Kingma, D., Ba, J.: ADAM: a method for stochastic optimization. In: International Conference for Learning Representations, ICLR (2015)
24. Srivastava, N., Hinton, G., Krizhevsky, A., Sutskever, I., Salakhutdinov, R.: Dropout: a simple way to prevent neural networks from overfitting. J. Mach. Learn. Res. JMLR **15**, 1929–1958 (2014)
25. Salamon, J., Bello, J.P.: Unsupervised feature learning for urban sound classification. In: IEEE International Conference on Acoustics, Speech, and Signal Processing (ICASSP) (2015)
26. Piczak, K.J.: Environmental sound classification with convolutional neural networks. In: IEEE International Workshop on Machine Learning For Signal Processing (MLSP) (2015)
27. Salamon, J., Bello, J.P.: Deep convolutional neural networks and data augmentation for environmental sound classification. IEEE Signal Process. Lett. **24**, 279–283 (2017)
28. Dhillon, I.S., Modha, D.S.: Concept decompositions for large sparse text data using clustering. Mach. Learn. **42**, 143–175 (2001)

Ensembles of Recurrent Neural Networks for Robust Time Series Forecasting

Sascha Krstanovic[✉] and Heiko Paulheim[✉]

Research Group Data and Web Science,
University of Mannheim, Mannheim, Germany
{sascha,heiko}@informatik.uni-mannheim.de

Abstract. Time series forecasting is a problem that is strongly dependent on the underlying process which generates the data sequence. Hence, finding good model fits often involves complex and time consuming tasks such as extensive data preprocessing, designing hybrid models, or heavy parameter optimization. Long Short-Term Memory (LSTM), a variant of recurrent neural networks (RNNs), provide state of the art forecasting performance without prior assumptions about the data distribution. LSTMs are, however, highly sensitive to the chosen network architecture and parameter selection, which makes it difficult to come up with a one-size-fits-all solution without sophisticated optimization and parameter tuning. To overcome these limitations, we propose an ensemble architecture that combines forecasts of a number of differently parameterized LSTMs to a robust final estimate which, on average, performs better than the majority of the individual LSTM base learners, and provides stable results across different datasets. The approach is easily parallelizable and we demonstrate its effectiveness on several real-world data sets.

Keywords: Time series · Ensemble · Meta-learning · Stacking · ARIMA · RNN · LSTM

1 Introduction

Tracking and logging information that is related to a timely dimension has been important in a variety of sectors such as energy, biology or meteorology. Using this data in order to estimate the future behavior is of high value since it has an immediate impact on decision making. Hence, time series forecasting is an established research field. State of the art solutions, among others, include recurrent neural networks, which have been shown to be very powerful for time series forecasting.

On the other hand, recurrent neural networks are not easy to configure for a given use case at hand. Configurations that work well for one setting can be sub-optimal for another problem. To account for that problem, we propose an approach which trains many recurrent neural networks with different parameter

© Springer International Publishing AG 2017
M. Bramer and M. Petridis (Eds.): SGAI-AI 2017, LNAI 10630, pp. 34–46, 2017.
https://doi.org/10.1007/978-3-319-71078-5_3

settings and combine their forecasts using ensemble methods. With that approach, we can provide robust results and circumvent the problem of finding the optimal parameters for a given dataset.

The rest of this paper is structured as follows. Section 2 gives an introduction to important concepts of time series analysis and ensemble learning that are essential for the further sections. Section 2.2 introduces Long Short-Term Memory, a central algorithm used in this work. We propose a concrete time series ensemble architecture in Sect. 3 and validate its performance in the subsequent section, as well as discussing implications and limitations of the approach. We show that the stacked LSTM forecasts beat, on average, the majority of the base learners in terms of root mean squared error (RMSE). Finally, areas holding potential for further improvement are outlined in Sect. 5.

2 Background and Related Work

Although a time series can formally be straightforwardly defined as "a set of observations y_t, each one being recorded at a specific time t" [21], it has a number of important characteristics with implications for data sampling, model training, and ensemble architecture.

2.1 Properties of Time Series Data

Time series forecasting is a special case of sequence modeling. This implicitly means that the observed values correlate with their own past values. The degree of similarity of a series with a lagged version of itself is called autocorrelation. As a consequence, individual observations can not be considered independently of each other, which demands the right sampling strategies when training prediction models. Autocorrelation leads to a couple of special time series properties; first and foremost, stationarity. A series Y is called stationary if its mean and variance stay constant over time, i.e., the statistical properties don't change [20]. Among other algorithms, autoregressive (AR) models theoretically assume stationarity.

Two further important properties are seasonality and trend. Seasonality means that there is some pattern in the series which repeats itself regularly. For example, the sales of ice cream in a year are higher in the summer months and decrease in the winter. Therefore, the seasonal period is fixed and known. We speak of a trend if a general change of direction in the series can be observed, for example if the average level of the series is steadily increasing over time. Identifying and extracting components like seasonality and trend is essential when dealing with state space model algorithms.

2.2 State of the Art Forecasting Algorithms

Very diverse application possibilities have been ensuring high interest in time series analysis and forecasting for decades. An extensive overview is given in [19]. One can arguably divide the majority of approaches to time series forecasting into two categories: autoregressive models for sequences generated by a linear process and artificial neural networks (ANNs) for nonlinear series.

Autoregressive Models

For time series that are generated by a linear process, autoregressive models constitute a popular family of algorithms used for forecasting, in particular, the Box-Jenkins autoregressive integrated moving average (ARIMA) model [18] and its variants. It performs well especially if the assumption that the time series under study is generated from a linear process is met [7], but it is generally not able to capture nonlinear components of a series. The ARIMA model has several subclasses such as the simple autoregressive (AR), the moving average (MA) and the autoregressive moving average (ARMA). ARIMA generated forecasts are composed of a linear combination of most recent series values and their past random errors, cf. [18] for mathematical details.

Artificial Neural Networks: Long Short-Term Memory

Autoregressive models are usually not suited for nonlinear time series. In this case, ANNs are the better alternative since they are capable of modeling non-linear relationships in the series. In fact, ANNs can approximate any continuous function arbitrarily well [4]. Recurrent neural networks (RNNs) are naturally suited for sequence modeling; we can think of them as forward networks with loops in them. [12] provides a detailed explanation of the various neural network architectures and their applications.

Although traditional RNNs can theoretically handle dependencies of a sequence even over a longer time interval, this is practically very challenging. The reason for this is the problem of vanishing or exploding gradients [13]. When training an RNN with hidden layers for a series with long-term dependencies, the model parameters are learned with the backpropagation through time and gradient descent algorithms. These gradient calculations imply extensive multiplications due to the chain rule, and this is where gradients tend to vanish (i.e., approach a value of zero) or explode. LSTM [1] overcomes the problem of unstable gradients. A coherent mathematical view on this is given in [15].

Hybrid Approaches

Since autoregressive models work well for linear series and ANNs suit nonlinear cases, it holds potential to use the two in combination. There have been several studies combining ARIMA and ANN models in a hybrid fashion [5,6,10,11]. In these approaches, an ARIMA model is used to model the linear component of the series, while an ANN captures the nonlinear patterns.

2.3   Approaches to Ensemble Learning

A comprehensive introduction to ensemble learning is given in [8]. Generally, there are different ways to combine a number of estimates to a final one. One popular approach known as *bagging* works by drawing N random samples (with replacement) from a dataset of size N. This is repeated m times such that m datasets, each of size N, are collected. A model is then trained on each of these data sets and the results are averaged (in case of a nominal outcome, the majority vote is taken). The goal here is to reduce variance. A highly popular and effective algorithm that incorporates bagging ideas is called Random Forest [16]. It extends bagging in the sense that also feature selection is randomized.

In the context of time series forecasting, bagging can not be applied in the defined manner since the values of a sequence are autocorrelated. Hence, random sampling of observations in order to train a forecasting model is not possible. Rather than that, it is necessary to develop reasonable sampling strategies instead of drawing random bootstrap samples.

Boosting constitutes another approach to ensembling. The core idea is that examples that were previously poorly estimated receive higher preference over well estimated examples. The objective is to increase the predictive strength of the model. Thinking of a reasonable sampling strategy in the context of sequence learning is essential for boosting. [17] combines a number of RNNs using a boosting approach for time series forecasting.

A more sophisticated ensemble approach is called *stacking*. In this case, a number of models are learned on various subsets of the data and a meta learner is then trained on the base models' forecasts. A meta-learner can theoretically be any model, e.g. Linear Regression or a Random Forest. The motivation is that the meta-learner successfully learns the optimal weights for combining the base learners, and, as a consequence, produces forecasts of higher quality compared to the individual base learners. Therefore, stacking aims at both reducing variance and increasing forecast quality.

3 An LSTM Ensemble Architecture

Finding optimal parameters of an RNN for a given dataset is generally a hard task, also for non-sequential tasks. Additionally, there exist no best parameters that are optimal for all data sets. As a consequence, an LSTM that was trained on a particular data set is very likely to perform poorly on an entirely different time series.

We overcome this problem by proposing an LSTM ensemble architecture. We show that the combination of multiple LSTMs enables time series forecasts that are more robust against variations of data compared to a single LSTM.

3.1 LSTM Base Learners and Diversity Generation

The models that are included in an ensemble are called base learners. In this work, we choose a number of differently constructed LSTMs as base learners. It is trivial to see that creating an ensemble of models is only reasonable if the included models sufficiently differ from one other. Otherwise, a single model would yield results of similar quality. In other words, the generated model forecast estimates should all differ significantly from one another. In our approach, diversity is introduced in two ways:

1. When designing the architecture of an LSTM, one crucial decision is the length of the training sequences that are fed into the network. We train one

LSTM for each user-specified length of the input sequences. Since the input sequence length directly affects the complexity of the learning problem, we change the sizes of the hidden layers accordingly. The applied rule is that the number of nodes in the two hidden layers is equal to the sequence length, respectively. For evaluation, we choose $S = \{50, 55, 60, 65, 70\}$ as sequence lengths under consideration.

2. Generally, LSTM expressibility is sensitive to parameter selection and much time-consuming tuning is required. We overcome this by training a number of LSTMs with different values for four parameters: dropout rate, learning rate, number of hidden layers, and number of nodes in the hidden layers. For each of these parameters, a set Δ of selected values is evaluated. For each of these parameters, we end up with $|S| \cdot |\Delta|$ LSTMs as base learners.

In order to measure the diversity and quality of the base learner forecasts, we compare the average pairwise Pearson correlation coefficients ρ as well as the mean RMSE of the individual sequence forecasts.

Training LSTMs on Temporal Data
In order to train an LSTM model for a sequence forecasting problem, it is necessary to split the training data into a number of sequences whose size depends on the input sequence length as well as the forecasting horizon. Given l past time steps that are used in order to forecast the next k values of the series, a sequence Y must be split into sequences of length $k + l$. These sequences are in turn split into two parts, where the first one represents the LSTM input sequence and the second one the target variable. Formally, the original training data $Y_{train} = [y_1, y_2, ..., y_T]$ of the standardized sequence $Y = [y_1, y_2, ..., y_N], N > T$ is firstly cut into

$$[y_1, ..., y_l, y_{l+1}, ..., y_{l+k}]$$
$$[y_2, ..., y_{l+1}, y_{l+2}, ..., y_{l+k+1}]$$
$$[y_3, ..., y_{l+2}, y_{l+3}, ..., y_{l+k+2}]$$
$$\vdots$$
$$[y_{T-l-k}, ..., y_{T-k-1}, y_{T-k}, ..., y_T]$$

Finally, these sequences are split into LSTM input sequences (left) and LSTM target sequences (right):

$$[y_1, ..., y_l] \qquad [y_{l+1}, ..., y_{l+k}]$$
$$[y_2, ..., y_{l+1}] \qquad [y_{l+2}, ..., y_{l+k+1}]$$
$$[y_3, ..., y_{l+2}] \qquad [y_{l+3}, ..., y_{l+k+2}]$$
$$\vdots$$
$$[y_{T-l-k}, ..., y_{T-k-1}] \qquad [y_{T-k}, ..., y_T]$$

The training data is now in a suitable shape for training an LSTM. The same procedure is applied to the holdout data in order to compute the models' forecast estimates.

3.2 Meta-Learning with Autocorrelation

After the individual LSTMs are trained, the key question is how to combine their individual forecast estimates. We use two approaches to combining:

1. Mean forecast: For each step in the forecasting horizon, take the mean of the base learners' forecasts for each future point.
2. Stacking: First, 70% of the holdout data $Y_{holdout}$ is used to generate the base learners' forecasts. In order to achieve this, the data is prepared as explained in Sect. 3.1. Since the true values of the forecasts are available, the forecasts (i.e., features of the meta-learners) are interpreted as the explanatory variables of the meta-learner and the true values are the target variable. We apply (1) Ridge Regression, (2) the Random Forest algorithm and (3) the xgboost algorithm as meta-learners, such that both linear relationships as well as non-linear ones can be modeled.

   Ridge Regression can be interpreted as linear least squares with L2 regularization of the coefficients. It is particularly effective if the number of predictors is high and if multicollinearity between the features is high. It is, however, a linear model, therefore suited for the case where the relationship between input features and target is linear.

   Random Forest constructs an ensemble of m decision trees, where each tree is trained on a bootstrap sample of the original training data. In addition to this, different random subsets of features are considered at each tree split. The trees usually remain unpruned such that they have high variance. Ultimately, individual tree predictions are averaged to a final estimate. This way, random forests can model non-linear relationships.

   Extreme Gradient Tree Boosting (xgboost) combines trees in a boosting manner and currently provides state of the art performance amongst several prediction challenges.

Independent of the combiner, all approaches are evaluated on the exact same data, i.e., the latter 30% of $Y_{holdout}$, in order to ensure result comparability.

3.3 Constructing the Ensemble

Concisely, the combined forecasts estimates for a univariate, continuous series $Y = \{y_1, y_2, ..., y_N\}$ are generated as follows:

1. Split Y into Y_{train} (85%) and $Y_{holdout}$ (15%).
2. Standardize training and test data:

$$Y_{train} = \frac{Y_{train} - \bar{y}_{train}}{sd_{train}}, \ Y_{holdout} = \frac{Y_{holdout} - \bar{y}_{train}}{sd_{train}}, \text{ where } \bar{y}_{train} = \frac{1}{T}\sum_{i=1}^{T} y_i \text{ and}$$

$sd_{train} = \sqrt{\frac{1}{T}\sum_{i=1}^{T}(y_i - \bar{y}_{train})^2}$. This step is essential when training neural networks due to gradient descent. $\bar{y}_{train}$ and sd_{train} are used to standardize both Y_{train} and $Y_{holdout}$ since $\bar{y}_{holdout}$ and $sd_{holdout}$ are unknown in a real-word scenario.

3. Split the standardized holdout data $Y_{holdout}$ into $Y_{metatrain}$ (first 70% of $Y_{holdout}$) and Y_{test} (last 30% of $Y_{holdout}$) data. $Y_{metatrain}$ is used to generate the training data for the meta-learners, and Y_{test} is unseen data that will be used for the final model evaluations.
4. Train $|S| \cdot |\Delta|$ LSTMs on the training data Y_{train} with given ensemble parameters $S = \{seqlen_1, seqlen_2, ...\}$ and $\Delta = \{\delta_1, \delta_2, ...\}$ as elaborated in Sect. 3.1.
5. Compute the individual LSTM forecasts on all sequences of the $Y_{metatrain}$ holdout data.
6. Train the meta-learners (Ridge Regression and Random Forest), where the individual LSTM forecasts serve as input features. The target variable is given by the actual values of the sequence forecasts.
7. Determine the sequence forecasts on the Y_{test} holdout data. Do this for the individual LSTMs as well as the stacking models. Further, calculate a mean forecast which, for each forecasted future point, takes the average of the LSTMs' individual forecasts for that point.
8. Transform all forecasts back to the original scale, i.e. $FC = FC \cdot sd_{train} + \bar{y}_{train}$ for each forecast vector FC.

Since the LSTMs in step 4 are independent of each other, they can be trained in parallel.

4   Experimental Analysis

We test the performance of the approach by applying it to four datasets of different size, shape and origin. The experimental analysis shows that the ensemble of LSTMs gives robust results across different data sets. Even more impressive is that stacking outperforms all other models, both base LSTM learners and baselines, in any considered case.

4.1   Setup

Figure 1 depicts the four datasets in their original shape, Table 1 describes their basic properties.

The algorithm specified in Sect. 3.3 is applied to each of the datasets. The following forecasting approaches are evaluated and compared:

- LSTM base models
- LSTM ensemble variants: mean forecast, stacking forecast via Ridge Regression (RR), Random Forest (RF) and xgboost (XGB)
- Simple moving average, predicting a constant value which is the mean of the input sequence
- Simple exponential smoothing. Here, the i-th forecasted value is given by

$$y_{t+i} = \alpha y_t + \alpha(1-\alpha)y_{t-1} + \alpha(1-\alpha)^2 y_{t-2} + ... + \alpha(1-\alpha)^{49} y_{t-49} \qquad (1)$$

- ARIMA

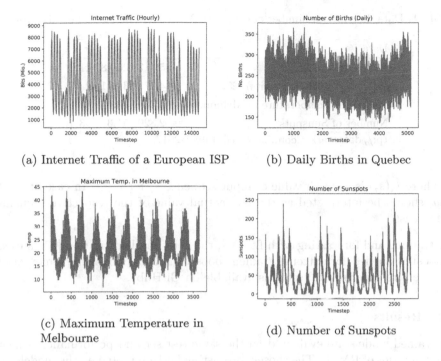

(a) Internet Traffic of a European ISP   (b) Daily Births in Quebec

(c) Maximum Temperature in
Melbourne

(d) Number of Sunspots

Fig. 1. Four time series in scope for the experimental analysis

– xgboost. Out-of-the-box xgboost is not capable of sequence forecasting. In order to account for this, we generate an additional variable which encodes forecasting step $1, 2, \ldots, 50$ of each example. Therewith, the feature matrix X and target variable y for the xgboost algorithm are

$$
X = \begin{pmatrix}
y_{t-49}(s_1) & y_{t-48}(s_1) & \cdots & y_t(s_1) & 1 \\
y_{t-49}(s_1) & y_{t-48}(s_1) & \cdots & y_t(s_1) & 2 \\
\vdots & \vdots & \vdots & \vdots & \vdots \\
y_{t-49}(s_1) & y_{t-48}(s_1) & \cdots & y_t(s_1) & 50 \\
y_{t-49}(s_2) & y_{t-48}(s_2) & \cdots & y_t(s_2) & 1 \\
y_{t-49}(s_2) & y_{t-48}(s_2) & \cdots & y_t(s_2) & 2 \\
\vdots & \vdots & \vdots & \vdots & \vdots \\
y_{t-49}(s_2) & y_{t-48}(s_2) & \cdots & y_t(s_2) & 50 \\
\vdots & \vdots & \vdots & \vdots & \vdots \\
y_{t-49}(s_N) & y_{t-48}(s_N) & \cdots & y_t(s_N) & 1 \\
y_{t-49}(s_N) & y_{t-48}(s_N) & \cdots & y_t(s_N) & 2 \\
\vdots & \vdots & \vdots & \vdots & \vdots \\
y_{t-49}(s_N) & y_{t-48}(s_N) & \cdots & y_t(s_N) & 50
\end{pmatrix}, y = \begin{pmatrix}
y_{t+1}(s_1) \\
y_{t+2}(s_1) \\
\vdots \\
y_{t+50}(s_1) \\
y_{t+1}(s_2) \\
y_{t+2}(s_2) \\
\vdots \\
y_{t+50}(s_2) \\
\vdots \\
y_{t+1}(s_N) \\
y_{t+2}(s_N) \\
\vdots \\
y_{t+50}(s_N)
\end{pmatrix} \quad (2)
$$

Table 1. Data description, number of examples N, mean μ, and standard deviation σ

Data	N	μ	σ
Births in Quebec [26]	5,113	250.8	41.9
Internet Traffic (Mio. bits) [25]	14,772	3,811	2,161
Maximum Temperature in Melbourne[a]	3,650	20.0	6.1
Number of Sunspots[a]	2,820	51.3	43.4

[a]http://datamarket.com, accessed July 7 2017.

where $y_i(s_j)$ is the i-th value of input sequence s_j for $i \leq t$. In case of $i > t$, y_i should be interpreted as the i-th actual value of the respective sequence forecast.

For training and forecasting with LSTMs, the keras implementation [27] is used. xgboost is applied for extreme gradient boosting. A functional implementation of the entire experimental setup is available on GitHub[1].

4.2   Results

All trained models are evaluated on the same test set and performance is measured in terms of RMSE. The chosen forecasting horizon is 50, i.e., the models are trained and tested to estimate the next 50 values of given input sequences. The average performance across all test sequences in the respective test set is shown in Tables 2 and 3. The first column indicates the diversity-generating parameter. For our experiments, we evaluate dropout values $\{0.1, 0.2, 0.3, 0.4, 0.5\}$, a number of hidden layers in $\{2, 3, 4, 5\}$, the number of nodes in the input and hidden layers varies between the length of the input sequence, half of the length, and quarter of the length. Learning rate is set to values $\{0.01, 0.001, 0.0001, 0.00001\}$.

As default values, we choose RMSProp [23] as optimizer, the learning rate is set to 0.001, the loss function is the mean squared error (MSE), batch size is 32 and training is performed over 15 epochs per LSTM. One LSTM input layer and two LSTM hidden layers are used, whose number of nodes is equal to the current sequence input length. Further, a dropout [22] of 0.3 is added to the LSTM layers in order to prevent model overfitting.

The second column represents the metric under consideration. We compare the model performance is terms of RMSE. Results are transformed back to their original scale prior to computing the RMSE for better interpretability. The cases where an ensemble beats all other tested models are marked in bold and the best performing combiner algorithm is stated in parentheses (RF: Random Forest, RR: Ridge Regression, XGB: xgboost). Additionally, we provide the average pairwise Pearson correlation ρ between the forecasts of the base LSTMs. The more the model forecasts differ from one another, the higher the potential improvement gained by an ensemble. The key observations are:

---

[1] https://github.com/saschakrs/TSensemble, accessed July 7 2017.

Table 2. Result summary for "Births" and "Traffic" datasets

Varied parameter	Performance measure	Dataset	
		Births	Traffic
-	Simple mean RMSE	42.19	1380.53
-	Exp. smoothing RMSE	49.36	1389.90
-	ARIMA RMSE	38.13	1224.83
-	xgboost RMSE	40.55	1033.65
Dropout	ρ between base LSTM forecasts	0.94	0.91
Dropout	Avg. base LSTM RMSE	27.76	991.41
Dropout	Best base LSTM RMSE	25.23	826.42
Dropout	Best ensemble RMSE	25.45 (XGB)	**652.42 (RF)**
#Hidden L	ρ between base LSTM forecasts	0.95	0.91
#Hidden L	Avg. base LSTM RMSE	27.77	726.20
#Hidden L	Best base LSTM RMSE	25.31	811.35
#Hidden L	Best ensemble RMSE	25.62 (XGB)	**656.97 (RF)**
#Nodes	ρ between base LSTM forecasts	0.95	0.91
#Nodes	Avg. base LSTM RMSE	28.55	944.92
#Nodes	Best base LSTM RMSE	25.65	826.42
#Nodes	Best ensemble RMSE	**25.57 (XGB)**	**630.85 (RF)**
Learning rate	ρ between base LSTM forecasts	0.56	0.80
Learning rate	Avg. base LSTM RMSE	42.85	1578.64
Learning rate	Best base LSTM RMSE	25.65	826.41
Learning rate	Best ensemble RMSE	**25.37 (RR)**	**667.26 (RF)**

- In 81% of all cases, an LSTM stacking model outperforms all other approaches. In the other cases, there is only one LSTM model (respectively) that slightly outperforms the stacked LSTMs.
- Although the ensemble architecture is identical for all data sets, there is no single best meta-learner for all data sets.
- Model diversity is essential: ρ is correlated to the best ensemble RMSE by more than 70%, i.e., a low ρ between forecasts tends to increase ensemble performance. This becomes visible especially in the context of the Sunspots data, where the stacked LSTMs outperform their base learners by more than 50% RMSE. Hence, combining many comparably weak LSTM predictors results in a greater performance win than the combination of a few good learners.

Table 3. Result summary for "Melbourne" and "Sunspots" datasets

Varied parameter	Performance measure	Dataset	
		Melbourne	Sunspots
-	Simple mean RMSE	7.44	74.88
-	Exp. smoothing RMSE	7.47	47.88
-	ARIMA RMSE	7.41	54.50
-	xgboost RMSE	5.90	47.09
Dropout	ρ between base LSTM forecasts	0.76	0.40
Dropout	Avg. base LSTM RMSE	6.94	79.39
Dropout	Best base LSTM RMSE	6.51	70.82
Dropout	Best ensemble RMSE	**6.10 (RR)**	**33.74 (RR)**
#Hidden L	ρ between base LSTM forecasts	0.69	0.39
#Hidden L	Avg. base LSTM RMSE	6.90	79.90
#Hidden L	Best base LSTM RMSE	6.70	67.53
#Hidden L	Best ensemble RMSE	**6.11 (RR)**	**31.69 (XGB)**
#Nodes	ρ between base LSTM forecasts	0.75	0.51
#Nodes	Avg. base LSTM RMSE	7.01	81.58
#Nodes	Best base LSTM RMSE	6.69	67.53
#Nodes	Best ensemble RMSE	**6.13 (RR)**	**32.91 (RR)**
Learning rate	ρ between base LSTM forecasts	0.59	0.59
Learning rate	Avg. base LSTM RMSE	7.36	85.42
Learning rate	Best base LSTM RMSE	5.91	67.53
Learning rate	Best ensemble RMSE	5.97 (RR)	**31.35 (XGB)**

- For all ensembles, it holds that its forecasts are significantly different from all baseline estimates. This result is based on the paired t-test for significance.[2]
- Out of the four investigated LSTM parameters, varying the learning rate leads to greatest diversity generation. The reason for this is that the learning rate has a strong effect on the local minimum that is reached. Varying the values for dropout, hidden layers and nodes tends to generate forecasts with higher correlation and less diversity.

5   Future Work and Conclusion

The experiments suggest that the LSTM ensemble forecast is indeed a robust estimator for multi-step ahead time series forecasts. Although there exist single models that perform better in terms of RMSE, the proposed ensemble approach

---

[2] Note that even if for smaller datasets, like the Sunspot dataset, the test set is fairly small, this shows that the results are still significant.

enables users to achieve solid forecasts without the need to focus on heavy parameter optimization. An interesting observation is that the outstanding performance of the ensemble forecast is valid across multiple datasets from entirely different domains. There remains, however, significant potential to further improve some aspects of the algorithm, especially with regard to the fundamental design of the ensemble.

The proposed LSTM ensemble architecture opens the door to lots of further potential. First and foremost, the meta-learner of the stacking model could be improved in two ways. One is to generate more features describing the dynamics of the series, especially that part immediately preceding the forecasting horizon. Additionally, the meta-learners' parameters could be tuned more heavily, or it could be replaced by an entirely different meta-learning algorithm.

Another area of improvement lies in the design of the ensemble itself. The selection of values for sequence lengths S and LSTM parameters Δ could further influence the final result, especially if some domain specific knowledge regarding the series is available.

Lastly, configuring the individual LSTMs may increase the general quality of the base learners. This can be achieved by tuning the LSTM parameters. It must be ensured, however, that the diversity between these models remains sufficiently large.

References

1. Hochreiter, S., Schmidhuber, J.: Long short-term memory. Neural Comput. **9**(8), 1735–1780 (1997)
2. Tsukamoto, K., Mitsuishi, Y., and Sassano, M.: Learning with multiple stacking for named entity recognition. In: Proceedings of the 6th Conference on Natural Language Learning, vol. 20, pp. 1–4. Association for Computational Linguistics (2002)
3. Lai, K.K., Yu, L., Wang, S., Wei, H.: A novel nonlinear neural network ensemble model for financial time series forecasting. In: Alexandrov, V.N., van Albada, G.D., Sloot, P.M.A., Dongarra, J. (eds.) ICCS 2006. LNCS, vol. 3991, pp. 790–793. Springer, Heidelberg (2006). https://doi.org/10.1007/11758501_106
4. Hornik, K., Stinchcombe, M., White, H.: Multilayer feedforward networks are universal approximators. Neural Netw. **2**(5), 359–366 (1989). Elsevier, Amsterdam
5. Zhang, G.P.: Time series forecasting using a hybrid ARIMA and neural network model. Neurocomputing **50**, 159–175 (2003). Elsevier, Amsterdam
6. Adhikari, R., Agrawal, R.K.: A linear hybrid methodology for improving accuracy of time series forecasting. Neural Comput. Appl. **25**(2), 269–281 (2014). Springer, London, UK
7. Adhikari, R.: A neural network based linear ensemble framework for time series forecasting. Neurocomputing **157**, 231–242 (2015). Elsevier, Amsterdam
8. Armstrong, J.S.: Combining forecasts. In: Armstrong, J.S. (ed.) Principles of Forecasting. ISOR, pp. 417–439. Springer, Boston (2001). https://doi.org/10.1007/978-0-306-47630-3_19
9. Babu, C.N., Reddy, B.E.: A moving-average filter based hybrid ARIMA-ANN model for forecasting time series data. Appl. Soft Comput. **23**, 27–38 (2014). Elsevier, Amsterdam

10. Wang, L., Zou, H., Su, J., Li, L., Chaudhry, S.: An ARIMA-ANN hybrid model for time series forecasting. Syst. Res. Behav. Sci. **30**(3), 244–259 (2013)
11. Aladag, C.H., Egrioglu, E., Kadilar, C.: Forecasting nonlinear time series with a hybrid methodology. Appl. Math. Lett. **22**(9), 1467–1470 (2009)
12. Goodfellow, I., Bengio, Y., Courville, A.: Deep Learning. MIT Press, Cambridge (2016). http://www.deeplearningbook.org
13. Bengio, Y., Simard, P., Frasconi, P.: Learning long-term dependencies with gradient descent is difficult. IEEE Trans. Neural Netw. **5**(2), 157–166 (1994)
14. Malhotra, P., Vig, L., Shroff, G., Agarwal, P.: Long short term memory networks for anomaly detection in time series. In: Proceedings of the 23rd European Symposium on Artificial Neural Networks. Computational Intelligence and Machine Learning, pp. 89–94. Presses universitaires de Louvain (2015)
15. Pascanu, R., Mikolov, T., Bengio, Y.: On the difficulty of training recurrent neural networks. In: Proceedings of the 30th International Conference on Machine Learning, ICML 2013, vol. 28, pp. 1310–1318 (2013)
16. Breiman, L.: Random forests. Mach. Learn. **45**(1), 5–32 (2001)
17. Assaad, M., Boné, R., Cardot, H.: A new boosting algorithm for improved time-series forecasting with recurrent neural networks. Inf. Fusion **9**(1), 41–55 (2008)
18. Durbin, J., Koopman, S.J.: Time Series Analysis by State Space Methods, vol. 38. Oxford University Press, Oxford (2012)
19. Hamilton, J.D.: Time Series Analysis, vol. 2. Princeton University Press, Princeton (1994)
20. Shumway, R.H., Stoffer, D.S.: Time Series Analysis and Its Applications: with R Examples. Springer Science & Business Media, Heidelberg (2010)
21. Brockwell, P.J., Davis, R.A.: Introduction to Time Series and Forecasting, 2nd edn. Springer, New York (2010)
22. Srivastava, N., Hinton, G.E., Krizhevsky, A., Sutskever, I., Salakhutdinov, R.: Dropout: a simple way to prevent neural networks from overfitting. J. Mach. Learn. Res. **15**(1), 1929–1958 (2014)
23. Tieleman, T., Hinton, G.: Lecture 6.5-rmsprop: divide the gradient by a running average of its recent magnitude. COURSERA: Neural Netw. Mach. Learn. **4**(2), 26–31 (2012)
24. Lichman, M.: UCI Machine Learning Repository. University of California, School of Information and Computer Science, Irvine, CA (2013). http://archive.ics.uci.edu/ml
25. Cortez, P., Rio, M., Rocha, M., Sousa, P.: Multi-scale Internet traffic forecasting using neural networks and time series methods. Expert Syst. **29**(2), 143–155 (2012)
26. Hipel, K.W., McLeod, A.I.: Time Series Modelling of Water Resources and Environmental Systems, vol. 45. Elsevier, Amsterdam (1994)
27. Chollet, F.: Keras (2015). https://github.com/fchollet/keras

A Blackboard Based Hybrid Multi-Agent System for Improving Classification Accuracy Using Reinforcement Learning Techniques

Vasileios Manousakis Kokorakis[1(✉)], Miltos Petridis[2],
and Stelios Kapetanakis[1]

[1] School of Computing, Engineering and Mathematics,
University of Brighton, Brighton, UK
{V.ManousakisKokorakis, S.Kapetanakis}@brighton.ac.uk
[2] Department of Computer Science, Middlesex University London, London, UK
M.Petridis@mdx.ac.uk

Abstract. In this paper, a general purpose multi-agent classifier system based on the blackboard architecture using reinforcement Learning techniques is proposed for tackling complex data classification problems. A trust metric for evaluating agent's performance and expertise based on Q-learning and employing different voting processes is formulated. Specifically, multiple heterogeneous machine learning agents, are devised to form the expertise group for the proposed Coordinated Heterogeneous Intelligent Multi-Agent Classifier System (CHIMACS). To evaluate the effectiveness of CHIMACS, a variety of benchmark problems are used, including small and high dimensional datasets with and without noise. The results from CHIMACS are compared with those of individual ML models and ensemble methods. The results indicate that CHIMACS is effective in identifying classifier agent expertise and can combine their knowledge to improve the overall prediction performance.

Keywords: Reinforcement learning · Hybrid systems · Q-learning · Machine learning · Agent voting · Multi-agent systems · Trust metric · Classification

1 Introduction

Machine learning models have been extensively used to solve problems in various application fields [1]. However, according to the "No Free Lunch Theorem" there is no model to tackle every kind of problem. This is due to the fact that individual machine learning models have limited capabilities [2, 3], e.g. deep learning models are very effective in learning representations from high dimensional unstructured data [4, 5], while others are more effective in learning from noisy data sets or numerical data or smaller datasets. At the same time, as reported in literature [6, 7] the concept of ensemble models is proposed to improve accuracy and stability of individual classifiers. The underlying rationale of an ensemble is to combine several individual and potentially weak models to produce a robust ensemble model. Multiple ensemble models have been proposed [5] and used to handle problems in various domains, e.g. Credit card fraud detection [8], medical diagnosis [9], etc. In the case of classification

© Springer International Publishing AG 2017
M. Bramer and M. Petridis (Eds.): SGAI-AI 2017, LNAI 10630, pp. 47–57, 2017.
https://doi.org/10.1007/978-3-319-71078-5_4

problems, the potential classes yielded by individual classifiers are combined using a set of predefined criteria in the ensemble algorithm.

In this study, the ensemble model is extended with the use of a Blackboard based Multi Agent System (MAS) for classification problems. In this approach classification problems are handled by a pool of heterogeneous autonomous classifier agents controlled by a Blackboard component. Each individual classifier provides an estimation of the target output of a new data observation. The Blackboard controller collects the prediction outcomes from all individual "expert" classifier agents and performs a set of voting rounds. Consequently, the Blackboard updates its trust score depending on the validity of the previous answers. Heterogeneity of data representation amongst the individual experts is translated in terms of a common internal structure and ontology. Classifier agents like logistic regression, k-NN, neural networks and Bayesian networks have been employed. Ensemble techniques like random forests and XGBoost have been integrated in the system too. A meta-reasoning ontology model has been formulated to capture the relationship between the individual agent knowledge representation and the knowledge contained inside the Blackboard based MAS.

In this study, we propose a blackboard based Multi Agent architecture as a framework to effectively combine predictions from multiple heterogeneous classifiers depending on the identified expertise context and competence for each classifier. The main objectives of this research are as follows:

- Formulating a protocol that effectively controls the operations of the heterogeneous agent members.
- Formulating a trust function for identifying the competence of each expert agent.
- Employing a mechanism for extracting distinct knowledge areas from the datasets.
- Devising a robust prediction fusion mechanism.

The rest of this paper is structured as follows: Sect. 2 looks at background literature especially in the area of MAS and Blackboard Systems for hybrid intelligent systems, Sect. 3 describes the approach and the Coordinated Heterogeneous Intelligent Multi-Agent Classifier System (CHIMACS) system and Sect. 4 describes the experiments and results, followed by conclusions and discussion of further work in Sect. 5.

2 Literature Review

2.1 Multi-Agent Systems

MAS implementations using different architectures have been used, investigated and applied to various domains, e.g. fault diagnosis [10], agriculture [11], medical diagnosis [12], etc. Broadly, a MAS is composed of multiple independent potentially intelligent agents interacting among themselves through a reasoning or inference scheme within a prescribed environment. Some implementations for air traffic control and classification performance, reported in [13, 14] utilize reinforcement learning techniques as reward function for its agent members. These systems are shown to be able to adapt to environment changes and present robust and accurate results. More specifically, the MAS system in [14] has the ability to figure out which of each agent ensembles are more competent and use their predictions for future classification problems.

2.2 Blackboard System Architectures

The Blackboard paradigm was introduced in the 80s and used on a number of applications of expert systems [18]. In the early 90s, Petridis et al. proposed a blackboard based architecture for the integration and combination of diverse hybrid Machine Learning, AI and mathematical models [15, 16]. A number of other blackboard based architectures and systems were proposed and shown to work effectively over a range of application areas [19]. Teodorescu [17] proposed a blackboard based architecture for a hybrid MAS to combine heterogeneous Case Based Reasoning classifiers. In this, she proposed a reinforcement learning algorithm based on the concept of agent confidence and agent trust and a weighted voting process. However, in this work, the hybrid element of the problem was based on similar agents operating on different datasets. In the work proposed in this paper, the approach applies on hybrid systems consisting of heterogeneous classifier agents operating on the same datasets. This presents the additional issue of different data representation and reasoning paradigm between agents that introduces the challenge of reconciliation and normalization of the various views of the dataset and the classification process among the agents.

3 The CHIMACS Model

In Fig. 1, the structure of the proposed Coordinated Heterogeneous Intelligent Multi-Agent Classifier System (CHIMACS) is depicted. It is based on the blackboard architecture and consists of three main modules. The blackboard-controller module is responsible for orchestrating the entire process which includes agent coordination, voting, trust update and final decision making. The knowledge area module represents the expertise of the knowledge sources and the agent repository module accommodates the agents. An approach using a trust measure based on the HMCBR system [17] and Q-learning [14], using Bayesian discounted future reward and two main voting procedures is proposed. The initialization of the trust score for each agent is random and in every execution cycle is updated depending on the validity of the predictions pertaining to each known data and class observation.

In terms of voting, different versions of the voting process have been implemented. However, only those presenting significantly different results are presented. Two main methods are implemented for the purposes of this study. The first voting is based on "best bid wins voting rule" and the second is based on the "majority voting rule" [20]. The winner for the first voting process is nominated through the highest bid submitted to the blackboard from the agent members. Each individual expert agent is evaluated from its bid score. Majority voting on the other hand, allows the expert agents to combine their knowledge and combine into one final proposal. The blackboard is then responsible for taking the final decision and updating trust measures for all agents.

The CHIMACS typical procedure is depicted in Fig. 2. The focus of this study is mainly on the measurement of agent trust, the impact it has on the voting process and

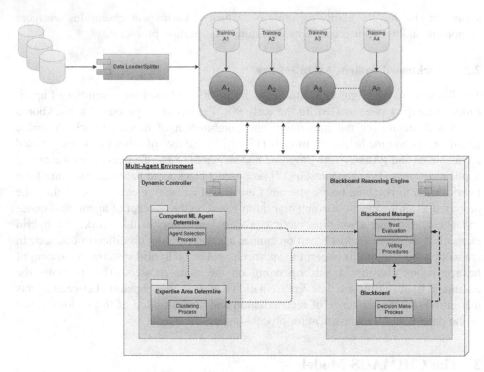

Fig. 1. The CHIMACS structure

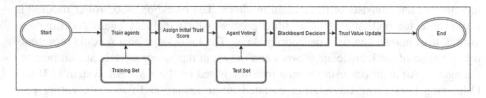

Fig. 2. Q-CHIMACS procedure

how the voting score influences the quality of an individual prediction and hence the increase of the overall prediction performance. The proposed method can be broken down into three steps.

In the first step, the initial trust score for each individual knowledge source is calculated using the Q-learning function. In the second, Q-learning function is employed to update the dedicated trust value of each knowledge source. The third step incudes the voting process. The blackboard initiates a series of voting procedures in which each expert expresses its opinion in a single or an aggregative manner. After voting is finished, blackboard concludes to a final decision. The next sections, describe in more detail the steps involved in the increase of prediction performance.

3.1 Trust Measurement of Agents

As mentioned earlier, the major factor for evaluating each expert agent's competence is through the trust score. Individual agents have a measure of their own confidence in the classification results they provide. This however, is difficult to use and compare on the blackboard due to the heterogeneity of the methods used by each agent and due to various other factors, such as the quality of training sets, the different semantics employed by each agent and the learning and feedback history of each agent. There-fore, there is a need to supplement and moderate the "local" agent confidence view by the central "trust" view of the blackboard that can be learned during the operation of the multi agent system. This approach has been first proposed by Teodorescu et al. [17] and was shown to work for agents operating on different datasets. In this work we inves-tigate the application of this approach to heterogeneous agents operating on the same dataset.

According to literature [17, 21] there many definitions of computational trust in regards to MAS. Commonly is defined as the degree of the trustworthiness an entity has towards another in regards to the reliability, truth or the ability to perform a task or how well it can perform a task in a multi-agent environment [22].

In this paper, we propose a model free method based on Q-learning, as a metric for personalized trust calculation and assertion. In each classification state the algorithm learns an action-utility representation. The value of choosing a class for each obser-vation i is the summation of the trust score in the previous state and the score of the state the agent currently is in. The trust score of each agent is calculated using Eq. (1):

$$Trust\,(i, a, c) = \sum \mu\left(r_{a,i}^c + \gamma \max{}_{Pr}\left(Pr(Y = y|X)_{a,i}^c\right)\right) \tag{1}$$

where $Trust\,(i, a, c)$ represents the trust value with regards to the i_{th} test observation belonging to the data cluster c and classified by the agent a, where $c = 1, \ldots, n$ and $a = 1, \ldots, m$. Total number of knowledge areas (data clusters) and total number of agents respectively. $\mu \in [0, 1]$ is the learning rate and $\gamma \in [0, 1]$ is the discount factor, and $Pr(Y = y|X)_{a,i}^c$ is the probability estimate of the predicted outcome.

3.2 Updating the Trust Measurement

Equation (2) is used during the entire classification process to update the trust value based on the predicted outcome for each observation for every agent member in the MAS. Depending on the validity of the examined test data observation, the blackboard manager increases or decreases the trust score accordingly by evaluating the reward for the current state and the discounted factor of the probability estimate enhanced by the learning rate μ. This is done for every identified data cluster (knowledge area), to capture the fact that different agent classifiers may be more or less accurate at different subdomains of the overall problem domain and dataset. The update function is depicted as follows:

$$Trust_a^c(i) = Trust_a^c(i-1) \pm \mu \left(r_{a,i}^c + \gamma \max_{Pr} \left(Pr(Y = y|X)_{a,i}^c \right) \right) \quad (2)$$

where $Trust_a^c(i-1)$ is the trust value of the previous state regarding the agent a classifying the observation i that belongs to the knowledge area (data cluster) c. The initialization of the Trust function and it's parameters is as follows, $Trust_a^c(i)t_0 = 0$, $\mu_{c,i-1}^a t_0 = 1$, $r_{c,i-1}^a t_0 = 0$ and $\gamma_{c,i-1}^a t_0 = 0.0001$. The blackboard uses the current state i, reward r and the estimated probability $Pr(Y = y|X)$ to evaluate the performance of each expert.

The score values are updated for every knowledge area until the systems reach an equilibrium. i.e. there is no change in the Q-Trust value for ten consecutive iterations. Once the Trust algorithm converges we can use these values to increase the overall accuracy performance. The Trust algorithm is given in Fig. 3.

Algorithm <u>CHIMACS</u>
 Input: Agents, Test Data
 Output: Accuracy Performance
 Determine Initial Trust (Eq.2)
 Until (True)
  For each Test Observation:
   For each agent:
    Collect votes
    Initialize Voting Procedure
    Finalize Decision Making
    Update Trust Score
   End for
   Increase gamma Factor
  End for
 End

Fig. 3. The trust algorithm.

3.3 Voting

From a social choice theory point of view, CHIMACS can be considered as a "society" [25] with a finite set of machine learning agents as its electorate or voters $N = \{1, 2, \ldots, n\}$ voting over an finite set of alternatives $A = \{1, 2, \ldots m\}$, $m \geq 2$. Each agent $i \in N$ holds a quasi-order P^i (ranking of the alternatives) over A, where transitivity, totality, reflexivity and antisymmetry are satisfied [26]. The set of all quasi-orders is denoted as $L = L(A)$, so for $i \in N$, $\mathcal{P}^i \in \mathcal{L}$ throughout. Thus, for each ML agent a preference rankings profile vector $i \in N$ is constructed.

In this research, a variety of social scoring functions (SCF) and social welfare functions (SWF) have been used but only the ones that produced significant increase in the overall prediction performance have been described. According to May's Theorem [26], considering two alternatives and any number of voters, majority rule declares as winner the most dominant between the two alternatives.

Majority SCF and judgment aggregation are used by the blackboard in order to conclude to an alternative either by nominating an agent as a winner in every epoch or by exploiting the diversity in capabilities. $Trust_a^c(i)$ the system has developed up to time t_{i-1}, has major impact to the agent's vote. Since Q-Trust is updated according to the validity of the answer for each agent, trust score reflects the quality of the answer and the expertise of every expert. Majority SCF and judgment aggregation voting are formulated as follows in Eqs. (3), (4):

$$Majority\ vote\mathcal{A}_n\ SCF = Trust_a^c(i) * \mathcal{E} \qquad (3)$$

$$Majority\ voteA_n\ SWF = \sum\nolimits_{voteA_n} Trust_a^c(i) * \mathcal{E} \qquad (4)$$

where $\mathcal{E}$ is the probability estimate over the alternative $\mathcal{A}_n$. Majority voting SCF declares a single alternative as the winner, whereas in judgment aggregation SWF every vote has its impact to the outcome. Both functions provide an output that is fed into (5).

$$Winner\ Vote = \text{argmax}_{p^i}\ \mathcal{P}^i \qquad (5)$$

Trust weighted voting presented an increase in the overall accuracy performance. In the next section, the results over three different benchmark datasets are described.

4   Experiments and Results

In this section, the results using a variety of datasets are presented. For the purposes of the evaluation, three very different publicly available datasets were chosen. The variety between the datasets is in terms of data types, dimensionality and quantity, but also in terms of the relative accuracy of best classifiers. Four datasets, noisy vs noise-free and balanced vs highly imbalanced benchmark problems have been selected to provide an evaluation of the approach. The performance of individual agent classifiers, including ensembles, sets the baseline for comparisons between them and CHIMACS.

First, the noisy Q&A extracted from StackOverflow and Prima Indian Diabetes problems were employed. Next, two noise-free but imbalanced benchmark problems (Credit Approval, Wine Quality) from the UCI machine learning repository [28], were employed. Details of the data sets are shown in Table 1. The results from CHIMACS were compared with those from its constituents.

4.1   Case Study Experiments

Two noisy and two noise-free but imbalanced problems used for evaluation are: (i) Q&A from Stack Exchange (ii) Prima Indian Diabetes (iii) Credit Approval and (iv) Wine Quality [28]. For every examined dataset, the same procedure was followed

Table 1. Datasets description

Dataset	Number of observations	Number of input features	Number of classes
Q&A	1.000.000	68	2
Wine quality	4898	12	2
Credit approval	690	15	2
PID	768	9	2

regarding the individual agent classifier training. 10-fold cross-validation and testing method was repeated 10 times, with 70% and 30% of the data samples used for training (80% for learning and 10% for validation) and test, respectively. The CHIMACS performance was evaluated against the same test bed the agents received. Table 2 shows the results for all data sets. It can clearly be seen that CHIMACS performed better in comparison with its counterparts. Also, it is observed that the accuracy rate for both individual agents as well as CHIMACS for the Q&A problem deteriorated due to increased noise levels. These datasets reflect real-word dataset structures, providing significant evaluation of the CHIMACS performance. However, more datasets from various domains are currently examined to further verify its prediction performance. Finally, in the "models" column the agent's names are not specified since a variety of algorithms have been employed depending on the dataset.

Table 2. Accuracy rates (%) for the examined datasets

Models	PID	Credit approval	Wine quality	Q&A
MAS agent 1	0.68	0.68	0.94	0.72
MAS agent 2	0.72	0.70	0.94	0.64
MAS agent 3	0.69	0.71	0.69	0.71
AdaBoostM1	0.67	0.70	0.99	0.67
Bagging	0.74	0.72	0.99	0.70
Stacking	0.72	0.72	0.99	0.70
Vote	0.71	0.74	0.99	0.71
CHIMACS	**0.78**	**0.78**	**0.99**	**0.74**

The output clearly show that CHIMACS has the ability not only to learn the expertise of every knowledge source inside its environment, but to combine the prediction outcome of its agent members to increase the overall prediction performance. The main advantages of CHIMACS emerge from the ability to realize the agent expertise by evaluating their competence and combining their knowledge.

The relative gains in the dataset where individual agents score quite high (Wine Quality) shows that there is still room for improvement by combining classifiers. We can see that the CHIMACS performance using the Q&A dataset did not extremely outperform any of its agent counterparts. This is observed because for this experiment we did not implement the concept of distinct knowledge areas (data clusters). Thus, the system could not realize which agents are more competent in certain knowledge area parts of the dataset. Similar results are observed in [14], where overall accuracy performance increased by that much as its best agent. However, further work under way has shown that further improvements can be achieved by defining clusters or "neighbourhoods" where the trust can be put in the context of classifier expertise in specific domain subdomains/areas.

The evaluation showed that the proposed approach is relatively poor in converging fast enough when it comes to datasets with little data observations since the gamma factor needs to increase very slowly and be more sensitive so that is able to capture the underlying trends. The CHIMACS approach may not be suitable for problems where a single agent performs very well or outperforms all other agents. However, in more complex and noisy problems, especially where each agent may be better at predicting different data cases, the CHIMACS approach can increase the overall prediction accuracy.

Finally, the CHIMACS approach as with most reinforcement learning approaches suffers from the "cold start" problem [17]. A pre-trained and initialized CHIMACS system can perform better than a "cold start" one, assuming no major paradigm or model sifts in the stream of data to be classified.

Further analysis is currently under way using different datasets and looking at clustering the datasets into areas of different expertise levels for different classifiers.

5 Conclusions and Future Work

In this paper, a blackboard based multi-agent classifier framework, namely CHIMACS has been proposed. A number of heterogeneous machine learning agents are used as the underlying reasoning sources. A trust metric based on Q-learning has been devised to capture the quality and the knowledge area expertise of each individual agent inside CHIMACS. Social score and welfare functions have been implemented to give the opportunity to each agent member to express their opinions related to an examined problem. Several benchmark problems with and without noise have been used to evaluate the efficiency of CHIMACS. The results have been compared with those from each individual agent and other ensemble methods. Although, each agent behaves differently, the system can exploit the capabilities deriving from the fact that each agent perceives the problem from its own knowledge and reasoning perspective. Thus, CHIMACS is able to improve the overall performance either by declaring a single agent as a winner or by aggregating agent preferences over an alternative. In addition, the approach can be considered as general purpose since it has no restrictions regarding domain applicability or the type of machine learning employed. The transparency and interoperability of the approach is a specific advantage of this approach, especially when compared to ensemble methods that hard-code classifiers together and usually do little or no learning and introspection. The use of confidence and trust and the use of a MAS around a blackboard provides extra transparency and it can support explanation of the classification decisions.

For further work, the effectiveness of CHIMACS is being evaluated using more binary and non-binary class datasets from the literature, training agents using clustered data, implementing different reinforcement learning trust score methods, adopt new voting procedures and transform the blackboard manager into an intelligent component for dynamically extracting knowledge areas (data clusters). Concluding, a more robust analysis of the accuracy results is essential. The addition of agent confidence and normalization of voting scores as well as tackling the "cold start" problem as well as that of model or paradigm shift in dataset streams will be explored.

References

1. Langley, P., Simon, H.A.: Applications of machine learning and rule induction. Commun. ACM **38**(11), 54–64 (1995)
2. Hoffmann, A.G.: General limitations on machine learning. In: ECAI, pp. 345–347 (1990)
3. Wolpert, D.H.: The supervised learning no-free-lunch theorems. In: Roy, R., Köppen, M., Ovaska, S., Furuhashi, T., Hoffmann, F. (eds.) Soft Computing and Industry: Recent Applications, pp. 25–42. Springer, London (2002). https://doi.org/10.1007/978-1-4471-0123-9_3
4. Işın, A., Direkoğlu, C., Şah, M.: Review of MRI-based brain tumor image segmentation using deep learning methods. Procedia Comput. Sci. **102**, 317–324 (2016)
5. LeCun, Y., Bengio, Y., Hinton, G.: Deep learning. Nature **521**(7553), 436–444 (2015)
6. Dietterich, T.G.: Ensemble methods in machine learning. In: Kittler, J., Roli, F. (eds.) MCS 2000. LNCS, vol. 1857, pp. 1–15. Springer, Heidelberg (2000). https://doi.org/10.1007/3-540-45014-9_1
7. Drucker, H., et al.: Boosting and other ensemble methods. Neural Comput. **6**(6), 1289–1301 (1994)
8. Zareapoor, M., Shamsolmoali, P.: Application of credit card fraud detection: based on bagging ensemble classifier. Procedia Comput. Sci. **48**, 679–685 (2015)
9. Dimililer, K., Ever, Y.K., Ratemi, H.: Intelligent eye tumour detection system. Procedia Comput. Sci. **102**, 325–332 (2016)
10. Mařik, V., Lhotská, L., Šedivá, I.: Blackboard control structure in the FEL-EXPERT system. IFAC Proc. Vol. **21**(19), 187–192 (1988)
11. Linkens, D.A., et al.: Intelligent control of a cryogenic cooling plant based on blackboard system architecture. ISA Trans. **39**(3), 327–343 (2000)
12. Iantovics, B.L.: A novel diagnosis system specialized in difficult medical diagnosis problems solving. In: Aziz-Alaoui, M., Bertelle, C. (eds.) Emergent Properties in Natural and Artificial Dynamical Systems. UCS, pp. 185–195. Springer, Heidelberg (2006). https://doi.org/10.1007/3-540-34824-7_10
13. Crespo, A.M.F., Weigang, L., de Barros, A.G.: Reinforcement learning agents to tactical air traffic flow management. J. Aviat. Manag. **1**(3), 145–161 (2012)
14. Pourpanah, F., et al.: A Q-learning-based multi-agent system for data classification. Appl. Soft Comput. **52**, 519–531 (2017)
15. Petridis, M., Knight, B., Edwards, D.: A design for reliable CFD software. In: Brebbia, C.A., Ferrante, A.J. (eds.) Reliability and Robustness of Engineering Software II, pp. 3–17. Elsevier, Amsterdam (1991)
16. Petridis, M., Knight, B.: The integration of an intelligent knowledge based system into engineering software using the blackboard structure. Adv. Eng. Softw. **25**, 141–147 (1996)
17. Teodorescu, E.I., Petridis, M.: An agent based framework for multiple, heterogeneous case based reasoning. In: Delany, S.J., Ontañón, S. (eds.) ICCBR 2013. LNCS, vol. 7969, pp. 314–328. Springer, Heidelberg (2013). https://doi.org/10.1007/978-3-642-39056-2_23

18. Engelmore, R., Morgan, T.: Blackboard Systems: Edited by Robert Engelmore, Tony Morgan. Addison Wesley Publishing Company, Boston (1988)
19. Nolle, L., Wong, K.C.P., Hopgood, A.A.: DARBS: a distributed blackboard system. In: Bramer, M., Coenen, F., Preece, A. (eds.) Research and Development in Intelligent Systems XVIII, pp. 161–170. Springer, London (2002). https://doi.org/10.1007/978-1-4471-0119-2_13
20. Endriss, U.: Tutorial on voting theory. In: AAAI (2010)
21. Adali, S.: Trust as a computational concept. In: Adali, S. (ed.) Modeling Trust Context in Networks, pp. 5–24. Springer, New York (2013). https://doi.org/10.1007/978-1-4614-7031-1_2
22. Witkowski, M., Pitt, J.: Objective trust-based agents: trust and trustworthiness in a multi-agent trading society. In: Proceedings Fourth International Conference on Multi Agent Systems (2000)
23. Kaelbling, L.P., Littman, M.L., Moore, A.W.: Reinforcement learning: a survey. J. Artif. Intell. Res. **4**, 237–285 (1996)
24. Komiyama, J., Honda, J., Nakagawa, H.: Optimal regret analysis of Thompson sampling in stochastic multi-armed bandit problem with multiple plays. In: Proceedings of the 32nd International Conference on International Conference on Machine Learning, Lille, France, vol. 37, pp. 1152–1161 (2015). JMLR.org
25. Endriss, U.: Computational social choice (with a special emphasis on the use of logic). In: Bezhanishvili, G., Löbner, S., Marra, V., Richter, F. (eds.) TbiLLC 2011. LNCS, vol. 7758, pp. 1–3. Springer, Heidelberg (2013). https://doi.org/10.1007/978-3-642-36976-6_1
26. Brandt, F., et al.: Handbook of Computational Social Choice, p. 548. Cambridge University Press, Cambridge (2016)
27. Endriss, U.: Social choice theory as a foundation for multiagent systems. In: Müller, J.P., Weyrich, M., Bazzan, A.L.C. (eds.) MATES 2014. LNCS, vol. 8732, pp. 1–6. Springer, Cham (2014). https://doi.org/10.1007/978-3-319-11584-9_1
28. Lichman, M.: UCI machine learning repository. University of California, School of Information and Computer Science, Irvine, CA (2017). http://archive.ics.uci.edu/ml

Machine Learning, Speech and Vision and Fuzzy Logic

Programming Without Program or How to Program in Natural Language Utterances

Martin J. Wheatman$^{(\boxtimes)}$

Yagadi Ltd., Withinreap Barn, Preston PR3 2ND, UK
martin@wheatman.net

Abstract. A new approach to programming computing machinery is presented, representing programming without a written software artifact—a program. The availability of numerous speech-to-text services, gives access to practical voice recognition. Enguage^{TM}is an open, programmable speech understanding engine, prototyped in Java, which is built into an app on Google Play, acting entirely as its user interface. Thus, devices can be instructed, and present results, in natural language utterances; engineers are afforded their own concepts and associated conversations. This paper shows how this can be turned in on itself, programming the interpretation of utterances, itself, purely through utterance.

Keywords: User interface programming · Interactive computation · Natural language understanding

1 Introduction

A talking interface has been sought since the dawn of the electronic computing age [1]. The first attempt, ELIZA [2], responds with stock replies generally related to keywords within an utterance. It has no grasp of an utterance as a whole amounting to no more than a guess at meaning. It has been described as a test of human gullibility, rather than of machine intelligence [3] If a keyword is not found, a subject changing reply is returned in an attempt to maintain the conversation, but in reality it gives the impression of evasiveness. A host of derivatives followed with the aim of passing what was to be known as the Turing Test [4].

Some degree of comprehension was achieved by SHRDLU [5], an interpreter which has the ability to conceptualize a limited world of blocks—*put X on top of Y*, etc. The main observation, here, is that it parses the entire statement: the whole utterance must be used to achieve this understanding. This in turn produces an impression of *listening*. Though this characteristic is not amenable to passing the Turing Test: a sheepdog may be considered intelligent because we can tell that it listens, but it has no chance of maintaining a conversation. Thus belies the dichotomy of specialization and generalization: do we want something that is deemed intelligent or something useful? There is the call for a better definition of intelligence [6].

© Springer International Publishing AG 2017
M. Bramer and M. Petridis (Eds.): SGAI-AI 2017, LNAI 10630, pp. 61–71, 2017.
https://doi.org/10.1007/978-3-319-71078-5_5

With the internet to plunder for context, further generalised applications have appeared. Google Now, Apple's SIRI, and IBM's Watson make use of online information for internet search or purchasing goods; Microsoft's Cortana and Amazon's Alexa provide an interface for the control of applications and devices. The latter, especially, shows some specialization in device control, with a skills interface e.g. *Alexa, tell X to do Y*. However, bespoke software, and the applications of not-so-giant corporations, also need access to vocal interfaces, as an accessibility feature for many technologically disenfranchised groups. Indeed, it was originally assumed that programming would benefit if software mimicked human communication, such as in COBOL and CORAL-66. However, these are rooted in the context-free programming languages; whereas, natural language, even for specialised interfaces, is *context-dependent*. While it is entirely possible that developers may hardwire their own understanding within a gigantic *if..then..elseif* structure, this would still lack many features common to all talking interface based systems: a disambiguation scheme, for example; or, given that language evolves, the ability to be updated at runtime.

To this end, Enguage™, the lang*uage eng*ine, is a programmable user interface (UI). Its source code is freely available on GitHub at martinwheatman/Enguage, along with its written language specifications. This paper presents a brief description of Enguage in Sect. 2. Then it describes the *intepret* concept in Sect. 3, which allows a user to construct interaction vocally. It then presents a simple example, in Sect. 4, of the construction of the instructions to use a variable to store a value. While we are used to seeing software, the specification of these instructions in this example as given in arbitrary strings, rather than in a context-free language. It must be stressed that the example in Sect. 4 is a working program. Given these instructions are designed for ease of reading, there is no punctuation to be read, which removes the need for a program as a written artefact. Not only can machines be directed by voice; this paper shows how they can also be programmed by voice.

2 Enguage

Language is an information bearing medium. It is context dependent—based on what has been already been said, and what is already known; and it is pragmatic—it is judged by its effect. Speech, as a transient mental process, is a social activity, with much repetition and often with little structure [7]; whereas, writing is a technology: it requires a well-structured written artefact; it shuns repetition, and is largely a solitary process.

Enguage is largely concerned with the spoken word. The transmission of ideas occurs by the swapping of one or more utterances; however, this mechanism is orthogonal to understanding—the impression of listening—which is achieved through confidence in the felicity of utterances [8]. This felicity is judged on the reaction to interpretation in a given context [9,10]: even an infelicitous reply— *sorry, I do not understand*—may increase the confidence in understanding within the system.

To Enguage, all utterances are simply an arbitrary list of strings [7,11]. Enguage maps user utterances onto machine replies, entirely by the interpretation of an internal list of utterances, or thoughts, associated with that utterance. An internal structure, known as *interpretant*, is composed of an ordered list of signs, each of which is used to interpret a specific utterance pattern. A *sign* is composed of a pattern, as an identifier, and the list of thoughts to be interpreted on an utterance being matched. The felicity of each utterance determines subsequent thoughts—if anything warrants Enguage to want to say *hang on a minute*, then the next utterance prefixed by *if not*, is interpreted. Each thought is therefore asserted.

There are three types of thought: *think*—more explicit utterances; *do*—interact with other software; or, *say*—the reply. For example, *I need X* can be deemed to mean *add X to my needs list*, which in turn may be conceptualized as *list.add (USER.needs, X)*, and the reply may be, *ok you need X*. The *meaning* of an utterance is therefore defined by the thoughts into which it is deconstructed.

Further, the interpretation of an utterance is context-dependent. Context is harvested both from the utterance itself and created during interpretation by explicitly setting values. In the above example, X will represent a value; $USER$ will have been ascertained earlier—if not, it may be infelicitous. Context is managed in an internal object database, and affords the elaboration of utterances. Applications built using Enguage also can have a *what can I say* mechanism, which guides the user to the directed concept. Interpretation concludes when a reply is reached.

A reply is a formatted answer, e.g. *reply my name is ...*, where the ellipsis represents the contextualized answer, and any variables are dereferenced. Replies need to be unequivocal, so typically, they begin with a hint as to their felicity, such as *ok, ...*, *yes, ...* and *no, ...* for positive replies, and *sorry, ...* for infelicitous replies. Replies are for human consumption, so vocal control of applciations requires another channel.

During interpretation, Enguage can interact with existing application code. The engine can directly call application code, as is the case with the context database. This mechanism has been recently adapted for a client to communicate through TCP/IP sockets. As such, it serves as an interface to software and online devices. In doing so, the application remains directed, while exercising some common features. Enguage:

- provides disambiguation, allowing the user to select the most appropriate interpretation of an utterance, see 2.1 below;
- it recognizes that language is self-authored—it defines itself in utterances, see 2.2 below; and,
- which in turn allows conversations to be organized into concepts, each of which is defined, appropriately, within a *.txt* file. It automatically loads any concept whose name is used within an utterance, and unloads them once used; allowing a virtually unlimited number of concepts to be supported. For

example, the *needs* concept is in the *need+needs.txt* file, which will be loaded on uttering *i need X* or *she needs Y*.

As a result, Enguage runs on modest hardware. It was intially validated against a complex contextual situation [12] to show it has a deep understanding of traditionally difficult to comprehend examples, e.g. *if we are holding hands then whose hand am i holding*. However, Enguage takes a non-traditional approach to text analysis.

2.1 Syntax, Considered Harmful

Let there be no doubt, syntax is key to the operation of context-free languages (the programming languages); its rules are used in determining the correctness of source code file. This does not necessarily mean that the programming languages are unambiguous, there may be times when a compiler will generate implementation dependent, or unspecified code; but, the thrust of language design, and the education of programmers, is towards unambiguous programs.

However, for the natural languages, meaning cannot be ascertained by structure; for example, *the Jumbo has landed* is an everyday phrase; whereas, *the Eagle has landed*, which has the same structure whilst being one of the most iconic phrases of the twentieth-century. While this is *contextual*, this is difficult to define. Meaning is more easily defined by Pragmatics; things are defined by their effect—while this may seem radical, it is certainly not a new approach [9,13].

Further, a syntax is used to deem what is grammatically correct: it has a Boolean outcome. If it is used to form language, gibberish may result, such as in Chomsky's *loud green flowers sleep furiously* examples [14] In this paper, however, concerned with pragmatics; what achieves the communication of ideas between human and machine. This may mean that double-negatives are entirely valid, such as *we ain't got no bananas* to mean we don't have any. This may be difficult for the structuralist to accept, as it points to the arbitrary link between what it said and what is meant; however, is not so radical [11] (although, some in turn may see this as a relativistic stance.) Again, this will be a disappointment to the Computational Linguistics community who tag corpora to achieve a statistical approach to meaning: we are neither looking for meaning in written text, nor for an all encompassing understanding. In this way, Enguage works like it is learning a second language—learning by example. Having argued against a syntactic approach, there is the caveat that basic data types following rigorous structure, explained in [15]. If the reader has any doubt about the efficacy of this approach, it is also the one taken by Amazon in their Alexa Skills Kit.

Enguage, therefore, turns to pattern matching, by which context-dependent language can be adequately analyzed [15]. A pattern is not a syntax: the focus is on the underlying word instances, rather than abstract word types where meaning is lost. For example, perhaps a trite example, but *help* has very little structure but a great deal of meaning. Andersen studied many cases of language use, finding that much spoken language is indeed such meaningful grunts and exclamations [7].

Utterance patterns in Engauge are specified in lowercase constants and uppercase variables. A pattern, such as *i need X*, is a straightforward way of defining an utterance, and therefore a concept. Typically, constants, which provide the framework for a pattern, are stop list words, those removed from internet search terms, and concept name themselves. From a pattern and an utterance context can be derived, e.g. given an utterance *My name is Martin* and the pattern [my, name, is, NAME], context, as named values are returned, e.g. NAME=martin. Such variables can also be configured: PHRASE-X represents one or more strings; and NUMERIC-X which has a numeric value, etc.

With pattern matching, several deemed meanings may be possible. This ambiguity needs to teased out, and that each potential meaning should be distinguished by an unequivocal reply. If an unintended, or misheard operation, is identified by the user, a simple mechanism enables it to be undone and another selected, see [16]. Thus, Engauge does not interpret a spoken language with an ultimate meaning, it mediates the most appropriate interpretation with the user, determined by outcome. By this felicity, Engauge follows speech act theory [9,10].

Finally, if an utterance cannot be matched to a pattern, the standard reply is *sorry, I do not understand*, indicating an infelicitous utterance.

2.2 Translation and Transformation

Central to the claim that Engauge can allow language to evlove, is that the interpretation of utterances is, itself, self-authored or *autopoietic*. In brief, autopoiesis comes from the informational basis of cellular biology; each cell contains the ability to self-replicate, whereas the production of non-informational entities—an *allopoietic* process—requires an external entity. For example, while a C compiler is written in C, motor vehicles require a motor vehicle factory. In this case, Engauge has a built-in concept which supports the creation of signs [17]. A concept file is largely, although not exclusively, comprised of autopoietic statements.

The utterances which construct signs fall into two categories [18]. Firstly, there are translations where one utterance directly means another. Typically, this is another way of saying the same thing, such as translating first-person utterances into the third person. See listing 1. Here _user refers to an unspeakable context which is the unnamed user.

```
On "I need PHRASE-OBJECTS", _user needs OBJECTS.
```

Listing 1. A translation from the need+needs.txt concept.

Secondly, there are transformations which are essentially a pattern and a list of utterances into which it is decomposed: a full sign represented as an English statement. Typically, thoughts are given as a more specific utterance.

```
On "SUBJECT needs PHRASE-OBJECTS":
set output format to "QUANTITY,UNIT of,,from FROM";
OBJECTS exists in SUBJECT needs list;
reply "I know";
if not, add / OBJECTS / to SUBJECT needs list;
then, reply "ok, SUBJECT needs ...".
```

Listing 2. A transformation from the need+needs.txt concept.

Note that this here includes slashes '/' to emphasize the objects list variable. While this is anachronistic, it shows that the repertoire is written, and that written statements—emails texts and the like—can contain slashes, and other ephemera, as emphasis. The current set of concepts can be found at github.com/martinwheatman/Enguage

3   Technical Contribution: Vocal Autopoiesis

This paper presents, here, a vocal autopoietic interface, which allows the user to create repertoire, and therefore instruction, by voice. To date, only a written autopoietic repertoire [17] has supported the creation of interpretant. A tool that provides a vocal interface is truly extensible if it creates that interface using the interface it, itself, uses. This is possible, given that utterances are able to work together.

Given an opening phrase, *interpret PATTERN thus*, the interpreter will build rules from utterances, rather than carry them out. The repertoire uses inductive language, phrases like *first*, *next* and *finally*, and *this implies*, rather than deductive one of imperative languages, like *add*, and *get* and *set*. To help signify that it is accepting a list of intentions, that the utterances are not actions in themselves, the vocal confirmation/prompt switches from *ok* to *goon*.

Following the openning interpret utterance, we have the *then* (or *next*) pattern. These append intentions to the sign under construction. Finally, there is a *finally* pattern, which creates a thought to be performed at the end of an interpretation, regardless of the felicity of outcome. An *ok* utterance finishes induction. For further definition see the full concept in *interpret.txt*, in Sect. 3.1 below.

Because we don't speak in capitalized sentences, or interject our speech with comma this or that question mark we need to carefully construct the repertoire to reply accurately to what we have said. Our patterns need to describe variables and constants carefully.

As we can introduce variables verbally, for example, variable name, we therefore need to say *variable variable* to mean the word variable. The phrase *phrase variable needs* results in PHRASE-NEEDS as a written variable, and similarly *numeric variable quantity* means NUMERIC-QUANTITY. So we may construct the longest pattern in the *needs* repertoire, thus:

> interpret variable subject needs numeric variable quantity variable unit of phrase variable needs thus

This is, quite frankly, a bit of a mouthful! But this work simplifies the written repertoire, by bringing *X means Y* and *X implies Y*, to the vocal autopoietic repertoire. affording a more natural sign construction. Next, the *interpret* concept is listed in full.

3.1 The Interpret Concept

The concept of interpret, available on GitHub as a written concept, is specified as follows:

```
On "start induction":
    perform "variable set induction true"; then, reply "ok".
On "stop induction":
    perform "variable set induction false"; then, reply "ok".
On "interpret PHRASE-X thus":
    start induction;
    perform "sign create X";
    then, reply "go on".
On "ok": stop induction; then, reply "ok".
On "that is it", ok.
On "that is all", ok.
On "finally PHRASE-X":
    perform "sign finally X"; then, reply "ok".
On "first PHRASE-X":
    perform "sign think X"; then, reply "go on".
On "then PHRASE-X":
    perform "sign think X"; then, reply "go on".
On "first perform PHRASE-X":
    perform "sign perform X"; then, reply "go on".
On "then perform PHRASE-X":
    perform "sign perform X"; then, reply "go on".
On "first reply PHRASE-X":
    perform "sign reply X"; then, reply "go on".
On "then reply PHRASE-X":
    perform "sign reply X"; then, reply "go on".
```

Listing 3. The written concept: interpret.txt (c/f Enguage 2nd May 2017).

Please note that none of these patterns contain any punctuation, as they reflect the spoken word: punctuation is not, by-and-large, enunciated—it is part of the technology of writing. While utterances do not contain any structure, in terms of keywords, as patterns they contain variables and constants. There are examples of both utterance types: translations and transformations, both interpreted by Enguage. The next section presents the output from a fully functioning, if simplistic, vocally programmed example within the Enguage test program itself.

4   Results

The Enguage test suite includes this demonstration of saving and retrieving a variable. These results can be confirmed by the source at GitHub.

```
enguage> my name is martin
I don't understand.
enguage> interpret my name is phrase variable name thus
Go on.
enguage> first perform variable variable set name variable name
Go on.
enguage> then perform variable variable get name
Go on.
enguage> then reply hello whatever
Go on.
enguage> and that is it
Ok.
enguage> my name is martin
Hello martin.
enguage> my name is ruth
Hello ruth.
```

Listing 4. Output from Enguage unit test, 2nd May 2017.

This example demonstrates program construction. It instructs the interpreter to construct a sign, a meaning, of *my name is NAME*, by attaching a variable set and get operations in the object database, and then to reply with a greeting. The ellipsis, an unspoken written artifact, representing the value returned from the previous utterance, is replaced vocally with *whatever*; this contextual reply can be configured at runtime. Further, the two performs are now replaced by utterances in the *get+set.txt* concept. Furthermore, the set utterance now also returns the value set, e.g. martin or ruth, as the contextual value, which could be returned as *whatever* without the get.

5   Discussion

This project is not text understanding, as sought by the Computation Linguistic community. It defines concepts using utterance, pattern and thought; it is not an algorithm to parse *any* text. Programming Enguage is more akin to teaching a language, rather than modelling the cognitive process for a native language. All software is directed: while Turing gave us a Univeral Machine [19], each application presents its own domain, its own business logic, to which a UI such as Enguage merely provides access.

While vocal autopoiesis demonstrates the extensibility of Enguage, the development of vocal autopoiesis has not been of a high priority, since it changes the balance from software being inviolate (something decided in the early days of software) to being modifiable by the user. If this is an issue—if, for example, you don't want your autopilot to be taught to play chess mid-flight(!)—the interpret concept can be removed from the installation, reverting it to written concepts alone.

Enguage is simply an interface; there are similarities between Enguage and GUIs. Certainly, Enguage works as a replacement for the GUI. In a GUI environment, the same function can be achieved through several routes: e.g. the click of a button, mouse operation of a menu system, or the keyboard operation of short-cuts. In Enguage, where one utterance means another, either can be used to obtain the same operation. In practice, when testing the disambiguation mechanism [16], it has been found an alternative utterance is often chosen, rather than disambiguating by repeating the misunderstood utterance.

For some, there will be the argument that Enguage merely mirrors the conventional programming model: that files containing concepts represent a textual instructions, or program source code; and, that interpretant—as an internal, linear list of signs—acts as an address space, each address containing a machine readable form of those concepts—a sign—as machine-level instructions. Further, some may also argue that there must be some artifact within the system which constitutes a program, because a program must persist; otherwise, we would have to reprogram it after each system restart. However, constructing vocally implies the management of persistence can also be vocal, and a mechanism (a concept) is currently being sought.

For others, this will not be real programming as it does not contain explicit loops, *for each X do Y*, or not being able to jump to arbitrary positions in the address space, it is therefore not Turing complete. However, speech does not contain explicit loops in the way that context-free languages do, much in the same way that SQL does not. In common parlance for example, *while* is more like a cobegin than a control structure: *listen to the raido while the kettle boils*. However, current research is into how Engauge can support recursion: Enguage is still in its infancy; what it lack is a comprehensive body of example concepts.

6   Conclusion and Further Work

While programming languages are defined in a formal structure, a *meta-language*, Enguage demonstrates a mechanical basis for utterance, but one which is contextual and self-defining. Inductive language supports the definition of language, in addition to the ordinary use of deductive language. All of this works by utterance, through Turing's teletype fed by freely available speech-to-text services. The distinction is more pronounced when the inductive English concept, interpret.txt, is used to define, say, French utterances: any utterance is simply an arbitrary list of strings. The goal is toward the mediation of the most appropriate, rather than some optimal, interpretation of an utterance. Utterances remain in the context-dependent domain, through more and more specific thoughts, until an unequivocal, context-free translation to a machine conceptualization is reached. Dava content is provided by the ability to create, as well as harvest, context;

for collaboration with further utterances. While Enguage supports arithmetical ability, and spatial and temproal concepts [15], it is largely directed towards software command and control. Further work includes the description of factorial, a positive outcome has come too late for this paper; and a reworking of what Engauge does, rather than how it does it, as a model of Informatics.

Until now, it could be claimed that while Enguage is vocally programmable, it follows the conventional Turing/Church model of algorithm specification mapping onto a virtual machine implementation. However, Enguage's vocal autopoiesis has made it possible to bridge the gap between user and developer, by removing the need for *a*—but not *to*—program. Not being based on written artifact, Enguage heralds a new computing paradigm. Although, it will not make users into developers overnight, and so is not the end of the programmer. What takes significant effort as a programmer still must be presented orally. However, with some thought we can *describe our world*: through this Turing's Imitation Game side-stepped the question of can machines think [1]. Enguage is an opportunity to side-step the Turing Test [4].

References

1. Turing, A.M.: Computing machinery and intelligence. Mind **59**, 433–460 (1950)
2. Weizenbaum, J.: Eliza–a computer program for the study of natural language communication between man and machine. Commun. ACM **9**(6), 36–45 (1966)
3. Schoenick, C., et al.: Moving beyond the turing test with the allen ai science challenge. Commun. ACM **60**(9), 60–64 (2017)
4. Loebner, H.G.: In response. Commun. ACM **37**(6), 79–82 (1994)
5. Winograd, T.: Understanding Natural Language. Edinburgh University Press, Edinburgh (1972)
6. Vardi, M.: Would turing have passed the turing test? Commun. ACM **57**(9), 5 (2014)
7. Andersen, P.B.: A Computer Theory of Semiotics. Cambridge University Press, Cambridge (1997)
8. Wheatman, M.J.: A semiotic model of information system. In: Jorna, R., Liu, K., Faber, N.R. (eds.) Proceedings of the 13th International Conference on Informatics and Semiotics in Organisations 13 (July 2011)
9. Austin, J.L.: How To Do Things With Words. Oxford University Press, Oxford (1962). Urmson, J.O., Sbisa, M., (eds.)
10. Searle, J.: Speech Acts. Cambridge University Press, Cambridge (1969)
11. de Saussure, F.: Course in General Linguistics, 3rd edn. Duckworth, London (1983, 1915). Bally, C., Sechehaye, A., Riedlinger, A. (eds.)
12. Wheatman, M.J.: A semiotic analysis of if we are holding hands, whose hand am i holding. Comput. Inform. Technol. **22**, 41–52 (2014). (special issue: LISS 2013, 2014)
13. Peirce, C.S.: Collected Papers. Vol. 2. Harvard University Press, Cambridge (1935–1958) Hartshorne, C., Weiss, P. (eds.)
14. Chomsky, N.: Syntatic Structures. Moulton and Co., Northamptonshire (1957)
15. Wheatman, M.J.: Context-dependent pattern simplication by extracting context-free floating qualiers. In: Proceedings of the Thirty-sixth SGAI International Conference. vol. 36, pp. 209–217 (2016)

16. Wheatman, M.: A pragmatic approach to disambiguation in text understanding. In: Baranauskas, M.C.C., Liu, K., Sun, L., Neris, V.P.A., Bonacin, R., Nakata, K. (eds.) ICISO 2016. IAICT, vol. 477, pp. 143–148. Springer, Cham (2016). https://doi.org/10.1007/978-3-319-42102-5_16
17. Wheatman, M.J.: An autopoietic repertoire. In: Proceedings of the Thirty-fourth SGAI International Conference. vol. 34 (2014)
18. Wheatman, M.J.: Translations and transformations in software engineering. In: Proceedings of the 11th ICISO, vol. 11, pp. 56–62 (2009)
19. Turing, A.M.: On computable numbers, with an application to the Entscheidungsproblem. In: Proceedings of the London Mathematical Society. vol. 2, no. 42, pp. 230–265 (1936)

Capturing the Dynamics of Cellular Automata, for the Generation of Synthetic Persian Music, Using Conditional Restricted Boltzmann Machines

Sahar Arshi[✉] and Darryl N. Davis

School of Engineering and Computer Science, University of Hull, Hull, UK
s.arshi@2014.hull.ac.uk, d.n.davis@hull.ac.uk

Abstract. In this paper the generative and feature extracting powers of the family of Boltzmann Machines are employed in an algorithmic music composition system. Liquid Persian Music (LPM) system is an audio generator using cellular automata progressions as a creative core source. LPM provides an infrastructure for creating novel Dastgāh-like Persian music. Pattern matching rules extract features from the cellular automata sequences and populate the parameters of a Persian musical instrument synthesizer [1]. Applying restricted Boltzmann machines, and conditional restricted Boltzmann machines as two family members of Boltzmann machines provide new ways for interpreting the patterns emanating from the cellular automata. Conditional restricted Boltzmann machines are particularly employed for capturing the dynamics of cellular automata.

Keywords: Computational creativity · Dastgāh · Persian music · Conditional Restricted Boltzmann Machines · Computer music · Cellular automata

1 Introduction

Persian traditional music is often recognized and investigated in the framework of Dastgāh music [2]. Each Dastgāh consists of smaller musical pieces called Gushe which share some similarity in respect to musical intervals, frequency of appearing notes, and repeated melodic motives. Different Dastgāh systems share some similar traits, for example the quality of the beginning and ending pieces and the presence of pieces having special characteristics as well as their respective time intervals. Dastgāhs, by their nature, have their complexities, which makes the emergence of new musical pieces reliant on the nascence of genius master musicians, who are intimately familiar with the concept of Dastgāh. This fact has made the creation of new Dastgāhs nearly impossible, and the quantity of compositions in different Dastgāhs intricate. Yet, there are immense possibilities for new music to be created in this genre [3, 4]. Techniques and tools from artificial intelligence are able to assist in the navigation of music space for creating the possibility of novel music.

One of the targets in the computational creativity arena is the manifestation of new artefacts with the help of computational algorithms. It is obvious that a clear viewpoint

© Springer International Publishing AG 2017
M. Bramer and M. Petridis (Eds.): SGAI-AI 2017, LNAI 10630, pp. 72–86, 2017.
https://doi.org/10.1007/978-3-319-71078-5_6

about the quality of creativity and how it happens is required from the outset. One of the ways for defining creativity is the study of its appearance or expression in human being when an artefact is created. Boden [5, 6] identifies three types of creativity in this respect: Combinational, Exploratory, and Transformational. In combinational creativity, previous ideas are populated and associated with each other in an artistic way. In exploratory creativity, a conceptual space is explored in the hope of finding novel forms; this navigation may result in transformational creativity by altering some of the involved dimensions of the elements and/or the conceptual space. Boden further describes creativity in two broad categories: Historical-Creativity, and Personal-Creativity with respect of their origin. H-creativity refers to a type of creativity that has never happened before within a civilization or society. P-creativity is allocated to a type of creativity that is new to the person who created it, though it has happened before throughout history. Observation of the requirements involved for the appearance of a creative act, provides guidelines in many respects for enabling the recreation process. Algorithmic music generation can be considered as a manifestation of computational creativity.

Algorithmic music composition have been performed for various purposes from generating musical motifs for inspiring musicians and usually in the form of computer aided algorithm composition software to more complex tasks as well as mechanization of music itself [7]. The later target is a hard core problem which needs the studying the creativity behavior in human. Likewise algorithmic composition can improve knowledge about how the creativity is performed by humans. Nevertheless various methodologies are applied for algorithmic composition; for example machine learning tools, knowledge based systems, evolutionary algorithms, and computational intelligence models [7]. Computational intelligence models as well as Cellular Automata (CA) are able to generate materials without contributing to human domain knowledge [4]. Therefore they have been in the attention of the computational creativity community. Noteworthy, hybrid methodologies which benefit from the characteristics of various tools are likely to be the subject of future research. In the current project the aim is to explore the possibility of creating new types of Persian music, by navigating the spectrum of various types of creativity by a hybrid approach consisting of CA, and a machine learning tool.

Liquid Persian Music (LPM) is a Cellular Automata based auditory system, which relies on pattern matching rules for extracting features from CA progressions, and feeding these to a Persian musical instrument synthesizer. Pattern matching rules extract features from consecutive CA progressions. The synthesizer accepts parameters such as the length of the musical instrument string, and the ADSR envelopes and produces the audio signal. More information about the software can be found in [8].

One of the aims in this paper is to elevate the pattern matching rules to the next level. For this work two major concepts have been taken into account. One of them refers to associative memories and their crystal like nature. Every time an associative memory system reaches its equilibrium stability, new associations are produced across their constituent elements. This in fact, determines their stochastic nature. The other concept refers to the nature of cellular automata, as stochastic, yet determinable systems which makes them storable.

Boltzmann machines are a type of associative memory, and in this paper two families of Boltzmann machines, Restricted Boltzmann Machines (RBM), and Conditional Restricted Boltzmann Machines (CRBM), are investigated. RBMs have been used for learning static data and producing new representations of data. Conditional Restricted Boltzmann machines expand RBM to be capable of prediction by learning time-series data. Cellular automata progressions are stored inside RBMs, and CRBMs. In this paradigm the stochastic nature of Boltzmann machine family have been used to benefit the generation of musical forms in the LPM system.

The arrangement of the sections of this paper are as follows: Sect. 2 presents Liquid Persian Music system, as a test bed for creating Persian-like music. Section 3 is dedicated to cellular automata, and basins of attraction models for studying the dynamics of CA. Section 4 is dedicated to Boltzmann machines in general and RBM, and CRBM in detail. The architectures of these two members of family of Boltzmann machines are described which then form the basis of the current experiments. The design approach and experiment are presented in Sects. 5 and 6. The results are available in Sect. 7. The paper concludes in Sect. 8, and future possibilities for research are presented.

2 Liquid Persian Music Software and Previous Research Agenda

The fundamental idea of LPM, likewise its former version Liquid Brain Music [9, 10] is the exploration of artificial life systems in the production of audio. Outputs of such system in relation to different parameterizations, are conventionally referred to as voices in the series of LPM associated publications. Voices resemble musical motives in music terminology. In [4, 11], it has been inferred that there are $88^7 * 20^7 * t$ number of such voices, considering the number of 88 unique CA behaviors, 20 pattern matching rules, t number of CA progressions, and 7 as the count of the synthesizer parameters.

One of the present considerations have been towards sequencing those voices in a musical manner. In [3], the LPM voices have been examined both individually and in relation to each other to study their aesthetical aspects regarding Zipf's law [12]. This study have been performed, acquiring suitable aesthetical means for evolving them in a musical manner. A computational framework for creating Persian Dastgāh-like music have been proposed in [4], in which sequencing the voices in a competent manner have been considered as a search problem. The musical critiques have been determined to be Zipfian metrics, and random sequences of voices as genotypes. Fitness functions based on Zipfian metrics are computable aesthetical critiques. In a later experiment in [3], Zipfian metrics have been extracted from a traditional Persian music data base. These metrics have been employed to train a Support Vector Machine Regression (SVMR) model, against, features extracted from LPM random sequences. The features which produced overlap between Persian music and LPM sequences were kept while the other ones have been discarded. This has been done due to the fact that SVMR model would decide solely based on a few strong detaching feature categories. On this basis, SVMR model would have cast off most of the LPM sequences without any chances for guiding them to the next evolutionary phase. On the other hand, it has been demonstrated that only a few number of features out of about 400 Zipfian features were sufficient for the conducting task. More details on this experiment can be found in [3].

The major issue in these experiments was the appearance of vivid jumps between the musical motives in some of the sequences. The randomized sequences in the initial population, left a dramatic effect throughout consequent generations which could not have been detected with the usage of Zipfian metrics solely. To counter this, there would be too many generations involved, and/or the fitness function possess sufficient amount of intelligence to unravel the competent individuals, and operators to erode the jumping effects and then evolve the pieces in a desired manner. Although fitness function based on Zipfian metrics are capable of discarding incompetent individuals and giving credits to those who have further similar Zipfian metrics to Persian music, the need for a more intelligent criticizer became self-evident. It should not be left unsaid that during algorithm execution some desirable pieces have been created which were detected while performing auditory investigations. Some of the LPM generated audio have also been evaluated in an auditory survey [13]; some examples are available in [8]. In the current paper, unlike the previous publications in this series [3, 4, 11], the aesthetical aspects of the produced audio are not directly and particularly the main focus. Instead the attention is shifted towards approaches for interpreting the patterns derived from cellular automata sequences and applying them in the problem of sequencing LPM voices. This kind of approach is not only considered as a generative model; multiplying the power of creativity of cellular automata; it also has the potential of maintaining and producing smoother transitions between LPM voices.

3   Cellular Automata

Cellular Automata are dynamical systems whose manifestation are assigned to Von Neumann back in 1940s [14, 15]. Later in 1960s CA have been investigated as dynamical systems [16]. In this viewpoint, CA are discrete dynamical systems consisting of identical elementary individuals with same set of defined behaviors, which account to the global dynamics of the whole system.

Elementary CA consists of an assembly of cells which are arranged in a sequence of one dimensional array. In this work, each of the cells take two binary states. The progression of CA in each time step t, emerges as a two-dimensional lattice. The state of a cell at a time step is determined by its state and the states of its adjacent neighbors at the previous time step. The neighborhood radius is defined by r, which accounts to 2^r specifications, resulting from permuting the states of a cell and its neighbors. Allocating these permutations to binary states produces 2^{2^r} CA rules [16]. Considering the states of the left, and right neighbors of a cell, the number of rules for an elementary CA becomes 256.

Wolfram recognized four major classes of behavior in CA, consisting of fixed, cyclic, chaotic, and complex behaviors [16]. In [18] the cyclic class is divided to further three sub classes, namely, heterogeneous, periodic, and locally chaotic. CA have been in the attention of artists' community as well, for their emergent behavior. Various attempts have taken place for contributing CA both independently as an inspiring source for artists, or as a computational creative tool for generating artefacts. Some of these works can be traced back in the works of pioneers as well as Iannis Xenakis in the generation of music. who used CA for attaining the general structure of compositions [7, 19]. However, these kind of compositions were often accompanied by heavy editing. Some others inferred CA as a source of raw material, which could not have been highly relied on for music composition in an independent manner [20].

Beyls Cellular Automata Explorer is one of the early musical systems based on CA. He experimented with various CA configurations including the cell neighborhood from previous and future CA progressions, and various rule specification in the search for finding complex musical structures [21]. Millen developed the CAM system, which exploits two and three dimensional game of life cellular automata, and maps the data to musical space for producing melody [7, 21]. CAMUS and Chaosynth [22, 23] are two other well-known CA musical generators. CAMUS uses Game of Life together with Demon Cyclic Space to simulate the diffusing effect of musical patterns in time. CAMUS system later exploits Cartesian mapping to achieve triplet musical forms [23]. Chaosynth is a CA based audio system which relies on producing sound granules resulting from additive synthesis; the produced audio is not presently similar to music as we know, it rather resembles the nature sounds as well as the flow of water, or a cluster of amphibians singing. Chaosynth underlying system is based on the model of the chemical reaction of a catalyst which in the visual domain appears as hypnotic contraction and detention effects of chemicals [20].

3.1   The Dynamics of Cellular Automata

The dynamics of cellular automata can be better illustrated in structures known as basin of attraction [24–26]. In order to clarify this notation, the meaning of state space is briefly overviewed. A state space consists of all possible configurations or patterns. For instance a binary vector of size N has 2^N patterns, and a binary matrix of size 4 * 4 has

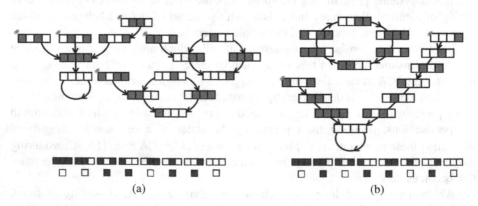

(a)   (b)

Fig. 1. Examples of basin of attraction for cellular automata configuration for (a) rule 54, and (b) rule 90. The star signs shows the Garden of Eden states. These graphs are manually obtained, however, there are algorithms available for obtaining basin of attraction models for any CA rule space with different configurations [17].

2^{16} different configurations. For a cellular automata rule number, this state space can be divided to sections with each section having a structure relating its consisting patterns. These structures are known as basins of attraction. They often consist of a central point or a collection of patterns arranged on a circular path. There might be branches with so many sub branches connecting to these figures. The links between patterns in a basin of attraction is formed according to the accessibility by previous observed patterns. These outer branches are pre-images of the inner ones.

The leaves are Garden of Eden states, which are not accessible by any previous states [24–26]. Figure 1 shows two examples of basin of attraction models for four-cell configurations for Wolfram rule numbers 54, and 90. Rule 54 produces 3 basins of attraction, while rule 90 produces 2 of them. Note that all different 16 configuration for 4 cells have been classified in the basin of attraction field model.

4 Restricted Boltzmann Machines

Boltzmann machines are stochastic neural networks invented by Hinton and Sejnowsky back in 1985 [27]. They can also be considered as Hopfield networks which replace the binary threshold rules associated to the units with stochastic decision rules [28]. Boltzmann machine dynamics revolve around an energy concept. Adhering to a fully connected architecture for Boltzmann machines make them inefficient for training. On the other hand, constraining the connections between the units will turn them into devices with tractable formulation for the required training procedures [29]. Restricted Boltzmann machines [30] are graphical models with undirected symmetrical connections which have only maintained their pair-wise connections between visible and hidden units. Figure 2(a) shows the architecture of RBM.

RBM are capable of modelling the probability distribution of the input data. These new representations of the observable data, are accumulated in the intra-layer weights. Consequently, these networks are widely used in feature extraction, dimensionality reduction, and classification applications. Some examples of these kinds are available in [31–33]. For instance, once this network is trained, the features which are now

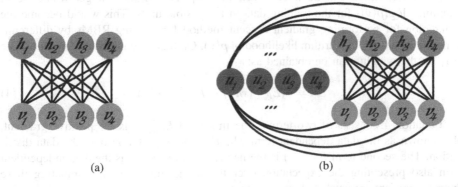

(a)   (b)

Fig. 2. The architectures of (a) Restricted Boltzmann machine, and (b) Conditional Restricted Boltzmann machine.

embedded in weights in the bipartite graph can be used as data for further machine learning applications [34, 35]. Boltzmann machines have also been utilized in music generation applications in [36], more examples of such systems are provided in the CRBM section.

The behavior of the RBM system is directed by the energy function defined in formula 1. In which v, and h, stand for visible and hidden layer units in vectors, W is the weight matrix. a, and b, are bias vectors. On this account, the energy function in RBM is a sum of the linear products of the hidden vector, the connection weights matrix, and the input vector. The remaining terms in the following formulas stand for the products of the visible and hidden units and their contributing bias terms.

$$E(v,h) = -\left(h^T Wx + a^T v + b^T h\right) \tag{1}$$

The probability of observation of a particular configuration over v visible input vectors and h hidden units are obtained by the notation 2, in which Z is the normalization term. The Z normalizing value is the result of calculating $e^{-E(v,h)}$ throughout all configurations for v, and h.

$$p(v,h) = e^{-E(v,h)}/Z \tag{2}$$

Obtaining Z (which is also known as the partition function) is nearly impossible, originating from the fact that so many binary units are involved. Inferring the joint probability distribution of v, and h can be performed by easier ways than computing the value of partition function. In order to track the value of the $p(v,h)$ a procedure is taken by marginalizing out the value of h from formula 2 [37].

The marginal probability distribution of a visible vector equals the sum of the exponential of the energy function over all possible configurations as

$$p(v) = \sum_h e^{-E(v,h)}/Z \tag{3}$$

This formulation provides a basis for attaining the logarithm likelihood of $p(v)$ which its derivation can be traced back in [38]. The ultimate target would be to maximize $\log(p(v))$ for the training data in the visible units. This would become the foundation for performing gradient descent method for training RBMs by differentiating the negative of logarithm likelihood of $p(v)$. On this account the parameter update [34] for the weights can be obtained as:

$$\Delta w = \gamma\left(E_{P_{data}}\left(vh^T\right) - E_{P_{model}}\left(vh^T\right)\right) \tag{4}$$

Equation 4 consists of two terms. The first term $E_{P_{data}}(.)$ is the positive gradient, also known as the data dependent term which is the expectation over the data distribution. The second term $E_{P_{model}}(.)$ is the negative gradient and is the data independent term also presenting the expectation over the model distribution. Computing these expectations are intractable, however, they are estimable by performing alternating

Gibbs sampling between hidden, and visible units. This procedure is followed in Contrastive Divergence algorithm.

4.1 Contrastive Divergence Algorithm

Contrastive Divergence algorithm [39, 40] is a sort of gradient descent method which is applied for training weights in RBMs.

The Contrastive Divergence algorithm works with the following procedure:
For each of training vectors the following steps are taken:

- The visible units are populated with a training vector.
- The probabilities of the units in the hidden layer are calculated and their states are determined by the following notation:

$$s(h_m) = \begin{cases} 1, & p(h_{m=1}|v) > rnd \\ -1, & otherwise \end{cases} \tag{5}$$

where rnd is a random number from uniform distribution in the range $[0, 1]$.

- k-levels of Gibbs sampling takes place: the vector v' is reconstructed by sampling from the hidden units and the hidden units h' are resampled from v'.
- The weights and biases are updated considering the following learning rules, in which γ is a learning rate:

$$W^t = W^{t-1} + \gamma \left(h^t v^{tT} - h'^t x'^{tT} \right) \tag{6}$$

$$a^t = a^{t-1} + \gamma (v^t - v'^t) \tag{7}$$

$$b^t = b^{t-1} + \gamma (h^t - h'^t) \tag{8}$$

- The algorithm iterates, until a stopping criteria is visited (as well as the number of Gibbs sampling to be performed).

4.2 Conditional Restricted Boltzmann Machines

Conditional restricted Boltzmann machines are an extended version of RBM systems, which model the dependability of data to its previous time frames. An architecture of CRBMs are shown in Fig. 2(b). They are best for capturing the dynamics of time-series data. CRBMs has had successful applications in modeling the dynamics of systems, as well as human motion [41, 42]. It is notable that there have been research in the area of music and CRBMs both for classification tasks, and for composition. CRBMs have been applied for the task of auto-tagging music in [43, 44]. This proposed model have been able to outperform some other machine learning classifiers, as well as support vector machines, and multi-layer perceptron. In [45] forward CRBMs have been employed to reconstruct music and improvise in the desired musical style, based on the provided first notes.

In CRBM model, the visible and hidden units are conditioned on n previous steps of visible states. Visible and hidden units receive this temporal information by established direct connection to an additional layer. Previous temporal information are provided in this new added layer. The topology of this model is illustrated in Fig. 2(b). The energy function of the system is inferred as:

$$E(v, h, u) = -v^T W h - u^T U^{uv} v - u^T U^{uh} h - v^T a - h^T b \qquad (9)$$

In which v, h, u correspondingly stand for observables, hidden neurons, and additional layer (associated to visible units in the previous time steps). Likewise, W are the weights between visible layer, and hidden layer, U^{uv} relates to the weights between visible layer and additional layer, and at last, U^{uh} is the weight matrix between conditional layer, and hidden units. a, b are bias matrixes. The weights, and biases in CRBM models can still be learned by the application of Contrastive Divergence algorithm.

5   Approach

The stochastic nature of Boltzmann machines proposes that there would be no unique equilibrium status for the system. This fact contributes to the generative nature of Boltzmann machine family models. This effect has been resembled to crystals which settle on their different facades (In fact Richards in [46] has first assimilated memories as crystals). A crystal with plasma like origin is gradually formed or crystallized. Starting from an initial configuration for the elements of the plasma, every time the system is run, different associations between the elements are formed. This causes for attaining various crystal shapes. However, using the term of a solid crystal for BMs is a little bit tricky. A stable equilibrium of the system is where a local minimum energy is achieved in the energy hyper-surface. This does not necessarily mean that the state of neurons are not changing any longer. Actually the states of the neurons may still be oscillating, but that is happening around the local minima. Therefore the states of the neurons are not necessarily frozen.

Since the dynamics of CA is stochastic yet determinable, they can be treated as static memories. This relaxes the architecture of the LPM system from the requirement of navigations in the search spaces as discussed previously. This provides the ability to apply associative memory architectures. The dynamics of CA can be stored as memories. This scheme lets the individuals of an associative memory model be resembled to fossilized ants (as an example of individuals in a swarm) in a crystal. The associations of the ants would be different in every single crystallization process. Moreover, the angle of looking into the crystal changes the relations and the proportions in which they are perceived. This latter phenomenon is an assimilation to show the importance of the choice of collecting output from different hidden units in various extensions of Boltzmann machines. To be clearer, it should be noted that, although all the hidden units can be used for populating the synthesizer parameter, the audio result would change, considering which neuron is taken. This is how the generative powers of Boltzmann machine family can be manifested in LPM system.

6   Experiments

In this section the details of the performed experiments are presented; there are different perspectives towards applying CA to Boltzmann machine model family. In one of the approaches, 88 one-dimensional CA progressions are considered as static images with white and black cells to be applied as input vectors to the visible units. In this approach the number of cells in the visible layer would equal the total number of cells of a cellular automata progression. The same visible units are associated with the same cells in the CA progression over all the training samples. It is obvious that various possible initial seeds exist for the CA progression, which determine the emerging patterns in the upcoming generations. In fact they would end up in different basin of attractions for a CA rule. For this experiment, all the possible binary configurations for the initial seed have been taken into account for all the 88 unique CA behaviors.

In the second experiment, various configurations of CA progression are provided for a Conditional Restricted Boltzmann machine. This model have been inspired from basin of attraction models which are applied for studying the dynamics of CA. There are also some literature about neural networks which learn the dynamics of CA [47]. Each of the CA rules have their own basin of attraction fields regarding the configurations in which the basin of attraction is studied for that CA rule. Identifying each of those attractors and employing them as inputs to CRBMs, requires the consideration of various topologies for the input layer, and the connecting weights. Although this is not an impossible task, it is a labor intensive one. Therefore, another tactic has been taken into account which is based on CA progressions history as training series. In this experiment all the transients starting from the initial seeds have been taken into account. Notably, all the possible initial seeds have been explored as well.

CA progressions can be trained to CRBMs for seizing their dynamics with various configurations. This work can be performed for each generation of CA, or even an arbitrary configuration from CA progression. For instance, one may wish to choose a complete number of cells from each CA generation, or partially select some of the cells. It is possible to include cells from more than one generation to form $p * q$ matrices of cells. The number of previous cells are also adjustable. For example, one may pick n number of $p * q$ previous configurations to constrain visible and hidden layers.

The number of the CA progressions to be trained by the CRBM system has been empirically determined by the behavior of CA rules themselves, whether they are in the classes of fixed, cyclic, chaotic, or complex. For instance, the number of the involved generations of CA rules in the fixed, and cyclic categories are noticeably less than the rules in the third, and fourth classes. These groups tend to achieve their stable behavior faster than the other groups, and would reach loopy behavior, and/or repetitions which would put more emphasis on these kinds of patterns and bring bias in the training set. Instead the possibility of having more generations out of the CA progressions have been allocated to chaotic, and complex behavior rule categories.

The experiments in this project are implemented in Matlab and with inspiration from the software and codes provided in [48–50].

7 Results

In this section more details on the conducted experiments are provided, and the results are presented. For the first experiment with RBM, a number of 88 main CA behaviors over 24 generations have been taken into account. The initial seeds have been taken constant for all the CA rules. The training set consists of 88, 25 * 25 metrics in 20 batches. This produces 625 visible units. The number of hidden neurons was selected to be 400 units. Overall number of 200 epochs were involved. Figure 3 demonstrates a portion of the connecting weights between visible, and hidden units. Each square presents one hidden unit. The square shapes are represented in this way to be analogous to the input metrics.

Fig. 3. Looking into the mind of RBM. Each of the small squares are associated to one of the units in the RBM architecture and all its connecting weights. These squares are a portion of 65 units out of the total hidden neurons.

In the second experiment which is performed with CRBM, the CA progression have been divided into a series of 3 * 3 metrics respecting their history of appearance. Each of these metrics have been conditioned to their three previous ancestors. This would result in having 9 visible units, and 27 past units. The count of hidden units are 400. Figure 4 demonstrates portions of weight metrics between visible-hidden, past-visible, and past-hidden. For this experiment all the 88 CA behaviors have been involved, and all the possible initial seeds have been allowed.

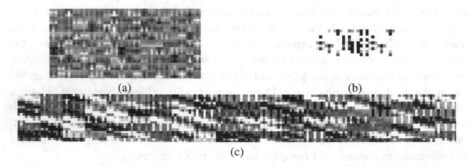

(a)   (b)

(c)

Fig. 4. Looking into the mind of CRBM. In the configuration of the CRBM for this experiment, (a) relates to the weights between the visible and hidden units, (b) demonstrates the weights in between past and visible units, while (c) shows the weight values between past and hidden units.

So far the experiments suggested in this paper have resulted in producing patterns which can later be accompanied in music production. This means that new pattern matching rules are introduced to LPM system. The interesting thing about this architecture is the generation of various patterns by changing the initial configuration of CA, the initial seeds, and the number of involved hidden units which also contribute to the generative power of Boltzmann machine family. The outputs of the pattern matching rules in the original LPM system are employed for feeding the parameters of a Persian musical instrument synthesizer. The parameters vary from the physical parameters of a musical instrument as well as string length to ADSR envelopes of musical notes.

What have been discussed in this paper are some technical issues revolving around the sub system of a bigger LPM architecture for creating Persian-Dastgāh like music. The presentation of the whole system is out of the scope of the current paper. The mapping of the results of this research to musical space would be in association to other parts of the system and subject to future publications. The interested readers are welcome to follow the creations of the system as the research progresses in [8], related to LPM web page.

8 Conclusions and Future Work

In this article, RBM and CRBM have been applied for capturing the dynamics of cellular automata. It has been illustrated that these models have generative characteristics. In fact the usage of these two models have manifold targets in LPM system. The first aim is to enhance the pattern matching rules in LPM system and taking them to another level. The other one is the exploitation of the generative, and stochastic nature of Boltzmann machine family themselves.

Elementary cellular automata have been used as a computational intelligence tool which provides raw material for creativity in LPM system. Complicating the initial configuration of CA, gives raise to the variety of the emerging patterns. Moreover, cellular automata are a sub type of Random Boolean Networks [51]. This fact expands the neighborhood configurations to multiply the level of complexity of the emerging patterns. It is obvious that taking account these types of configurations would increase the generality of the whole system, however, the integrity is suppressed by the current computational resources while the results of this stage are sufficient guidelines for entering the next phases of research.

Deep neural networks have been generating interest in the area of computational creativity due to the resemblance their underlying processes bear to the procedures taking place in human brain. In this work an infrastructure for employing deep architectures are employed which are built on Boltzmann machines. Extending the architecture of RBM into deep Boltzmann machine or a deep belief net [52] architecture by building further hidden layers would provide additional feature extractors or in another viewpoint higher level of features. This implies that further representations of data will be reflected in the top layers which can be derived correspondingly.

Other future steps of this research includes the design of the mapping mechanism to musical space of LPM voices while delving deeper into the sequencing problem. The produced mechanism is capable of being generalized to include various sources of raw materials for creativity rather than CA and different genres of music besides Persian music or any other creative artefacts.

References

1. Arshi, S.: An implementation of Santur musical instrument and the synthesis of music pieces using learning machines. Master thesis (2012)
2. Farhat, H.: The Dastgah Concept in Persian Music. Cambridge University Press, Cambridge (1990)
3. Arshi, S., Davis, D.N.: Generating synthetic Persian music. In: Chapter one in Third International Conference on New Music Concepts, ICNMC 2016, pp. 11–43. ABEditore s. r.1, Academia Musicale, Milano (2016)
4. Arshi, S., Davis, D.N.: A computational framework for aesthetical navigation in musical search space. In: AISB Symposium on Computational Creativity, Sheffield, UK (2016)
5. Boden, M.: Computer models of creativity. Psychologist **13**, 72–76 (2000)
6. Boden, M.: Computer models of creativity. Artif. Intell. Mag. **30**, 23–34 (2009)
7. Fernández, J.D., Vico, F.: AI methods in algorithmic composition: a comprehensive survey. J. Artif. Intell. Res. **48**, 513–582 (2013)
8. Davis, D.N.: Computer and Artificial Music: Liquid Persian Music. http://www2.dcs.hull.ac.uk/NEAT/dnd/music/lpm.html
9. Turner, C.: Liquid Brain Music (2008)
10. Woods: Liquid Brain Music: Phase II. http://www2.dcs.hull.ac.uk/NEAT/dnd/. Computer Science, University of Hull (2009)
11. Arshi, S., Davis, D.N.: Towards a fitness function for musicality using LPM. In: 6th York Doctoral Symposium on Computer Science and Electronics (2015)
12. Manaris, B., Sessions, V., Wilkinson, J.: Searching for Beauty in Music. vol. 1, pp. 1–10 (2001)
13. Arshi, S.: Liquid Persian Music Survey. https://www.surveymonkey.co.uk/r/QPQ77JB
14. Burks, A.W.: Von Neumann's Self-Reproducing Automata (1970)
15. Burks, A.: Essays on Cellular Automata. University of Illinois Press, Champaign (1970)
16. Wolfram, S.: A New Kind of Science. Wolfram media Champaign, Champaign (2002)
17. Wuensche, A.: Discrete dynamics lab: tools for investigating cellular automata and discrete dynamical networks. Artif. Life Model. Softw. pp. 215–258 (2009). (2nd edn.)
18. Li, W., Packard, N.: The structure of the elementary cellular automata rule space. Complex Syst. **4**, 281–297 (1990)
19. Hoffmann, P.: Towards an automated art: algorithmic process in Xenakis' composition. Contemp. Music Rev. **21**, 121–131 (2002)
20. Miranda, E.R.: Cellular automata music: from sound synthesis to musical forms. Evol. Comput. Music. **8**, 170–193 (2007)
21. Burraston, D., Edmonds, E., Livingstone, D., Miranda, E.R.: Cellular automata in MIDI based computer music. In: Proceedings of International Computer Music Conference, vol. 4, pp. 71–78 (2004)
22. Miranda, E.R.: Evolving cellular automata music: from sound synthesis to composition. In: Proceedings of Workshop on Artificial Life Models for Musical Applications, vol. 12 (2001)
23. Miranda, E.R.: Sounds of artificial life. In: Proceedings of the 4th Conference on Creativity and Cognition, pp. 173–177. ACM (2002)
24. Wuensche, A.: Basins of attraction in network dynamics: a conceptual framework for biomolecular networks. Modul. Dev. Evol. pp. 288–314 (2004)

25. Wuensche, A.: Classifying cellular automata automatically. Complexity **4**, 1–26 (1999)
26. Wuensche, A., Lesser, M.: The Global Dynamics of Cellular Automata. Addison-Wesley, Boston (1992)
27. Ackley, D., Hinton, G., Sejnowski, T.: A learning algorithm for boltzmann machines. Cogn. Sci. **9**, 147–169 (1985)
28. Hinton, G.E.: Boltzmann Machines. Tutorial. pp. 1–7 (2007)
29. Carreira-Perpiñán, M.Á., Hinton, G.E.: On contrastive divergence learning. In: Proceedings of Artificial Intelligence and Statistics (2005)
30. Smolensky, P.: Information processing in dynamical systems: foundations of harmony theory. In: Rumelhart, D.E., Mcclelland, J.L. (eds.) Parallel Distributed Processing: Explorations in the Microstructure of Cognition, Volume 1: Foundations, pp. 194–281. MIT Press, Cambridge (1986)
31. Larochelle, H., Bengio, Y.: Classification using discriminative restricted Boltzmann machines. In: ICML, pp. 536–543 (2008)
32. Gehler, P.V., Holub, A.D., Welling, M.: The rate adapting poisson model for information retrieval and object recognition. In: Proceedigs 23rd International Conference on Machine Learning. – ICML 2006, pp. 337–344 (2006)
33. Salakhutdinov, R., Hinton, G.: Replicated softmax: an undirected topic model. In: Proceedings of 2009 Conference on Advances in Neural Information Processing Systems, vol. 22, pp. 1607–1614 (2009)
34. Salakhutdinov, R., Hinton, G.: An efficient learning procedure for deep Boltzmann machines. Neural Comput. **24**, 1967–2006 (2012)
35. Hinton, G.E., Salakhutdinov, R.R.: Reducing the Dimensionality of Data with Neural Networks. Science (80-) **313**, 504–507 (2006)
36. Lauly, S.: Music generation using Dynamically Linked Boltzmann Machines, pp. 1 8 (2007)
37. Mnih, V., Larochelle, H., Hinton, G.: Conditional restricted Boltzmann machines for structured output prediction. In: UAI, pp. 514–522 (2011)
38. Hinton, G., Sejnowski, T.J.: Optimal perceptual inference. In: Proceedings of the IEEE Conference on Computer Vision and Pattern Recognition, Washington, D.C. (1983)
39. Hinton, G.: A practical guide to training restricted Boltzmann machines. Comput. (Long. Beach. Calif) **9**, 1 (2010)
40. Hinton, G.E.: Training products of experts by minimizing contrastive divergence. Neural Comput. **14**, 1771–1800 (2002)
41. Taylor, G.W., Hinton, G.E.: Factored conditional restricted Boltzmann Machines for modeling motion style. In: Proceedings of 26th Annual International Conference on Machine Learning, ICML 2009, pp. 1025–1032 (2009)
42. Taylor, G.W.: School: learning representations of sequences with applications to motion capture and video analysis. In: CVPR (2012)
43. Mandel, M., Pascanu, R., Larochelle, H., Bengio, Y.: Autotagging music with conditional restricted Boltzmann machines (2011)
44. Mandel, M., Eck, D., Bengio, Y.: Learning tags that vary within a song. In: Proceedings of 11th International Conference on Music Information Retrieval, pp. 399–404 (2010)
45. Loeckx, A.J., Bultheel, J.: Forward conditional restricted Boltzmann machines for the generation of music. In: 17th International Conference on Computational Creativity, ICCC 2015, Zurich, Switzerland (2015)
46. Richards, I.A.: Principles of Literary Criticism (Routledge Classics). Routledge, Abingdon (1924)
47. Wulff, N.H., Hertz, J.A.: Learning Cellular Automation Dynamics with Neural Networks. In: Advances in Neural Information Processing Systems, vol. 5, pp. 631–638 (1993)

48. Tanaka, M.: Deep Neural Network, Mathworks, Matlab. https://uk.mathworks.com/matlabcentral/fileexchange/42853-deep-neural-network
49. Salakhutdinov, R.R.: Learning deep Boltzmann machines software. http://www.cs.toronto.edu/~rsalakhu/code.html
50. Taylor, G.W.: Matlab implementation of implicit mixtures of conditional restricted Boltzmann machines. https://github.com/gwtaylor/imCRBM
51. Kauffman, S.: Homeostasis and differentiation in random generic control networks. Nature **224**, 177–178 (1969)
52. Hinton, G.E., Osindero, S., Teh, Y.W.: A fast learning algorithm for deep belief nets. Neural Comput. **18**, 1527–1554 (2006)

Measuring Relations Between Concepts
in Conceptual Spaces

Lucas Bechberger[(✉)] [iD] and Kai-Uwe Kühnberger

Institute of Cognitive Science, Osnabrück University, Osnabrück, Germany
{lucas.bechberger,kai-uwe.kuehnberger}@uni-osnabrueck.de

Abstract. The highly influential framework of conceptual spaces provides a geometric way of representing knowledge. Instances are represented by points in a high-dimensional space and concepts are represented by regions in this space. Our recent mathematical formalization of this framework is capable of representing correlations between different domains in a geometric way. In this paper, we extend our formalization by providing quantitative mathematical definitions for the notions of concept size, subsethood, implication, similarity, and betweenness. This considerably increases the representational power of our formalization by introducing measurable ways of describing relations between concepts.

Keywords: Conceptual spaces · Fuzzy sets · Measure

1 Introduction

One common criticism of symbolic AI approaches is that the symbols they operate on do not contain any meaning: For the system, they are just arbitrary tokens that can be manipulated in some way. This lack of inherent meaning in abstract symbols is called the "symbol grounding problem" [18]. One approach towards solving this problem is to devise a grounding mechanism that connects abstract symbols to the real world, i.e., to perception and action.

The framework of conceptual spaces [16,17] attempts to bridge this gap between symbolic and subsymbolic AI by proposing an intermediate conceptual layer based on geometric representations. A conceptual space is a high-dimensional space spanned by a number of quality dimensions that are based on perception and/or subsymbolic processing. Regions in this space correspond to concepts and can be referred to as abstract symbols.

The framework of conceptual spaces has been highly influential in the last 15 years within cognitive science and cognitive linguistics [14,15,28]. It has also sparked considerable research in various subfields of artificial intelligence, ranging from robotics and computer vision [11,12] over the semantic web [2] to plausible reasoning [13,25].

One important aspect of conceptual representations is however often ignored by these research efforts: Typically, the different features of a concept are correlated with each other. For instance, there is an obvious correlation between

© Springer International Publishing AG 2017
M. Bramer and M. Petridis (Eds.): SGAI-AI 2017, LNAI 10630, pp. 87–100, 2017.
https://doi.org/10.1007/978-3-319-71078-5_7

the color and the taste of an apple: Red apples tend to be sweet and green apples tend to be sour. Recently, we have proposed a formalization of the conceptual spaces framework that is capable of representing such correlations in a geometric way [6]. Our formalization not only contains a parametric definition of concepts, but also different operations to create new concepts from old ones (namely: intersection, union, and projection).

In this paper, we provide mathematical definitions for the notions of concept size, subsethood, implication, similarity, and betweenness. This considerably increases the representational power of our formalization by introducing measurable ways of describing relations between concepts.

The remainder of this paper is structured as follows: Sect. 2 introduces the general framework of conceptual spaces along with our recent formalization. In Sect. 3, we extend this formalization with additional operations and in Sect. 4 we provide an illustrative example. Section 5 contains a summary of related work and Sect. 6 concludes the paper.

2   Conceptual Spaces

This section presents the cognitive framework of conceptual spaces as described in [16] and as formalized in [6].

2.1   Dimensions, Domains, and Distance

A conceptual space is a high-dimensional space spanned by a set D of so-called "quality dimensions". Each of these dimensions $d \in D$ represents a way in which two stimuli can be judged to be similar or different. Examples for quality dimensions include temperature, weight, time, pitch, and hue. The distance between two points x and y with respect to a dimension d is denoted as $|x_d - y_d|$.

A domain $\delta \subseteq D$ is a set of dimensions that inherently belong together. Different perceptual modalities (like color, shape, or taste) are represented by different domains. The color domain for instance consists of the three dimensions hue, saturation, and brightness. Distance within a domain δ is measured by the weighted Euclidean metric d_E.

The overall conceptual space CS is defined as the product space of all dimensions. Distance within the overall conceptual space is measured by the weighted Manhattan metric d_M of the intra-domain distances. This is supported by both psychological evidence [5,19,26] and mathematical considerations [3]. Let Δ be the set of all domains in CS. The combined distance d_C^Δ within CS is defined as follows:

$$d_C^\Delta(x, y, W) = \sum_{\delta \in \Delta} w_\delta \cdot \sqrt{\sum_{d \in \delta} w_d \cdot |x_d - y_d|^2}$$

The parameter $W = \langle W_\Delta, \{W_\delta\}_{\delta \in \Delta} \rangle$ contains two parts: W_Δ is the set of positive domain weights w_δ with $\sum_{\delta \in \Delta} w_\delta = |\Delta|$. Moreover, W contains for each domain $\delta \in \Delta$ a set W_δ of dimension weights w_d with $\sum_{d \in \delta} w_d = 1$.

The similarity of two points in a conceptual space is inversely related to their distance. This can be written as follows:

$$Sim(x, y) = e^{-c \cdot d(x,y)} \quad \text{with a constant } c > 0 \text{ and a given metric } d$$

Betweenness is a logical predicate $B(x, y, z)$ that is true if and only if y is considered to be between x and z. It can be defined based on a given metric d:

$$B_d(x, y, z) : \iff d(x, y) + d(y, z) = d(x, z)$$

The betweenness relation based on d_E results in the line segment connecting the points x and z, whereas the betweenness relation based on d_M results in an axis-parallel cuboid between the points x and z. One can define convexity and star-shapedness based on the notion of betweenness:

Definition 1 *(Convexity)*.
A set $C \subseteq CS$ is convex under a metric d : $\iff$
$$\forall x \in C, z \in C, y \in CS : (B_d(x, y, z) \rightarrow y \in C)$$

Definition 2 *(Star-shapedness)*.
A set $S \subseteq CS$ is star-shaped under a metric d with respect to a set $P \subseteq S$: $\iff$
$$\forall p \in P, z \in S, y \in CS : (B_d(p, y, z) \rightarrow y \in S)$$

2.2 Properties and Concepts

Gärdenfors [16] distinguishes properties like "red", "round", and "sweet" from full-fleshed concepts like "apple" or "dog" by observing that properties can be defined on individual domains (e.g., color, shape, taste), whereas full-fleshed concepts involve multiple domains. Each domain involved in representing a concept has a certain importance, which is reflected by so-called "salience weights". Another important aspect of concepts are the correlations between the different domains, which are important for both learning [8] and reasoning [23, Chap. 8].

Based on the principle of cognitive economy, Gärdenfors argues that both properties and concepts should be represented as convex sets. However, as we demonstrated in [6], one cannot geometrically encode correlations between domains when using convex sets: The left part of Fig. 1 shows two domains, age and height, and the concepts of child and adult. The solid ellipses illustrate the intuitive way of defining these concepts. As domains are combined with the Manhattan metric, a convex set corresponds in this case to an axis-parallel cuboid. One can easily see that this convex representation (dashed rectangles) is not satisfactory, because the correlation of the two domains is not encoded. We therefore proposed in [6] to relax the convexity criterion and to use star-shaped sets, which is illustrated in the right part of Fig. 1. This enables a geometric representation of correlations while still being only a minimal departure from the original framework.

We have based our formalization on axis-parallel cuboids that can be described by a triple $\langle \Delta_C, p^-, p^+ \rangle$ consisting of a set of domains Δ_C on which this cuboid C is defined and two points p^- and p^+, such that

$$x \in C \iff \forall \delta \in \Delta_C : \forall d \in \delta : p_d^- \leq x_d \leq p_d^+$$

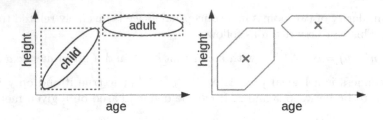

Fig. 1. Left: Intuitive way to define regions for the concepts of "adult" and "child" (solid) as well as representation by using convex sets (dashed). Right: Representation by using star-shaped sets with central points marked by crosses.

These cuboids are convex under d_C^A. It is also easy to see that any union of convex sets that have a non-empty intersection is star-shaped [27]. We define the core of a concept as follows:

Definition 3 *(Simple star-shaped set).*
A simple star-shaped set S is described as a tuple $\langle \Delta_S, \{C_1, \ldots, C_m\}\rangle$. $\Delta_S \subseteq \Delta$ is a set of domains on which the cuboids $\{C_1, \ldots, C_m\}$ (and thus also S) are defined. Moreover, it is required that the central region $P := \bigcap_{i=1}^m C_i \neq \emptyset$. Then the simple star-shaped set S is defined as

$$S := \bigcup_{i=1}^m C_i$$

In order to represent imprecise concept boundaries, we use fuzzy sets [7,30, 31]. A fuzzy set is characterized by its membership function $\mu : CS \to [0,1]$ that assigns a degree of membership to each point in the conceptual space. The membership of a point to a fuzzy concept is based on its maximal similarity to any of the points in the concept's core:

Definition 4 *(Fuzzy simple star-shaped set).*
A fuzzy simple star-shaped set $\widetilde{S}$ is described by a quadruple $\langle S, \mu_0, c, W\rangle$ where $S = \langle \Delta_S, \{C_1, \ldots, C_m\}\rangle$ is a non-empty simple star-shaped set. The parameter $\mu_0 \in (0,1]$ controls the highest possible membership to $\widetilde{S}$ and is usually set to 1. The sensitivity parameter $c > 0$ controls the rate of the exponential decay in the similarity function. Finally, $W = \langle W_{\Delta_S}, \{W_\delta\}_{\delta \in \Delta_S}\rangle$ contains positive weights for all domains in Δ_S and all dimensions within these domains, reflecting their respective importance. We require that $\sum_{\delta \in \Delta_S} w_\delta = |\Delta_S|$ and that $\forall \delta \in \Delta_S : \sum_{d \in \delta} w_d = 1$. The membership function of $\widetilde{S}$ is then defined as follows:

$$\mu_{\widetilde{S}}(x) = \mu_0 \cdot \max_{y \in S}(e^{-c \cdot d_C^A(x,y,W)})$$

The sensitivity parameter c controls the overall degree of fuzziness of $\widetilde{S}$ by determining how fast the membership drops to zero. The weights W represent

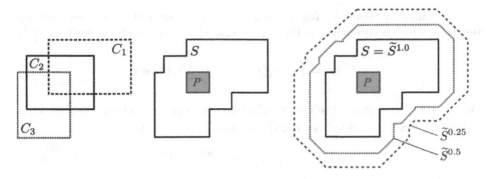

Fig. 2. Left: Three cuboids C_1, C_2, C_3 with nonempty intersection. Middle: Resulting simple star-shaped set S based on these cuboids. Right: Fuzzy simple star-shaped set $\tilde{S}$ based on S with three α-cuts for $\alpha \in \{1.0, 0.5, 0.25\}$.

not only the relative importance of the respective domain or dimension for the represented concept, but they also influence the relative fuzziness with respect to this domain or dimension. Note that if $|\Delta_S| = 1$, then $\tilde{S}$ represents a property, and if $|\Delta_S| > 1$, then $\tilde{S}$ represents a concept. Figure 2 illustrates this definition (the x and y axes are assumed to belong to different domains and are combined with d_M using equal weights).

In our previous work [6], we have also provided a number of operations, which can be used to create new concepts from old ones: The intersection of two concepts can be interpreted as the logical "and" – e.g., intersecting the property "green" with the concept "banana" results in the set of all objects that are both green and bananas. The union of two concepts can be used to construct more abstract categories (e.g., defining "fruit" as the union of "apple", "banana", "coconut", etc.). Projecting a concept onto a subspace corresponds to focusing on certain domains while completely ignoring others.

3   Defining Additional Operations

3.1   Concept Size

The size of a concept gives an intuition about its specificity: Large concepts are more general and small concepts are more specific. This is one obvious aspect in which one can compare two concepts to each other.

One can use a measure M to describe the size of a fuzzy set. It can be defined in our context as follows (cf. [10]):

Definition 5. *A measure M on a conceptual space CS is a function $M : \mathcal{F}(CS) \to \mathbb{R}_0^+$ with $M(\emptyset) = 0$ and $\tilde{A} \subseteq \tilde{B} \Rightarrow M(\tilde{A}) \leq M(\tilde{B})$, where $\mathcal{F}(CS)$ is the fuzzy power set of CS and where $\tilde{A} \subseteq \tilde{B} :\Longleftrightarrow \forall x \in CS : \mu_{\tilde{A}}(x) \leq \mu_{\tilde{B}}(x)$.*

A common measure for fuzzy sets is the integral over the set's membership function, which is equivalent to the Lebesgue integral over the fuzzy set's α-cuts[1]:

$$M(\widetilde{A}) := \int_{CS} \mu_{\widetilde{A}}(x) \, dx = \int_0^1 V(\widetilde{A}^\alpha) \, d\alpha \tag{1}$$

We use $V(\widetilde{A}^\alpha)$ to denote the volume of a fuzzy set's α-cut. Let us define for each cuboid $C_i \in S$ its fuzzified version $\widetilde{C}_i$ as follows (cf. Definition 4):

$$\mu_{\widetilde{C}_i}(x) = \mu_0 \cdot \max_{y \in C_i}(e^{-c \cdot d_C^\triangle(x,y,W)})$$

It is obvious that $\mu_{\widetilde{S}}(x) = \max_{C_i \in S} \mu_{\widetilde{C}_i}(x)$. It is also clear that the intersection of two fuzzified cuboids is again a fuzzified cuboid. Finally, one can easily see that we can use the inclusion-exclustion formula (cf. e.g., [9]) to compute the overall measure of $\widetilde{S}$ based on the measure of its fuzzified cuboids:

$$M(\widetilde{S}) = \sum_{l=1}^m \left((-1)^{l+1} \cdot \sum_{\substack{\{i_1,\ldots,i_l\} \\ \subseteq \{1,\ldots,m\}}} M\left(\bigcap_{i \in \{i_1,\ldots,i_l\}} \widetilde{C}_i \right) \right) \tag{2}$$

The outer sum iterates over the number of cuboids under consideration (with m being the total number of cuboids in S) and the inner sum iterates over all sets of exactly l cuboids. The overall formula generalizes the observation that $|\widetilde{C}_1 \cup \widetilde{C}_2| = |\widetilde{C}_1| + |\widetilde{C}_2| - |\widetilde{C}_1 \cap \widetilde{C}_2|$ from two to m sets.

In order to derive $M(\widetilde{C})$, we first describe how to compute $V(\widetilde{C}^\alpha)$, i.e., the size of a fuzzified cuboid's α-cut. Using Eq. 1, we can then derive $M(\widetilde{C})$, which we can in turn insert into Eq. 2 to compute the overall size of $\widetilde{S}$.

Figure 3 illustrates the α-cut of a fuzzified two-dimensional cuboid both under d_E (left) and under d_M (right). Because the membership function is defined based on an exponential decay, one can interpret each α-cut as an ϵ-neighborhood of the original cuboid C, where ϵ depends on α:

$$x \in \widetilde{C}^\alpha \iff \mu_0 \cdot \max_{y \in C}(e^{-c \cdot d_C^\triangle(x,y,W)}) \geq \alpha \iff \min_{y \in C} d_C^\triangle(x,y,W) \leq -\frac{1}{c} \cdot \ln(\frac{\alpha}{\mu_0})$$

$V(\widetilde{C}^\alpha)$ can be described as a sum of different components. Let us use the shorthand notation $b_d := p_d^+ - p_d^-$. Looking at Fig. 3, one can see that all components of $V(\widetilde{C}^\alpha)$ can be described by ellipses[2]: Component I is a zero-dimensional ellipse (i.e., a point) that was extruded in two dimensions with extrusion lengths of b_1 and b_2, respectively. Component II consists of two one-dimensional ellipses (i.e., line segments) that were extruded in one dimension, and component III is a two-dimensional ellipse.

---

[1] The α-cut of a fuzzy set $\widetilde{A}$ is defined as $\widetilde{A}^\alpha = \{x \in CS \mid \mu_{\widetilde{A}}(x) \geq \alpha\}$.
[2] Note that ellipses under d_M have the form of streched diamonds.

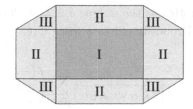

Fig. 3. α-cut of a fuzzified cuboid under d_E (left) and d_M (right), respectively.

Let us denote by $\Delta_{\{d_1,\dots,d_i\}}$ the domain structure obtained by eliminating from Δ all dimensions $d \in D \setminus \{d_1,\dots,d_i\}$. Moreover, let $V(r,\Delta,W)$ be the hypervolume of a hyperball under $d_C^\Delta(\cdot,\cdot,W)$ with radius r. In this case, a hyperball is the set of all points with a distance of at most r (measured by $d_C^\Delta(\cdot,\cdot,W)$) to a central point. Note that the weights W will cause this ball to have the form of an ellipse. For instance, in Fig. 3, we assume that $w_{d_1} < w_{d_2}$ which means that we allow larger differences with respect to d_1 than with respect to d_2. This causes the hyperballs to be streched in the d_1 dimension, thus obtaining the shape of an ellipse. We can in general describe $V(\widetilde{C}^\alpha)$ as follows:

$$V(\widetilde{C}^\alpha) = \sum_{i=0}^{n} \left(\sum_{\substack{\{d_1,\dots,d_i\} \\ \subseteq D}} \left(\prod_{\substack{d \in \\ D\setminus\{d_1,\dots,d_i\}}} b_d \right) \cdot V\left(-\frac{1}{c}\cdot\ln\left(\frac{\alpha}{\mu_0}\right), \Delta_{\{d_1,\dots,d_i\}}, W \right) \right)$$

The first sum of this formula runs over the number of dimensions with respect to which a given point $x \in \widetilde{C}^\alpha$ lies outside of C. We then sum over all combinations $\{d_1,\dots,d_i\}$ of dimensions for which this could be the case, compute the volume of the i-dimensional hyperball under these dimensions ($V(\cdot,\cdot,\cdot)$) and extrude this intermediate result in all remaining dimensions ($\prod_{d \in D\setminus\{d_1,\dots,d_i\}} b_d$).

Let us illustrate this formula for the α-cuts shown in Fig. 3: For $i = 0$, we can only select the empty set for the inner sum, so we end up with $b_1 \cdot b_2$, which is the size of the original cuboid (i.e., component I). For $i = 1$, we can either pick $\{d_1\}$ or $\{d_2\}$ in the inner sum. For $\{d_1\}$, we compute the size of the left and right part of component II by multiplying $V\left(-\frac{1}{c}\cdot\ln\left(\frac{\alpha}{\mu_0}\right), \Delta_{\{d_1\}}, W\right)$ (i.e., their combined width) with b_2 (i.e., their height). For $\{d_2\}$, we analogously compute the size of the upper and the lower part of component II. Finally, for $i = 2$, we can only pick $\{d_1,d_2\}$ in the inner sum, leaving us with $V\left(-\frac{1}{c}\cdot\ln\left(\frac{\alpha}{\mu_0}\right), \Delta, W\right)$, which is the size of component III. One can easily see that the formula for $V(\widetilde{C}^\alpha)$ also generalizes to higher dimensions.

Proposition 1. $V(r,\Delta,W) = \frac{1}{\prod_{\delta\in\Delta} w_\delta \cdot \prod_{d\in\delta} \sqrt{w_d}} \cdot \frac{r^n}{n!} \cdot \prod_{\delta\in\Delta}\left(|\delta|! \cdot \frac{\pi^{\frac{|\delta|}{2}}}{\Gamma(\frac{|\delta|}{2}+1)} \right)$

Proof. See appendix (http://lucas-bechberger.de/appendix-sgai-2017/).

Defining $\delta(d)$ as the unique $\delta \in \Delta$ with $d \in \delta$, and $a_d := w_{\delta(d)} \cdot \sqrt{w_d} \cdot b_d \cdot c$, we can use Proposition 1 to rewrite $V(\widetilde{C}^\alpha)$:

$$V(\widetilde{C}^\alpha) = \frac{1}{c^n \prod_{d \in D} w_{\delta(d)} \sqrt{w_d}} \sum_{i=0}^{n} \left(\frac{(-1)^i \cdot \ln\left(\frac{\alpha}{\mu_0}\right)^i}{i!} \cdot \sum_{\substack{\{d_1,\dots,d_i\} \\ \subseteq D}} \left(\prod_{\substack{d \in \\ D \setminus \{d_1,\dots,d_i\}}} a_d \right) \cdot \right.$$
$$\left. \prod_{\substack{\delta \in \\ \Delta_{\{d_1,\dots,d_i\}}}} \left(|\delta|! \cdot \frac{\pi^{\frac{|\delta|}{2}}}{\Gamma(\frac{|\delta|}{2} + 1)} \right) \right)$$

We can solve Eq. 1 to compute $M(\widetilde{C})$ by using the following lemma:

Lemma 1. $\forall n \in \mathbb{N} : \int_0^1 \ln(x)^n dx = (-1)^n \cdot n!$

Proof. Substitute $x = e^t$ and $s = -t$, then apply the definition of the Γ function.

Proposition 2. *The measure of a fuzzified cuboid $\widetilde{C}$ can be computed as follows:*

$$M(\widetilde{C}) = \frac{\mu_0}{c^n \prod_{d \in D} w_{\delta(d)} \sqrt{w_d}} \sum_{i=0}^{n} \left(\sum_{\substack{\{d_1,\dots,d_i\} \\ \subseteq D}} \left(\prod_{\substack{d \in \\ D \setminus \{d_1,\dots,d_i\}}} a_d \right) \cdot \right.$$
$$\left. \prod_{\substack{\delta \in \\ \Delta_{\{d_1,\dots,d_i\}}}} \left(|\delta|! \cdot \frac{\pi^{\frac{|\delta|}{2}}}{\Gamma(\frac{|\delta|}{2} + 1)} \right) \right)$$

Proof. Substitute $x = \frac{\alpha}{\mu_0}$ in Eq. 1 and apply Lemma 1.

Note that although the formula for $M(\widetilde{C})$ is quite complex, it can be easily implemented via a set of nested loops. As mentioned earlier, we can use the result from Proposition 2 in combination with the inclusion-exclusion formula (Eq. 2) to compute $M(\widetilde{S})$ for any concept $\widetilde{S}$. Also Eq. 2 can be easily implemented via a set of nested loops. Note that $M(\widetilde{S})$ is always computed only on Δ_S, i.e., the set of domains on which $\widetilde{S}$ is defined.

3.2   Subsethood

In order to represent knowledge about a hierarchy of concepts, one needs to be able to determine whether one concept is a subset of another concept. The classic definition of subsethood for fuzzy sets reads as follows:

$$\widetilde{S}_1 \subseteq \widetilde{S}_2 : \iff \forall x \in CS : \mu_{\widetilde{S}_1}(x) \le \mu_{\widetilde{S}_2}(x)$$

This definition has the weakness of only providing a binary/crisp notion of subsethood. It is desirable to define a *degree* of subsethood in order to make more fine-grained distinctions. Many of the definitions for degrees of subsethood proposed in the fuzzy set literature [10,29] require that the underlying universe is discrete. The following definition [20] works also in a continuous space and is conceptually quite straightforward:

$$Sub(\widetilde{S}_1, \widetilde{S}_2) = \frac{M(\widetilde{S}_1 \cap \widetilde{S}_2)}{M(\widetilde{S}_1)} \quad \text{with a measure } M$$

One can interpret this definition intuitively as the "percentage of $\widetilde{S}_1$ that is also in $\widetilde{S}_2$". It can be easily implemented based on the measure defined in Sect. 3.1 and the intersection defined in [6]. If $\widetilde{S}_1$ and $\widetilde{S}_2$ are not defined on the same domains, then we first project them onto their shared subset of domains before computing their degree of subsethood.

When computing the intersection of two concepts with different sensitivity parameters $c^{(1)}, c^{(2)}$ and different weights $W^{(1)}, W^{(2)}$, one needs to define new parameters c' and W' for the resulting concept. In our earlier work [6], we have argued that the sensitivity parameter c' should be set to the minimum of $c^{(1)}$ and $c^{(2)}$. As a larger value for c causes the membership function to drop faster, this means that the concept resulting from intersecting two imprecise concepts is at least as imprecise as the original concepts. Moreover, we defined W' as a linear interpolation between $W^{(1)}$ and $W^{(2)}$. The importance of each dimension and domain to the new concept will thus lie somewhere between its importance with respect to the two original concepts.

Now if $c^{(1)} > c^{(2)}$, then $c' = \min(c^{(1)}, c^{(2)}) = c^{(2)} < c^{(1)}$. It might thus happen that $M(\widetilde{S}_1 \cap \widetilde{S}_2) > M(\widetilde{S}_1)$, and that therefore $Sub(\widetilde{S}_1, \widetilde{S}_2) > 1$. As we would like to confine $Sub(\widetilde{S}_1, \widetilde{S}_2)$ to the interval $[0,1]$, we should use the same c and W for computing both $M(\widetilde{S}_1 \cap \widetilde{S}_2)$ and $M(\widetilde{S}_1)$.

When judging whether $\widetilde{S}_1$ is a subset of $\widetilde{S}_2$, we can think of $\widetilde{S}_2$ as setting the context by determining the relative importance of the different domains and dimensions as well as the degree of fuzziness. For instance, when judging whether tomatoes are vegetables, we focus our attention on the features that are crucial to the definition of the "vegetable" concept. We thus propose to use $c^{(2)}$ and $W^{(2)}$ when computing $M(\widetilde{S}_1 \cap \widetilde{S}_2)$ and $M(\widetilde{S}_1)$.

3.3   Implication

Implications play a fundamental role in rule-based systems and all approaches that use formal logics for knowledge representation. It is therefore desirable to define an implication function on concepts, such that one is able to express facts like *apple* $\Rightarrow$ *red* within our formalization.

In the fuzzy set literature [22], a fuzzy implication is defined as a generalization of the classical crisp implication. Computing the implication of two fuzzy sets typically results in a new fuzzy set which describes for each point in the space the validity of the implication. In our setting, we are however more interested in a single number that indicates the overall validity of the implication $apple \Rightarrow red$. We propose to reuse the definition of subsethood from Sect. 3.2: It makes intuitive sense in our geometric setting to say that $apple \Rightarrow red$ is true to the degree to which $apple$ is a subset of red. We therefore define:

$$Impl(\widetilde{S}_1, \widetilde{S}_2) := Sub(\widetilde{S}_1, \widetilde{S}_2)$$

3.4   Similarity and Betweenness

In our prior work [6] (cf. Sect. 2.1), we have already provided definitions for similarity and betweenness of points. We can naively define similarity and betweenness for concepts by applying the definitions from Sect. 2.1 to the midpoints of the concepts' central regions P (cf. Definition 3). Betweenness is a binary relation and independent of dimension weights and sensitivity parameters. For computing the similarity, we propose to use both the dimension weights and the sensitivity parameter of the second concept, which again in a sense provides the context for the similarity judgement. If the two concepts are defined on different sets of domains, we use only their common subset of domains for computing the distance of their midpoints and thus their similarity.

4   Illustrative Example

4.1   A Conceptual Space and Its Concepts

We consider a very simplified conceptual space for fruits, consisting of the following domains and dimensions:

$$\Delta = \{\delta_{color} = \{d_{hue}\}, \delta_{shape} = \{d_{round}\}, \delta_{taste} = \{d_{sweet}\}\}$$

d_{hue} describes the hue of the observation's color, ranging from 0.00 (purple) to 1.00 (red). d_{round} measures the percentage to which the bounding circle of an object is filled. d_{sweet} represents the relative amount of sugar contained in the fruit, ranging from 0.00 (no sugar) to 1.00 (high sugar content). As all domains are one-dimensional, the dimension weights w_d are always equal to 1.00 for all concepts. We assume that the dimensions are ordered like this: $d_{hue}, d_{round}, d_{sweet}$. Table 1 defines several concepts in this space and Fig. 4 visualizes them.

4.2   Computations

Table 2 shows the results of using the definitions from Sect. 3 on the concepts defined in Sect. 4.1. Note that $M(\widetilde{S}_{lemon}) \neq M(\widetilde{S}_{orange})$ because the two concepts have different weights and different sensitivity parameters. Also all relations involving the property "red" tend to yield relatively high numbers – this is because all computations only take place within the single domain on which

Table 1. Definitions of several concepts.

Concept	Δ_S	p^-	p^+	μ_0	c	W $w_{\delta_{color}}$	$w_{\delta_{shape}}$	$w_{\delta_{taste}}$
Orange	Δ	(0.80, 0.90, 0.60)	(0.90, 1.00, 0.70)	1.0	15.0	1.00	1.00	1.00
Lemon	Δ	(0.70, 0.45, 0.00)	(0.80, 0.55, 0.10)	1.0	20.0	0.50	0.50	2.00
Granny Smith	Δ	(0.55, 0.70, 0.35)	(0.60, 0.80, 0.45)	1.0	25.0	1.00	1.00	1.00
Apple	Δ	(0.50, 0.65, 0.35)	(0.80, 0.80, 0.50)	1.0	10.0	0.50	1.50	1.00
		(0.65, 0.65, 0.40)	(0.85, 0.80, 0.55)					
		(0.70, 0.65, 0.45)	(1.00, 0.80, 0.60)					
Red	$\{\delta_{color}\}$	(0.90, -∞, -∞)	(1.00, +∞, +∞)	1.0	20.0	1.00	–	–

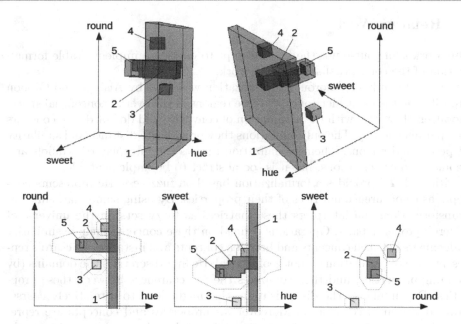

Fig. 4. Top: Three-dimensional visualization of the fruit space (only cores). Bottom: Two-dimensional visualizations of the fruit space (cores and 0.5-cuts). The concepts are labeled as follows: red (1), apple (2), lemon (3), orange (4), Granny Smith (5). (Color figure online)

"red" is defined. The numbers computed for the subsethood/implication relation nicely reflect our intuitive expectations. Finally, both the values for similarity and betweenness can give a rough idea about the relationship between concepts, but can only yield relatively shallow insights. This indicates that a less naive approach is needed for these two relations. Especially a fuzzy betweenness relation yielding a degree of betweenness seems to be desirable.

Table 2. Computations of different relations. Note that $Impl(\widetilde{S}_1, \widetilde{S}_2) = Sub(\widetilde{S}_1, \widetilde{S}_2)$.

$\widetilde{S}_1$	$\widetilde{S}_2$	$M(\widetilde{S}_1)$	$M(\widetilde{S}_2)$	$Sub(\widetilde{S}_1, \widetilde{S}_2)$	$Sub(\widetilde{S}_2, \widetilde{S}_1)$	$Sim(\widetilde{S}_1, \widetilde{S}_2)$	$Sim(\widetilde{S}_2, \widetilde{S}_1)$
Granny Smith	Apple	0.0042	0.1048	1.0000	0.1171	0.1353	0.0010
Orange	Apple	0.0127	0.1048	0.1800	0.0333	0.0036	0.0006
Lemon	Apple	0.0135	0.1048	0.0422	0.0054	0.0005	0.0000
Red	Apple	0.2000	0.1048	1.0000	0.3333	0.3679	0.0183

$\widetilde{S}_1$	$\widetilde{S}_2$	$\widetilde{S}_2$	$B(\widetilde{S}_1, \widetilde{S}_2, \widetilde{S}_3)$
Lemon	Apple	Orange	True
Lemon	Granny Smith	Orange	False
Granny Smith	Apple	Orange	False

5   Related Work

Our work is of course not the first attempt to devise an implementable formalization of the conceptual spaces framework.

An early and very thorough formalization was done by Aisbett and Gibbon [4]. Like we, they consider concepts to be regions in the overall conceptual space. However, they stick with the assumption of convexity and do not define concepts in a parametric way. The only operations they provide are distance and similarity of points and regions. Their formalization targets the interplay of symbols and geometric representations, but it is too abstract to be implementable.

Rickard [24] provides a formalization based on fuzziness. He represents concepts as co-occurence matrices of their properties. By using some mathematical transformations, he interprets these matrices as fuzzy sets on the universe of ordered property pairs. Operations defined on these concepts include similarity judgements between concepts and between concepts and instances. Rickard's representation of correlations is not geometrical: He first discretizes the domains (by defining properties) and then computes the co-occurences between these properties. Depending on the discretization, this might lead to a relatively coarse-grained notion of correlation. Moreover, as properties and concepts are represented in different ways, one has to use different learning and reasoning mechanisms for them. His formalization is also not easy to work with due to the complex mathematical transformations involved.

Adams and Raubal [1] represent concepts by one convex polytope per domain. This allows for efficient computations while being potentially more expressive than our cuboid-based representation. The Manhattan metric is used to combine different domains. However, correlations between different domains are not taken into account and cannot be expressed in this formalization as each convex polytope is only defined on a single domain. Adams and Raubal also define operations on concepts, namely intersection, similarity computation, and concept combination. This makes their formalization quite similar in spirit to ours.

Lewis and Lawry [21] formalize conceptual spaces using random set theory. They define properties as random sets within single domains and concepts as random sets in a boolean space whose dimensions indicate the presence or absence of properties. In order to define this boolean space, a single property is taken from each domain. Their approach is similar to ours in using a distance-based membership function to a set of prototypical points. However, their work purely focuses on modeling conjunctive concept combinations and does not consider correlations between domains.

As one can see, none of the formalizations listed above provides a set of operations that is as comprehensive as the one offered by our extended formalization.

6   Conclusion and Future Work

In this paper, we extended our previous formalization of the conceptual spaces framework by providing ways to measure relations between concepts: concept size, subsethood, implication, similarity, and betweenness. This considerably extends our framework's capabilities for representing knowledge and makes it (to the best of our knowledge) the most thorough and comprehensive formalization of conceptual spaces developed so far.

In future work, we will implement this extended formalization in software. Moreover, we will provide more thorough definitions of similarity and betweenness for concepts, given that our current definitions are rather naïve. A potential starting point for this can be the betwenness relations defined by Derrac and Schockaert [13]. Finally, our overall research goal is to use machine learning in conceptual spaces, which will put this formalization to practical use.

References

1. Adams, B., Raubal, M.: A metric conceptual space algebra. In: Hornsby, K.S., Claramunt, C., Denis, M., Ligozat, G. (eds.) COSIT 2009. LNCS, vol. 5756, pp. 51–68. Springer, Heidelberg (2009). https://doi.org/10.1007/978-3-642-03832-7_4
2. Adams, B., Raubal, M.: Conceptual space markup language (CSML): towards the cognitive semantic web. In: IEEE International Conference on Semantic Computing, September 2009
3. Aggarwal, C.C., Hinneburg, A., Keim, D.A.: On the surprising behavior of distance metrics in high dimensional space. In: Bussche, J., Vianu, V. (eds.) ICDT 2001. LNCS, vol. 1973, pp. 420–434. Springer, Heidelberg (2001). https://doi.org/10.1007/3-540-44503-X_27
4. Aisbett, J., Gibbon, G.: A general formulation of conceptual spaces as a meso level representation. Artif. Intell. 133(1–2), 189–232 (2001)
5. Attneave, F.: Dimensions of similarity. Am. J. Psychol. 63(4), 516–556 (1950)
6. Bechberger, L., Kühnberger, K.U.: A thorough formalization of conceptual spaces. In: Kern-Isberner, G., Fürnkranz, J., Thimm, M. (eds.) KI 2017. LNCS, vol. 10505, pp. 58–71. Springer, Heidelberg (2017). https://doi.org/10.1007/978-3-319-67190-1_5
7. Bělohlávek, R., Klir, G.J.: Concepts and Fuzzy Logic. MIT Press, Cambridge (2011)

8. Billman, D., Knutson, J.: Unsupervised concept learning and value systematicitiy: a complex whole aids learning the parts. J. Exp. Psychol.: Learn. Memory Cogn. **22**(2), 458–475 (1996)
9. Bogart, K.P.: Introductory Combinatorics, 2nd edn. Saunders College Publishing, Philadelphia (1989)
10. Bouchon-Meunier, B., Rifqi, M., Bothorel, S.: Towards general measures of comparison of objects. Fuzzy Sets Syst. **84**(2), 143–153 (1996)
11. Chella, A., Frixione, M., Gaglio, S.: Conceptual spaces for computer vision representations. Artif. Intell. Rev. **16**(2), 137–152 (2001)
12. Chella, A., Frixione, M., Gaglio, S.: Anchoring symbols to conceptual spaces: the case of dynamic scenarios. Robot. Auton. Syst. **43**(2–3), 175–188 (2003)
13. Derrac, J., Schockaert, S.: Inducing semantic relations from conceptual spaces: a data-driven approach to plausible reasoning. Artif. Intell. **228**, 66–94 (2015)
14. Douven, I., Decock, L., Dietz, R., Égré, P.: Vagueness: a conceptual spaces approach. J. Philos. Logic **42**(1), 137–160 (2011)
15. Fiorini, S.R., Gärdenfors, P., Abel, M.: Representing part-whole relations in conceptual spaces. Cogn. Process. **15**(2), 127–142 (2013)
16. Gärdenfors, P.: Conceptual Spaces: The Geometry of Thought. MIT Press, Cambridge (2000)
17. Gärdenfors, P.: The Geometry of Meaning: Semantics Based on Conceptual Spaces. MIT Press, Cambridge (2014)
18. Harnad, S.: The symbol grounding problem. Phys. D: Nonlinear Phenom. **42**(1–3), 335–346 (1990)
19. Johannesson, M.: The problem of combining integral and separable dimensions. Technical report HS-IDA-TR-01-002, University of Skövde, School of Humanities and Informatics (2001)
20. Kosko, B.: Neural Networks and Fuzzy Systems: A Dynamical Systems Approach to Machine Intelligence. Prentice Hall, Upper Saddle River (1992)
21. Lewis, M., Lawry, J.: Hierarchical conceptual spaces for concept combination. Artif. Intell. **237**, 204–227 (2016)
22. Mas, M., Monserrat, M., Torrens, J., Trillas, E.: A survey on fuzzy implication functions. IEEE Trans. Fuzzy Syst. **15**(6), 1107–1121 (2007)
23. Murphy, G.: The Big Book of Concepts. MIT Press, Cambridge (2002)
24. Rickard, J.T.: A concept geometry for conceptual spaces. Fuzzy Optim. Decis. Making **5**(4), 311–329 (2006)
25. Schockaert, S., Prade, H.: Interpolation and extrapolation in conceptual spaces: a case study in the music domain. In: Rudolph, S., Gutierrez, C. (eds.) RR 2011. LNCS, vol. 6902, pp. 217–231. Springer, Heidelberg (2011). https://doi.org/10.1007/978-3-642-23580-1_16
26. Shepard, R.N.: Attention and the metric structure of the stimulus space. J. Math. Psychol. **1**(1), 54–87 (1964)
27. Smith, C.R.: A characterization of star-shaped sets. Am. Math. Monthly **75**(4), 386 (1968)
28. Warglien, M., Gärdenfors, P., Westera, M.: Event structure, conceptual spaces and the semantics of verbs. Theoret. Linguis. **38**(3–4), 159–193 (2012)
29. Young, V.R.: Fuzzy subsethood. Fuzzy Sets Syst. **77**(3), 371–384 (1996)
30. Zadeh, L.A.: Fuzzy sets. Inf. Control **8**(3), 338–353 (1965)
31. Zadeh, L.A.: A note on prototype theory and fuzzy sets. Cognition **12**(3), 291–297 (1982)

Towards a Deep Reinforcement Learning Approach for Tower Line Wars

Per-Arne Andersen[✉], Morten Goodwin, and Ole-Christoffer Granmo

University of Agder, Grimstad, Norway
per-arne.andersen@uia.no

Abstract. There have been numerous breakthroughs with reinforcement learning in the recent years, perhaps most notably on Deep Reinforcement Learning successfully playing and winning relatively advanced computer games. There is undoubtedly an anticipation that Deep Reinforcement Learning will play a major role when the first AI masters the complicated game plays needed to beat a professional Real-Time Strategy game player. For this to be possible, there needs to be a game environment that targets and fosters AI research, and specifically Deep Reinforcement Learning. Some game environments already exist, however, these are either overly simplistic such as Atari 2600 or complex such as Starcraft II from Blizzard Entertainment.

We propose a game environment in between Atari 2600 and Starcraft II, particularly targeting Deep Reinforcement Learning algorithm research. The environment is a variant of Tower Line Wars from Warcraft III, Blizzard Entertainment. Further, as a proof of concept that the environment can harbor Deep Reinforcement algorithms, we propose and apply a Deep Q-Reinforcement architecture. The architecture simplifies the state space so that it is applicable to Q-learning, and in turn improves performance compared to current state-of-the-art methods. Our experiments show that the proposed architecture can learn to play the environment well, and score 33% better than standard Deep Q-learning—which in turn proves the usefulness of the game environment.

Keywords: Reinforcement Learning · Q-Learning · Deep Learning · Game environment

1 Introduction

Despite many advances in AI for games, no universal reinforcement learning algorithm can be applied to Real-Time Strategy Games (RTS) without data manipulation or customization. This includes traditional games such as Warcraft III, Starcraft II, and Tower Line Wars. Reinforcement Learning (RL) has been applied to simpler games such as games for the Atari 2600 platform but has to the best of our knowledge not successfully been applied to RTS games. Further, existing game environments that target AI research are either overly simplistic such as Atari 2600 or complex such as Starcraft II.

© Springer International Publishing AG 2017
M. Bramer and M. Petridis (Eds.): SGAI-AI 2017, LNAI 10630, pp. 101–114, 2017.
https://doi.org/10.1007/978-3-319-71078-5_8

Reinforcement Learning has had tremendous progress in recent years in learning to control agents from high-dimensional sensory inputs like vision. In simple environments, this has been proven to work well [1], but are still an issue for complex environments with large state and action spaces [2]. In games where the objective is easily observable, there is a short distance between action and reward which fuels the learning. This is because the consequence of any action is quickly observed, and then easily learned. When the objective is more complicated the game objectives still need to be mapped to the reward function, but it becomes far less trivial. For the Atari 2600 game Ms. Pac-Man this was solved through a hybrid reward architecture that transforms the objective to a low-dimensional representation [3]. Similarly, the OpenAI's bot is able to beat world's top professionals at 1v1 in DotA 2. It uses reinforcement learning while it plays against itself, learning to predict the opponent moves.

Real-Time Strategy Games, including Warcraft III, is a genre of games much more comparable to the complexity of real-world environments. It has a sparse state space with many different sensory inputs that any game playing algorithm must be able to master in order to perform well within the environment. Due to the complexity and because many action sequences are required to constitute a reward, standard reinforcement learning techniques including Q-learning are not able to master the games successfully.

This paper introduces a two-player version of the popular Tower Line Wars modification from the game Warcraft III. We refer to this variant as Deep Line Wars. Note that Tower Line Wars is not an RTS game, but has many similar elements such as time-delayed objectives, resource management, offensive, and defensive strategy planning. To prove that the environment is working we, inspired by recent advances from van Seijen et al. [3], apply a method of separating the abstract reward function of the environment into smaller rewards. This approach uses a Deep Q-Network using a Convolutional Neural Network to map actions to states and can play the game successfully and perform better than standard Deep Q-learning by 33%.

Rest of the paper is organized as follows: We first investigate recent discoveries in Deep RL in Sect. 2. We then briefly outline how Q-Learning works and how we interpret Bellman's equation for utilizing Neural Networks as a function approximator in Sect. 3. We present our contribution in Sect. 4 and present a comparison of other game environments that are widely used in reinforcement learning. We introduce a variant of Deep Q-Learning in Sect. 5 and present a comparison to other RL models used in state-of-the-art research. Finally we show results in Sect. 6, define a roadmap of future work in Sect. 7 and conclude our work in Sect. 8.

2   Related Work

There have been several breakthroughs related to reinforcement learning performance in recent years [4]. Q-Learning together with Deep Learning was a game-changing moment, and has had tremendous success in many single agent environments on the Atari 2600 platform [1]. Deep Q-Learning as proposed by Mnih et al. [1] as shown in Fig. 1 used a neural network as a function approximator and outperformed human expertise in over half of the games [1].

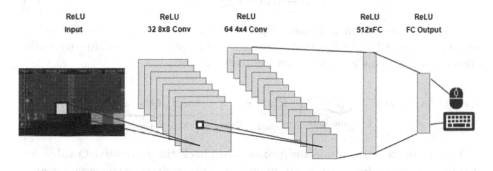

ReLU | ReLU | ReLU | ReLU | ReLU
Input | 32 8x8 Conv | 64 4x4 Conv | 512xFC | FC Output

Fig. 1. Deep Q-Learning architecture

Hasselt et al. proposed Double DQN, which reduced the overestimation of action values in the Deep Q-Network [5]. This led to improvements in some of the games on the Atari platform.

Wang et al. then proposed a dueling architecture of DQN which introduced estimation of the value function and advantage function [6]. These two functions were then combined to obtain the Q-Value. Dueling DQN were implemented with the previous work of van Hasselt et al. [6].

Harm van Seijen et al. recently published an algorithm called Hybrid Reward Architecture (HRA) which is a divide and conquer method where several agents estimate a reward and a Q-value for each state [3]. The algorithm performed above human expertise in Ms. Pac-Man, which is considered one of the hardest games in the Atari 2600 collection and is currently state-of-the-art in the reinforcement learning domain [3]. The drawback of this algorithm is that generalization of Minh et al. approach is lost due to a huge number of separate agents that have domain-specific sensory input.

There have been few attempts at using Deep Q-Learning on advanced simulators specifically made for machine-learning. It is probable that this is because there are very few environments created for this purpose.

3   Q-Learning

Reinforcement learning can be considered hybrid between supervised and unsupervised learning. We implement what we call an agent that acts in our environment. This agent is placed in the unknown environment where it tries to maximize the environmental reward [7].

Markov Decision Process (MDP) is a mathematical method of modeling decision-making within an environment. We often use this method when utilizing model-based RL algorithms. In Q-Learning, we do not try to model the

MDP. Instead, we try to learn the optimal policy by estimating the action-value function $Q^*(s, a)$, yielding maximum expected reward in state s executing action a. The optimal policy can then be found by

$$\pi(s) = argmax_a Q^*(s, a) \tag{1}$$

This is derived from *Bellman's Equation*, because we can consider $U(s) = max_a Q(s, a)$, the Utility function to be true. This gives us the ability to derive following update-rule equation from Bellman's work:

$$Q(s, a) \leftarrow Q(s, a) + \underbrace{\alpha}_{\text{Learning Rate}} \left(\underbrace{R(s)}_{\text{Reward}} + \underbrace{\gamma}_{\text{Discount}} \underbrace{max_{a'} Q(s', a')}_{\text{New Estimate}} - \underbrace{Q(s, a)}_{\text{Old Estimate}} \right) \tag{2}$$

This is an iterative process of propagating back the estimated Q-value for each discrete time-step in the environment. It is guaranteed to converge towards the optimal action-value function, $Q_i \rightarrow Q^*$ as i $\rightarrow \infty$ [1,7]. At the most basic level, Q-Learning utilize a table for storing (s, a, r, s') pairs. But we can instead use a non-linear function approximation in order to approximate $Q(s, a; \theta)$. θ describes tunable parameters for approximator. Artificial Neural Networks (ANN) are a popular function approximator, but training using ANN is relatively unstable. We define the loss function as following.

$$L(\theta_i) = E\left[(r + \gamma max_{a'} Q(s', a'; \theta_i) - Q(s, a; \theta_i))^2 \right] \tag{3}$$

As we can see, this equation uses Bellman equation to calculate the loss for the gradient descent. To combat training instability, we use *Experience Replay*. This is a memory module which stores memories from experienced states and draws a uniform distribution of experiences to train the network [1]. This is what we call a *Deep Q-Network* and are as described in its most primitive form. See related work for recent advancements in DQN.

4   Deep Line Wars

For a player to play RTS games well, he typically needs to master high difficulty strategies. Most RTS strategies incorporate

- Build strategies,
- Economy management,
- Defense evaluation, and
- Offense evaluation.

These objectives are easy to master when separated but become hard to perfect when together. Starcraft II is one of the most popular RTS games, but due to its complexity, it is not expected that an AI-based system can beat this game anytime soon. At the very least, state-of-the-art Deep Q-Learning is not directly applicable. Blizzard entertainment and Google DeepMind has collaborated on an interface to the Starcraft II game [8,9]. Starcraft II is for many researchers considered the next big goal in AI research. Warcraft III is relatable to Starcraft II as they are the same genre and have near identical game mechanics.

Current state-of-the-art algorithms struggle to learn objectives in the state-space because the action-space is too abstract [10]. State and action spaces define the range of possible configurations a game board can have. Existing DQN models use pixel data as input and objectively maps state to action [1]. This works when the game objective is closely linked to an action, such as controlling a paddle in Breakout, where the correct action is quickly rewarded, and a wrong action quickly punished. This is not possible in RTS games. If the objective is to win the game, an action will only be rewarded or punished after minutes or even hours of gameplay. Furthermore, gameplay would consist of thousands of actions and only combined will they result in a reward or punishment.

Game Property Chart

Game	Stochastic	Partial Observable	Simultaneous	Solved	Date
Tic Tac Toe					1970's
Connect Four		NO			1970's
Chess				YES	Deep Blue 1996
GO (19x19)					DeepMind 2015
Backgammon	YES	NO	NO		1979
Deep Line Wars	YES	BOTH	YES		NO
Ms. Pac Man	NO	NO	YES	YES	Microsoft 2017
Starcraft II		YES			NO

Fig. 2. Properties of selected game environments

Collected data in Fig. 2 argues that games that have been solved by current state-of-the-art is usually non-stochastic and is fully observable. Also, current AI prefers environments which are not simultaneous, meaning they can be paused between each state transition. This makes sense because hardware still limits advances in AI.

By doing rough estimations of the state-space in-game environments from Fig. 2, it is clear that state-of-the-art has done a big leap in recent years. With the most recent contribution being Ms. Pac-Man [3]. However, by computing the state-space of a regular Starcraft II map only taking unit compositions into account, the state space can be calculated to be $(128x128)^{400} = 16384^{400} = 10^{1685}$ [11].

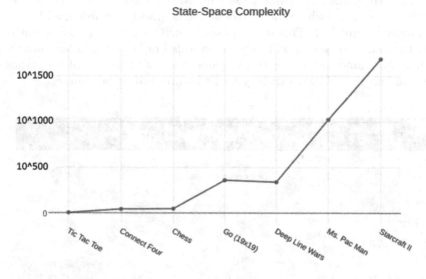

Fig. 3. State-space complexity of selected game environments

The predicament is that the difference in complexity between Ms. Pac-Man and Starcraft II is tremendous. Figure 3 illustrates a relative and subjective comparison between state-complexity in relevant game environments. State-space complexity describes approximately how many different game configurations a game can have. It is based on map size, unit position, and unit actions. The comparison is a bit arbitrary because the games are complex in different manners. However, there is no doubt that the distance between Ms. Pac-Man, perhaps the most advanced computer game mastered so far, and Starcraft II is colossal. To advance AI solutions towards Starcraft II, we argue that there is a need for several new game environments that exceed the complexity of existing games and challenge researches on multi-agent issues closely related to Starcraft II [12]. We, therefore, introduce Deep Line Wars as a two-player variant of Tower Line Wars. Deep Line Wars is a game simulator aimed at filling the gap between Atari 2600 and Starcraft II. It features the most important aspects of an RTS game.

The objective of this game is as seen in Fig. 4 to invade the opposing player with units until all health is consumed. The opposing player's health is reduced for each friendly unit that enters the red area of the map. A unit spawns at a random location on the red line of the controlling player's side and automatically

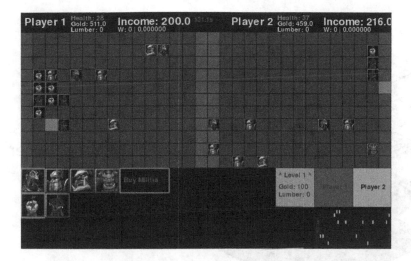

Fig. 4. Graphical interface of Deep Line Wars

walks towards the enemy base. To protect your base against units, the player can build towers which shoot projectiles at enemy units. When an enemy unit dies, a fair percentage of the unit value is given to the player. When a player sends a unit, the income variable is increased by a defined percentage of the unit value. Players gold are increased at regular intervals determined in the configuration files. To master Deep Line Wars, the player must learn following skill-set:

- offensive strategies of spawning units,
- defending against the opposing player's invasions, and
- maintain a healthy balance between offensive and defensive in order to maximize income

and is guaranteed a victory if mastered better than the opposing player.

Because the game is specifically targeted towards machine learning, the game-state is defined as a multi-dimensional matrix. Figure 5 represents a $5 \times 30 \times 11$ state-space that contains all relevant board information at current time-step. It is therefore easy to cherry-pick required state-information when using it in algorithms. Deep Line Wars also features possibilities of making an abstract representation of the state-space, seen in Fig. 6. This is a heat-map that represent the state (Fig. 5) as a lower-dimensional state-space. Heat-maps also allows the developer to remove noise that causes the model to diverge from the optimal policy, see Formula 3.

We need to reduce the complexity of the state-space to speed up training. Using heat-maps made it possible to encode the five-dimensional state information into three dimensions. These dimensions are RGB values that we can find in imaging. Figure 6 show how the state is seen from the perspective of player 1 using gray-scale heatmaps. We define

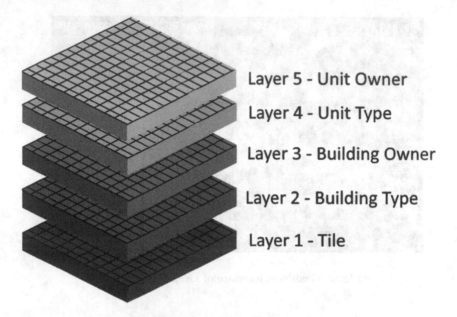

Fig. 5. Game-state representation

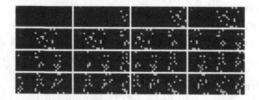

Fig. 6. State abstraction using gray-scale heat-maps

- red pixels as friendly buildings,
- green pixels as enemy units, and
- teal pixels as the mouse cursor.

We also included an option to reduce the state-space to a one-dimensional matrix using gray-scale imaging. Each of the above features is then represented by a value between 0 and 1. We do this because Convolutional Neural Networks are computational demanding, and by reducing input dimensionality, we can speed up training. [1] We do not down-scale images because the environment is only 30×11 pixels large. The state cannot be described fully by these heat-maps as there are economics, health, and income that must be interpreted separately. This is solved by having a 1-dimensional vectorized representation of the data, that can be fed into the model.

5 DeepQRewardNetwork

The main contribution in this paper is the game environment presented in Sect. 4. A key element is to show that the game environment is working properly and we, therefore, introduce a learning algorithm trying to play the game. This is in no way meant as a perfect solver for Deep Line Wars, but rather as a proof of concept that learning algorithms can be applied in the Deep Line Wars environment. In our solution we consider the environment as a MDP having state set S, action set A, and a reward function set R. Each of the weighted reward functions derives from a specific agent within the MDP and defines the absolute reward of the environment R_{env} with following equation:

$$R_{env}(s, a) = \sum_{i=1}^{n} w_i R_i(s, a) \tag{4}$$

where $R_{env}(s, a)$ is the weighted sum w_i of reward function(s) $R_i(s, a)$. The proposed algorithm model is a method of dividing the ultimate problem into separate smaller problems which can be trivialized with certain kinds of generic algorithms.

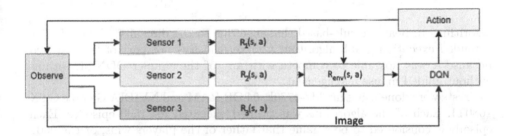

Fig. 7. Separation of the reward function

When reward for the observed state is calculated, we calculate the Q-value of $Q(s, a)$ utilizing R_{env} by using a variant of DQN.

6 Experiments

We conducted experiments with several deep learning algorithms in order to benchmark current state-of-the-art put up against a multi-agent, multi-sensory environment. The experiments were conducted in Deep Line Wars, a multi-agent, multi-sensory environment. All algorithms were benchmarked with identical game parameters.

We tested *DeepQNetwork*, a state-of-the-art DQN from Mnih et al. [1], *DeepQRewardNetwork*, rule-based, and random behaviour. Each of the algorithms was tested with several configurations, seen in Fig. 8. We did not expect any of these

Algorithm	Double Q-Learning	Prioritized Replay	Dueling DQN
Deep Q-Network	YES	YES/NO	NO
DeepQRewardNet...	NO	NO	NO
Random	N/A	N/A	N/A
Rule Based	N/A	N/A	N/A

Fig. 8. Property matrix of tested algorithms

algorithms to beat the rule-based challenge due to the difficulty of the AI. The extended execution graph algorithm (see Sect. 7) was not part of the test bed because it was not able to compete with any of the simpler DQN algorithms without guided mouse management.

Tests were done using Intel I7-4770k, 64 GB RAM and NVIDIA Geforce GTX 1080TI. Each of the algorithms was trained/executed for 1500 episodes. Each episode is considered to be a game that either of the players wins, or the 600 s time limit is reached. DQN had a discount-factor of 0.99, learning rate of 0.001 and batch-size of 32.

Throughout the learning process, we can see that DeepQNetwork and DeepQRewardNetwork learn to perform resource management correctly. Figure 9 illustrates income throughout learning from 1500 episodes. The random player is presented as an aggregated average of 1500 games, but the remaining algorithms are only single instances. It is not practical to perform more than a single run of the Deep Learning algorithms because it takes several minutes per episode to finish which sums up to a huge learning time.

Figure 9 shows that the proposed algorithms outperform random behavior after relatively few episodes. DeepQRewardNetwork performs approximately 33% better than DeepQNetwork. We believe that this is because the reward function $R(s, a)$ is better defined and therefore easier to learn the optimal policy in a shorter period of time. These results show that DeepQRewardNetwork converges towards the optimal policy better, but as seen in Fig. 9 diverges after approximately 1300 games. The reason for the divergence is that experience replay does not correctly batch important memories to the model. This causes

Gold Income per game

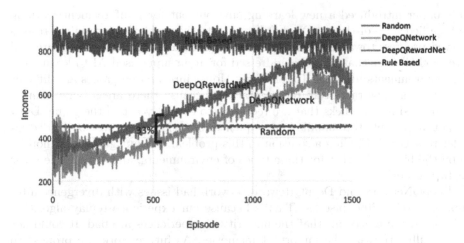

Fig. 9. Income after each episode

the model to train on unimportant memories and diverges the model. This is considered a part of future work and is addressed more thoroughly in Sect. 7. The rule-based algorithm can be regarded as an average player and can be compared to human level in this game environment.

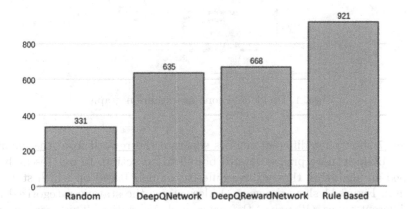

Fig. 10. Victory distribution of tested algorithms

Figure 10 shows that DeepQNetwork and DeepQRewardNetwork have about 63–67% win ratio throughout the learning process. Compared to the rule-based AI it does not qualify to be near mastering the game, but we can see that it outperforms random behavior in the game environment.

7   Future Work

This paper introduced a new learning environment for reinforcement learning and applied state-of-the-art Deep-Q Learning to the problem. Some initial results showed progress towards an AI that could beat a rule-based AI. There are still several challenges that must be addressed for an unsupervised AI to learn complex environments like Line Tower Wars. Mouse input based games are difficult to map to an abstract state representation, because there are a huge number of sequenced mouse clicks that are required, to correctly act in the game. DQN cannot at current state handle long sequences of actions and must be guided in-order to succeed. Finding a solution to this problem without guiding is thought to be the biggest blocker for these types of environments, and will be the focus for future work.

DeepQNetwork and DeepQRewardNetwork had issues with divergence after approximately 1300 episodes. This is because our experience replay algorithm did not take into account that the majority of experiences are bad. It could not successfully prioritize the important memories. As future work, we propose to instead use prioritized experience replay from Schaul et al. [13].

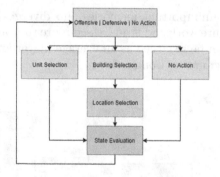

Fig. 11. Divide and conquer execution graph

Figure 7 show that different sensors separate the reward from the environment to obtain a more precise reward bound to an action. In our research, we developed an algorithm that utilizes different models based on which state the player has. Figure 11 show the general idea, where the state is categorized into three different types *Offensive*, *Defensive*, and *No Action*. This state is evaluated by a Convolutional Neural Network and outputs a one-hot vector that signal which state the player is currently in. Each of the blocks in Fig. 11 then represents a form of state-modeling that is determined by the programmer. Our initial tests did not yield any promising results, but according to the Bellman equations, it is a qualified way of evaluating the state and successfully perform learning, on an iterative basis.

8   Conclusion

Deep Line Wars is a simple but yet advanced Real-Time (strategy) game simulator, which attempts to fill the gap between Atari 2600 and Starcraft II. DQN shows promising initial results but is far from perfect in current state-of-the-art. An attempt in making abstractions in the reward signal yielded some improved performance, but at the cost of a more generalized solution. Because of the enormous state-space, DQN cannot compete with simple rule-based algorithms. We believe that this is caused by specifically the mouse input which requires some understanding of the state to perform well. This also causes the algorithm to overestimate some actions, specifically the offensive actions, because the algorithm is not able to correctly build defensive without getting negative rewards. It is imperative that a solution of the mouse input actions are found before DQN can perform better. A potential approach could be using the StarCraft II API to get additional training data, including mouse sequences [14].

References

1. Mnih, V., Kavukcuoglu, K., Silver, D., Graves, A., Antonoglou, I., Wierstra, D., Riedmiller, M.: Playing ATARI with deep reinforcement learning. In: NIPS Deep Learning Workshop (2013)
2. Mirowski, P., Pascanu, R., Viola, F., Soyer, H., Ballard, A.J., Banino, A., Denil, M., Goroshin, R., Sifre, L., Kavukcuoglu, K., Kumaran, D., Hadsell, R.: Learning to navigate in complex environments. CoRR abs/1611.03673 (2016)
3. van Seijen, H., Fatemi, M., Romoff, J., Laroche, R., Barnes, T., Tsang, J.: Hybrid reward architecture for reinforcement learning. abs/1706.04208 (2017)
4. Gosavi, A.: Reinforcement learning: a tutorial survey and recent advances. INFORMS J. Comput. 21(2), 178–192 (2009)
5. van Hasselt, H., Guez, A., Silver, D.: Deep reinforcement learning with double q-learning. CoRR abs/1509.06461 (2015)
6. Wang, Z., de Freitas, N., Lanctot, M.: Dueling network architectures for deep reinforcement learning. CoRR abs/1511.06581 (2015)
7. Sutton, R.S., Barto, A.G.: Reinforcement Learning: An Introduction. MIT Press (1998)
8. Traysent: Starcraft ii api - technical design, November. https://us.battle.net/forums/en/sc2/topic/20751114921
9. Vinyals, O.: Deepmind and blizzard to release starcraft ii as an ai research environment, November 2016. https://deepmind.com/blog/deepmind-and-blizzard-release-starcraft-ii-ai-research-environment/
10. Lillicrap, T.P., Hunt, J.J., Pritzel, A., Heess, N., Erez, T., Tassa, Y., Silver, D., Wierstra, D.: Continuous control with deep reinforcement learning. CoRR abs/1509.02971 (2015)
11. Uriarte, A., Ontañón, S.: Game-tree search over high-level game states in RTS games, October 2014
12. Bellemare, M.G., Naddaf, Y., Veness, J., Bowling, M.: The arcade learning environment: an evaluation platform for general agents. CoRR abs/1207.4708 (2012)
13. Schaul, T., Quan, J., Antonoglou, I., Silver, D.: Prioritized experience replay. CoRR abs/1511.05952 (2015)

14. Vinyals, O., Ewalds, T., Bartunov, S., Georgiev, P., Sasha Vezhnevets, A., Yeo, M., Makhzani, A., Küttler, H., Agapiou, J., Schrittwieser, J., Quan, J., Gaffney, S., Petersen, S., Simonyan, K., Schaul, T., van Hasselt, H., Silver, D., Lillicrap, T., Calderone, K., Keet, P., Brunasso, A., Lawrence, D., Ekermo, A., Repp, J., Tsing, R.: StarCraft II: a new challenge for reinforcement learning. ArXiv e-prints, August 2017

Improving Modular Classification Rule Induction with G-Prism Using Dynamic Rule Term Boundaries

Manal Almutairi[1]([✉]), Frederic Stahl[1], and Max Bramer[2]

[1] Department of Computer Science, University of Reading, Reading, UK
Manal.Almutairi@pgr.reading.ac.uk, F.T.Stahl@reading.ac.uk
[2] School of Computing, University of Portsmouth, Portsmouth, UK
Max.Bramer@port.ac.uk

Abstract. Modular classification rule induction for predictive analytics is an alternative and expressive approach to rule induction as opposed to decision tree based classifiers. Prism classifiers achieve a similar classification accuracy compared with decision trees, but tend to overfit less, especially if there is noise in the data. This paper describes the development of a new member of the Prism family, the G-Prism classifier, which improves the classification performance of the classifier. G-Prism is different compared with the remaining members of the Prism family as it follows a different rule term induction strategy. G-Prism's rule term induction strategy is based on Gauss Probability Density Distribution (GPDD) of target classes rather than simple binary splits (local discretisation). Two versions of G-Prism have been developed, one uses fixed boundaries to build rule terms from GPDD and the other uses dynamic rule term boundaries. Both versions have been compared empirically against Prism on 11 datasets using various evaluation metrics. The results show that in most cases both versions of G-Prism, especially G-Prism with dynamic boundaries, achieve a better classification performance compared with Prism.

Keywords: Modular classification rule induction · Dynamic rule term boundaries · Gaussian probability density distribution

1 Introduction

The general consensus in the data mining community is that there is no single best technique that can work successfully on every dataset. However, decision tree induction is one of the most popular and most widely used algorithms. It produces classification rules in the form of a tree structure and uses a 'divide-and-conquer' strategy to construct the tree from training data. A considerable amount of literature has been published discussing and referring to this approach and a popular and widely used algorithm is C4.5 [13]. However, decision tree based algorithms suffer from several drawbacks such as redundant rule

© Springer International Publishing AG 2017
M. Bramer and M. Petridis (Eds.): SGAI-AI 2017, LNAI 10630, pp. 115–128, 2017.
https://doi.org/10.1007/978-3-319-71078-5_9

terms, overfitting, and replicated subtrees [5]. This paper will revisit some of these problems in Sect. 2. Decision rules can be extracted from a decision tree [4] by transforming each leaf in the tree into a rule [8]. Despite its simplicity, this process ends up with a set of rules that may inherit all the shortcomings of decision trees and thus might become more difficult to understand [8,16]. The author of [4] argues that the major cause of overfitting problem is the tree representation itself and suggests that the solution is to look at another representation which extracts rules directly from data. Examples of classifiers that are based on the induction of classification rules directly from training dataset are, among others, RIPPER [7] CN2 [6] and Prism [5]. Cendrowska's original Prism algorithm started a range of different Prism variations and improvements over the years, also known as the Prism family of algorithms. Some of the members of the Prism family are PrismTCS which improves original Prism's computational efficiency [3] and PMCRI [15], a parallel version of Prism. Originally Prism was only applicable on categorical data, however, all aforementioned Prism variations are also applicable on numerical attributes as will be explained in Sect. 2.

In [1] we provided a proof of concept (evaluated only on 2 datasets) for a potentially efficient method to induce such rule terms based on Gauss Probability Density Distribution (GPDD) of attribute values. The method was termed G-Prism. There are two contributions in this paper: (1) a more dynamic rule term boundary allowing larger rule terms to be built (in terms of data coverage) and (2) a thorough empirical evaluation of both, the original G-Prism, the new version of G-Prism with dynamic rule term boundaries and original Prism.

This paper is organised as follows: Sect. 2 introduces Prism and Sect. 3 describes and positions the development of a new version of Prism based on Gauss Probability Density Distribution. Section 4 provides an empirical evaluation of G-Prism in comparison with Prism. Section 5 describes our ongoing and future work and concluding remarks are provided in Sect. 6.

2   Related Work: The Prism Family of Algorithms for Inducing Modular Classification Rules

A major critique of rule representation in the form of trees is the replicated subtree problem. First discussed in [5] and later termed replicated subtree problem in [16]. For example, consider a training dataset with 4 attributes a, b, c and d. Each attribute can take 2 possible values T (true) and F (false). There are also two possible class values *stop* and *go*. The rules below encode a pattern that predicts class *stop* and all remaining instances would lead to class *go*.

$$\text{IF } a \text{ AND } b \rightarrow \text{Stop}$$
$$\text{IF } c \text{ AND } d \rightarrow \text{Stop}$$

Labelling instances *go* and *stop* using a tree will require replicated subtrees to be induced as illustrated in Fig. 1. An alternative to decision trees are classifiers that induce modular IF-THEN classification rules directly from a training

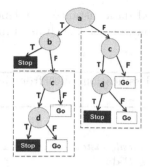

Fig. 1. Replicated subtree problem

dataset. Each rule can be separately handled or even removed without needing to reconstruct the whole classifier or affect its accuracy. Cendrowska's Prism algorithm [5] can induce such modular IF-THEN rules that do not necessarily contain any redundancies.

Algorithm 1 depicts Prism based on Cendrowska's original publication [5]. It also incorporates a method of handling continuous attributes using a local discretisation technique called cut-points calculations [4], as the original version of Prism does not consider numerical attributes for inducing rule terms. ChiMerge [10] and Chi Square [9] are alternative discretisation methods that could convert the values of continuous attributes into a small number of intervals as a pre-processing step. Prism generates rules by appending rule terms (using a logical *AND*) that maximise the conditional probability with which the rule covers a target class. A rule is complete if it only covers instances of the target class or if it cannot be specialised further. Once the rule has been generated all instances covered by the rule are removed from the training data and the next rule is constructed from the remaining instances. This is repeated until no instances that match the target class remain. Then the same process is repeated for the next target class for the entire original training dataset. This is also known as 'separate-and-conquer' approach. Basically Prism classifiers generate rule terms from numerical attributes α through binary splitting [4], potentially resulting in rule term combinations such as $(10 \leq \alpha)$ or $(20 > \alpha)$ to describe an interval of attribute values. Binary splitting is also very inefficient due to a potentially large number of probability calculations which can be quantified as $N \cdot m \cdot 2$, where N is the number of training instances and m the number of numerical attributes. A better way of representing such a rule term is $(10 \leq \alpha < 20)$ instead of two separate rule terms. This would greatly enhance readability of the individual rules and potentially reduce overfitting. The in this paper presented G-Prism approach, is able to induce such more readable rule terms.

Another interesting property of the Prism family of algorithms is that it by default does not force a classification. If a data instance is unknown to the classifier, i.e. it is not covered by a Prism rule, it will simply remain unclassified. We refer to this property as abstaining. Abstaining may be desirable in application where an incorrectly classified data instance could be potentially very costly, such as in financial applications, or risky, such as in medical applications.

Algorithm 1. Learning classification rules from labelled data instances using Prism.

---

1 **for** $i = 1 \rightarrow C$ **do**
2   D ← Dataset;
3   **while** D *does not contain only instances of class* ω_i **do**
4   **forall** *attributes* $\alpha_j \in D$ **do**
5   **if** *attribute* α_j *is categorical* **then**
6   Calculate the conditional probability, $\mathbb{P}(\omega_i | \alpha_j = x)$ for all possible attribute-value $(\alpha_j = x)$ from attribute α;
7   **else if** *attribute* α_j *is numerical* **then**
8   sort D according to x values;
9   **foreach** x *value of* α_j **do**
10   calculate $\mathbb{P}(\omega_i | \alpha_j \leq x)$ and $\mathbb{P}(\omega_i | \alpha_j > x)$;
                end
12   **end**
        end
15   Select the $(\alpha_j = x)$, $(\alpha_j > x)$, or $(\alpha_j \leq x)$ with the maximum conditional probability as a rule term;
16   D ← S, create a subset S from D containing all the instances covered by selected rule term at line 15;
    end
18   The induced rule R is a conjunction of all selected $(\alpha_j = x)$, $(\alpha_j > x)$, or $(\alpha_j \leq x)$ at line 15;
19   Remove all instances covered by rule R from original Dataset;
20   **repeat**
21   lines 2 to 19;
    until *all instances of class* ω_i *have been removed*;
23   Reset input Dataset to its initial state;
  end
25 **return** induced rules;

---

3   G-Prism: Inducing Rule Terms Directly from Numerical Attributes

This section describes rule induction directly from numerical attributes using Gauss Probability Density Distribution (GPDD) termed G-Prism. Section 3.1 introduces the in [1] published proof of concept for G-Prism with fixed rule term boundaries and Sect. 3.2 introduces the new version of G-Prism using dynamic rule term boundaries.

3.1 Prism using GPDD to induce Rule Terms for Numerical Attributes

The work described in this section is inspired by a data stream classifier that also uses GPDD to induce rule terms from numerical real-time data sources [11]. We have incorporated this rule term structure into G-Prism. The Gaussian distribution is calculated with mean μ and variance σ^2 for the values of a numerical attribute α matching a given target class ω_i in the training dataset. The most relevant value for a numerical attribute α for the given target class ω_i is obtained from this Gaussian distribution. Equation 1 can be used to calculate the conditional probability for class ω_i for a given attribute value α_j:

$$\mathbb{P}(\alpha_j|\omega_i) = \mathbb{P}(\alpha_j|\mu,\sigma^2) = \frac{1}{\sqrt{2\pi\sigma^2}}exp(-\frac{(\alpha_j-\mu)^2}{2\sigma^2}) \qquad (1)$$

A value for $\mathbb{P}(\omega_i|\alpha_j)$ or $log(\mathbb{P}(\omega_i|\alpha_j))$ can be calculated using Eq. 2. This value is then used to acertain the probability of class label ω_i for a valid value of attribute α_j.

$$log(\mathbb{P}(\omega_i|\alpha_j)) = log(\mathbb{P}(\alpha_j|\omega_i)) + log(\mathbb{P}(\omega_i)) - log(\mathbb{P}(\alpha_j)) \qquad (2)$$

The Gaussian distribution for a class label can then be used to determine the probability of an attribute value α_j belonging to class label ω_i, assuming that α_j lies between an upper and lower bound Ω_i. This is based on the assumption that the values close to μ represent the most common values of numerical attribute α_j for ω_i. This is depicted in Fig. 2, values in the shaded area are more relevant for ω_i than those outside the shaded area.

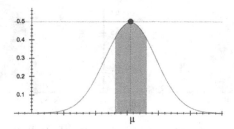

Fig. 2. Gaussian distribution of a classification from a continuous attribute

G-Prism uses the next smaller attribute value x and next larger attribute value y from μ to build a rule term $(x < \alpha_j \leq y)$. Then G-Prism calculates $\mathbb{P}(\omega_i|x < \alpha_j \leq y)$. G-Prism does this for each numerical attribute and selects the rule term with the highest conditional probability to specialise the rule further. In this process G-Prism also considers categorical rule terms which are induced in the same way as in the original Prism algorithm. Otherwise G-Prism follows the same rule specialisation process as outlined in Algorithm 1.

A test of normal distribution may be applied prior to applying this method. Attributes that are not normally distributed can alternatively be dealt with by binary splitting as outlined in the Prism algorithm in Sect. 2.

3.2 Prism Using GPDD with Dynamic Rule Term Boundaries

As explained in Sect. 3.1 above, Gaussian distribution is calculated for a continuous attribute α with mean μ and σ^2. The range of values which extends to both sides from μ of the distribution should represent the most common values of attribute α_j for the target class ω_i. For each continuous attributes in a dataset, the original G-Prism uses the class conditional density probability of the Gaussian distribution to find a rule term in the form of $(x < \alpha \leq y)$, which can maximise the probability with which the rule term covers the target class. As illustrated in Fig. 3(a), the mean value (μ) of the attribute in the middle of the shaded area represents the highest posterior class probability while x and y are the next smaller and larger values from μ. A rule term is produced using these two values.

However, this is a very conservative strategy for finding good rule term boundaries as the GPDD for a range beyond the current fixed boundaries may still be very high. Thus the approach taken in G-Prism may result in the rules only covering few instances, which in turn may lead to overfitting of rules and more rules to be induced.

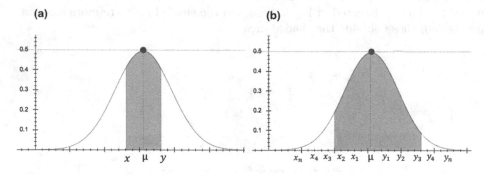

Fig. 3. The shaded area represents a range of values of attributes α_j for class ω_i. **(a)** 68% of all possible values, **(b)** 95% of all possible values

To overcome this problem, the shaded area under the curve is expanded as shown in Fig. 3(b). Thus, more attribute values are tested before choosing a highly relevant range of values that maximises the coverage of a rule for a target class. This means that instead of generating one range in the form of $(x < \alpha \leq y)$ by selecting the next lower bound (x) and the next upper bound (y), more ranges can be dynamically produced in such as $(x_1 < \alpha \leq y_3)$, $(x_3 < \alpha \leq y_5)$, $(x_2 < \alpha \leq y_4)$,... $(x_n < \alpha \leq y_k)$.

Algorithm 2. Learning classification rules from labelled data instances using G-Prism with Dynamic Bounds.

```
1   for i = 1 → C do
2   |   D ← input Dataset;
3   |   while D does not contain only instances of class ωᵢ do
4   |   |   forall attributes αⱼ ∈ D do
5   |   |   |   if attribute αⱼ is categorical then
6   |   |   |   |   Calculate the conditional probability, ℙ(ωᵢ|αⱼ) for all possible
                    attribute-value (αⱼ = x) from attribute α;
7   |   |   |   else if attribute αⱼ is numerical then
8   |   |   |   |   calculate mean μ and variance σ² of continuous attribute α for class ωᵢ;
9   |   |   |   |   foreach value αⱼ of attribute α do
10  |   |   |   |   |   calculate ℙ(αᵢ|ωᵢ) based on created Gaussian distribution created in
                        line 8;
    |   |   |   |   end
12  |   |   |   |   for n = maxBound → 1 do
13  |   |   |   |   |   for k = 1 → maxBound do
14  |   |   |   |   |   |   calculate ℙ(xₙ < αⱼ ≤ yₖ) ;
    |   |   |   |   |   end
    |   |   |   |   end
    |   |   |   end
    |   |   end
19  |   |   select (αⱼ = x) or (xₙ < αⱼ ≤ yₖ) with the maximum conditional probability as a
            rule term ;
20  |   |   D ← S, create a subset S from D containing all the instances covered by selected
            rule term at line 19;
    |   end
22  |   The induced rule R is a conjunction of all selected rule terms built at line 19;
23  |   Remove all instances covered by rule R from original Dataset;
24  |   repeat
25  |   |   lines 2 to 23;
    |   until all instances of class ωᵢ have been removed;
27  |   Reset input Dataset to its initial state;
    end
29  return induced rules;
```

In the current implementation the user can choose the maximum upper and lower bound considered from μ and any combination of rule terms within these bounds is considered. For example, if the user has chosen a bound of 3, then there are (3^2) possible rule terms that are considered for this attribute. Theoretically it is possible not to impose a bound (apart form the minimum and maximum values of the attribute) and allow any possible rule term combinations fanning out from μ. However, this is likely to result in a computationally very expensive approach especially if there are many distinct values for a particular attribute. Also it is statistically unlikely that rule terms spanning far from the μ will cover many instances of the target class. In our current implementation the default boundary is 6, which is also used in all of the experiments presented in Sect. 4. This setting worked well in most case. However, the user is able to specify a different lower and upper boundary. We termed this improved version of G-Prism *Dynamic Bound G-Prism*, which is illustrated in the Algorithm 2. The algorithm uses the Prism rule induction strategy as outlined in Algorithm 1 combined with the in this Section presented generation of rule terms which is contained in lines 7–19 in Algorithm 2. As the algorithm follows a 'separate-and-conquer' strategy the number of training instances decreases over time. Thus after each iteration μ

and σ^2 are updated and the bounds are selected from the currently available values of the numerical attribute.

As mentioned in Sect. 2 the Prism family, including the new Dynamic Bound G-Prism has the ability to abstain from a classification if it is uncertain. This is desirable in applications where incorrectly classified instances are either costly or risky. This abstaining property is retained in both versions of G-Prism.

4   Empirical Evaluation

The main goal of the experimental evaluation is to compare the performance of the dynamic rule term boundary approach with binary splitting in Prism and the fixed boundary approach in G-Prism. Binary splitting is the discretisation method that has been applied to Prism in [4] to deal with numerical attributes. Therefore, our comparison is against this implementation of Prism.

4.1   Experimental Setup

The algorithms used for the evaluation are Prism [2] incorporating the rule induction strategy for numerical attributes as outlined in Sect. 2 as a baseline, G-Prism as published in [1] with fixed size rule term boundaries which is termed G-Prism-FB and G-Prism as described in this paper with dynamic rule term boundaries which is termed G-Prism-DB. Please note that the original publication of G-Prism-FB [1] produced a proof of concept with limited empirical evaluation, thus this paper also aims to provide a more detailed empirical analysis of G-Prism-FB. All algorithms have been implemented in the statistical programming language R [14]. The fixed sized boundary of G-Prism-FB was set to one value smaller and one value larger than μ, which is how is was originally implemented in [1]. The dynamic sized boundary was set to allow a range up to 6 smaller and 6 larger values from μ. The algorithms have been applied to 11 datasets from the UCI repository [12]. These datasets were chosen randomly from all datasets in the UCI repository that comprise numerical attributes only and require classification tasks. The reason for choosing datasets with numerical attributes only is because the G-Prism-FB and G-Prism-DB algorithms are distinct from the baseline Prism only with respect to processing numerical attributes. The datasets have been randomly sampled without replacement into train and test datasets, whereas the testset comprises 30% of the data. On each of the datasets the algorithms were evaluated against 6 evaluation metrics for classifiers which are described below:

- *Abstaining Rate:* Prism, G-Prism-FB and G-Prism-DB abstain from a classification if a case is not covered in the ruleset. This would be very useful in applications where a wrong classification potentially leads to costly or dangerous consequences. The abstain rate is the ratio of instances that remain unclassified in the testset. A low abstain rate may be desired, however, this may be at the expense of accuracy. This is a number between 0 and 1.

- *Accuracy:* This is the ratio of data instances that have been correctly classified. Unclassified instances are classified using the majority class strategy. A high classification accuracy is desired. This is a number between 0 and 1.
- *Tentative Accuracy (Precision):* Different compared with the accuracy above, the tentative accuracy is the ratio of correctly classified instances based only on the number of instances that have been assigned a classification. A high tentative accuracy is desired. This is a number between 0 and 1.
- *Recall:* The recall is the probability with which a data instance is classified correctly. A high recall is desired. This is a number between 0 and 1.
- *F1 Score:* This is the product of recall and tentative accuracy divided by their average. This is also known as the harmonic mean of precision and recall. A high F1 Score is desired. This is a number between 0 and 1.
- *Number of rules induced:* This is simply the total number of rules induced.

One should note that there is a direct relationship between accuracy, tentative accuracy and abstaining rate as abstained instances are counted as misclassifications in the accuracy measure, but are not considered at all in the tentative accuracy measure. Thus a higher abstain rate will also result in a lower accuracy and a higher tentative accuracy.

Metric	Method		iris	seeds	wine	blood transfusio	banknote	ecoli	yeast	page blocks	user modeling	breast tissue	glass
Number of Rules	Prism		12	19	12	19	13	51	78	138	26	31	54
	G-Prism	DB	9	30	16	46	176	49	287	465	41	23	46
		FB	20	37	55	109	466	113	595	1236	122	42	77
Abstaining Rate	Prism		0.04	0.02	0.06	0.00	0.00	0.04	0.00	0.00	0.29	0.13	0.09
	G-Prism	DB	0.04	0.10	0.11	0.10	0.08	0.21	0.12	0.03	0.17	0.31	0.48
		FB	0.02	0.06	0.19	0.32	0.09	0.28	0.28	0.03	0.28	0.44	0.46
Recall	Prism		0.90	0.87	0.98	1.00	0.99	0.39	0.20	0.49	0.65	0.69	0.47
	G-Prism	DB	0.93	0.92	0.95	0.99	0.98	0.68	0.41	0.70	0.90	0.94	0.67
		FB	0.93	0.93	0.88	0.99	0.98	0.64	0.44	0.71	0.82	0.73	0.51
Precision	Prism		0.91	0.90	0.98	0.76	0.66	0.36	0.56	0.71	0.68	0.73	0.67
	G-Prism	DB	0.93	0.93	0.96	0.81	0.95	0.86	0.50	0.92	0.93	0.92	0.80
		FB	0.93	0.94	0.90	0.82	0.94	0.75	0.44	0.95	0.85	0.85	0.39
F1 Score	Prism		0.90	0.88	0.98	0.87	0.80	0.37	0.29	0.58	0.66	0.71	0.55
	G-Prism	DB	0.93	0.93	0.96	0.89	0.96	0.76	0.45	0.79	0.92	0.93	0.73
		FB	0.93	0.94	0.89	0.90	0.96	0.69	0.44	0.82	0.84	0.79	0.44
Accuracy	Prism		0.87	0.87	0.92	0.76	0.72	0.67	0.37	0.95	0.53	0.66	0.52
	G-Prism	DB	0.91	0.86	0.89	0.77	0.92	0.75	0.43	0.95	0.78	0.66	0.66
		FB	0.91	0.87	0.79	0.77	0.90	0.65	0.40	0.95	0.66	0.50	0.51
Tentative Accuracy	Prism		0.91	0.87	0.98	0.76	0.72	0.68	0.36	0.95	0.72	0.75	0.53
	G-Prism	DB	0.93	0.93	0.96	0.81	0.96	0.88	0.48	0.96	0.91	0.95	0.82
		FB	0.93	0.93	0.88	0.82	0.95	0.84	0.47	0.96	0.83	0.89	0.54

Fig. 4. Overview of empirical results. DB denotes Dynamic Boundaries and FB denotes Fixed Boundaries

4.2 Empirical Results

Figure 4 gives an overview of the results obtained using the datasets and evaluation metrics explained in Sect. 4.1. A more detailed breakdown of the results is given in the following illustrations in this section. For easier description we refer to G-Prism with Dynamic Boundaries as G-Prism-DB and G-Prism with Fixed Boundaries as G-Prism-FB.

Figure 5 illustrates the difference of the accuracies and tentative accuracies of G-Prism-DB and G-Prism-FB compared with Prism. As can be seen in the figure G-Prism-DB achieves a better accuracy compared with Prism in 7 out of 11 datasets. In 7 out of 11 cases G-Prism-DB is considerably better and in one case (blood transfusion) only marginally better. However, in the cases where G-Prism-DB has a lower accuracy this accuracy is only marginally lower. G-Prism-FB does not seem to outperform Prism, in 5 cases it has a higher accuracy and in 7 it does not. With respect to tentative accuracy both versions of G-Prism clearly outperform Prism, both achieve a higher tentative accuracy in 10 out of 11 cases. Furthermore G-Prism-DB in comparison with G-Prism-FB achieves a better accuracy in 7 out of 11 cases and in all cases where G-Prism-DB did not perform better than G-Prism-FB, it achieved only marginally lower accuracy.

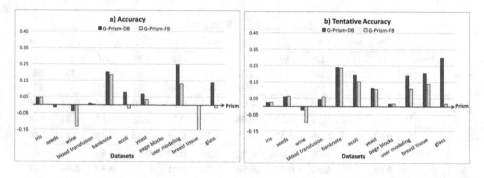

Fig. 5. Difference of accuracy and tentative accuracy of G-Prism-DB and G-Prism-FB compared with Prism

Figure 6 illustrates the difference of the F1 Score and Recall of G-Prism-DB and G-Prism-FB compared with Prism. Both versions of G-Prism outperform Prism in 8 out of 11 cases. G-Prism-DB seems to be the better of the two G-Prism versions with G-Prism-DB achieving a higher recall in 7 out of 11 cases compared with G-Prism-FB. With respect to the F1 Score G-Prism achieves a higher score compared with Prism in 10 out of 11 cases. Again, G-Prism-DB seems to be the better of the two G-Prism versions with G-Prism-DB achieving a higher F1 Score in 7 out of 11 cases compared with G-Prism-FB.

Regarding abstaining rate as illustrated in Fig. 7 the predecessor Prism seems to have a lower abstain rate in most cases (9 out of 11). Comparing both version of G-Prism, G-Prism-DB achieves a lower abstain rate compared with G-Prism-FB in 8 out of 11 cases.

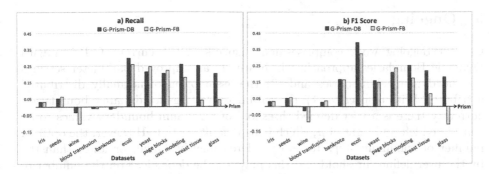

Fig. 6. Difference of Recall and F1 Score of G-Prism-DB and G-Prism-FB compared with Prism

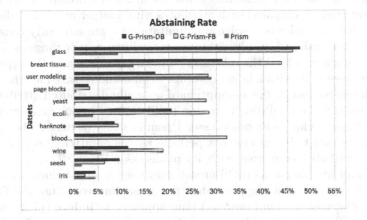

Fig. 7. Abstaining rates of G-Prism-DB, G-Prism-FB and Prism

4.3   Summary of Evaluation

Overall it can be seen that G-Prism outperforms Prism in most cases with regards to all evaluation metrics except for the abstaining rate where Prism performs better. This could potentially be linked to the high number of rules induced by G-Prism approaches as can be seen in Fig. 4. A high number of rules suggests that the rule terms for each rule covers a lower number of instances compared with Prism. However, what can also be seen is that G-Prism-DB induces less rules compared with G-Prism-FB and also has a lower abstain rate compared with G-Prism-FB. The difference between both G-Prism approaches is that G-Prism-DB had a dynamic rule term boundaries that are either the same or cover a wider range and thus also produce potentially less rules but covering a larger number of training instances. Overall G-Prism-DB achieves a better classification performance compared with Prism and G-Prism-FB. Alternative descritisation methods, such as ChiMerge [10] and Chi square [9], prior to the application of Prism will also be considered in the future.

5   Ongoing

Current ongoing work comprises four aspects of the current G-Prism with Dynamic Boundaries approach, which are (1) an improved parameter settings for the dynamic boundaries and (2) the assumption of normally distributed attributes. With respect to (1), the parameter settings for dynamic boundaries, currently there is a user defined threshold of maximum boundary values to be considered left and right of μ, which is by default set to 6. However, the optimal number of maximum steps to be considered may be higher or lower than the by the user define threshold and this may also be dependent on the number of training instances as a larger number of training instances is likely to produce a larger number of distinct values. For attributes with a smaller number of distinctly different values it is more likely that the maximum boundary threshold is further away from μ compared with attributes with a larger number of distinctly different values. In order to resolve this limitation we are currently considering implementing a version of the algorithm using the interquartile range as an upper rule term boundary to limit the rule term boundary search space. We expect that this will produce rules with a larger coverage of data and thus reduce the abstain rate. With respect to (2), the assumption of normally distributed attributes, we have not tested for normal distribution in the data used in our experiments, yet G-Prism-DB outperforms its predecessor Prism in many respects. Thus there is the possibility that G-Prism may not perform as well on attributes that are not normally distributed compared with its predecessor Prism. Therefore, we are currently implementing a hybrid approach that tests if an attribute's values are normally distributed, if it they are, then the algorithm would use the G-Prism approach, otherwise it would use the Prism approach to induce rule terms from that a particular attribute. Moreover, future work comprises the development of novel methods for rule term induction taking different underlying attribute value distributions into consideration, such as i.e. Poison distribution. Also the implementation of other discretisation methods based on ChiMerge [10] and Chi square [9] for a further comparisons is planned in the future work.

6   Conclusion

The paper introduced a new rule term induction method based on Gauss Probability Density Distribution to produce a new rule term structure that improves classification performance of the Prism family of algorithms. The new rule term structure is an alternative structure to the currently used rule terms in the Prism family of algorithms. The basic idea of the new rule term structure had been introduced by the authors in [1] in a short paper but only limited evaluation was conducted at the time. This paper offers two contributions (1) a thorough evaluation of the originally proposed G-Prism algorithm and (2) an improvement to the G-Prism rule term induction method by using more dynamic maximum rule term boundaries. Both G-Prism approaches (with fixed and dynamic rule term boundaries) and their predecessor Prism have been evaluated empirically and comparatively using various metrics and datasets. Overall G-Prism with dynamic boundaries outperforms Prism and G-Prism with fixed boundaries in most cases. Regarding abstain rate we saw a larger number of rejected test instances by using G-Prism than by using Prism. We also observed that G-Prism (either of the two versions) produces more rules and we assume that this is related to a higher abstaining rate of G-Prism. Thus we are currently working on a more elastic dynamic rule term boundary selection that will likely lead to a higher coverage of data instances and thus is expected to reduce the abstaining rate of G-Prism. Other ongoing work comprises also the development of approaches that can be used to induce rule terms if an attribute is not normally distributed.

References

1. Almutairi, M., Stahl, F., Jennings, M., Le, T., Bramer, M.: Towards expressive modular rule induction for numerical attributes. In: Bramer, M., Petridis, M. (eds.) Research and Development in Intelligent Systems XXXIII, pp. 229–235. Springer, Cham (2016). https://doi.org/10.1007/978-3-319-47175-4_16
2. Bramer, M.: Automatic induction of classification rules from examples using N-prism. In: Research and development in Intelligent Systems XVI, pp. 99–121. Springer, Heidelberg (2000). https://doi.org/10.1007/978-1-4471-0745-3_7
3. Bramer, M.: An information-theoretic approach to the pre-pruning of classification rules. In: Neumann, B., Musen, M., Studer, R. (eds.) Intelligent Information Processing, pp. 201–212. Kluwer, Dordrecht (2002)
4. Bramer, M.: Principles of Data Mining, vol. 131. Springer, Heidelberg (2016). https://doi.org/10.1007/978-1-4471-4884-5
5. Cendrowska, J.: Prism: an algorithm for inducing modular rules. Int. J. Man-Mach. Stud. **27**(4), 349–370 (1987)
6. Clark, P., Niblett, T.: The CN2 induction algorithm. Mach. Learn. **3**(4), 261–283 (1989)
7. Cohen, W.: Fast effective rule induction. In: Proceedings of the Twelfth International Conference on Machine Learning, pp. 115–123 (1995)
8. Han, J., Pei, J., Kamber, M.: Data Mining: Concepts and Techniques. Elsevier, Amsterdam (2011)
9. Imam, I., Michalski, R., Kerschberg, L.: Discovering attribute dependence in databases by integrating symbolic learning and statistical analysis techniques. In: Proceeding of the AAAI 1993 Workshop on Knowledge Discovery in Databases, Washington DC (1993)
10. Kerber, R.: Chimerge: discretization of numeric attributes. In: Proceedings of the Tenth National Conference on Artificial Intelligence, pp. 123–128. Aaai Press (1992)
11. Le, T., Stahl, F., Gomes, J., Gaber, M., Di Fatta, G.: Computationally efficient rule-based classification for continuous streaming data. In: Research and Development in Intelligent Systems XXXI, pp. 21–34. Springer, Heidelberg (2014). https://doi.org/10.1007/978-3-319-12069-0_2
12. Lichman, M.: UCI machine learning repository (2013)
13. Quinlan, J.: C4. 5: Programs for Machine Learning. Elsevier, Amsterdam (2014)

14. R Core Team. R: A Language and Environment for Statistical Computing. R Foundation for Statistical Computing, Vienna, Austria (2014)
15. Stahl, F., Bramer, M.: Computationally efficient induction of classification rules with the PMCRI and J-PMCRI frameworks. Knowl.-Based Syst. **35**, 49–63 (2012)
16. Witten, I., Frank, E., Hall, M., Pal, C.: Data Mining: Practical Machine Learning Tools and Techniques. Morgan Kaufmann, Burlington (2016)

Short Technical Papers

Inference and Discovery in Remote Sensing Data with Features Extracted Using Deep Networks

Isabel Sargent[1,2]([☒]), Jonathon Hare[2], David Young[2], Olivia Wilson[1],
Charis Doidge[1], David Holland[1], and Peter M. Atkinson[3]

[1] Ordnance Survey, Southampton SO16 0AS, UK
isabel.sargent@os.uk
[2] University of Southampton, Southampton SO17 1BJ, UK
[3] Lancaster University, Lancaster LA1 4YW, UK

Abstract. We aim to develop a process by which we can extract generic features from aerial image data that can both be used to infer the presence of objects and characteristics and to discover new ways of representing the landscape. We investigate the fine-tuning of a 50-layer ResNet deep convolutional neural network that was pre-trained with ImageNet data and extracted features at several layers throughout these pre-trained and the fine-tuned networks. These features were applied to several supervised classification problems, obtaining a significant correlation between the classification accuracy and layer number. Visualising the activation of the networks' nodes found that fine-tuning had not achieved coherent representations at later layers. We conclude that we need to train with considerably more varied data but that, even without fine tuning, features derived from a deep network can produce better classification results than with image data alone.

Keywords: Remote sensing · Deep learning · Feature extraction

1 Introduction

To serve its public task and meet customers' requirements, Ordnance Survey, Britain's mapping agency, interprets the landscape to create digital representations portraying and characterising human-made (e.g. pylons, buildings, roads) and natural (e.g. rivers, moorland, boulder fields) real-world objects for a wide range of applications such as routing, asset management, planning and geospatial modelling. Increasingly diverse and subtle objects and landscape characteristics are required such as the location of hedgerows or the age of buildings. In a rapidly changing commercial environment, it is essential that mapping agencies build approaches that can respond quickly to customers' changing needs - both in response to customers' requests and in anticipation of their future requirements.

Both field survey and remote sensing survey are used to create and maintain detailed mapping products. The majority of information extraction from remote sensing data is done so by expert interpreters using manual processes. For example, digital plotting using stereo imagery is employed to define the perimeter of

© Copyright Ordnance Survey Limited 2017
M. Bramer and M. Petridis (Eds.): SGAI-AI 2017, LNAI 10630, pp. 131–136, 2017.
https://doi.org/10.1007/978-3-319-71078-5_10

real-world objects. With better instrumentation and the pressure to improve data currency, the volume of data being acquired is increasing. Clearly, manual capture methods will struggle to scale with increased data and demand. A few, rules-based, automatic approaches are also used but as data and products develop, these rules need to be manually updated, usually at considerable cost.

Machine learning offers an approach that allows models to develop as the real world, data and customer needs change. Recent breakthroughs in image interpretation have used deep learning [8,9], which has the ability to extract "hierarchies of representations" [4]. However, most applications focus on only the the final layers of the network: either training the network to find the classes of interest [2,10] or using the features extracted by the penultimate layer as inputs to a shallow learning algorithm [6,7].

Given the complexity of the model being learned [12], deep networks require a considerable amount of data. Adequate labelled data are rarely available and so it is impractical to train a deep model for each customer requirement. Instead, we aim to extract, from remote sensing data, features that are generic to our existing and future inference problems. Our hypothesis is that we can decode the signatures of human activities and non-human processes that have shaped the landscape - Bengio *et al.*'s "underlying explanatory factors hidden in the observed data" [1] - to extract descriptors of the landscape. These descriptors can then be applied as input features to infer the presence of real-world objects or landscape characteristics. As well as this *inference* goal, we conjecture that these features will serve a second, *discovery*, goal by providing new ways of describing the landscape. For example, the features may represent the era in which regions were developed (as is evident in the layout of roads and buildings) or they may pertain to the risk of flood inundation (as results in identifiable patterns of vegetation). This presented work focuses on our inference goal by testing extracted features against a set of classification problems. We also begin to address our discovery goal by interrogating the weights in the trained networks.

2   Approach

We used the 3-band aerial imagery that makes up our OS MasterMap® Imagery Layer (Imagery Layer) product. These images are orthorectified to 25 cm spatial resolution and are available for all of Great Britain. We also have a topographic vector product, OS MasterMap® Topography Layer (Topography Layer), that portrays real-world objects, such as buildings, roads and fields, as area, line and point vectors with a range of descriptive attributes. Because the aerial imagery is orthorectified using detailed terrain and object height data, Topography Layer has a strong correspondence to Imagery Layer.

In essence, our problem is one of unsupervised learning in that we want to transform our input data in such a way that draws out factors that we have only loosely defined in advance - the underlying explanatory factors, or descriptors, of the landscape. Unsupervised targets can be difficult to specify and so we opted to set a supervised target for training - Topography Layer data. Our assumption is that this target will 'guide' training towards forming a hierarchy of representations of the factors that, in combination, define the landscape as described in Topography Layer.

From Imagery Layer, we extracted overlapping patches of 224×224 pixels, corresponding to a square of $56\,m \times 56\,m$ on the ground. Each patch was labelled with attribution taken from the vector feature in Topography Layer that overlaid its centre. To achieve this, we combined the 'Theme' attributes for the vector feature into a string resulting in the following 22 classes: {ROADS TRACKS AND PATHS; LAND; WATER; RAIL; BUILDINGS; STRUCTURES; HERITAGE AND ANTIQUITIES; LAND,WATER; RAIL,ROADS TRACKS AND PATHS; BUILDINGS,STRUCTURES; ROADS TRACKS AND PATHS,STRUCTURES; LAND,STRUCTURES; LAND,ROADS TRACKS AND PATHS; ROADS TRACKS AND PATHS,RAIL; STRUCTURES,WATER; WATER,STRUCTURES; RAIL,STRUCTURES; WATER,LAND; ROADS TRACKS AND PATHS,WATER; LAND,RAIL; HERITAGE AND ANTIQUITIES,LAND; BUILDINGS,ROADS TRACKS AND PATHS}.

To investigate the features learned at depth, we chose to adapt a 50-layer ResNet [5] (ResNet50) that had been trained on the ImageNet dataset [11] (weights available in Keras [3]) by performing a fine-tuning operation to enable the network to better learn internal representations of our aerial imagery. With limited processing capacity, fine-tuning allowed the re-use of learned low-level image features, such as edge and color filters, focusing the computational effort on tailoring the network to a new data domain. Fine-tuning was performed by fixing all layers of the network except the last one for 50 epochs, and then training all layers for a further 50 epochs. We used a stochastic gradient descent optimiser with an initial learning rate of $1e{-}4$ and momentum of 0.8 for fine-tuning. Each epoch consisted of approximately 1.2 million image-class pairs sampled from the Southampton area in the South of the UK (containing a mix of water, urban and rural settings). The training pairs were sampled randomly against the same underlying distribution as the training region. Because of the vast size of the data used for training it is extremely unlikely that the network saw the same training instance more than once during the entire training process. With a batch size of 32, training the last layer alone took slightly over $9000\,s$ per epoch on a single Titan X GPU, and training the entire network took around $23000\,s$ for each epoch. Overall training accuracy was 84.3% and validation accuracy (on 16000 image-class pairs taken from a region that was not used during training) was 78.2%.

Towards our inference goal, we performed a series of trials of the features extracted from the ResNet50 networks for a small labelled dataset from Lincolnshire in the East Midlands of the UK. Three different classification problems were investigated: (1) finding inland water; (2) finding roads and tracks; and (3) differentiating metalled roads and tracks, unmetalled roads and tracks and a mixture of other classes. These classification problems were selected from a wider set of manually labelled data because they were particularly difficult for our rules-based approaches. We did not perform any further training of the deep networks for these trials. It was noted that they were similar, but not identical, to classes in the target data.

A patch of 224×224 pixels, centred on the location of the class label, was extracted from the image data. For each classification problem, an 'other' class was drawn from labelled patches not currently being used (these included classes such as 'scrub', 'solar panels'). The patches were shuffled and balanced such that the same number of patches was available for each class, including the 'other' class, in each trial. The numbers of examples were approximately 100, 90 and 40 for problems (1), (2) and (3), respectively. Each patch was forward-propagated through both the ImageNet and fine-tuned ResNet50 networks and the maximum activation at each node was returned forming a feature set for each selected layer. For comparison, we also created a feature set from values taken directly from the central 12 by 12 pixels of each patch, which resulted in a vector of similar magnitude to feature sets from the later layers of the deep networks. Feature sets were input to linear support vector machine classifiers, which were trained against each of the 3 classification problems. For each classification problem and feature set combination, training was performed over 10 different folds of the data. For 5 of these, the regularization parameter, C, was tuned using 10 folds of a separate verification dataset. For the other 5 folds, the C parameter was set to 1.0. For each test, the average classification accuracy was taken over the 5 folds of the data. The resulting accuracies are compared in Fig. 1. Towards our discovery goal, we studied the nodes' receptive fields by visualising the parts of the data that most activated each node using a similar method to [14].

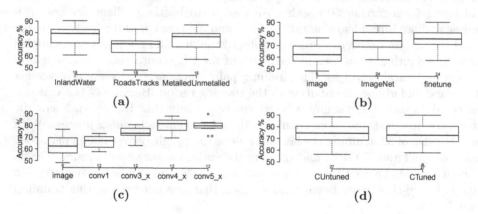

Fig. 1. Boxplots showing the accuracy against (1a) the classification problem, (1b) the network weights, (1c) the layer from which the features were extracted and (1d) whether or not the C parameter was tuned. In (1b) and (1c), 'image' refers to the trials using pixel values as input features. 'conv1', 'conv3_x', 'conv4_x' and 'conv5_x' are regions increasingly deep within the network as described in [11]. The number of trials for each plot is given above the x-axis. Outliers are represented by dots.

Over the 54 tests, the classification accuracy averaged 73.8%. It is evident in 1b that using features derived from the deep networks increases classification accuracy but that there is only a small improvement with fine-tuning. In Fig. 1c, deeper features tend to result in higher classification accuracy and a large correlation (r = .70) was found between layer number and classification accuracy.

The early layers of the network responded to our data as would be expected for any image data, having nodes that are activated by edges and colors and, at intermediary layers, particular shapes such as circles. However, although we observed a divergence between the receptive fields in the ImageNet and the fine-tuned network, at later layers, no discernable label could be applied to the activations of the nodes, even with fine-tuned weights.

3   Discussion and Conclusions

We have initiated research into extracting generic features from remote sensing data and applied these to our inference and discovery goals. Topography Layer provided labels for a large training dataset. However, the chosen 22 classes were poorly balanced resulting in few examples for some classes. For future work, we are developing a more balanced set of labels based on Topography Layer.

The large correlation between accuracy and layer number is evidence that more useful features are learned deeper within the network. Even features taken from deep layers of the network trained only with ImageNet achieved promising classification accuracies. Our investigation of the receptive fields demonstrated that early layers of the network represented generic image features, yet we were not able to interpret the representations at later layers even following fine-tuning. Further, it is likely that concepts are represented as a combination of activations within the network (and not just high activations). Future research will therefore investigate how the whole layer represents the input data using techniques such as clustering and dimensionality reduction on outputs at each layer.

Most image datasets applied to deep learning, such as the ImageNet challenge data, comprise scenes in which the labelled objects are well framed within the view. Even aerial image benchmark datasets, such as UC Merced Land Use Dataset [13], feature objects centred within the frame. In contrast, region- and country-wide aerial imagery comprise continuous real-world features that occur with equal probability anywhere within the view, at any orientation. Further, the kinds of real-world objects that remote sensing is often concerned with (roads, fields, buildings, etc.) are extremely variable in scale and shape. One way of interpreting a trained CNN is as a set of templates that represent the most commonly encountered structure within the dataset. The variation in position, orientation, scale and shape presents a particular problem for feature learning from remote sensing data. Thus, the training data for our classification problems were not typical of most patches from remote sensing data because the objects were centred in the patch, even for the 'other' class. Whilst the classification accuracy within these tests was promising, when we applied the classifier to whole images the results were noisy and demonstrated that more typical training examples are needed to develop a usable inference tool for our data. This principle is also pertinent to training and fine-tuning a deep network and may explain why fine-tuning did not result in interpretable representations in later layers.

To date, we have not extracted the underlying explanatory factors that we desire from our remote sensing data. We conclude that greater consideration of the training data is required to ensure that datasets, for both deep networks and shallow inference networks, portray real-world objects with the full variance of position, orientation, scale and shape.

References

1. Bengio, Y., Courville, A., Vincent, P.: Representation learning: a review and new perspectives. IEEE Trans. Pattern Anal. Mach. Intell. **35**(8), 1798–1828 (2013)
2. Castelluccio, M., Poggi, G., Sansone, C., Verdoliva, L.: Land use classification in remote sensing images by convolutional neural networks. ArXiv e-prints abs/1508.00092 (2015). http://arxiv.org/abs/1508.00092
3. Chollet, F., et al.: Keras (2015). https://github.com/fchollet/keras
4. Deng, L., Yu, D.: Deep learning: methods and applications. Technical report, Microsoft Research Lab., Redmond, May 2014. https://www.microsoft.com/en-us/research/publication/deep-learning-methods-and-applications/
5. He, K., Zhang, X., Ren, S., Sun, J.: Deep residual learning for image recognition. In: 2016 IEEE Conference on Computer Vision and Pattern Recognition (CVPR) (2016)
6. Hu, F., Xia, G.S., Hu, J., Zhang, L.: Transferring deep convolutional neural networks for the scene classification of high-resolution remote sensing imagery. Remote Sens. **7**(11), 14680–14707 (2015)
7. Huang, F.J., LeCun, Y.: Large-scale learning with SVM and convolutional nets for generic object categorization. In: Proceedings of Computer Vision and Pattern Recognition Conference (2006)
8. Le, Q.V., Ranzato, M., Monga, R., Devin, M., Chen, K., Corrado, G.S., Dean, J., Ng, A.Y.: Building high-level features using large scale unsupervised learning. In: Proceedings of the Twenty-Ninth International Conference on Machine Learning, Edinburgh, Scotland (2012)
9. Lee, H., Grosse, R., Ranganath, R., Ng, A.Y.: Convolutional deep belief networks for scalable unsupervised learning of hierarchical representations. In: ICML 2009 Proceedings of the 26th Annual International Conference on Machine Learning, pp. 609–616 (2009). http://www.cs.toronto.edu/rgrosse/icml09-cdbn.pdf
10. Mnih, V., Hinton, G.E.: Learning to label aerial images from noisy data. In: International Conference on Machine Learning (2012)
11. Russakovsky, O., Deng, J., Su, H., Krause, J., Satheesh, S., Ma, S., Huang, Z., Karpathy, A., Khosla, A., Bernstein, M., Berg, A.C., Fei-Fei, L.: Imagenet large scale visual recognition challenge. Int. J. Comput. Vis. **115**, 211–252 (2015)
12. Vapnik, V.N.: Statistical Learning Theory. Wiley, New York (1998)
13. Yang, Y., Newsam, S.: Bag-of-visual-words and spatial extensions for land-use classification. In: ACM SIGSPATIAL International Conference on Advances in Geographic Information Systems (ACM GIS) (2010)
14. Zeiler, M.D., Fergus, R.: Visualizing and understanding convolutional networks. In: Fleet, D., Pajdla, T., Schiele, B., Tuytelaars, T. (eds.) ECCV 2014. LNCS, vol. 8689, pp. 818–833. Springer, Cham (2014). https://doi.org/10.1007/978-3-319-10590-1_53

Quantization Error-Based Regularization in Neural Networks

Kazutoshi Hirose$^{(\boxtimes)}$, Kota Ando, Kodai Ueyoshi, Masayuki Ikebe,
Tetsuya Asai, Masato Motomura, and Shinya Takamaeda-Yamazaki

Hokkaido University, Sapporo, Japan
{hirose,ando,ueyoshi}@lalsie.ist.hokudai.ac.jp,
{ikebe,asai,motomura,takamaeda}@ist.hokudai.ac.jp

Abstract. Deep neural network is a state-of-the-art technology for achieving high accuracy in various machine learning tasks. Since the available computing power and memory footprint are restricted in embedded computing, precision quantization of numerical representations, such as fixed-point, binary, and logarithmic, are commonly used for higher computing efficiency. The main problem of quantization is accuracy degradation due to its lower numerical representation. There is generally a trade-off between numerical precision and accuracy. In this paper, we propose a quantization-error-aware training method to attain higher accuracy in quantized neural networks. Our approach appends an additional regularization term that is based on quantization errors of weights to the loss function. We evaluate the accuracy by using MNIST and CIFAR-10. The evaluation results show that the proposed approach achieves higher accuracy than the standard approach with quantized forwarding.

Keywords: Deep neural network · Quantization · Regularization

1 Introduction

Deep neural network (DNN) is a widely-used technology for various machine learning applications, such as image recognition, speech recognition [9], and translation [6]. While DNNs are very powerful, the computing resource demands of DNNs are huge. In server environments, high-performance but power-consuming GPUs are essential for both training and inference. In contrast, since recent IoT purposes do not allow employment of such power-consuming accelerators due to the cost and energy requirements, a more hardware-aware approach with a smaller energy and memory footprint must be considered.

One of the hardware-aware DNN approaches is quantization which replaces floating point representations with low-complexity representations, such as fixed-point [11], binary [2], and logarithmic [12]. These reduce both computing complexity and memory footprint. For example, binary-weight and binary-activation computation no longer requires energy- and area-consuming multiplication.

© Springer International Publishing AG 2017
M. Bramer and M. Petridis (Eds.): SGAI-AI 2017, LNAI 10630, pp. 137–142, 2017.
https://doi.org/10.1007/978-3-319-71078-5_11

Instead, the multiplications are replaced with XNOR operations, which can be implemented by a very simple circuit, so that energy consumption is dramatically reduced [1].

The main problem of quantization is accuracy degradation due to its lower numerical representation. With quantization, pre-learned weights in the full-precision representation are converted into the quantized values. Therefore, there are certainly quantization errors between the original and quantized values. While a lower precision quantization can effectively reduce the computation complexity and memory footprint, it also degrades the accuracy of the neural network. Therefore, a training technology for both low-precision and high-accuracy is desired for low power neural network hardware.

In this paper, we propose a quantization-error-aware training method for higher accuracy of quantized neural networks. Our method focuses on the quantization error at the training phase. Our method introduces a novel regularization term based on the quantization error. Since quantization errors usually degrade accuracy, the errors must be reduced at the training phase. The proposed method appends an additional regularization term calculated by quantization errors in weights to the loss function.

2   Quantized Neural Network

Quantization in neural network represents original floating point values by using reduced information, such as fixed point and binary. A recent advanced technique of quantization uses logarithmic representation to increase both dynamic range and resolution of numerical values. In this work, we focus on logarithmic quantization and binarization. Note that we do not consider quantization of activation values in this paper.

We first present the logarithmic quantization as follows:

$$LogQuant(w, bitwidth, maxV) = Clip(AP2(w), minV, maxV) \qquad (1)$$
$$AP2(w) = sign(w) \times 2^{round(log_2|w|)} \qquad (2)$$

where w is original weight, $bitwidth$ is a bit width of the quantized weights which contain a sign bit, and $maxV$ and $minV$ are the maximum and minimum scale ranges, respectively. $AP2(\cdot)$ is the approximate power-of-2. Figure 1(a) shows the value conversions from original real values to logarithmic quantized values. Quantized values are obtained by the round operation. The typical round operation is defined as follows:

$$round(x) = \begin{cases} ceil(x) & (x - \lfloor x \rfloor \geq 0.5) \\ floor(x) & (x - \lfloor x \rfloor < 0.5) \end{cases} \qquad (3)$$

However, the round operation by the following expression reduces quantization errors in Eq. (2) more than the previous expression:

$$round(x) = \begin{cases} ceil(x) & (x - \lfloor x \rfloor \geq log_2(\frac{3}{2})) \\ floor(x) & (x - \lfloor x \rfloor < log_2(\frac{3}{2})) \end{cases} \qquad (4)$$

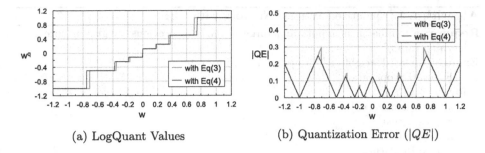

(a) LogQuant Values   (b) Quantization Error ($|QE|$)

Fig. 1. Quantized value and error by LogQuant(w, 3, 1)

Figure 1(b) shows the quantization errors by the above expressions. In addition to the logarithmic quantization, the binary quantization is defined as follows:

$$Binarize(w) = sign(w) = \begin{cases} +1 & (if \ w \geq 0) \\ -1 & (otherwise) \end{cases} \tag{5}$$

3   QER: Quantization Error-Based Regularization

Quantization errors (QE) have never been considered in past approaches of quantized neural networks. We propose a quantization-error-aware training method, which uses the QE as a regularization term.

QE is defined by following expression:

$$QE(w) = w - w^q \tag{6}$$

where w^q is the quantized weight values whose expressions are represented by logarithmic quantization or binarization. Then we define the QER (Quantization Error-based Regularization) term as follows:

$$QER(w) = \|w - w^q\|_2 \tag{7}$$

The QER term is appended to the objective function as follows:

$$L(w) = E(w) + \eta_2 QER(w) \tag{8}$$

where $E(w)$ is the loss function. Thus, the weights are updated via the following optimization problem, as well as the general neural network training.

$$\min_w L(w) \tag{9}$$

L2-norm regularization is a common technique in neural network training for the generalization of weights to prevent overfitting [5]. L2-norm regularization works to limit weight divergence. In contrast, QER works to force weights closer to values of AP2. By updating the weights to minimize $L(w)$, both quantization errors and loss are gradually reduced.

Algorithm 1. Quantized-Weights Network with QER

Require: a minibatch of inputs and targets (x_0, x^*), previous weights w, previous
learning rate η^t.
Ensure: updated weights w^{t+1}, updated learning rate η^{t+1}
  1. Forward propagation
  for $l = 1$ to L **do**
    $w_l^q \Leftarrow \text{Quantize}(w_l)$
    $u_l \Leftarrow x_{l-1} \cdot w_l$
    if $l < L$ **then**
      $x_l \Leftarrow \text{ReLU}(u_l)$
    end if
  end for
  2. Backward propagation
  Compute $\frac{\partial E}{\partial u_L}$ knowing u_L and x^*
  for $l = L$ to 1 **do**
    $\frac{\partial E}{\partial u_{l-1}^q} \Leftarrow \frac{\partial E}{\partial u_l} \cdot w_l^q$
    $\frac{\partial E}{\partial w_l} \Leftarrow \frac{\partial E}{\partial u_l}^T \cdot u_{l-1}^q$
  end for
  3. Accumulating the parameter gradients
  for $l = 1$ to L **do**
    $\frac{\partial QER(w_l)}{\partial w_l} \Leftarrow QE(w_l)$
    $w_l^{t+1} \Leftarrow w_l - \eta_1^t \cdot \frac{\partial E}{\partial w_l} - \eta_2^t \cdot \frac{\partial QER(w_l)}{\partial w_l}$
    $\eta^{t+1} \Leftarrow \lambda \eta^t$
  end for

---

4 Experiments

We performed experiments on the proposed method to apply QER in neural
network training. We compared the proposed method to the original quantized
network without QER in terms of accuracy. Numerical representations used are
logarithmic quantization and binarization. In the logarithmic quantization, all
weights were obtained by $LogQuant(w, 4, 1)$. Algorithm 1 describes the training
algorithm used in this evaluation, where η_1 is 0.001, η_2 starts at 0.00001, and is
amplified by a factor 1.2 every 10 epochs. The optimization solver is Adam [7].
The used benchmarks are MNIST [10] and CIFAR-10 [8].

For MNIST, we used a multi-layer perceptron that consists of 2 hidden
layers. For CIFAR-10, we used a simple convolutional neural network (CNN)
that consists of 2 convolution layers, 2 max-pooling layers, and 3 full-connection
layers.

Table 1 shows the results of the test classification accuracy. Figure 2 shows
their convergence graph. In both benchmarks and both cases of the logarithmic
quantization and binarization, the proposed approach using QER achieves a
higher accuracy. Especially, the logarithmic quantization with QER exceeds the
baseline network trained and tested in floating point.

Table 1. Test accuracy for neural network models

		MNIST	CIFAR-10
Float		0.9777	0.6941
LogQuantize (4 bit)	w/o QER	0.9773	0.6844
	w/ QER	0.9783	0.7031
Binarize (1 bit)	w/o QER	0.9664	0.6724
	w/ QER	0.9709	0.6839

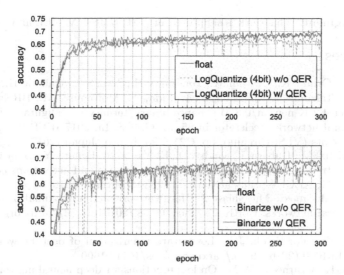

Fig. 2. Convergence of test accuracy on CIFAR-10

5   Related Works

Some quantization- or hardware-aware weight compression techniques have been proposed. Shin et al. proposed a weight compression technique by using a look up table (LUT) [13]. Gysel et al. proposed a fine-tuning technique for hardware-oriented weight quantization [3]. These approaches aimed to optimize weights with high prediction accuracy for limited numerical representations. Our work differs from these approaches in terms of quantization error consideration, but can be used simultaneously with these techniques.

Loss-aware binarization [4] uses a proximal Newton algorithm with diagonal Hessian approximation that directly minimizes the loss with respect to the binarized weights. Our work is similar to this work since it also focuses on the adverse effect of quantization. Since our approach aims to improve prediction accuracy via the regularization term, it can be applied to quantization types other than binarization.

6   Conclusion

We proposed a quantization-error-aware training method for hardware-oriented neural network implementations. Our approach appends an additional regularization term, based on quantization errors of weights, to the loss function.

A major future work is to apply the proposed method to more complicated neural network structures. Additionally, adoption and evaluation for linear quantizations are essential. Since there are some coefficients about the quantization-error term, dynamic optimization techniques should be considered.

Acknowledgment. This work is supported in part by JST ACCEL and Technova.

References

1. Ando, K., Orimo, K., Ueyoshi, K., Yonekawa, H., Sato, S., Nakahara, H., Ikebe, M., Asai, T., Takamaeda-Yamazaki, S., Kuroda, T., Motomura, M.: BRein memory: a 13-layer 4.2 K neuron/0.8 M synapse binary/ternary reconfigurable in-memory deep neural network accelerator in 65 nm CMOS. In: 2017 IEEE Symposium on VLSI Circuits (VLSI-Circuits), pp. C24–C25, Kyoto, Japan (2017)
2. Courbariaux, M., Hubara, I., Soudry, D., El-Yaniv, R., Bengio, Y.: Binarized neural networks: training deep neural networks with weights and activations constrained to +1 or −1. ArXiv e-prints arXiv:1602.02830, February 2016
3. Gysel, P., Motamedi, M., Ghiasi, S.: Hardware-oriented approximation of convolutional neural networks. CoRR abs/1604.03168 (2016). http://arxiv.org/abs/1604.03168
4. Hou, L., Yao, Q., Kwok, J.T.: Loss-aware binarization of deep networks. CoRR abs/1611.01600 (2016). http://arxiv.org/abs/1611.01600
5. Janocha, K., Czarnecki, W.M.: On loss functions for deep neural networks in classification. CoRR abs/1702.05659 (2017). http://arxiv.org/abs/1702.05659
6. Johnson, M., Schuster, M., Le, Q.V., Krikun, M., Wu, Y., Chen, Z., Thorat, N., Viégas, F., Wattenberg, M., Corrado, G., Hughes, M., Dean, J.: Google's multilingual neural machine translation system: enabling zero-shot translation. ArXiv e-prints, Nov 2016
7. Kingma, D.P., Ba, J.: Adam: a method for stochastic optimization. CoRR abs/1412.6980 (2014). http://arxiv.org/abs/1412.6980
8. Krizhevsky, A., Nair, V., Hinton, G.: Cifar-10 (Canadian institute for advanced research). http://www.cs.toronto.edu/kriz/cifar.html
9. LeCun, Y., Bengio, Y., Hinton, G.: Artificial intelligence: deep neural reasoning. Nature **538**, 467–468 (2016)
10. LeCun, Y., Cortes, C.: MNIST handwritten digit database (2010). http://yann.lecun.com/exdb/mnist/
11. Lin, D.D., Talathi, S.S., Annapureddy, V.S.: Fixed point quantization of deep convolutional networks. CoRR abs/1511.06393 (2015). http://arxiv.org/abs/1511.06393
12. Miyashita, D., Lee, E.H., Murmann, B.: Convolutional neural networks using logarithmic data representation. CoRR abs/1603.01025 (2016). http://arxiv.org/abs/1603.01025
13. Shin, D., Lee, J., Lee, J., Yoo, H.J.: 14.2 DNPU: an 8.1TOPS/W reconfigurable CNN-RNN processor for general-purpose deep neural networks. In: 2017 IEEE International Solid-State Circuits Conference (ISSCC), pp. 240–241, February 2017

Knowledge Transfer in Neural Language Models

Peter John Hampton[✉], Hui Wang, and Zhiwei Lin

Artifcial Intelligence Research Group, Ulster University,
Co. Antrim, Northern Ireland
{hampton-p1,h.wang,z.lin}@ulster.ac.uk
https://ulster.ac.uk

Abstract. The complexity and depth of Information Extraction becomes increasingly apparent as time goes on. Heuristics, shocastic and more recently, neural models have proved challenging to scale into and out of various domains. In this paper we discuss the limitations of current approaches and explore if transferring human knowledge into a neural language model could improve performance in an deep learning setting. We approach this by constructing gazetteers from existing public resources. We demonstrate that leveraging existing knowledge we can increase performance and train such networks faster. We argue a case for further research into leveraging pre-existing domain knowledge and engineering resources to train neural models.

Keywords: Named Entity Recognition · Information Extraction

1 Introduction

In 2016, Natural Language Processing (NLP) has been dubbed a *rabbit in the headlights of Deep Learning* [1]. It is certainly plausible given the recent achievements of Deep Learning in the image classification and object recognition space [2,3]. In addition, open source communities have worked to commoditize deep learning capabilities through high-level frameworks thus lowering the barrier to entry for new research and greenfield projects [4,6]. In this vast growing research field, it is of interest to revisit research from previous years and look to how systems can be potentially improved with legacy learning methods. Information Extraction (IE) is regarded as an umbrella term for classification tasks such as Named Entity Recognition, Relation Extraction and Coreference Resolution but is typically used in other areas such as Information Retrieval (Entity Search), stylometry, vocabulary analysis and so on [8]. This paper focuses on established research in the areas of Named Entity Recognition applying a Bidirectional Long-Short Term Memory with two shallow classifiers to the CoNLL 2003 shared task [5]. Leveraging open data we achieve performance greater than shallow methods than those with stringent heuristics. We conclude this preliminary study by discussing future directions for hybrid-specific deep learning based entity mining.[1,2]

---

[1] Implementation: https://github.com/zhiweiuu/SGAITagger.
[2] This work is partially supported by the EPSRC (Grant REF: EP/P031668/1).

© Springer International Publishing AG 2017
M. Bramer and M. Petridis (Eds.): SGAI-AI 2017, LNAI 10630, pp. 143–148, 2017.
https://doi.org/10.1007/978-3-319-71078-5_12

2   Information Extraction

It would be rational to assume true understanding of language requires consciousness similar to that experienced by human beings. Language not only evolves over time, it arguably evolves in one's mind based on their interactions with the world. The longevity of information extraction tasks has been sustained due to the exponential growth in unstructured content in previous years and the need to computationally understand human language. Various languages, document genres, entity types and knowledge connections have interested researchers and practitioners in this area for decades [10]. It is still common to find researchers adopting rules or gazetteers when identifying entities. This works well in narrow cases, but this approach alone is often unscalable, deterministic and doesn't handle the ambiguous nature of natural languages. Researchers have popularized stochastic methods such as markovian classification models and Conditional Random Fields (the current state of the art) to classify named entities [9,10].

Attention has been focused on activations, model optimization, training networks and architectures and learning from data with no explicit feature engineering, thus reflecting the real world. These architectures include, but not limited to, Convolutional Neural Networks (ConvNets), Recurrent Neural Networks (RNNs) [7]. In this study, we focus on a Hybrid LSTM-CRF leveraging gazetteers built from open GATE (ANNIE) data.

CoNLL. For the experiments described we use the CoNLL 2003 English dataset [5]. This popular dataset is split into three parts: Training (train), Validation (testa) and Testing (testb). The data set is split at a document, sentence, and word level. The data has two features included: *Part of Speech* (POS) and *Chunk Tags*.

Gazetteers. Gazetteers are a common input format for rule based methods. It is not uncommon to see applications leverage them as organizations tend to be abundant in columnar data. They are employed in various studies with often random results. This is because there is no predefined agreed upon set of gazetteers. It is possible to create *task specific* gazetteers. Although these types of gazetteers produce great results in various IE tasks, they don't generalize well to external unseen data. This is why we create the gazetteers used in this study from the ANNIE system as described by [13].

Word Embeddings. Word embeddings are the result of mapping semantic meaning into a highly dimensional geometric space. This is done by associating a numeric vector to every word in a dictionary. In this study we use the Glove pretrained word embeddings with 100 dimensions that were trained on the 2014 English Wikipedia data dump [12].

3   Methodology

3.1   Long-Short Term Memory Network

Long-Short Term Memory (LSTM) Networks are a type of training method to overcome the general Recurrent Neural Networks (RNN) bias for more recent inputs and help learn long-term dependencies. RNNs are networks whose connections between units form a directed cycle which in turn make it good when working with sequential data. This is achieved by introducing memory cells and implementing gates to control the proportion of the input to given and what proportion of the previous state to forget, in essence carrying memory forward.

$$h_t := \theta(Wx_t + Uh_{t-1}) \tag{1}$$

where h_t is the hidden state at that time step and $\theta(\cdot)$ is an activation function that is applied to the sum of the weight input W and hidden states U. Although there are other interesting hybrid variations of LSTMs with convolutional layers and other exotic variations, one promising approach which we have based our initial implementation is the work of [11] who designed the following:

$$i_t = \sigma(W_{xi}x_t + W_{hi}h_{t-1} + W_{ci}c_{t-1} + b_i) \tag{2}$$
$$c_t = (1 - i_t) \cdot c_{t-1} + i_t \cdot \tanh(W_{xs}x_t + W_{hc}h_{t-1} + b_c) \tag{3}$$
$$o_t = \sigma(W_{xo}x_t + W_{ho}h_{t-1} + W_{co}c_t + b_o) \tag{4}$$
$$h_t = o_t \cdot \tanh(c_t) \tag{5}$$

where σ is an element-wise *hard* sigmoid function. When training in both directions (with different parameters) the word representations are learned by concatenating the right and left context representations, $h_t = [h_t\rightarrow; h_t\leftarrow]$. Another interesting product of their research was adoption of the IOBES tagging scheme, an evolution of IOB (Inner-Outer-Beginning) which marks entities (s) and the end of entities (e). However, they claim their early work didn't yield any noteworthy improvements. In this work we re-introduce a forget gate, $f_t = \sigma(W_{xf}x_t + W_{hf}h_{t-1} + W_{cf}c_{t-1} + b_f)$, to discard long-term dependencies.

3.2   Conditional Random Fields

CRFs have remained the state of the art for quite some time in the Named Entity Recognition space and are good for encoding known relationships between observations and construct consistent interpretations. The conditional probability of a state sequence $X = (x_1, x_2, ..., x_n)$ given some form of observation sequence $Y = (y_1, y_2, ..., y_n)$ is

$$P(X|Y) = \frac{1}{Z_o}exp\left(\sum_{t=1}^{T}\sum_{k} \lambda_k f_k(X_{t-1}, X, Y, t)\right) \tag{6}$$

where $f_k(X_{t-1}, X, Y, t)$ is a feature function whose weight λ_k is to be learned in the training process with Z_o as a normalization function (7). These models define the conditional probability of a label sequence based on total probability over the state sequences (8):

$$Z_o = \sum_x \sum_{t=1}^{T} \lambda_k f_k(x_{t-1}, x, y, t) \tag{7}$$

$$P(1|Y) = \sum_{x:1(X)=1} P(X|Y) \tag{8}$$

4 Experiments and Results

4.1 Preprocessing

After loading the CoNLL data, we convert all numbers to 0 and lowercase all the as this showed marginal improvements. We also move off the IOB format for the Chunk and NER tags and convert them to IOBES tags to make the compositionality more deducible. We further normalize the Part of Speech tags by removing any invalid alphabetical based tags. When analysing the training, validation and testing data we found that an **average of 96% of Named Entities had the chunk tag I-NP and an average of 90% of the POS tags were NNP**. We therefore expanded the gazetteers by labelling all of the words with these Chunk and POS tags and generating tuples like the CoNLL datasets. We finish by **concatenating the processed gazetteers onto the training data**.

4.2 Topology

In our experiment we implement a LSTM (example depiction Fig. 1) network with a softmax output layer that feeds into a CRF classifier. The 3 vectors in the embedding layer are merged together and passed to $LSTMF$ and $LSTMB$. $LSTMF_n$ represents the LSTM training forward and $LSTMB_n$ represents the LSTM training backwards. The number of neurons in the softmax layer is related to the number of position output (y_n) values. The output of the softmax layer is then passed to the CRF which outputs a vector index corresponding to a Named Entity tag. A **dropout rate of 0.4** is applied between the BLSTM and the softmax layer to prevent overfitting. Each **LSTM has 100 units** and we have a **batch size of 64**. A **RMSProp optimizer with a learning rate of 0.005** was adopted as it trains the model fast and we found it to generate the best results.

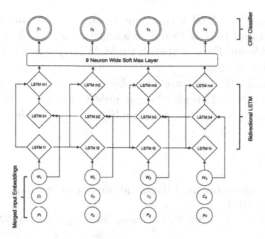

Fig. 1. A visual depiction of our employed network topology. W_i is the embedding for each word, C_i and P_i and the respective Chunk and POS tags at timestep T_i. y_i is the outputed Named Entity

4.3 Results

Our results are presented in Table 1. After running each model for 5 epochs we uncovered two things:

1. A performance gain of 2.25% FB1 (87.98%) was observed (Precision: 88.43% Recall: 87.53%).
2. The network trained much faster.

Table 1. Results of our experiments compared to the baseline

Model	F1
Proposed (No Gaz)	85.73
Proposed (inc Gaz)	**87.98**
LSTM-CRF [11][a]	83.63
Stacked LSTM [11][a]	80.88

[a]We baseline the results without the closed source pre-trained word embeddings.

5 Conclusions and Future Work

We argue that there is an abundance of data that researchers could leverage to train such models. We demonstrate promising performance gains by creating gazetteers out of GATE's ANNIE gazetteers and adding it to the existing training set. In the near future we plan to:

1. Implement a separate feed forward network to learn the gazetteer/Named Entity relations and pass it to our existing topology in Fig. 1, merging with the Word, Chunk and Part of Speech tuple. We hypothesize this would enable an additional feature gain.
2. Enhance the utilization of gazetteers by generating or retrieving sentences containing the entries. This should give greater context between words in the context and allow the network to disambiguate the ambiguous terms.

References

1. Manning, C.D.: Computational linguistics and deep learning. Comput. Linguist. **41**(4), 701–707 (2015)
2. LeCun, Y., Bengio, Y., Hinton, G.: Deep learning. Nature **521**(7553), 436–444 (2015)
3. Schmidhuber, J.: Deep learning in neural networks: an overview. Neural Netw. **61**, 85–117 (2015)
4. Bahrampour, S., Ramakrishnan, N., Schott, L., Shah, M.: Comparative study of caffe, neon, theano, and torch for deep learning. arXiv preprint arXiv:1511.06435 (2015)
5. Tjong Kim Sang, E.F., De Meulder, F.: Introduction to the CoNLL-2003 shared task: language-independent named entity recognition. In: Proceedings of the Seventh Conference on Natural Language Learning at HLT-NAACL 2003, vol. 4. Association for Computational Linguistics (2003)
6. Pedregosa, F., Varoquaux, G., Gramfort, A., Michel, V., Thirion, B., Grisel, O., Blondel, M., Prettenhofer, P., Weiss, R., Dubourg, V., Vanderplas, J.: Scikit-learn machine learning in Python. J. Mach. Learn. Res. **12**(Oct), 2825–2830 (2011)
7. Ma, X., Hovy, E.: End-to-end sequence labeling via bi-directional LSTM-CNNs-CRF. arXiv preprint arXiv:1603.01354 (2016)
8. Schmitz, M., Bart, R., Soderland, S., Etzioni, O.: Open language learning for information extraction. In: Proceedings of the 2012 Joint Conference on Empirical Methods in Natural Language Processing and Computational Natural Language Learning, pp. 523–534. Association for Computational Linguistics, July 2012
9. Zhu, J., et al.: 2D conditional random fields for web information extraction. In: Proceedings of the 22nd International Conference on Machine Learning. ACM (2005)
10. Sarawagi, S.: Information extraction. Found. Trends Databases **1**(3), 261–377 (2008)
11. Lample, G., Ballesteros, M., Subramanian, S., Kawakami, K., Dyer, C.: Neural architectures for named entity recognition. arXiv preprint arXiv:1603.01360 (2016)
12. Pennington, J., Socher, R., Manning, C.D.: Glove: global vectors for word representation. In: EMNLP, vol. 14, pp. 1532–1543, October 2014
13. Bontcheva, K., Derczynski, L., Funk, A., Greenwood, M.A., Maynard, D., Aswani, N.: TwitIE: an open-source information extraction pipeline for microblog text. In: RANLP, pp. 83–90, September 2013

Emotion Recognition in Text Using PPM

Amer Almahdawi[(⊠)] and William John Teahan

School of Computer Science, Bangor University, Bangor, North Wales, UK
{a.j.almahdawi,w.j.teahan}@bangor.ac.uk

Abstract. In this paper we investigate the automatic recognition of emotion in text. We propose a new method for emotion recognition based on the PPM (PPM is short for Prediction by Partial Matching) character-based text compression scheme in order to recognize Ekman's six basic emotions (*Anger, Disgust, Fear, Happiness, Sadness, Surprise*). Experimental results with three datasets show that the new method is very effective when compared with traditional word-based text classification methods. We have also found that our method works best if the sizes of text in all classes used for training are similar, and that performance significantly improves with increased data.

Keywords: Text categorisation · Emotion recognition · PPM compression

1 Introduction

There are many ways to recognize a person's emotional state such as from their facial expressions, their voice, or by their behaviour. With the growth of the Internet, social media and the use of smart mobile devices, much of the communication between people is through written text such as email, texting, blogs and tweets. It would be interesting to recognize the emotional state of the person or persons producing the text.

Emotion recognition can be considered a specific form of text categorisation. One of the aims of this paper was to see how well a compression-based method performed at recognizing fine-grained emotions in the form of the six basic emotions as proposed by Ekman—*Anger, Disgust, Fear, Happiness, Sadness*, and *Surprise*. Ekman argued that these emotions are common across all cultures as evidenced by very brief facial expressions that occur when a person either deliberately or unconsciously conceals an emotion [5].

The rest of this paper is organised as follows. The related work is discussed next along with the PPM-based classification method we adopt. Experimental results are then discussed, followed by the conclusion.

2 Related Work

Early work on emotion recognition from text was accomplished by Alm et al. [1] who used 22 children's fairy tales as the dataset to recognize the emotions defined

© Springer International Publishing AG 2017
M. Bramer and M. Petridis (Eds.): SGAI-AI 2017, LNAI 10630, pp. 149–155, 2017.
https://doi.org/10.1007/978-3-319-71078-5_13

by Ekman. Aman and Szpakowicz [2] composed a corpus from web blogs based on Ekman's six basic emotions. They used the Naïve Bayes and the support vector machine (SMO) classifiers to classify Ekman's basic emotions. Keshtkar [7] used a corpus taken from LiveJournal[1] web blogs. What distinguished these web blogs from others is that they also provided 132 moods (such as *excited* and *astonished*) that the writer used to describe their mood or moods. Keshtkar used similar techniques combined with decision trees to classify emotions from test data. Moreover, there have been other studies that have used the same Live-Journal blogs dataset [9,10]. Chaffer and Inkpen [3] used heterogeneous datasets including Alm's and Aman's dataset in their work on emotion recognition from text. They investigated four classifiers: the ZeroR classifier as a base line, the Naïve Bayes classifier, the J48 classifier and the SMO classifier [3]. Ghazi et al. [6] also experimented with Alm's dataset and Aman's dataset. They used a multilevel hierarchy to classify Ekman's six basic emotions, combined with the support vector machine SMO as the classifier.

One approach found to be effective for many text categorisation tasks adopts an approach based on the PPM text compression scheme that avoids various issues to do with feature extraction simply by processing all the characters in the text [11]. However, the success of this approach on the specific problem of emotion recognition has yet to be investigated in the literature. Therefore the primary purpose of this paper is to address this gap in the research.

PPM is a lossless text compression method first published in 1984 [4]. It is usually adaptive: that is, it dynamically processes the text one character at a time in an on-line manner, updating its model as it goes. The context-based model adopts a maximum fixed order context length to encode the symbols. The method essentially estimates probabilities using a Markov based approach, and when the upcoming symbol is unseen in the context, the model will smooth the probability estimates by "escaping" to a shorter context (recursively if necessary) in order to make the prediction. Different escape methods can be chosen based on how the escape probability is estimated with Method D usually leading to the best compression. (This is described in the literature as using method PPMD). Text categorisation using PPM is performed by first training models for each class. Then the text is compressed using each model with the class being chosen from the model that compresses the text best.

3   Experimental Results

Our experimental results are presented in this section. Three datasets have been used for the experiments: the LiveJournal dataset [7], Alm's dataset [1] and Aman's dataset [2]. The TMT Toolkit developed by Teahan[2] was used to obtain the PPM compression codelength estimates. This toolkit allows PPM models to be constructed from training text. Although standard dynamic PPM models are possible using the toolkit, we chose to use a static variation where once the

---

[1] http://www.LiveJournal.com/.
[2] Contact author for a copy of the latest distribution.

models have been trained, they are not updated subsequently as the testing text is being processed since previous text categorisation experiments [11] have shown these models to be just as effective as dynamic models.

For our experiments, we used order 5 PPM models with escape method D as this usually leads to the best compression for English text. Static models were created while training, and then used to classify the separate testing data. Ten-fold cross validation was then applied to evaluate the classification of the text according to Ekman's six basic emotions for all three datasets using the static models. Prior to each of the experiments described below, we applied the following pre-processing steps to the various datasets. Aman and Alm's datasets are directly labelled by Ekman's basic emotions. An extra label is used for blogs that do not contain emotions in Aman's dataset. For Alm's dataset, each sentence is classified with its equivalent emotion label. However, for the LiveJournal dataset, the following pre-processing is required. Firstly, the XML tags were removed; secondly, all punctuation and URLs were removed; and thirdly, blogs labelled in the same class were extracted from the LiveJournal data and concatenated together to form six separate text files for Ekman's classes. Aman and Szpakowicz [2] describe how to collect blogs from the web by using seed words. Each one of these seed words have its equivalent mood in the LiveJournal weblogs so we use these to map the 132 moods to the six Ekman emotions using synonyms (for example, *awesome* and *fantastic* are some synonyms for the *Happiness* emotion).

In order to improve the effectiveness of the PPM classifier, we have found that balancing the training data for the different PPM models works best. Where there is an imbalance in training data for a particular class or classes, then the performance of the PPM classifier can be improved by essentially truncating the amount of training data used for all classes to the smallest class training size with any unused training data discarded. The rationale behind using balanced sizes for class training data is as follows. If the training size for one class were to predominate, for example, then that class model will often become a better predictor of the general language (e.g. English) compared to the individual class models at predicting the language specific to each class. (Just as idiolects are associated with the speech peculiarities of an individual person, the language of each class will also have its own peculiarities, but this can be dominated if one has a better model of the standard variety of the language). In order to overcome this issue, a simple expedient is to truncate training sizes for each class so that they are the same for each even if this means truncating training text in most classes down to the smallest class training size. As far as we are aware, this paper is the first to report this result that balancing of class training size often leads to noticeably improved classification performance for the PPM classifier.

The text files for each dataset were first split into ten partitions in order to perform ten-fold cross-validation where different folds were used for training and testing ensuring that text was split on a blog boundary rather than in the middle of the blog. For the LiveJournal dataset, in order to obtain roughly equal sized training text for each class, the files were reduced in size to just over 2.4 MB each using the text from the beginning of each file. For Aman's dataset, text related to each of the six Ekman emotions was extracted directly according to the blog annotations. This resulted in just 10 KB being available when using balanced text sizes as Aman's dataset is much smaller than the LiveJournal dataset. Similarly, for Alm's dataset, the text for each emotion could be extracted directly, with 12 KB of text available for each emotion. Table 1 summarises the best results obtained for the three datasets in terms of accuracy, precision, recall and F-measure.

Table 1. PPM classification results for Ekman's emotions for the three datasets.

Dataset	Accuracy	Precision	Recall	F-measure
LiveJournal	96.1 %	0.90	0.88	0.88
Aman	95.6 %	0.89	0.87	0.87
Alm	88.0 %	0.71	0.70	0.67

Table 2 compares the PPM results with previously published results for the classification of Ekman's emotions for the three datasets. Leshed and Kaye [8] used SVMlight as a classifier on the LiveJournal dataset. Chaffer and Inkpen [3] used various traditional classifiers (ZeroR, Naïve Bayes, J48, SMO) implemented using Weka on both Aman's and Alm's datasets. Ghazi et al. [6] used both a flat SMO classifier and a two-level SMO classifier on the same two datasets. PPM clearly outperforms the other methods. Possible reasons for this are that testing was done on all the blogs together as one file rather than separately, and that the previous studies did not use classifiers potentially more effective at processing text such as Naïve Bayes Multinomial in Weka. However, note that direct comparison between these studies is difficult due to the different processing and data selection methods used.

Table 2. Comparing accuracy results for Ekman's emotions for the three datasets.

Dataset	PPM	SVMlt. [8]	ZeroR [3]	NB [3]	J48 [3]	SMO [3]	Fl. SMO [6]	2Lv. SMO [6]
LiveJournal	**96.1**	74.0						
Aman	**95.6**		68.5	73.0	71.4	81.2	61.7	65.5
Alm	**88.0**		36.9	54.9	47.5	61.9	57.4	56.6

Further experiments on the LiveJournal, Aman, and Alm datasets to classify Ekman's emotions have been performed to determine what effect the training text size has and how using balanced or unbalanced training sizes for classes affects the classification accuracy, precision, recall, and F-measure (see Table 3). First, we used equal-sized texts used for training from the LiveJournal dataset for each of the six classes that ranged in size from 100 KB to 2.4 MB. We compared this to several cases where the text sizes used were not balanced—one where

3 MB was used for all classes except for *Disgust* which used 2.4 MB which was the maximum available for that class; and one where the full text that was available in the dataset was used for each class (so the training text sizes across the six classes was very unbalanced ranging from 2.4 MB for *Disgust* up to 78 MB for *Happiness*, with the latter class having a size greater than the combined sizes for the other five classes).

The results listed in Table 3 for the LiveJournal dataset are striking and show two noticeable trends. Firstly, the results consistently improve with training size, rising from an accuracy of 78.9% when as little as 100 KB is used up to 96.1% when 2.4 MB is used instead. And secondly, if unbalanced sizes are used between classes, this leads to a noticeable drop in performance, dropping down to an accuracy of 76.6% when training size is maximised across the classes but is very unbalanced as a result. Even when only one class is unbalanced (as when 3 MB is used for all classes except *Disgust*), the negative effect of unbalancing the class sizes outweighs the positive effect of using a larger size for the other classes.

Table 3. PPM classification results for Ekman's emotions for the three datasets.

Datas.	Training size	Acc.	Prec.	Rec.	F-m.
LiveJ.	100 KB *for each class*	78.9 %	0.35	0.37	0.31
	500 KB *for each class*	87.8 %	0.73	0.63	0.60
	1 MB *for each class*	91.7 %	0.83	0.75	0.74
	2 MB *for each class*	95.6 %	0.87	0.87	0.87
	2.4 MB *for each class*	96.1 %	0.90	0.88	0.88
	3 MB *except class for Disgust* (2.4 MB)	88.3 %	0.74	0.65	0.62
	Anger (22.1 MB), *Disgust* (2.4 MB), *Fear* (11.9 MB), *Happi.* (78 MB), *Sadness* (24.7 MB), *Surpr.* (8.8 MB)	76.6 %	0.53	0.30	0.25
Aman	10 KB *for each class except Surprise* (9.8 KB)	95.6 %	0.89	0.87	0.87
	Anger (17.5 KB), *Disgust* (13.5 KB), *Fear* (12.4 KB), *Happi.* (38.8 KB), *Sad.* (13.5 KB), *Surpr.* (9.8 KB)	78.9 %	0.70	0.37	0.36
Alm	12 KB *for each class*	88.0 %	0.71	0.70	0.67
	Anger-Disgust (23.7 KB), *Fear* (20 KB), *Happiness* (59.9 KB), *Sadness* (36.4), *Surprise* (12.3 KB)	75.6 %	0.65	0.42	0.38

We also explored the effect of training size for both Aman's dataset and Alm's dataset. These datasets have an order of magnitude less text available compared to the LiveJournal dataset so it is not possible to explore what effect increasing the size of the text has in any depth. However, we did compare the two cases when the class training text sizes were mostly balanced (approx. 10 KB for Aman's dataset and 12 KB for Alm's dataset), and when the sizes were unbalanced using the full text that was available in each class. In this case, the *Happiness* class again had the largest size compared with the other five classes, and was just over 4 times the size for the smallest class *Surprise*. The results in Table 3 clearly shows that using balanced class sizes compared to using unbalanced sizes for these datasets has a significant impact on classification performance, dropping from 95.6% to 78.9% accuracy for Aman's dataset and from 88.0% to 75.6% accuracy for Alm's dataset.

4   Conclusion

This paper has described how the Prediction by Partial Matching (PPM) text compression scheme can be applied to the problem of emotion recognition in text. Experimental results show that our new method is very effective when compared with other traditional data mining methods at recognizing emotions in text. The proposed method processes all characters in the text without explicit feature extraction while the other research methods have relied on processing words as features.

One important issue with our proposed method should be considered. It is often the case that the amount of text available for training purposes in different classes is mis-matched. In performing the experiments reported in this paper, we have found that our method works best if the sizes of text in all classes are the same, even if this means truncating text in most classes down to the smallest class size. This is because if the size for one class is much larger than for other classes, for example, then that class model will often become a better predictor of the general language (e.g. English) compared to the individual class models at predicting the language specific to each class.

References

1. Alm, C.O., Roth, D., Sproat, R.: Emotions from text: machine learning for text-based emotion prediction. In: Proceedings of the Conference on Human Language Technology and Empirical Methods in Natural Language Processing. pp. 579–586. ACL (2005)
2. Aman, S., Szpakowicz, S.: Identifying expressions of emotion in text. In: Matoušek, V., Mautner, P. (eds.) TSD 2007. LNCS, vol. 4629, pp. 196–205. Springer, Heidelberg (2007). https://doi.org/10.1007/978-3-540-74628-7_27
3. Chaffar, S., Inkpen, D.: Using a heterogeneous dataset for emotion analysis in text. In: Butz, C., Lingras, P. (eds.) AI 2011. LNCS, vol. 6657, pp. 62–67. Springer, Heidelberg (2011). https://doi.org/10.1007/978-3-642-21043-3_8
4. Cleary, J., Witten, I.: Data compression using adaptive coding and partial string matching. IEEE Trans. Commun. **32**(4), 396–402 (1984)
5. Ekman, P.: Basic emotions. Handb. Cognit. Emot. **16**, 45–60 (1999)
6. Ghazi, D., Inkpen, D., Szpakowicz, S.: Hierarchical versus flat classification of emotions in text. In: Proceedings of the NAACL HLT 2010 Workshop on Computational Approaches to Analysis and Generation of Emotion in Text, pp. 140–146. ACL (2010)

7. Keshtkar, F.: A computational approach to the analysis and generation of emotion in text. Ph.D. thesis, Université d'Ottawa/University of Ottawa (2011)
8. Leshed, G., Kaye, J.: Understanding how bloggers feel: recognizing affect in blog posts. In: CHI 2006 Extended Abstracts on Human Factors in Computing Systems, pp. 1019–1024. ACM (2006)
9. Mihalcea, R., Liu, H.: A corpus-based approach to finding happiness. In: AAAI Spring Symposium: Computational Approaches to Analyzing Weblogs, pp. 139–144 (2006)
10. Mishne, G., et al.: Experiments with mood classification in blog posts. In: Proceedings of ACM SIGIR 2005 Workshop on Stylistic Analysis of Text for Information Access, vol. 19, pp. 321–327 (2005)
11. Teahan, W.J., Harper, D.J.: Using compression-based language models for text categorization. In: Croft, W.B., Lafferty, J. (eds.) Language Modeling for Information Retrieval. The Springer International Series on Information Retrieval, pp. 141–165. Springer, Dordrecht (2003). https://doi.org/10.1007/978-94-017-0171-6_7

An Experimental Comparison of Ensemble Classifiers for Evolving Data Streams

Ahmad Idris Tambuwal$^{(\boxtimes)}$, Daniel Neagu, and Marian Gheorghe

University of Bradford, Bradford, UK
A.IdrisTambuwal@bradford.ac.uk

Abstract. Today, there is a tremendous growth in the amount of data being generated from various fields (such as smartphones, social networks, emails, customer click streams, different types of sensors and Internet of Things) that show Big Data attributes. Recently efforts have been made towards developing models for knowledge discovery from such data under the research area of stream mining or data stream classification in particular. Ensemble learners have become the popular approach in data stream classification because of their stability-elasticity property, which enables handling data stream challenges such as concept drift, recurrent concepts, novel class detection, and class imbalance. In this paper, we compare ten ensemble classifiers with respect to concept drift and class imbalance using Prequential AUC. In addition, Friedman nonparametric statistical test and Nemenyi post-hoc test were used to identify the best approach among them. This work to some extent can serve as part of a review of existing ensemble classifier algorithms for non-stationary data streams.

Keywords: Concept drift · Data stream · Class imbalance · Ensemble learners

1 Introduction

Today, there is tremendous growth in the amount of data being generated from various fields (e.g. smartphones, social networks, emails, customer click streams, different types of sensors and Internet of Things) that show Big Data attributes. This data is useful only if properly analyzed so that individuals and organizations can make real-time decisions. The major feature of this data is its streaming nature. Recently efforts have been made towards developing models for knowledge discovery from such data under the research area of stream mining [1]. Data stream mining poses many challenges which include: a large volume of data in real time, concept drifts, temporal dependencies, limited class label, class imbalance, noise, and limited computational resources requirements.

However, concept drift and class imbalance become major challenges for stream mining and received major research attention. In literature, many approaches are used for handling concept drift which is generally classified into active and passive approaches [2]. These approaches are developed based on single classifier and ensemble classifiers. Even though, single classifier approaches provide a lower computational cost than ensemble approaches that tend to consume more computational resources. Ensemble learners have become the popular approach in data stream

© Springer International Publishing AG 2017
M. Bramer and M. Petridis (Eds.): SGAI-AI 2017, LNAI 10630, pp. 156–162, 2017.
https://doi.org/10.1007/978-3-319-71078-5_14

classification because of their stability-elasticity property which makes it easy to incorporate new data into the model, by training and adding new members to the ensemble, and naturally, forget irrelevant knowledge by removing the old members from the ensemble [2].

The objective of this paper is to experimentally compare the performance of these ensemble methods to concept drift and class imbalance. Ten ensemble classifiers are compared using an evaluation method called Prequential AUC, that is more robust to class imbalance and concept drift [3]. The ensemble classifiers were chosen from the ones with a high number of citation and implemented in MOA framework [4].

The rest of this paper is organized as follows: Sect. 2 provides a background knowledge. Experimental description and results are given in Sects. 3 and 4. Finally, Sect. 5 presents our conclusion and future works.

2   Background

In this section, we start by introducing class imbalance and concept drift followed by a review of ensemble classification techniques existing in the literature.

2.1   Concept Drift and Class Imbalance

There are many definitions of concept drift, but a more probabilistic view is given in [5], where concept drift is set to have occurred when for two distinct points of time t and $t + k$, there exist x such that $P_t(x, y) \neq P_{t+k}(x, y)$. Concept drift can be classified based on the rate at which the changes occurs which includes

Sudden Drift. This type of drift is characterized by x_t being rapidly replace by x_{t+k}, where $P_t(x, y) \neq P_{t+k}(x, y)$.

Gradual Drift. This is considered as transition state where instances in x_{t+k} are generated by a mixture of $P_t(x, y)$ and $P_{t+k}(x, y)$ in different proportions.

Incremental Drift. This type of drift occurred when instances are derived from more than one probability distributions $P_t(x, y)$ and $P_{t+k}(x, y)$ where the difference between them is not significant.

Recurrent Drift. This is where the distribution of an instance may reappear after unknown period, i.e. $P_t(x, y) = P_{t-k}(x, y)$.

Concept drift can also be classified based on the nature of the changes which include

Real Drift. That involves change in posterior probability distribution (i.e. $P(y|x)$).

Virtual Drift. That involves changes in prior probability (i.e. $P(y)$) and change in class conditional probability distribution (i.e. $P(x|y)$). However, changes in prior probability result to the class imbalance where one class serve as majority class and the other as the minority.

2.2   Ensemble Classifiers

Ensemble classifiers involve the combination of many classification models whose individual predictions are combined in some format (e.g. averaging or voting). Several ensemble techniques have already been proposed, but this paper concentrates on those that are used for classification in non-stationary data streams, which are divided into chunk-based and online approaches. Table 1 summarizes these approaches with their performance evaluation metrics. We refer the reader to [5] for a detailed survey of these approaches.

Table 1. Ensemble Classifiers for non-stationary data streams.

	Approaches	Description	Evaluation Metrics
Chunk	AWE [6]	Accuracy weighted ensemble	Accuracy and error rate
	Learn++.NSE [7]	Incremental learning	Accuracy and time
	AUE [8]	Accuracy updated ensemble	Accuracy, memory, time
	RCD [9]	Recurrent concept drift	Accuracy
	EB [10]	Ensemble building	Classification error
Online	DWM [11]	Dynamic weighted majority	Accuracy
	OAUE [12]	Online accuracy updated ensemble	Accuracy, memory, time
	LB [13]	Leveraging bagging	Accuracy, memory, time
	OzaBagASHT [14]	Bagging with adaptive size hoeffding tree	Accuracy, memory, time
	OzaBagADWIN [15]	Bagging with adaptive windowing	Accuracy, memory, time

3   Experiment Description

This section starts with the description of the datasets used, followed by the experimental settings and evaluation methodology used in the experiment.

3.1   Datasets

To compare and analyze the performance of the classifiers, both artificial and real datasets are used with different class imbalance ratio and affected by both sudden and gradual concept drifts. Detailed characteristics of the datasets are given in Table 2.

3.2   Experimental Settings

The experiment was carried out using MOA software tool for stream mining [4]. For ensemble classifiers with decision tree structure, we used 10 Very Fast Decision Trees

Table 2. Datasets and their characteristics

Datasets	Instances	Attributes	Class ratio	Noise	Drift type
SEA$_{ND}$	100 k	3	–	10%	None
SEA$_{SD}$	100 k	3	–	10%	Sudden
HYP$_{GD}$	100 k	3	–	10%	Gradual
Imb1	100 k	5	1:1	10%	None
Imb2	100 k	5	1:10	10%	None
Imb3	100 k	5	1:20	10%	None
Imb4	100 k	5	1:100	10%	None
SEA$_{SC}$	100 k	3	1:1/1:100/1:10/1:1	10%	Sud. Virt.
HYP$_{GC}$	100 k	3	1:1 to 1:100	10%	Grad.
MinMaj	100 k	5	1:20/20:1	10%	Virt.
Air	539 k	7	~24:30	–	Sud. Virt.
Elect	45 k	8	~19:26	–	Unknown
KDDCup	494 k	41	~1:4	–	Unknown
PAKDD	50 k	30	~1:4	–	Unknown

(VFDT) [16] as base learners with Adaptive Naive Bayes leaf predictions with a grace period $n_{min} = 100$, split confidence $\delta = 0.01$, and tie-threshold $\varphi = 0.05$ [3]. The choice of VFDT as a base learner is due to its ability in monitoring differences between two class distributions [1], and availability in MOA. Similarly, error-based pruning strategy was used for Learn^{++}.NSE while for RCD, we used DDM [17] as drift detection method. A chunk size of 500 was chosen for all chunk-based approach and lastly, we maintain default settings for the rest of parameters on all ensemble classifiers.

3.3 Evaluation Setup

To evaluate the ensemble approaches using the presented datasets, a methodology similar to that described in [3] was used where a prequential evaluation is carried out with an evaluation method called ImbalancePerformanceEvaluator. Friedman non-parametric statistical test and Nemenyi post-hoc test [18], were used to compare and identify the best approach among the choosing ensemble classifiers.

4 Experimental Results

This section presents the result of the experiments carried out with the ensemble classifiers using the datasets presented, regarding predicted AUC.

4.1 Predictive Performance Evaluation

The performance of all the ensemble classifiers was accessed using Prequential AUC. Table 3, shows the average Prequential AUC, individual rank, and average ranks of all the classifiers under the used datasets. It can be observed that all classifiers nearly have

Table 3. Average prequential AUC

Datasets	AWE	NSE	AUE	RCD	EB	DWM	OAUE	LB	ASHT	ADWIN
SEA$_{ND}$	0.87(6)	0.86(9.5)	0.87(6)	0.87(6)	0.86(9.5)	0.87(6)	0.87(6)	0.88(2)	0.88(2)	0.88(2)
SEA$_{SD}$	0.74(7.5)	**0.73**(10)	0.74(7.5)	0.76(5)	0.74(7.5)	0.74(7.5)	0.78(4)	0.87(1)	0.81(3)	0.83(2)
HYP$_{GD}$	0.78(7.5)	**0.74**(10)	0.78(7.5)	0.80(5)	0.76(9)	0.84(2.5)	0.79(6)	0.88(1)	0.82(4)	0.84(2.5)
Imb1	0.99(9)	0.99(9)	0.99(9)	0.99(9)	0.99(9)	1.00(2.5)	0.99(9)	1.00(2.5)	1.00(2.5)	1.00(2.5)
Imb2	0.99(2)	**0.69**(10)	0.99(2)	0.96(6)	0.86(9)	0.90(8)	0.99(2)	0.94(7)	0.98(4.5)	0.98(4.5)
Imb3	0.99(4.5)	0.97(9)	0.99(4.5)	0.98(7.5)	0.96(10)	0.98(7.5)	0.99(4.5)	0.99(4.5)	1.00(1.5)	1.00(1.5)
Imb4	0.99(6)	0.98(9)	0.99(6)	0.99(6)	0.97(10)	0.99(6)	0.99(6)	1.00(1.5)	1.00(1.5)	1.00(1.5)
SEA$_{SC}$	0.78(4.5)	0.76(9)	0.78(4.5)	0.77(8)	0.75(10)	0.78(4.5)	0.78(4.5)	0.79(1)	0.78(4.5)	0.78(4.5)
HYP$_{GC}$	0.66(4)	0.62(8)	0.66(4)	0.66(4)	0.64(7)	0.66(4)	0.66(4)	0.67(1)	0.58(10)	0.59(9)
MinMaj	0.99(5)	**0.85**(10)	0.99(5)	0.99(5)	0.96(9)	0.98(8)	0.99(5)	0.99(5)	1.00(1.5)	1.00(1.5)
Air	0.67 (2.5)	0.57 (9)	0.67 (2.5)	0.64 (5)	0.56 (10)	0.62 (7)	0.63 (6)	0.60(8)	0.68 (1)	0.65 (4)
Elect	0.84 (7.5)	0.73 (9)	0.84 (7.5)	0.87 (6)	0.56 (10)	0.94 (3)	0.94 (3)	0.96 (1)	0.93 (5)	0.94 (3)
KDD	0.96 (6)	0.94 (8)	0.92 (10)	0.99 (4.5)	0.95 (7)	1.00 (2)	0.93 (9)	1.00 (2)	1.00 (2)	0.99 (4.5)
PAKDD	0.61 (5)	0.50 (10)	0.61 (5)	0.60 (7)	0.56 (8)	0.51 (9)	0.62 (3)	0.63 (1.5)	0.61 (5)	0.63 (1.5)
Average	5.50	**7.89**	5.79	6.00	**8.93**	5.54	5.14	**2.79**	3.43	3.18

the same performance on the datasets with no concept changes (SEA$_{ND}$). In the overall consideration of all the datasets with concept drift and class imbalance problems, LB is the best classifier in terms AUC having the lowest average rank, while EB and Learn[++]. NSE has the lowest performance. Figure 1, represents the results of Nemenyi's test, by grouping ensemble classifiers that are not significantly different. The result shows that online ensemble approaches perform better than chunk-based approaches for learning in a non-stationary streaming environment. Specifically, tree based online ensemble learners were group together showing significant difference to other chunk-based ensembles like EB and Learn[++].NSE.

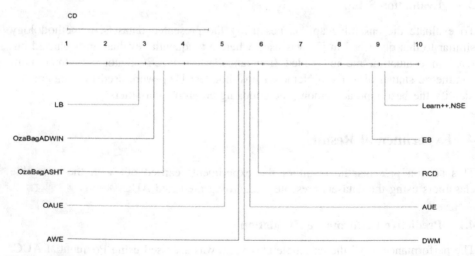

Fig. 1. AUC comparison of ensemble classifiers with Nemenyi test (at $p < 0.00001$ and $\alpha = 0.05$).

5 Conclusion and Future Work

This paper compared Ten (10) ensemble classifiers and studied their performance in the presence of concept drift and class imbalance, using artificial and real datasets. In the overall consideration of datasets, LB is the best classifier in terms AUC having the lowest average rank, while EB and Learn^{++}.NSE, having the lowest performance. The result also shows online ensemble approaches perform better than chunk-based approaches and specifically, tree based ensemble learners having the highest performance for learning in a non-stationary streaming environment with concept drift and class imbalance problems. Future work would be to consider varying the parameter values to determine their effects in the performance of ensemble classifiers.

References

1. Gama, J., Rodrigues, P.P., Spinosa, E., Carvalho, A.: Knowledge discovery from data streams. In: Web Intelligence and Security – Advances in Data and Text Mining Techniques for Detecting and Preventing Terrorist Activities on the Web, pp. 125–138 (2010)
2. Ditzler, G., Roveri, M., Alippi, C., Polikar, R.: Learning in nonstationary environments: a survey. IEEE Comput. Intell. Mag. **10**(4), 12–25 (2015)
3. Brzezinski, D., Stefanowski, J.: Prequential AUC: properties of the area under the ROC curve for data streams with concept drift. Knowl. Inf. Syst. **52**, 531–562 (2017)
4. Bifet, A., Holmes, G., Kirkby, R., Pfahringer, B.: MOA massive online analysis. J. Mach. Learn. Res. **11**, 1601–1604 (2011)
5. Krawczyk, B., Minku, L.L., Gama, J., Stefanowski, J., Woźniak, M.: Ensemble learning for data stream analysis: a survey. Inf. Fusion **37**, 132–156 (2017)
6. Wang, H., Fan, W., Yu, P.S., Han, J.: Mining concept-drifting data streams using ensemble classifiers. In: Proceedings of the Ninth ACM SIGKDD International Conference on Knowledge Discovery and Data Mining, vol. 2, no. 1, pp. 226–235 (2003)
7. Elwell, R., Polikar, R.: Incremental learning of concept drift in nonstationary environments. IEEE Trans. Neural Netw. **22**(10), 1517–1531 (2011)
8. Brzezinski, D., Stefanowski, J.: Reacting to different types of concept drift: the accuracy updated ensemble algorithm. IEEE Trans. Neural Netw. Learn. Syst. **25**(1), 81–94 (2014)
9. Gonçalves Jr., P.M., de Barros, R.S.M.: RCD: a recurring concept drift framework. Pattern Recognit. Lett. **34**(9), 1018–1025 (2013)
10. Metzen, J.H., Edgington, M., Kassahun, Y., Kirchner, F.: Tracking recurrent concept drift in streaming data using ensemble classifiers. In: Proceedings of the 6th International Conference on Machine Learning and Applications ICMLA 2007, pp. 342–347 (2007)
11. Kolter, J., Maloof, M.: Dynamic weighted majority: an ensemble method for drifting concepts. J. Mach. Learn. Res. **8**, 2755–2790 (2007)
12. Brzezinski, D., Stefanowski, J.: Combining block-based and online methods in learning ensembles from concept drifting data streams. Inf. Sci. (Ny) **265**, 50–67 (2014)
13. Bifet, A., Holmes, G., Pfahringer, B.: Leveraging bagging for evolving data streams. In: Balcázar, J.L., Bonchi, F., Gionis, A., Sebag, M. (eds.) ECML PKDD 2010. LNCS, vol. 6321, pp. 135–150. Springer, Heidelberg (2010). 10.1007/978-3-642-15880-3_15
14. Bifet, A., Holmes, G., Pfahringer, B., Kirkby, R., Gavaldà, R.: New ensemble methods for evolving data streams. In: Proceedings of the 15th ACM SIGKDD International Conference Knowledge Discovery data Mining – KDD 2009, p. 139 (2009)

15. Bifet, A., Gavaldà, R.: Learning from time-changing data with adaptive windowing. In: Proceedings of the 2007 SIAM International Conference on Data Mining, Philadelphia, PA: Society for Industrial and Applied Mathematics, pp. 443–448 (2007)
16. Domingos, P., Hulten, G.: Mining high-speed data streams. In: Proceedings of the Sixth ACM SIGKDD International Conference Knowledge Discovery Data Mining, pp. 71–80 (2000)
17. Gama, J., Medas, P., Castillo, G., Rodrigues, P.: Learning with drift detection. In: Bazzan, Ana L.C., Labidi, S. (eds.) SBIA 2004. LNCS, vol. 3171, pp. 286–295. Springer, Heidelberg (2004). 10.1007/978-3-540-28645-5_29
18. Demšar, J.: Statistical comparisons of classifiers over multiple data sets. J. Mach. Learn. Res. **7**, 1–30 (2006)

A Learning Automata Local Contribution Sampling Applied to Hydropower Production Optimisation

Jahn Thomas Fidje[(✉)], Christian Kråkevik Haraldseid,
Ole-Christoffer Granmo, Morten Goodwin, and Bernt Viggo Matheussen

Centre for Artificial Intelligence Research, University of Agder, Grimstad, Norway
jtfidje@gmail.com

Abstract. Learning Automata (LA) is a powerful approach for solving complex, non-linear and stochastic optimisation problems. However, existing solutions struggle with high-dimensional problems due to slow convergence, arguably caused by the global nature of feedback. In this paper we introduce a novel Learning Automata (LA) scheme to attack this challenge. The scheme is based on a parallel form of Local Contribution Sampling (LCS), which means that the LA receive *individually* directed feedback, designed to speed up convergence. Furthermore, our scheme is highly decentralized, allowing parallel execution on GPU architectures. To demonstrate the power of our scheme, the LA LCS is applied to hydropower production optimisation, involving several particularly challenging optimisation scenarios. The experimental results show that LA LCS is able to quickly find optimal solutions for a wide range of problem configurations. Our results also demonstrate that local directed feedback provides significantly faster convergence than global feedback. These results lead us to conclude that LA LCS holds great promise for solving complex, non-linear and stochastic optimisation problems, opening up for improved performance in a number of real-world applications.

Keywords: Reinforcement learning · Local feedback · Learning Automata

1 Introduction

The global feedback scheme has been widely used to train teams of Learning Automata (LA) that jointly solve complex problems [1]. Individually, each LA is a decision making mechanism that performs actions sequentially in an environment. Each action triggers a reward or a penalty, and the goal of the LA is to identify an action that provides the maximal expected reward. In the global feedback scheme, multiple LA work together as a team to optimize a joint objective function, often modelled as a common payoff game [1].

A prominent property of LA teams is that they operate in a fully decentralized manner, without the need for inter-communication. Remarkably, they still

© Springer International Publishing AG 2017
M. Bramer and M. Petridis (Eds.): SGAI-AI 2017, LNAI 10630, pp. 163–168, 2017.
https://doi.org/10.1007/978-3-319-71078-5_15

are able to find the optimal solution, jointly agreeing upon a common strategy. The problem with this approach is that as the team of LA grows in size, the influence of each LA on the global feedback becomes minuscule. This in turn leads to a progressively smaller signal-to-noise ratio. In complex scenarios this effect will increase the convergence time and, in some cases, even keep the algorithm from finding the optimal solution within a practical amount of time.

2   Related Work

A diverse selection of approaches exists for hydropower optimisation, drawn from multiple fields. Previously, classical optimization algorithms, like linear programming, have been extensively discussed in the literature [2–5].

One typical approach is dynamic programming (DP). There exists several hydropower optimization algorithms building upon DP [6,7], inspired by the Stochastic Dynamic Programming algorithm (SDP) introduced by Bellman in 1957 [8]. The SDP algorithm suffers from the *curse of dimensionality*[8], which becomes particularly critical in multi-reservoir systems. These suffers an an exponential increase in candidate solutions, both in the number of reservoirs and the number of production choices [7].

To the best of our knowledge, LA have not previously been applied to hydropower optimization. Although LA falls under the group of policy iterators in reinforcement learning (directly manipulating the policy π), they are relatively simple, yet powerful. A LA can learn the optimal actions when acting against a stochastic environment. They further have a low computational cost combined with rapid and accurate convergence.

Previous results have shown that LAs are capable of solving complex combinatorial optimization problems when interacting with unknown stochastic environments [9–11], and is thus a promising candidate for solving complex issues related to hydropower optimisation.

3   Hydropower Optimisation

In this paper we study multi-reservoir systems for hydropower production. The optimization problem that we address concerns finding the production strategy that yields the highest profit. To elaborate, in discrete time, we need to decide when to turn on/or production for each dam in the reservoir system. Thus, the solution space consists of action sequences, referred to as *production strings*, representing the actions *Produce electricity* (1) and *Pause production* (0), respectively.

The multi-reservoir system is simulated so as to estimate the profit of any given production string, thus acting as the environment for the LA. The *production string* informs the simulation on the production strategy over the next t_n time steps, which in turn allows the total profit to be obtained, measuring success. In the experiments, one time step is defined as 24 h.

The simulation is based on a simple graph structure where each *vertex* is an element from a hydropower system. The vertices are connected using *edges* which simulates water-flow in the system. A one dam system consists of a *reservoir* which is attached to a *turbine* that produces energy from the water. Reservoirs are filled with water, called inflow. The inflow can be rain, rivers or tail-water[1]. In a real-world scenario the inflow and prices are seen as stochastic and requires a multitude of simulations to be run in parallel to determine the best strategy. This is possible with our GPU optimized implementation of the algorithm.

4   Learning Automata with Local Contribution Sampling

Traditionally the collective set of actions derived from internal states of the LA is the only input that the environment will take into account. We denote this behaviour global feedback, a method where each automaton is either rewarded or punished based on their collective contribution, and not their individual contribution.

4.1   Action Change

In this paper we propose Action Change (Fig. 1), a method that gives the environment the possibility to individually evaluate the contribution of each automaton. By first creating a base set of actions G from the internal states of the LA, modified sets G'_i can be derived from this base. For each LA A_i , its corresponding action A_i^x in G is changed to its opposite action and stored in a new set G'_i.

By evaluating all actions sets G and G'_i, we get a set set of fitness scores $X = (x_0, \ldots, x_i)$ where x_0 is the fitness returned from action set G, and $x_1, \ldots, x_i$ is the fitness returned from action sets G'_i. Equation 1 is then used to calculate individual reward probabilities for each of the LA.

$$p(x_i) = 1 - \frac{(x_i - X_{min}) \cdot 0.6}{X_{max} - X_{min}} + 0.2 \qquad (1)$$

5   Results

5.1   Hydropower Optimization in Short Time Periods

We here provide our empirical results for the LA LCS algorithm on a scenario of 10 time steps and three dams. With such a small number of time steps we are able to find the optimal solution(s) by brute force, making it possible to compare the results with the optimal production string. Figure 2 shows LA LCS converging after very few iterations. Table 1 compares the results of LA LCS with LA using a global reward scheme. We see that LA LCS converges to the optimal solution 100% of the runs, while the global LA never reaches optimal with the tested number of iterations.

---

[1] **Tail-water:** water downstream from the turbine is called tail-water.

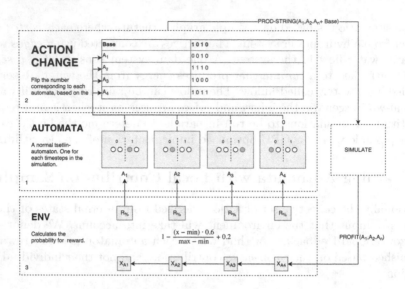

Fig. 1. Local contribution change on hydropower optimisation problem

Table 1. Comparing results of LA LCS with LA Global after 100 and 10000 iterations on a 10-timestep scenario.

Algorithm	Initialization	Iterations	
		1000	10000
LA Global	0	0.0	0.0
LA Global	1	0.0	0.0
LA Global	Random	0.0	0.0
LA LCS	0	1.0	1.0
LA LCS	1	1.0	1.0
LA LCS	Random	1.0	1.0

5.2 Hydropower Optimization in Longer Time Periods

By increasing the number of time steps to 50, we are no longer able to find the optimal solution(s) by brute force. A 50 time step scenario has therefore been designed such that there exists only one solution which is always known, enabling the possibility to compare the results of the algorithms with the true solution.

LA LCS is unable to converge to the optimal solution in this scenario. Despite this, Table 2 shows that the algorithm is still able to find the optimal solution in nearly 50% of the test runs, displaying a capability of searching beyond local optimums.

Table 2. Comparing results of LA LCS with LA Global after 100 and 10000 iterations on a 50-timestep scenario.

Algorithm	Initialization	Iterations	
		1000	10000
LA Global	0	-	-
LA Global	1	-	-
LA Global	Random	-	-
LA LCS	0	0.125 ± 0.0205	0.494 ± 0.0310
LA LCS	1	0.037 ± 0.0117	0.441 ± 0.0308
LA LCS	Random	0.0	0.0

Table 3. Comparing results of LA LCS with LA Global after 100 and 10000 iterations on a 100-timestep scenario. LA Global did not find the optimal.

Algorithm	Initialization	Iterations	
		1000	10000
LA LCS	0	0.012 ± 0.0067	0.011 ± 0.0064
LA LCS	1	0.0	0.0
LA LCS	Random	0.0	0.0

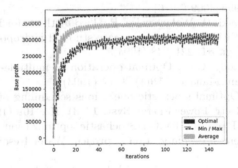

Fig. 2. Convergence graph on a 10-timestep scenario.

However, increasing the time period to 100 time steps using the same scenario, LA LCS cannot be said to reliably converge to a state where it is able to find an optimal solution. This is shown from the results in Table 3.

6   Conclusion

In this paper, we have proposed the use of Local Contribution Sampling (LCS), a method for evaluating the individual contribution of each Learning Automaton (LA) in a team of LA. We have shown that significant improvements can be achieved compared to using so-called global feedback (common payoff) In brief, LA LCS is able to perform more precise reward/punish actions, resulting in significantly faster convergence. Finally, our LCS LA allow parallel GPU computing that can be utilized to address large scale optimization problems.

As further work, one could enhance the parallel process that has been designed for the GPU to allow executing of multiple scenarios in parallel, addressing uncertainty in price and inflow forecasts. Further testing of scalability in more comprehensive and complex simulation of hydropower is of interest.

Finally, it would be interesting to introduce LA LCS in other application areas, such as warehouse optimization or evacuation planning, in comparison with other algorithms such as GA (Genetic Algorithm) and PSO (Particle Swarm Optimization).

References

1. Thathachar, M.A.L., Sastry, P.S.: Varieties of learning automata: an overview. IEEE Trans. Syst. Man Cybern. Part B (Cybern.) **32**(6), 711–722 (2002)
2. Archibald, T.W., McKinnon, K.I.M., Thomas, L.C.: An aggregate stochastic dynamic programming model of multireservoir systems. Water Resour. Res. **33**(2), 333–340 (1997)
3. Azizipour, M., Ghalenoei, V., Afshar, M.H., Solis, S.S.: Optimal operation of hydropower reservoir systems using weed optimization algorithm. Water Resour. Manag. **30**(11), 3995–4009 (2016)
4. Arnold, E., Tatjewski, P., Wołochowicz, P.: Two methods for large-scale nonlinear optimization and their comparison on a case study of hydropower optimization. J. Optim. Theory Appl. **81**, 221–248 (1994)
5. Crawley, P.D., Dandy, G.C.: Optimal operation of multiple-reservoir system. J. Water Resour. Plan. Manage. **119**(1), 1–17 (1993)
6. Pereira, M.V.F.: Optimal stochastic operations scheduling of large hydroelectric systems. Int. J. Electr. Power Energy Syst. **11**(3), 161–169 (1989)
7. Pereira, M.V.F., Pinto, L.M.V.G.: Stochastic optimization of a multireservoir hydroelectric system: a decomposition approach. Water Resour. Res. **21**(6), 779–792 (1985)
8. Bellman, R.: Dynamic Programming, vol. 1, no. 2, p. 3. Princeton University Press, Princeton (1957)
9. Granmo, O.-C., Bouhmala, N.: Solving the satisfiability problem using finite learning automata. IJCSA **4**(3), 15–29 (2007)
10. Oommen, B.J., de St Croix, E.V.: Graph partitioning using learning automata. IEEE Trans. Comput. **45**(2), 195–208 (1996)
11. Granmo, O.-C., Oommen, B.J.: Solving stochastic nonlinear resource allocation problems using a hierarchy of twofold resource allocation automata. IEEE Trans. Comput. **59**(4), 545–560 (2010)

Toward Component-Based Self-Adaptive Multi-Strategic Pedagogical Agents

Soufiane Boulehouache[1](✉), Ramdane Maamri[2], and Zaidi Sahnoun[2]

[1] 20 Août 1955-Skikda University, Skikda, Algeria
sboulehouache@yahoo.com
[2] Abdelhamid Mehri Constantine 2 University, Constantine, Algeria
rmaamri@yahoo.fr, sahnounz@yahoo.fr

Abstract. Multi-Strategic Pedagogical Systems (MSPSs) achieve effective learning by dynamically switching to the Pedagogical Strategy (PS) appropriate to the student mental state. Since, within the same session, the Student Cognitive State (SCS) frequently changes as a consequence of learning. However, the integration of different PSs and the mixture of the Pedagogical Strategy Switching (PSS) logic with the pedagogical logic in a single closed monolithic cognitive entity was making this kind of pedagogical systems too complex to construct and non-reusable in most cases. To overcome the above mentioned deficiencies, within this paper, we propose a new design model of MSPSs. We call this model a Multi-Strategic Pedagogical Agent (MSPA) and it is devoted to construct MSPSs that self-reconfigure their internal structure to implement the appropriate PS regarding the SCS.

Keywords: Agents · Pedagogical Agents · Pedagogical strategy adapting · Fractal Component Model · Components selection

1 Introduction

Multi-Strategic Pedagogical Systems (MSPSs) achieve effective learning by reproducing the flexibility of human teachers switching of the teaching methods. This vision fills the gap of the one size fit all philosophy of mono-strategic pedagogical systems by integrating multiple SCSs related PSs and PSS logic. Since, each strategy has specific advantages and it appears useful to use adequately the strategy that will strengthen the acquisition process for a given learner [1].

However, the conventional engineering of such type of system has intensified drastically their complexity. Since, they integrate multiple PSs and a PSS logic in addition to the different types of expertise. In short, we must reconsider the engineering of these systems if we want to make the best possible use of them.

In fact, the Component-based Agents seems appropriate to construct efficient MSPSs. Since, they deal with the structuring of the Agents. According to [2], the component concept and technology may help in the actual construction of MASs at agent level as it provides some support for structuring, (de)composing

© Springer International Publishing AG 2017
M. Bramer and M. Petridis (Eds.): SGAI-AI 2017, LNAI 10630, pp. 169–174, 2017.
https://doi.org/10.1007/978-3-319-71078-5_16

and reusing of its internal architecture. Thus, within this paper, we use the component based agent model to propose a new design model that permits to construct MSPAs that self-reconfigure their internal structure and behavior to achieve the PSS.

We discuss the proposition in the remainder of this paper as following. In section two, we introduce the PSS concept and its importance. The next section describes the architecture of our Component Based Self-Adaptive Multi-Strategic Pedagogical Agent model. The Sect. 4 presents conclusions and perspectives.

2 Multi-Strategic Pedagogical Systems

Despite the importance of using multiple SCSs related PSs, little works were proposed that focus on the improvement of the outcomes of learning by dynamically and automatically triggering multiple PSs. Here, we present Multi-Strategic Pedagogical Systems based, mainly, on the works of *Claude Frasson*, *Esma Aïmeur* and their colleagues.

2.1 Cooperative Pedagogical Strategies

PSs are policies to decide the next system action when there are multiple ones available [3]. It means to decide what knowledge to present, when to present and how to present in correspondence with the SCS. From another point of view, they are the set of teaching events (actions and decisions) that motivate and interest the learner while improving his performance [4].

Cooperative Pedagogical Strategies (CPSs) are strategies that implement the Social Learning Theory. Example of systems that implement the CPSs are ITS, Pedagogical Agents, etc. According to [5], the roles played by the Intelligent Agent as a cognitive tool can be decomposed in four tutorial strategies: (1) Tutor-Tutee, (2) Learning Companion, (3) Learning by Disturbing, (4) Learning by Teaching.

2.2 Student Cognitive Levels

Generally, the Student Cognitive (knowledge) Level (SCL) is evaluated at the concept level and it reflects the understanding of the learner. [4] have defined a *Student Model* with four different knowledge levels: (1) Novice, (2) Beginner, (3) Intermediate and (4) the Expert [4]. It ranges from no prior understanding of the concept at all to extensive understanding. At the Expert Level, the students have acquired extensive knowledge that affects what they notice and how they organize, represent, and interpret information in their environment. This, in turn, affects their abilities to remember, reason, and solve problems [6].

2.3   CPSs and SCLs Correlation

The evaluation of the four CPSs shows a correlation with the SCLs. The Tutor-Tutee strategy works better with a Beginner [4]. For the novice knowledge level, [4] were selected the Tutor-Tutee. The use of the Tutor-Tutee model proved best for the novice. Concerning the Learning Companion strategy, usually works better with a novice or a beginner [4]. Working with a companion would suit a learner whose knowledge level is low and who requires assistance or who needs to be motivated by cooperation [1]. The Learning by Disturbing is more efficient with an intermediate [7]. In a Learning by Disturbing approach, the learner needs to defend his point of view. He must know how to retrieve information that has been previously stored. This strategy reinforces good learners but discourages poor ones [1]. The use of the Troublemaker with novices creates confusion [4]. However, it proved more efficient with the expert. The Learning by Teaching works better with an expert. For students with insufficient training on the target problems, Learning by Teaching may have limited benefits compared to learning by tutored problem solving [8].

3   A Components Based Self-Adaptive Multi-Strategic Pedagogical Agent

Within this section we present our MSPA model. This model, that is designed based on software architectures, is general and can be applied to various types of User-Aware Self-Adaptive Agents but its design is particularly adapted to the PSS. It adopts a subdivision of the internal structure of the PA using components as a style of both the Managed (functional) and the Manager (PSS Engine) Sub-Systems. The design of the internal structure of our MSPA is achieved using the Fractal Component Model that provides the suitable abstraction level and re-configuration mechanisms to achieve the PSS.

The Fig. 1 shows the architecture of our MSPA. It is a composite component that is constituted of a set of sub-components. These sub-components bounded each to other cooperate to provide dynamic switches to appropriate PS. The design of the MdSS structure, FCs local Repository and the FCs Repositories as distinct components is to promote their sharing and reusing. The following is a description of the components constituting the MSPA.

- **Managed Sub-System.** The component based design of the Managed Sub-System (MdSS), represented by the Fractal-Based Generalized Pedagogical Agent Model (FBGPA) [9], aims to provide a fine-tuned, cost-effective and flexible PSS. It is a composite sub-component of the MSPA where the PSS is accomplished, on the fly, by (re)-configuring its sub-components. The Fig. 2 shows the architecture of the MdSS. It is constituted of sub-components of the well known modules of pedagogical systems and bindings between the required (right) interfaces and the provided (left) interfaces to each other. The sub-components correspond to the sub-modules of the Generalized Pedagogical Agent (GPA) Model proposed by [10]. However, against the original GPA

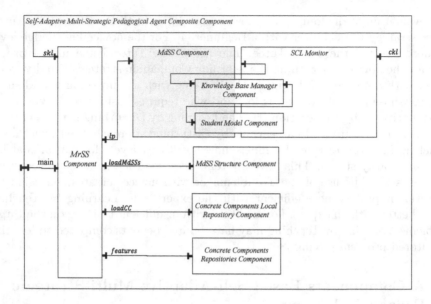

Fig. 1. MSPA architecture.

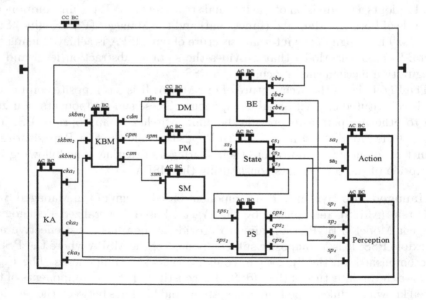

Fig. 2. Assembly of the Managed Sub-System

pattern, using the Fractal Model, the MdSS does not represent explicitly the data-flow direction. They are hidden within the interfaces constituting the components.

- **Manager Sub-System.** Since the PSS is frequently triggered, the Manager Sub-System (MrSS) performs on the fly PSS. This (re)configuration of the MdSS aims to implement the appropriate PS corresponding to the current SCL. The selection process of the MrSS can be implemented using a genetic search algorithm like in [11]. Next, it assembles the appropriate linear combination of the pre-built components to implement the appropriate PS.

- **MdSS Structure Component.** It is a distinct component that wraps the MdSS Structure as Fractal ADL. It is used by the MrSS to get the Concrete Components related to the Abstract Component constituting the MdSS Structure during the reconfiguration process. The MdSS Structure Component simplifies the replacement of MdSS.

- **Concrete Components Repositories Component.** It is a Fractal Component that wraps the distributed FCs repositories. These last contain the Concrete Components that can be selected to implement the MdSS (the PA characters). This component is bound to the MrSS to provide the specified services. I is used by the MrSS to retrieve the selected components to assemble the MdSS.

- **Concrete Components Local Repository Component.** It is a Fractal Component that wraps the features of the Fractal Component indexed by the Search Engine. It is a local Concrete Components repository that is used by the MrSS to select the appropriate set of components to construct the MdSS.

- **Student Model Component.** Since the SCL change as a consequence of learning, the Student Model Component captures the SCL for each concept of the Domain Model. So, in order to switch the PS, the MrSS needs an informative and an updated SCL Model. It is a shared component between the SCL Monitor Component and the MdSS. Thus, the MdSS updates the SCL that is intercepted by the SCL Monitor Component to notify the MrSS that decides if a reconfiguration is required.

- **Knowledge Base Manager Component.** The Knowledge Base Manager (KBM) is a component that controls the access and the updates to/of the Knowledge Base [10]. Each module of the MdSS can access the knowledge base only through the functions of the Knowledge Base Manager [10]. The KBM has a required interface that is used by the SCL Monitor Component to access the Student Model Component.

4   Conclusions and Perspectives

Within this paper we have presented a MSPA model that is designed as Component Based Agent. Exploiting the composition feature of the Fractal model, the MSPA is designed incrementally. Each time, we have a composite component that integrates the previous sub-components. In addition to the flexibility of the PSS, this design principal makes the MSPA strategy independent. Furthermore, the use of one re-configurable Pedagogical Agent really imitates the strategy switching achieved by the human tutors.

As perspectives, we work on the construction of Multi-Strategic Animated Pedagogical Agents using Autonomic related principals and mechanisms. Also, we work on the study of using different control loops with Multi-Objective Adapting goals.

References

1. Frasson, C., Mengelle, T., Ameur, E.: Using pedagogical agents in a multi-strategic intelligent tutoring system. In: Workshop on Pedagogical Agents in AI-ED, vol. 97, pp. 40–47 (1997)
2. Briot, J.-P., Meurisse, T., Peschanski, F.: Architectural design of component-based agents: a behavior-based approach. In: Bordini, R.H., Dastani, M., Dix, J., Seghrouchni, A.E.F. (eds.) ProMAS 2006. LNCS, vol. 4411, pp. 71–90. Springer, Heidelberg (2007). https://doi.org/10.1007/978-3-540-71956-4_5
3. Chi, M.T.H., Roy, M.: How adaptive is an expert human tutor? In: Aleven, V., Kay, J., Mostow, J. (eds.) ITS 2010. LNCS, vol. 6094, pp. 401–412. Springer, Heidelberg (2010). https://doi.org/10.1007/978-3-642-13388-6_44
4. Abou-Jaoude, S.C., Frasson, C.: An agent for selecting learning strategy. In: Proceedings of the World Conference on Nouvelles Technologies de la Communication et de la Formation (NTICF), Rouen, pp. 353–358 (1998)
5. Bandura, A., McClelland, D.C.: Social learning theory (1977)
6. Bransford, J.D., Brown, A.L., Cocking, R.R.: How People Learn: Brain, Mind, Experience, and School. National Academy Press, Washington, D.C. (1999)
7. Jaques, P., Andrade, A., Jung, J., Bordini, R., Vicari, R.: Using pedagogical agents to support collaborative distance learning. In: Proceedings of the Conference on Computer Support for Collaborative Learning: Foundations for a CSCL Community, International Society of the Learning Sciences, pp. 546–547 (2002)
8. Matsuda, N., Yarzebinski, E., Keiser, V., Raizada, R., Stylianides, G.J., Cohen, W.W., Koedinger, K.R.: Learning by teaching simstudent—an initial classroom baseline study comparing with cognitive tutor. In: Biswas, G., Bull, S., Kay, J., Mitrovic, A. (eds.) AIED 2011. LNCS, vol. 6738, pp. 213–221. Springer, Heidelberg (2011). https://doi.org/10.1007/978-3-642-21869-9_29
9. Boulehouache, S., Maamri, R., Sahnoun, Z., Larguet, A.: A fractal based generalized pedagogical agent model. In: Badica, A., Trawinski, B., Nguyen, N. (eds.) Recent Developments in Computational Collective Intelligence, vol. 513, pp. 47–57. Springer, Cham (2014). https://doi.org/10.1007/978-3-319-01787-7_5
10. Devedzic, V., Harrer, A.: Software patterns in its architectures. Int. J. Artif. Intell. Educ. **15**(2), 63–94 (2005)
11. Boulehouache, S., Sahnoun, Z.: A genetic based components selection. Softw. Knowl. Inf. Manage. Appl. 667–672 (2009)

Application Stream Papers

Papers Included in the Application Stream of AI-2017

The following seven sections comprise refereed papers accepted for the application stream of AI-2017 divided into the following categories:

- Best Application Paper
- AI for Healthcare
- Applications of Machine Learning
- Applications of Neural Networks and Fuzzy Logic
- Case-Based Reasoning
- AI Techniques
- Short Application Papers

The winner of the Rob Milne Memorial Award for the best refereed application paper in the conference was the paper "Cable Belief Networks" by A. Ferguson and S. Thompson (BT Labs, UK).

The final section comprises the text of short application papers which were presented as posters at the conference.

Cable Belief Networks
(Best Application Paper)

Andrew Ferguson[(✉)] and Simon Thompson

BT Labs, Ipswich, UK
{andrew.ferguson, simon.2.thompson}@bt.com

Abstract. Telecommunication networks are developed over many years (over 100 in the case of the UK) and buried underground. Creating and maintaining accurate inventories of the materials used in their construction is challenging, when these systems were implemented electronic records did not exist and large scale surveys are uneconomic and unreliable. A Bayesian model of the network structure is developed and it is shown how this can be used in combination with the telemetry derived from a DSL network to create estimates that repair the inventory records. This approach was evaluated using a physical investigation of a sample of network elements and these results are presented along with a discussion of the limitations of the approach that have been identified. This result was derived vs an inventory system of approximately 7 million entries and required data processed from approximately 130 Tb of telemetry an applied to over 2 million cable records. This technique is now used to deliver broadband services in the UK.

Keywords: Bayesian networks and stochastic reasoning · Industrial applications of artificial intelligence · Machine learning

1 Introduction

The delivery of broadband through xDSL (Digital Subscriber Line) technologies is reliant on our existing metallic phone network. The network is comprised of cable segments of different materials (mostly copper, but a substantial minority of aluminium), gauges, and pair counts. Figure 1 shows how each circuit in a broadband network is composed. The DSLAM (DSL Access Multiplexer) connects the circuit to the backhaul network, a tie cable is used to connect the DSLAM to the PCP (Principle Connection Point) which is wired into the circuit. Each circuit is composed of multiple cable legs which are shared between multiple circuits, finally the last cable leg is connected to a drop wire which is only used for this circuit and any internal wiring reaching to the modem/hub in the customers premises.

The loss properties (measured here as Hlog by tone) of the cables that make up the route to the customer premise are a dominant factor in determining the speed of the broadband service that the customer can receive. The inventory records approach to estimating loss relies on the records of the lengths of the cable segments combined with the average expected loss per kilometre for the given material and gauge (known as the 'cable constant'). Residual error for this estimate relative to empirically observed loss figures can have multiple contributing factors:

© Springer International Publishing AG 2017
M. Bramer and M. Petridis (Eds.): SGAI-AI 2017, LNAI 10630, pp. 177–189, 2017.
https://doi.org/10.1007/978-3-319-71078-5_17

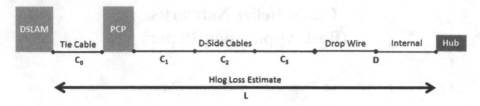

Fig. 1. The different components of a d-side circuit that connects a customer's hub to the DSLAM comprise the tie cable (connecting the PCP and DSLAM), the d-side cables from the PCP to the DP, the drop wire from the DP to the premise, and any internal wiring within the premise. The total insertion loss (in decibels) is the sum of the insertion losses of all these components.

- Measurement error.
- Incorrect drop/internal wiring estimates.
- Between-pair length variance (due to twisting).
- Physical impairments such as an HR joint.
- Incorrect material or gauge in inventory records.

Some of these factors can be mitigated: such as calibrating Hlog inputs by CPE (Customer Premise Equipment) and DSLAM to offset measurement errors, or baselining measurements over time to filter out transient fault effects. Others cannot but the uncertainty can be estimated reasonably such as between-pair variance (BPV) or drop wire estimate errors (DWE).

The most difficult error to overcome is that of the wrong material and/or gauge being present in the inventory records as there is no way, a priori, of knowing where it occurs. In principle this error could have a positive (i.e. better quality cable than records) or a negative effect, but in practice the most common error of this kind is a cable segment that is labelled as copper but is in fact aluminium. This is due to legacy issues with the digitisation of inventory records that has results in a proportion of the cable records being "generic" or "inferred" which meant that a default value of 0.5 gauge copper was used.

The trend in broadband delivery has been to move away from (longer reaching) exchange based technology such as ADSL through to the FTTC technologies VDSL and now G.Fast and as such the service a customer receives is becoming more sensitive to the noise these errors can introduce as they are becoming larger as a proportion of total circuit length.

This paper outlines an approach to using loss estimates derived from VDSL diagnostic data combined with the existing inventory records to try and algorithmically identify the material and gauge of cable segments and subsequently cleanse the incorrect cable records.

The structure of the paper is as follows. Section 2 is an overview of the structure and nature of the inventory system to be repair and shows why it was intuited that the development of and application of the technique was required. Section 3 provides an overview of related work. In Sect. 4 the model developed is presented, and Sect. 5 shows how it was practically applied using the data available. Section 6 provides the results that were obtained by calculation and during a field investigation. Section 7 provides an evaluation of the technique including a number of limitations that have been identified. Section 8 is a review of the claims that have been made for the work presented.

2 Inventory Records Overview

Each of the cable segment records can be uniquely identified by a field called the "Transmedia Name", e.g. "COP:PET:U5465599". The prefix preceding the first colon indicates the material of the segment if it was known when the record was created:

- AL: Aluminium.
- COAX: Coaxial.
- COP: Copper.
- FIB: Fibre.
- DATA: Generic or inferred.

Here we are concerned with the metallic d-side network and so will be only be analysing records with the AL, COP, or DATA prefixes that pertain to d-side cables.

Where we have reliable records they can be used to calculate the proportion of AL to COP d-side segments. Assuming that the incidence of DATA records occurs at random on aggregate then a reasonable prior belief is that a similar proportion of those records are in fact aluminium cables, knowledge of the presence of this population of aluminium legs has the potential to influence the technology chosen to deliver broadband connections and influence the success of investment in network uplift.

We can gain an overall impression of the aggregate error between records estimates of circuit loss and empirical Hlog (insertion loss of signal in the circuit) estimates from the histogram of the residual difference between these values as a ratio to the d-side records loss:

We can see from Fig. 2 that this distribution is not normally distributed around 0 as you would expect if the records estimates were accurate and the difference would be purely due to BPV. We can note three interesting features of this graph:

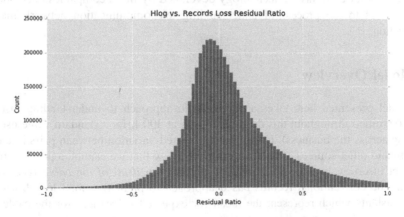

Fig. 2. Histogram of (Hlog Loss − Records Loss) /(D-side Loss)

- The mode is slightly negative which suggests d-side losses are usually slightly better than records suggest. A fact we now believe to be accounted for by the 0.5 Cu cable constant being incorrect (was 11.47 instead of 10.5).
- The bulk of records are between -0.2 and 0.2 which could be due to normal BPV.
- There is a considerable right skew which can be explained by d-side losses calculated incorrectly due to generic/inferred cables being labelled as 0.5 Cu instead of 0.5–0.8 Al.

3   Related Work

Bayesian networks have been well described by a number of authors and popularised by Heckerman and Wellman [4]. A comprehensive and accessible description is provided in relation to the Trueskill system [5] by Bishop [2]. Trueskill was used to evaluate the relative ranking of video game players in the Microsoft x-box 360 gaming system ensuring that prior information about player performance was properly used to generate rankings. Applications of Bayesian Networks to domains more analogous to the Cable Belief Networks application can be found in Cyr et al. [3] where a description of using a Bayesian network to unify beliefs from two fragmentary databases in order to assess forest fire risk is given. We note that whereas CBN is used to understand the probability of individual records being correct and to estimate individual material probabilities Cyr et al.'s paper describes using the technique to generate overall estimates.

Steinder and Sethi [7] describe applying Bayesian networks in the context of telecommunication networks to estimate the probability of faults being embedded in particular elements of a network based on the combination of data from across the infrastructure, but does not describe inventory repair or bearer inference. In the commercial world Gamalon is a start-up company in Boston which uses Bayesian program synthesis to generate mechanisms for repairing mistakes in retailers inventory records by combining various data sources, and Tamr is a start-up company which uses statistical machine learning to generate decision rules that repair corrupted data in databases. In neither case has the technology developed by these companies been adapted to or applied to the process of understanding telecommunication network material composition.

4   Model Overview

The model presented here takes a probabilistic approach to understanding insertion losses (assumed throughout this document to be at 300 kHz, a standard value used for planning across the business). Given the engineered variation between pairs in a cable segment and other sources of noise or error we know that we cannot, a priori, estimate the exact insertion loss for an individual circuit *even if all of the cable records are correct*. The conventional records based approach to predicting total loss L uses the cable constants which represent the mean (or expected value) loss for the cable C in addition to the drop wire estimate (which we mean here to include internal wiring also) D and splitter loss of 0.2 dB:

$$L = \sum_{i=0}^{n} E[C_i] + E[D] + 0.2 \tag{1}$$

We can rewrite Eq. (1) to provide an estimator for the distribution of losses for an individual cable given the other cables on the route and a total loss measurement:

$$\hat{C}_j = L - D - 0.2 - \sum_{i=0}^{n} I_{i \neq j} \cdot C_i \tag{2}$$

Note that if you simply tried to estimate the loss of a cable using the point estimates then you would ascribe all of the discrepancy in loss to that single cable. As such we replace the point estimates with distributions to reflect the fact that we are uncertain about the values we are using to estimate the cable loss under consideration. We can express this relationship between circuits and the cables as a Bayes Network (or Belief Network) graphical model as shown in Fig. 3.

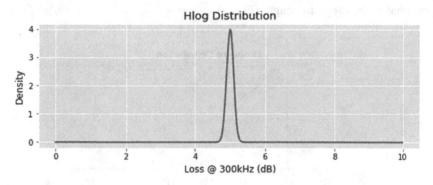

Fig. 3. An example loss distribution for a Hlog measurement.

In the context of analysing the types of cables we can fix the estimates (or distributions) of the nodes representing the loss measurements and dropwire losses and perform inference on the cable nodes. Below we describe the implementation of the representations and inference technique used to perform the cable type analysis. This also attempts to utilise the domain specific knowledge and intuitions we have about the d-side cable network and the uncertainty we have about various aspects of it:

- Cables have a predictable amount of variation between pairs.
- Cables can be one of a limited number of material gauge combinations.
- Hlog loss estimates are limited by the accuracy of the measurement equipment.
- Dropwire estimates exclude the internal wiring of a premise.

Because we have prior knowledge of these components we can select probability distributions that reflect these beliefs.

5   Cable Analysis Implementation

5.1   Hlog Measurements

Hlog loss measurements, **k,** are provided as exact point estimates using quantile regression on VDSL Hlog data calibrated to the CPE and DSLAM vendor. However to reflect that the input data is only provided to a resolution of 0.1 dB we represent the small degree of uncertainty in this measurement by modelling the loss **L** using a Gaussian distribution with a standard deviation of 0.1 (Fig. 3).

5.2   Dropwire Estimates

Dropwire estimates, **d,** are conventionally produced by using the straight line or Manhattan distance between the DP and the premise depending on the type of DP. As such they usually represent a lower bound on the dropwire loss given that they do not attempt to account for internal wiring. To represent this uncertainty we model the dropwire loss D using a rectified (i.e. one half of) Gaussian with a standard deviation proportional to the dropwire length (Fig. 4).

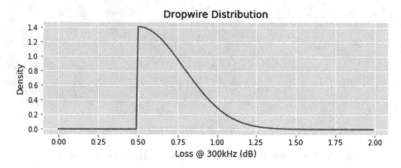

Fig. 4. An example loss distribution for a dropwire estimate.

5.3   Cable Segments

The conventional records based approach to estimating the loss for a cable uses an average loss per kilometre figure called the cable constant. In reality the different pairs in a segment have different losses due to twisting effects. For example, for a cable segment of 100 m in length we would expect the loss distributions for the different cable types to look like this:

By using weighted sums of these probability distributions (Fig. 5) we can represent a loss distribution of a cable segment whose material and gauge we are uncertain about.

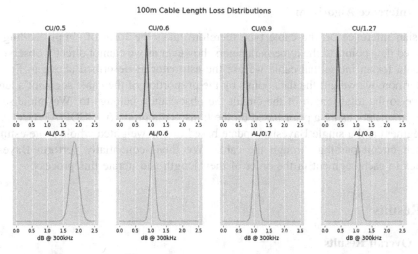

Fig. 5. Example loss distributions for a cable 100 m long for each of the different material and gauge combinations using Gaussian (normal) distributions.

For a given cable of a certain type we model the uncertainty caused by between pair variance using a Gaussian distribution with a mean and standard deviation proportional to the length of the cable segment as per the records cable constant figure giving the standard deviation a value of 5% of the mean (an approximate figure derived from empirical measurements on long lines).

As described above, each cable segment is modelled as a mixture of Gaussians (Fig. 6), where the weights reflect our beliefs as to which cable type the segment actually is made from. Since we are using Bayesian inference to update our beliefs of the cable types we use a Dirichlet-Multinomial variable to model the mixture weights.

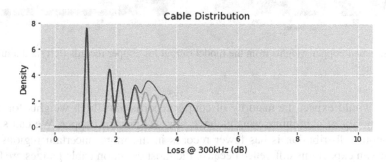

Fig. 6. Example of a mixture distribution representing the belief that the cable could equally be any of the different cable types.

5.4   Inference Algorithm

Bayesian inference on the cable type therefore takes the form of simply adding the observed data points to the hyperparameters, however as we cannot directly observe the loss data for an individual cable we use the estimator as described above in Eq. (2). Furthermore we weight the data points by the proportion of the cable segment's length relative to the total length of the circuit the observation belongs to. We initialise the hyperparameters using a prior based on the transmedia prefix (i.e. COP/AL/DATA) of the segment and a single Bayesian update based on the weighted whole route estimate of each circuit passing through the cable. We then sequentially perform Bayesian updates to each segment in the order of their length and iterate this process.

6   Results

6.1   Overall Results

A number of validation exercises were undertaken using data resources and expert opinion. These studies established confidence in the technique such that it was possible to conduct field inspections validating the performance and behaviour of the algorithm.

The first validation exercise was to compare the output of the model to the subset of our cable data with material labels. Figure 7 below shows the sum of copper weights for each of these categories:

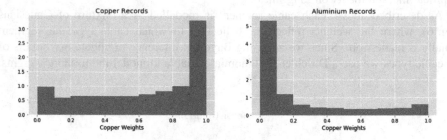

Fig. 7. Summed copper weights from the model output for copper records (left) and aluminium records (right).

As we would expect the majority of copper records have high weights for copper and the majority of aluminium weights have low weights for copper. We can see that the aluminium distribution is has fewer records in the more uncertain regions. Intuitively we can expect this difference because the most common cable gauges are 0.5 for both types of material. In the aluminium case 0.5/Al is the furthest cable type in terms of loss characteristics from the copper types, however 0.5/Cu is the closest copper cable type to the aluminium. Therefore data pointing towards 0.5/Cu is more likely to produce some aluminium weighting than data pointing to 0.5/Al would produce copper weighting.

6.2 South West Regional Inspection

Engineers visited the following 26 cable segments in the South West region to take loop resistance measurements to compare against the output of the algorithm (note that this was not a random sample and these segments were selected to demonstrate properties of the model performance). The primary use cases for the model with respect to repairing our inventory records were:

- Cables labelled as aluminium because an old cable has been replaced at some point and the records have not been updated.
- Generic or inferred cable records that are assumed to be copper.

The results are shown in Table 1. In terms of the material of the cables we can see that amongst the 8 segments labelled as aluminium that 5 of the records were incorrect (although one of these is 0.4/Cu which is functionally equivalent to 0.5/Al). Out of the 4 cables that turned out to be 0.5/Cu in reality the model correctly predicted (i.e. the sum of the copper weights was greater than the aluminium weights) 3 of them and was uncertain about the 4th. This suggests that the model is a good way to repair these potentially outdated records.

Table 1. Model output on the case study segments showing the relative weights (i.e. the expected values of the Dirichlet prior of each cable's mixture distribution).

	Samples	Al/0.5	0.6	0.7	0.8	Cu/0.5	0.6	0.9	1.27	???	Record	Measured	Al	Cu	Record	Material	Gauge
1	11	0.01	0.12	0.29	0.29	0.28	0.00	0.00	0.00	0.00	0.5/Al	0.5/Al	0.12	0.28	X	X	
2	2	0.45	0.21	0.21	0.10	0.02	0.00	0.00	0.00	0.00	0.5/Al	0.4/Cu*	0.97	0.02	X	X	X
3	6	0.00	0.00	0.01	0.04	0.94	0.00	0.00	0.00	0.00	0.5/Al	0.5/Cu	0.06	0.94		X	X
4	5	0.00	0.10	0.25	0.31	0.34	0.00	0.00	0.00	0.00	0.5/Al	0.5/Al	0.66	0.34	X	X	
5	14	0.03	0.17	0.26	0.33	0.21	0.00	0.00	0.00	0.00	0.8/Al	0.8/Al	0.79	0.21	X	X	X
6	2	0.00	0.03	0.06	0.12	0.78	0.00	0.00	0.00	0.00	0.5/Al	0.5/Cu	0.22	0.78		X	X
7	9	0.00	0.01	0.04	0.09	0.86	0.00	0.00	0.00	0.00	0.5/Al	0.5/Cu	0.14	0.86		X	X
8	6	0.00	0.08	0.22	0.25	0.45	0.00	0.00	0.00	0.00	0.5/Al	0.5/Cu	0.55	0.45			X
9	2	0.00	0.00	0.00	0.00	0.41	0.59	0.00	0.00	0.00	0.5/Cu Generic	0.5/Cu	0.00	1.00	X	X	
10	12	0.99	0.01	0.00	0.00	0.00	0.00	0.00	0.00	0.00	0.5/Cu Generic	0.5/Al	1.00	0.00		X	X
11	2	0.02	0.03	0.03	0.06	0.46	0.19	0.18	0.03	0.00	0.5/Cu Generic	0.5/Cu	0.13	0.87	X	X	
12	16	0.00	0.00	0.01	0.03	0.15	0.24	0.57	0.00	0.00	0.5/Cu Generic	0.5/Cu	0.03	0.96	X	X	
13	6	0.12	0.04	0.02	0.02	0.15	0.01	0.04	0.60	0.00	0.5/Cu Generic	0.5/Cu	0.20	0.80	X	X	
14	2	0.00	0.00	0.00	0.00	0.01	0.97	0.02	0.00	0.00	0.5/Cu Generic	0.5/Cu	0.00	1.00	X	X	
15	10	0.52	0.12	0.06	0.06	0.21	0.02	0.01	0.00	0.00	0.5/Cu Generic	0.5/Cu	0.76	0.24	X		
16	20	0.97	0.03	0.00	0.00	0.00	0.00	0.00	0.00	0.00	0.5/Cu Generic	0.5/Al	1.00	0.00		X	X
17	4	0.00	0.00	0.00	0.01	0.50	0.22	0.26	0.00	0.00	0.5/Cu Generic	0.5/Cu	0.01	0.99	X	X	X
18	7	0.00	0.00	0.01	0.10	0.40	0.37	0.12	0.00	0.00	0.5/Cu Generic	0.5/Cu	0.11	0.89	X	X	X
19	5	0.00	0.00	0.00	0.01	0.94	0.05	0.00	0.00	0.00	0.5/Cu Generic	0.5/Cu	0.01	0.99	X	X	X
20	1	0.01	0.00	0.00	0.00	0.00	0.00	0.00	0.00	0.98	0.5/Cu Generic	0.63/Cu	0.01	0.00			
21	9	0.64	0.00	0.00	0.00	0.00	0.00	0.00	0.00	0.36	0.5/Cu Generic	0.4/Cu*	0.64	0.00		X	X
22	18	0.80	0.12	0.03	0.02	0.03	0.00	0.00	0.00	0.00	0.5/Cu Generic	0.5/Cu	0.96	0.04	X		
23	4	0.00	0.00	0.00	0.00	0.00	0.16	0.37	0.46	0.00	0.5/Cu Generic	0.5/Cu	0.00	1.00	X	X	
24	8	0.00	0.00	0.00	0.00	0.01	0.35	0.63	0.01	0.00	0.5/Cu Generic	0.5/Cu	0.00	1.00	X	X	
25	3	0.00	0.00	0.00	0.00	0.05	0.91	0.04	0.00	0.00	0.5/Cu Inferred	0.5/Cu	0.00	1.00	X	X	
26	5	0.00	0.01	0.02	0.03	0.11	0.13	0.68	0.01	0.00	0.5/Cu Inferred	0.5/Cu	0.06	0.94	X	X	

Amongst the generic cable records 3 turned out to be incorrect and the model correctly predicted all of these. However the model made 2 false positive predictions which suggests some care must be taken as to which predictions are to be used to alter these records. It is encouraging to observe that at least 1 of these false positives would be filtered out by taking only predictions with very high weights.

In terms of predicting both the material and gauge we can see that in the case study examples the model has a tendency to be overly optimistic in predicting higher gauge copper. The reasons that flaws in the input data can cause this behaviour are discussed below.

7   Evaluation

Here we describe some of the vulnerabilities that the model faces because of common problems in the input data and the mitigating techniques we use within the model or as a post-processing filter on the use of the results.

7.1   Address Matching Error

One of the most basic and damaging issues is the potential for a customer to be matched to the wrong premise in our records. This means that the Hlog measurement is ascribed to completely the wrong premise and as a consequence has the wrong route corrupting the analysis of these cables. Within the model we have mitigated this problem by using 'phantom' cable types with a wide variance to capture when a Hlog measurement is above or below the expected losses from the plausible combinations of cable types on the given route. For those values that lie within the plausible range there is very little we can do from within the model, except hope that other data points drown out the rogue data or hope that it is a sparse data point we can filter out, see 'Sparse Data' below.

7.2   Incorrect/Badly Inferred Routes

Optimising the parameters of a model that doesn't reflect the reality on the ground is clearly a pointless pursuit, however when the routes are wrong (in the most extreme cases completely wrong as in the address matching above) this is exactly what we're doing. The common instance of this problem is due to inferred cable routes. This is when we didn't have records for the cables but knew there are ducts and customers and so we inferred (guessed) the route and, and as in the case of generic cables, assumed they were 0.5 gauge copper.

Unsurprisingly this process was not perfect. The problem usually manifests itself in inferred cables and routes that actually take a longer path than in reality (one example is shown in Fig. 8). This phantom length then makes the measured Hlog values appear more optimistic (from our perspective) than the reality. For the short d-side circuits this can even take the Hlog values out of the plausible range and be caught by the phantom cable type (helping us potentially spot where the worst of these problems exist in the records) but in other cases it may just make, for example, a 0.5 gauge copper cable look like a 0.9 gauge.

To mitigate this problem we currently filter out inferred cabling showing higher gauge copper in the record updates. We allow inferred cables to take aluminium values because it's much more difficult for this problem to manifest itself as a route length that is shorter than the reality.

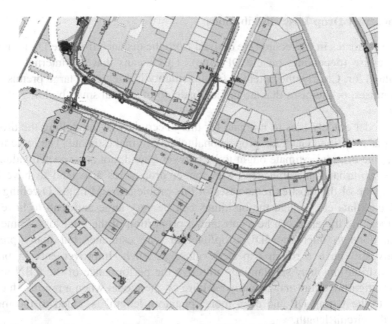

Fig. 8. Example of an incorrectly inferred route adding 'phantom length' from a case study.

7.3 Sparse Data

For some cable segments we may only have one circuit passing through with a VDSL Hlog measurement. This occurs most often as you get deeper into the d-side network and in rural areas. The danger in these circumstances is that the variation of one circuit and/or the records errors concerning lengths and drop wire estimates means that the algorithm may give a reasonably "confident" false positive for a cable type, for example if the dropwire was substantially underestimated then the model will infer that a copper cable looks like an aluminium cable. We can see that a similar problem occurred in case study 20 but the sample was sufficiently far from the plausible truth the model flagged it up as anomalous – indicating a different kind of record error.

Currently simplest way to mitigate this problem is to only use inferred cable types that have more than one circuit passing through them to provide a higher level of confidence in the results. In the future improvements in analysing cable lengths, routes, and drop/internal wiring estimates could encode the appropriate uncertainty in the model to deal with this issue.

Another kind of sparse data problem is when there are cable segments in a sequence without any observations between them, but may be different materials and/or gauges. In this case the segments will effectively operate as one segment and appear as a weighted average of the two cable characteristics.

7.4   Incorrect Drop Loss Distributions

Dropwire estimates in the records are derived from the distance from the DP to the edge of the premise (depending on the DP type). This means that the internal wiring is unaccounted for. Clearly, the potential for uncertainty is greater for large premises than small premises, or premises that are in fact made up of several small building clustered together.

The model crudely tries to mitigate for this uncertainty by modelling the dropwire estimates as a rectified Gaussian proportional to the original estimate. The logic for this is that (1) the original estimate ought to be a lower bound, not an expected value. And (2) more sub-urban and rural areas with longer drop wires also tend to have larger premises. One of the most extreme cases of this problem are Multiple Dwelling Units (MDUs, e.g. flats etc.) where the buildings can be very large and tend to have short d-sides meaning the error can be a substantial proportion of the total loss. Some work has been done to improve MDU drop/internal wire estimates but many premises essentially still have a rough expected value. As such, Improvements in premise specific distributions may substantially improve the performance of the CBN model.

This mitigating effort may actually backfire on the model when a premise has been matched to the wrong DP and even more 'phantom length' is added to the model's view of the circuit length.

8   Conclusion

The provision of broadband services is extremely important for the UK [1] and the delivery of the best network that can be obtained for a given investment in a given time could enhance the environmental, financial and social well-being of people that live there. The work presented here showed that there was an opportunity to identify and repair the inventory of network links in the broadband network and described an approach to do this.

These techniques have been successfully applied vs a national network and are now in production. By combining Bayesian modelling, priors from legacy data and large scale telemetry data this work shows how state of the art machine learning can have a significant societal impact. The limitations of the work relate to uncertainty in the real world data available in this practical setting, it is encouraging to note both the interesting approaches to mitigating these and the many opportunities for similar applications in other settings.

References

1. POSTnote 494: UK Broadband Infrastructure, The Parliamentary Office of Science and Technology, May 2015. http://researchbriefings.files.parliament.uk/documents/POST-PN-0494/POST-PN-0494.pdf. Accessed July 2017
2. Bishop, C.M.: A new framework for machine learning. In: Zurada, J.M., Yen, G.G., Wang, J. (eds.) WCCI 2008. LNCS, vol. 5050, pp. 1–24. Springer, Heidelberg (2008). https://doi.org/10.1007/978-3-540-68860-0_1

3. Cyr, D., Gauthier, S., Etheridge, D.A., Kayahara, G.J., Bergeron, Y.: A simple Bayesian Belief Network for estimating the proportion of old-forest stands in the Clay Belt of Ontario using the provincial forest inventory. Can. J. For. Res. **40**(3), 573–584 (2010)
4. Heckerman, D., Wellman, M.P.: Bayesian networks. Commun. ACM **38**(3), 27–31 (1995)
5. Herbrich, R., Minka, T., Graepel, T.: TrueSkill™: a Bayesian skill rating system. In: Advances in Neural Information Processing Systems, pp. 569–576 (2007)
6. Pearl, J.: Probabilistic Reasoning in Intelligent Systems: Networks of Plausible Inference. Representation and Reasoning Series. Morgan Kaufmann, San Mateo (1988). ISBN 0-934 613-73-7
7. Steinder, M., Sethi, A.S.: Probabilistic fault localization in communication systems using belief networks. IEEE/ACM Trans. Netw. **12**(5), 809–822 (2004)
8. Zhao, T., Nehorai, A.: Distributed sequential Bayesian estimation of a diffusive source in wireless sensor networks. IEEE Trans. Signal Process. **55**(4), 1511–1524 (2007)

AI for Healthcare

Towards the Integration of Prescription Analytics into Health Policy and General Practice

Brian Cleland[1]([✉]), Jonathan Wallace[1], Raymond Bond[1],
Michaela Black[1], Maurice Mulvenna[1], Deborah Rankin[1],
and Austin Tanney[2]

[1] Ulster University, Coleraine, Northern Ireland, UK
{b.cleland, jg.wallace, rb.bond, mm.black,
md.mulvenna}@ulster.ac.uk
[2] Analytics Engines, Belfast, Northern Ireland, UK
a.tanney@analyticsengines.com

Abstract. The phenomenon of big data and data analytics is impacting many sectors, including healthcare. Practical examples of the application of big data to health policy and health service delivery remain scarce, however. In this paper, which summarises findings from an ongoing research project, we explore the potential for applying data analytics and anomaly detection to open data in order to support improved policy design and to enable better clinical decisions in primary care. The policy context of mental health in Northern Ireland is described, and its importance as a public health issue is explained. Based on previous work, it is proposed that depression prevalence is a mediating factor between economic deprivation and antidepressant prescribing. This hypothesis is tested by analysing a variety of open datasets. The methodology is described, including datasets used, the data processing pipeline, and analysis tools. The results are presented, identifying correlations between the three main variables, and highlighting anomalies in the data. The findings are discussed and implications and opportunities for further research are described.

Keywords: Health policy · Data analytics · Big data · Prescribing · Prevalence · Deprivation

1 Introduction

The increasing impact of data analytics on industry and society is often discussed under the banner of "big data". Just as the growth of data analytics has impacted many economic sectors, so healthcare is being transformed by this phenomenon [1, 14, 29]. In 2016, the UK House of Commons noted that big data had "huge unrealised potential, both as a driver of productivity and as a way of offering better products and services to citizens" [12]. Nevertheless, with the exception of some public health surveillance [5, 31] and pharmacovigilance systems [33], exploration of the application of big data to health policy and service delivery remains limited.

© Springer International Publishing AG 2017
M. Bramer and M. Petridis (Eds.): SGAI-AI 2017, LNAI 10630, pp. 193–206, 2017.
https://doi.org/10.1007/978-3-319-71078-5_18

This paper will present a summary of work to date on an ongoing research project exploring the application of data analytics and machine learning techniques to policy development and service delivery. Specifically, it will examine how open data from various different sources - including antidepressant prescribing data, depression prevalence data and economic deprivation data - can be integrated and analysed in order to provide actionable information for primary care clinicians and public health policy-makers.

2   Related Work

2.1   Mental Health Policy in Northern Ireland

In Northern Ireland, as in other parts of the UK [26] mental health has been identified as a priority policy area for service provision. In a report produced for the Northern Ireland Assembly, Betts and Thompson [4] state that mental illness is the single largest cause of ill health and disability. They note that 318 suicides were registered in NI during 2015, the highest since records began in 1970 and a 19% increase on the suicides recorded in 2014. The report refers to calls for a ten-year regional mental health strategy and a mental health champion to lead work across government departments. Specific policy challenges identified by the authors include the need for more personalised models of care, the need to address stigmas around mental health, improved access to services and more GP training. The study also notes that Northern Ireland is also lagging in the provision of psychological therapies such as psychotherapy, cognitive behavioural therapy (CBT), and trauma therapy.

Factors that particularly impact mental health policy in Northern Ireland include:

- **Higher rates of mental health issues than the rest of the UK** - According to the Department of Health, Social Services and Public Safety, Northern Ireland has a 25% higher prevalence of mental illness compared to England.
- **Lower levels of public spending on health services** - In Northern Ireland health services account for 19.7% of the public budget, in comparison with 22% in England, 20.4% in Scotland, and 20.3% in Wales [16].
- **Higher levels of suicide** - According to Office of National Statistics figures (2016), suicide rates in Northern Ireland are 16.4 per 100,000 population. The equivalent rates in England, Wales and Scotland are 10.3, 9.2 and 15.4.
- **Post-Conflict Factors** - Mental health-related issues in Northern Ireland may be due at least in part to the historical conflict [6]. Some authors have suggested that the traumatic impacts of the conflict can be passed from generation to generation [3].
- **Economic Factors** - In Northern Ireland, the number of economically inactive adults is 28.4% - 5% above the UK average [27].

2.2   Antidepressant Prescribing in Northern Ireland

In a report on mental health in Northern Ireland, the Mental Health Foundation [21] states that "According to prescribing trends, Northern Ireland has significantly higher levels of depression than the rest of the UK." This statement assumes that prescribing data can be used as an indicator for underlying health phenomena, and more specifically, that antidepressant prescribing in particular reflects levels of depression in the wider population. This use of prescribing data as a proxy variable for the prevalence of mental illness is not limited to this particular report.

Another example of this assumption being adopted is a pair of studies looking at mental health impacts and burdens in Northern Ireland using administrative data [17, 18]. In these analyses, prescribing and other forms of administrative data, such as social and economic indicators and life event data, are used to determine the effect on mental health of factors such as deprivation, bereavement, care-giving and transition into care. Findings from these studies suggest that the impact on the mental health of individuals of such circumstances are very significant. The authors also found that prescribing rates varied widely between GP practices, although they speculate that this might be explained by differences in practice population composition or levels of deprivation in the practice area.

Another interesting, non-academic, analysis of the same subject using similar data sources was published by the Detail Data [19]. This data journalism piece points out that compared with a major international study by the OECD, antidepressant usage in Northern Ireland is significantly higher than any of the 23 countries surveyed [19]. Antidepressant prescription rates in Northern Ireland stand at 129 daily doses per thousand, compared with the overall UK figure of 72 daily doses per thousand. The authors also demonstrate that there was a strong correlation between economic deprivation and levels of antidepressant usage. Interestingly, their analysis shows that depression prevalence is not correlated with either economic deprivation or antidepressant prescribing. When asked what factors might be behind increasing levels of antidepressant prescribing, GPs point to growing public awareness and patient demand as a driver.

2.3   Summary of Northern Ireland Mental Health Policy

Looking at mental health in Northern Ireland, it is clear that the region has important challenges in this area, and there are some very specific political, social and economic factors that must be taken into account. The burden of mental health issues in Northern Ireland is significantly greater than in other parts of the UK. While the region experiences higher rates of suicide and illnesses such as depression and anxiety, it is also faced with lower levels of public spending on health compared to other parts of the UK. There has been some use of administrative data to try to understand the policy implications of issues in Northern Ireland. Such studies have attempted to illustrate the impact of factors such as economic deprivation and bereavement on illnesses such as depression and anxiety. In some of these studies prescribing rates have been used as a proxy variable for mental health issues. There is some evidence, however, that the link between prescribing and prevalence is not straightforward.

3 Methodology

3.1 The Hypothesis

Much of the literature on the use of prescribing data as a proxy for public health suggests that the correlation between disease prevalence and prescribing is sufficiently strong to make such analyses useful in the development of public policy [10, 11]. Based on this assumption, a number of studies have examined the correlation between economic deprivation and prescribing and used this to propose that economic factors have a measurable impact on mental health. We argue that these studies contain an implicit assumption that *depression prevalence is a mediating factor in the relationship between economic deprivation and antidepressant prescribing* (see Fig. 1). There is, however, some evidence that the link between disease prevalence and prescribing levels is not straightforward or reliable [16].

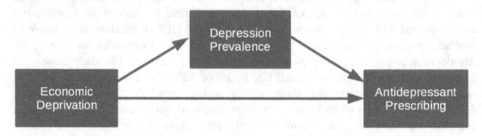

Fig. 1. Hypothesis: mental health is a mediating factor linking economic deprivation and antidepressant prescribing.

In this study, we will be testing the hypothesis presented in Fig. 1 by using open data drawn from multiple publicly available sources. Specifically, we will examine the links between three major variables - economic deprivation, depression prevalence and antidepressant prescribing - in order to explore the correlations between them. We will also be examining the data for anomalies in depression prevalence and antidepressant prescribing, which may present opportunities to apply machine learning methods to mental health policy development in Northern Ireland.

3.2 Datasets

Antidepressant Prescribing Data. Antidepressant prescribing data was downloaded from the Open Data NI portal, operated by the Northern Ireland Department of Finance. For the purposes of this study, only data for October 2016 was used. In order to provide a direct comparison with international figures, it was necessary to classify the data according to the international Anatomical Therapeutic Chemical (ATC) Classification System. Since UK prescribing data is encoded using the British National Foundry (BNF) standard, each drug had to be re-classified. This was done using a dataset provided by NHS Dictionary of Medicines and Devices (dm + d). Classifying the data according to the ATC system also allowed prescribing levels to be compared across different drugs. This was done using a "defined daily dose" (DDD), defined by the World Health Organisation as "the assumed average maintenance dose per day for a drug used for its main indication in adults".

Economic Deprivation Data. The metric for economic deprivation used in this study was the Multiple Deprivation Measure (MDM), which is published by the Northern Ireland Statistics and Research Agency (NISRA). Unlike in other parts of the UK, individual GP practice data does not include deprivation measures. In order to link GP practices to the MDM data, the postcode for each practice was obtained from the Detail Data portal, an open data resource provided by the Northern Ireland Council for Voluntary Action. The online MySociety Mapit service was then used to convert the postcode data into super output areas (SOA). By linking each practice to a specific SOA we could then assign a deprivation measure for each prescriber, based on the data supplied by NISRA. While deprivation measures are available for other geographic boundaries, super output areas were chosen due to their relatively high granularity and stability compared to other boundaries such as electoral wards.

Depression Prevalence Data. Depression prevalence data, that is the number of patients per 1000 diagnosed as suffering from depression, is available across most of the UK under the Quality Outcomes Framework (QOF), a collection of data which is designed to measure GP performance in order to support GP payments. In Northern Ireland the QOF data no longer includes disease prevalence figures, but fortunately these are still published separately by the Department of Health. Since the prevalence data is linked directly to GP practice identifiers, it allows for a direct comparison between the number of patients being diagnosed with depression and the amount of antidepressants being prescribed.

3.3   Data Analytics Tools and Pipeline

Microsoft Excel was used to view each dataset and to do basic cleaning and validation. For the formal analysis, Jupyter Notebooks using were used to algorithmically restructure, transform and merge datasets were required. Pandas and NumPy were used for the statistical analysis. Visualisation of the data was also done through Jupyter Notebooks using MatPlotLib and Seaborn for charts and graphs and iPyLeaflet for maps. Correlations between the key variables were explored using Pearson correlations and p-values.

A major challenge of the study was identifying, cleaning and integrating multiple datasets from diverse open data sources. This involved the assembly of a "data pipeline" that could be tracked and audited, and was capable of bringing together heterogeneous datasets in a way that allowed them to be meaningfully compared and analysed using the analytics stack defined above. The resulting process is outlined in Fig. 2.

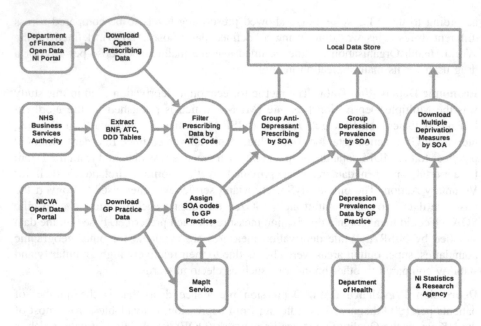

Fig. 2. Data flow diagram illustrating the main data sources and data processing activities.

3.4   Results

Correlation Between Prescribing and Deprivation. The analysis showed that there was strong correlation ($r = 0.51$) between levels of antidepressant prescribing and the multiple deprivation measure for each practice (see Fig. 3). Two outlying points are

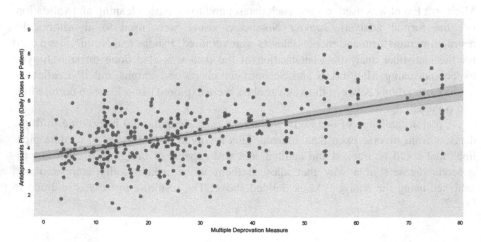

Fig. 3. Chart showing a strong correlation between antidepressant prescribing (daily doses per patient) and multiple deprivation measure for each GP practice.

also visible, which show high levels of antidepressant prescribing relative to the level of deprivation. These anomalies are examined in more detail in the discussion (Sect. 3).

Correlation Between Prevalence and Deprivation. The analysis showed that there was a weak correlation ($r = 0.12$) between the prevalence of depression among patients of a given GP practice and the multiple deprivation measure for the area in which the practice resides (see Fig. 4).

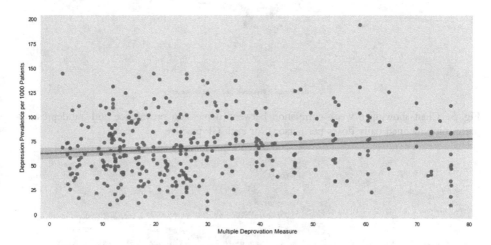

Fig. 4. Chart showing a weak correlation between depression prevalence and multiple deprivation measure for each GP practice.

Correlation Between Prevalence and Prescribing. The analysis showed that there was a weak correlation ($r = 0.15$) between the prevalence of depression among patients of a given GP practice and the multiple deprivation measure for the area in which the practice resides (see Fig. 5). From the chart it can be seen that some anomalies exist. Specifically, there is a single practice in the top right of the chart which demonstrates exceptionally high levels on depression prevalence, and a cluster of practices in the lower right which combine relatively low levels of prevalence with high levels of prescribing. These outliers are explored in more detail in the discussion (Sect. 3).

Variability in Prescribing and Prevalence. One of the interesting phenomena that can be seen from the data is the high variability in antidepressant prescribing and depression prevalence among GP practices that are located either closely together or on the same site. This can be seen more clearly if we focus on a specific area, such as Belfast (see map-based visualisations Figs. 6 and 7, and box plot in Fig. 8). This suggests that local differences in social or economic deprivation may not be able to account for much of the variation in diagnosing and prescribing behaviours.

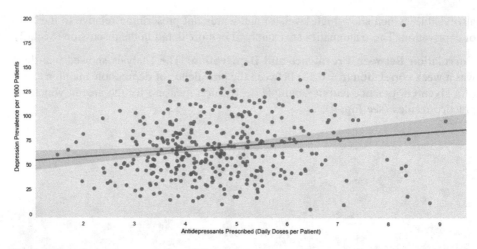

Fig. 5. Chart showing a weak correlation between depression prevalence and antidepressant prescribing (defined daily doses per person) for each GP practice.

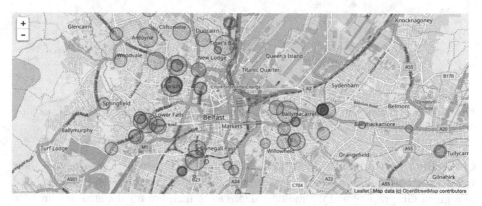

Fig. 6. Map showing relative levels of antidepressant prescribing for GP practices in Belfast (radius of circle is proportional to defined daily doses per patient).

Fig. 7. Map showing relative levels of depression prevalence for GP practices in Belfast (radius of circle is proportional to depression prevalence per 1000 patients per practice)

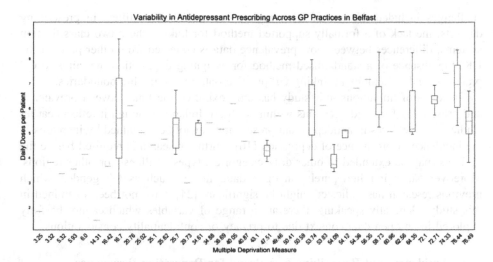

Fig. 8. Box plot illustrating variability in prescribing levels across GP practices in Belfast.

4 Summary and Discussion

4.1 Summary of Main Findings

The issue of relatively greater incidence of mental health issues in Northern Ireland compared to other parts of the UK remains an important public health challenge in the region. Numerous studies have pointed to a range of factors that might be impacting the prevalence of such illnesses. Some studies have noted the higher levels of antidepressant prescribing compared to other countries and have suggested that there is a link between such prescribing rates and underlying mental health issues. These links are not well proven or understood, however, and require further investigation.

This study explored correlations between three main variables - economic deprivation, depression prevalence and antidepressant prescribing - based on open GP prescribing data. The results showed that while there was a strong correlation between economic deprivation and antidepressant prescribing, the correlations between deprivation and prevalence and between prevalence and prescribing were weak. We therefore propose that the hypothesis that depression is a mediating factor between deprivation and prescribing is not supported by the available data. Moreover, the lack of a clear link between depression prevalence and prescribing rates suggest that the clinical basis for increased antidepressant prescribing requires further investigation.

4.2 Challenges and Limitations of the Study

The major challenges for the study to date have been in identifying, integrating and analysing open datasets from diverse sources. Data provided by the public sector in Northern Ireland differs in a number of ways from that provided in other parts of the UK, or by other nations, which makes valid comparisons more difficult. Specific challenges included the use of BNF as opposed to ATC identifiers in prescribing datasets, the lack of a formally supported method for linking these two classification systems, differences between how prevalence data is collected from other parts of the UK, the absence of a standardised method for assigning deprivation measures to GP practices, and difficulties in linking GP practice data to geographic boundaries.

In terms of limitations, this study has only explored the link between prevalence and prescribing for antidepressants within Northern Ireland, although it reflects earlier studies that increases in antidepressant prescribing cannot be explained by increases in the incidence of prevalence of depression [16]. Further research is required before the findings may be extended to other drug categories, types of illness, or other regions. Moreover, since it relied purely on open data, factors such as GP gender, which previous research has indicated might be significant [24], have not been examined in this study. Generally speaking, there are a range of variables which cannot be fully explored in an open data context due to privacy or confidentiality considerations.

4.3 Antidepressant Prescribing as a Proxy for Depression Prevalence

There has been some exploration within the literature of the validity of using pharmaceutical data as a proxy for measuring clinical conditions in a given population [8, 9, 13]. The arguments in favour of such an approach include that fact that disease prevalence data is often difficult to capture accurately [32], may be inconsistently [8], and in some cases may not be available at all [9]. In such situations, prescribing data, if available, may offer an attractive alternative for studying public health issues. Indeed, some studies have suggested a strong correlation between some antidepressants and clinical diagnoses. Gardarsdottir et al. [10] for example observed that 73% of patients on an SSRI had a diagnosis of depression or anxiety, while Henriksson et al. [11] found that 82% using SSRIs had been diagnosed with depression.

While the case for using pharmaceutical data as a tool for public health surveillance may seem fairly strong, there are a number of important caveats that should be taken into consideration. Firstly, as Henriksson et al. [11] shows, not all drugs are equally strongly correlated with specific illnesses. Many drugs have more than one use, and many antidepressants are used for a wide range of disorders including fibromyalgia, chronic pain, eating disorders, insomnia and migraine [10]. An analysis by Mercier et al. [22] of antidepressant prescribing among French GPs found that 20% of prescriptions are potentially unrelated to any psychiatric condition. The perceived "safety" of SSRIs may exacerbate the tendency towards prescribing for a wider range of conditions [16].

The results of this study show that the link between depression prevalence and antidepressant prescribing is weak. One implication of this is that antidepressant prescribing data cannot be used to be an effective proxy for depression prevalence in Northern Ireland - although it may be that some specific drugs within the overall category of antidepressants are more reliable indicators.

4.4   Understanding the Factors Driving Antidepressant Prescribing

If, as the data suggests, dramatic increases in the levels of antidepressant prescribing are not being motivated by corresponding increases in depression prevalence, the question arises as to what other factors might be behind these trends. A number of studies have attempted to answer this question by interviewing GPs in order to get their perspective on the problem. McDonald et al. [16] proposes that few GPs believe that depression levels has actually risen, and that there were some concerns about whether current prescribing levels were appropriate. When asked to identify factors that were driving the increase in prescribing rates, suggestions included: successful awareness-raising campaigns on depression, the perceived safety of selective serotonin reuptake inhibitors (SSRIs), and a willingness among patients to ask for help. Some clinicians believed that normal human "unhappiness" was being inappropriately interpreted as a medical condition.

Other authors have attempted to examine the problem from the perspective of the patient rather than the clinician. An example of this is Schofield et al. [30], which explores how patient attitudes influence the usage of antidepressants over time. This study found that many patients discontinue medication early due to a complex range of factors, including: symptoms improving or worsening, side-effects or adverse events, social stigma, adverse media coverage and preference for psychological therapies. Interestingly, Schofield et al. [30], and other studies focus on the challenge of getting patients to adhere to treatment [23, 28]. This suggests that patient behaviour will tend to reduce prescription levels over time, possible working against the prescription-increasing factors identified in GP-centred studies.

An alternative explanation is offered by Moore et al. [25], who argue that increasing antidepressant prescribing can be explained by small changes in the numbers of patients undergoing long term treatment, and that the focus on initiation and targeting of antidepressants is misdirected. However, even this explanation would imply that the greater numbers of patients receiving antidepressants should be reflected in a growing number of patients registered as having depression. This link is not supported by the data from our study.

4.5   Prescribing and Prevalence Anomaly Detection

The scatter plots in Figs. 3 and 5 show a number of anomalous data points and clusters. In Fig. 3, there are two outlying points at the top left of the chart, indicating an unusually high level of antidepressant prescribing relative to the deprivation score for those practices. Although both of these practices share a similar deprivation score, they are not geographically closely connected, with one prescriber being based in Belfast and the other over 100 km away. Similarly, Fig. 5 exhibits a single outlier in the top right of the chart, and a cluster of points in the lower right quadrant. The former stands out due to an unusually high level of depression prevalence compared to other practices, while the latter is distinguished by a combination of relatively low depression prevalence and high antidepressant prescribing. Within this cluster of 11 points, 9 are in Belfast, while the other two are in Omagh and Ballymena.

Although it is impossible to say what factors are leading to such anomalies without further research, the presence of these outliers suggests that there may be opportunities to provide useful feedback to both policy-makers and GPs. In the case of policy-makers, this data could be used as the basis for either further investigation, or for targeted interventions or "nudges" [15, 20]. For GPs, direct access to such information may support greater self-awareness and better clinical decisions. The application of automated solutions such as machine learning and data mining to anomaly detection is well established in fields such as security, finance and law enforcement [2, 7]. Similarly, anomalies in health service delivery might in future be automatically identified through the analysis of open data and flagged for human review and intervention.

5 Conclusion

It is well established in Northern Ireland and other parts of the UK that mental health services need greater investment, and that policy-making should target effectiveness and efficiency in the delivery of those services. The growth of data science and big data creates an opportunity to meet some of these needs. In this paper we examined the potential for applying analytics to open prescribing data, disease prevalence data and deprivation in order to enhance policy-making and service delivery. The findings highlight some limitations in such an approach, and in particular they call into question the use of prescribing data as a proxy for public health.

The apparently weak correlation between depression prevalence and antidepressant prescribing also raises important questions about the clinical basis for rising pre-scription rates. This is particularly important in the context of Northern Ireland, where antidepressant prescribing is exceptionally high compared to international norms. Our analysis also demonstrated the existence of anomalous practices in terms of antide-pressant prescribing and depression prevalence, which suggests the potential for tar-geted interventions by the Department of Health, as well as useful feedback for clinicians.

Opportunities for future research exist in automating anomaly detection using statistical or machine learning techniques. While this study has examined correlations with prevalence and antidepressant prescribing as a whole, further investigation is required into individual drug correlations. Finally, useful insights for policy develop-ment might be achieved by combining open data with more granular, non-open datasets such as individual GP and patient information.

References

1. Andreu-Perez, J., Poon, C.C.Y., Merrifield, R.D., Wong, S.T.C., Yang, G.Z.: Big data for health. IEEE J. Biomed. Health Inform. **19**, 1193–1208 (2015). https://doi.org/10.1109/JBHI.2015.2450362
2. Akoglu, L., Tong, H., Koutra, D.: Graph based anomaly detection and description: a survey. Data Mining Knowl. Discov. **29**(3), 626–688 (2015)

3. Bamford Review of Mental Health and Learning Disability: A Vision of a Comprehensive Child and Adolescent Mental Health Service (CAMHs). DHSSPS, Belfast (2006)
4. Betts, J., Thompson, J.: Mental Health in Northern Ireland: Overview, Strategies, Policies, Care Pathways, CAMHS and Barriers to Accessing Services (2017)
5. Birkhead, G.S., Klompas, M., Shah, N.R.: Uses of electronic health records for public health surveillance to advance public health. Annu. Rev. Public Health **36**, 345–359 (2015). https://doi.org/10.1146/annurev-publhealth-031914-122747
6. Bunting, B.P., Murphy, S.D., O'Neill, S.M., Ferry, F.R.: Lifetime prevalence of mental health disorders and delay in treatment following initial onset: evidence from the Northern Ireland Study of Health and Stress. Psychol. Med. **42**(8), 1727–1739 (2011). https://doi.org/10.1017/S0033291711002510
7. Chandola, V., Banerjee, A., Kumar, V.: Anomaly detection: a survey. ACM Comput. Surv. **41**, 1 (2009). https://doi.org/10.1145/1541880.1541882
8. Chini, F., Pezzotti, P., Orzella, L., Borgia, P., Guasticchi, G.: Can we use the pharmacy data to estimate the prevalence of chronic conditions? A comparison of multiple data sources. BMC Public Health **11**, 688 (2011)
9. Cossman, R.E., Cossman, J.S., James, W.L., Blanchard, T., Thomas, R., Pol, L.G., Cosby, A.G.: Correlating pharmaceutical data with a national health survey as a proxy for estimating rural population health. Popul. Health. Metr. **8**, 25 (2010). https://doi.org/10.1186/1478-7954-8-25
10. Gardarsdottir, H., Heerdink, R., van Dijk, L., Egberts, A.: Indications for antidepressant drug prescribing in general practice in the Netherlands. J. Affect. Disord. **98**(1), 109–115 (2007)
11. Henriksson, S., Boëthius, G., Hakansson, J., Isacsson, G.: Indications for and outcome of antidepressant medication in a general population: a prescription database and medical record study in Jämtland county, Sweden, 1995. Acta. Psychiatr. Scand. **108**(6), 427–431 (2016)
12. House of Commons: The Big Data Dilemna (2016). https://www.publications.parliament.uk/pa/cm201516/cmselect/cmsctech/468/46802.htm
13. Huber, C.A., Szucs, T.D., Rapold, R., Reich, O.: Identifying patients with chronic conditions using pharmacy data in Switzerland: an updated mapping approach to the classification of medications. BMC Public Health **13**, 1030 (2013)
14. Krumholz, H.M.: Big data and new knowledge in medicine: the thinking, training, and tools needed for a learning health system. Health. Aff. (Millwood). **33**, 1163–1170 (2014). https://doi.org/10.1377/hlthaff.2014.0053
15. Loewenstein, G., Asch, D.A., Friedman, J.Y., Melichar, L.A., Volpp, K.G.: Can behavioural economics make us healthier? (2012)
16. Macdonald, S., Morrison, J., Maxwell, M., Munoz-Arroyo, R., Power, A., Smith, M., Sutton, M., Wilson, P.: "A coal face option": GPs' perspectives on the rise in antidepressant prescribing. Br. J. Gen. Pract. **59**, e299–e307 (2009)
17. Maguire, A., Hughes, C., Cardwell, C., O'Reilly, D.: Psychotropic medications and the transition into care: a national data linkage study. J. Am. Geriatr. Soc. **61**, 215–221 (2013). https://doi.org/10.1111/jgs.12101
18. Maguire, A., McCann, M., Moriarty, J., O'Reilly, D.: The grief study: using administrative data to understand the mental health impact of bereavement. Eur. J. Public Health. (2014). https://doi.org/10.1093/eurpub/cku165.058
19. McClure, J.: The Script Report (2014). http://script-report.thedetail.tv/
20. Meeker, D., Knight, T.K., Friedberg, M.W., Linder, J.A., Goldstein, N.J., Fox, C.R., Rothfeld, A., Diaz, G., Doctor, J.N.: Nudging guideline-concordant antibiotic prescribing: a randomized clinical trial. JAMA Int. Med. **174**, 425–431 (2014)

21. Mental Health Foundation: Mental Health in NI: Fundamental Facts 2016 (2016). http://www.mentalhealth.org.uk/sites/default/files/FF16%20Northern%20ireland.pdf
22. Mercier, A., Auger-Aubin, I., Lebeau, J.-P., Van Royen, P., Peremans, L.: Understanding the prescription of antidepressants: a qualitative study among french GPs. BMC Family Pract. **12**, 99 (2011)
23. Mitchell, A.J.: Adherence behaviour with psychotropic medication is a form of self-medication. Med. Hypotheses **68**(1), 12–21 (2016)
24. Morrison, J., Anderson, M.-J., Sutton, M., Munoz-Arroyo, R., McDonald, S., Maxwell, M., Power, A., Smith, M., Wilson, P.: Factors influencing variation in prescribing of antidepressants by general practices in Scotland. Br. J. Gen. Pract. **59**, e25–e31 (2009)
25. Moore, M., Yuen, H.M., Dunn, N., Mullee, M.A., Maskell, J., Kendrick, T.: Explaining the rise in antidepressant prescribing: a descriptive study using the general practice research database. BMJ **339**, b3999 (2009). https://doi.org/10.1136/bmj.b3999
26. NHS England: The Five Year Forward View for Mental Health (2016). http://www.england.nhs.uk/wp-content/uploads/2016/02/Mental-Health-Taskforce-FYFV-final.pdf
27. O'Neill, C., McGregor, P., Merkur, S.: United Kingdom (Northern Ireland). Health System Review. Health. Syst. Transit. **14**(10), 1–90 (2012)
28. Pampallona, S., Bollini, P., Tibaldi, G., et al.: Patient adherence in the treatment of depression. Br. J. Psychiatry **180**(2), 104–109 (2002)
29. Rahman, F., Slepian, M.J.: Application of big-data in healthcare analytics #8212; Prospects and challenges. In: 2016 IEEE-EMBS International Conference on Biomedical and Health Informatics (BHI), pp. 13–16 (2016)
30. Schofield, P., Crosland, A., Waheed, W., Aseem, S., Gask, L., Wallace, A., Dickens, A., Tylee, A.: Patients' views of antidepressants: from first experiences to becoming expert. Br. J. Gen. Pract. **61**, e142–e148 (2011)
31. Velasco, E., Agheneza, T., Denecke, K., Kirchner, G., Eckmanns, T.: Social media and internet-based data in global systems for public health surveillance: a systematic review. Milbank Q. **92**, 7–33 (2014). https://doi.org/10.1111/1468-0009.12038
32. Vercambre, M., Gilbert, F.: Respondents in an epidemiologic survey had fewer psychotropic prescriptions than nonrespondents: an insight into health-related selection bias using routine health insurance data. J. Clin. Epidemiol. (2012). https://doi.org/10.1016/j.jclinepi.2012.05.002
33. Yang, M., Kiang, M., Shang, W.: Filtering big data from social media – Building an early warning system for adverse drug reactions. J. Biomed. Inform. **54**, 230–240 (2015). https://doi.org/10.1016/j.jbi.2015.01.011

An Ontology to Support Knowledge Management in Behaviour-Based Healthcare

John Kingston[✉] and Nathaniel Charlton

University of Brighton, Brighton, UK
j.k.kingston@brighton.ac.uk

Abstract. A Do Something Different (DSD) behaviour change programme consists of a series of digitally delivered behavioural prompts, or "Dos", for targeted behaviour change designed to aid people to achieve personal goals or to break bad habits. "Dos" may address for example behaviour connected with exercise, smoking, diet, sleep or diabetes self-management, or personal development objectives such as leadership. DSD's current database contains thousands of such "Dos", developed by behaviour change experts.

We have developed an ontology to organise the large database of behavioural prompts in order to help DSD with its knowledge management. We began by developing an ontology of function, bottom-up; then we expanded this into a multi-perspective ontology covering WHO, WHAT, HOW, WHEN, WHERE and WHY perspectives.

The expected benefits from our ontology are: 1. response data from users can be aggregated by ontology category to get insights into users' behaviour, 2. the ontology enables the implementation of smarter algorithms for selecting which "Dos" to suggest to which users, and 3. the ontology assists in the process of generating new "Dos", either by domain experts or by crowd-sourcing.

Finally we follow an ontology-theoretic approach to argue that our ontology should be re-usable across other behaviour change applications, but maybe not across other application types.

Keywords: Ontology · Knowledge management · Healthcare · Health · Behaviour change · Case based reasoning

1 Introduction

Since 2012, Do Something Different Ltd (DSD) has designed and delivered a wide range of behaviour change interventions, addressing health and wellbeing issues such as stress reduction, weight loss and diabetes self-management, and broader personal and organisational development objectives such as leadership, diversity and management skills. It has been argued that the most effective way of changing thoughts and attitudes is via behaviours [1, 2]. Results have been reported in [3, 4].

Each DSD intervention begins with an online pre-programme diagnostic questionnaire, where the user answers questions about their behaviours, habits, wellbeing, thoughts and feelings. Then over the next few weeks, the participant receives a series of personalised recommendations of small activities, called "Dos", that are outside their

© Springer International Publishing AG 2017
M. Bramer and M. Petridis (Eds.): SGAI-AI 2017, LNAI 10630, pp. 207–216, 2017.
https://doi.org/10.1007/978-3-319-71078-5_19

normal habits [2]. For example, on a smoking cessation programme, a user who has answered that they often smoke "while sitting in your favourite place/chair/spot on the sofa" might be advised "Today break one connection: only smoke when standing up. Don't take one sitting down!".

"Dos" are sent by smartphone app, email or SMS, and supported with an online forum and motivational messaging. Participants are offered the chance to complete the questionnaire again after their programme; doing so gives them access to a personalised report comparing their pre- and post-programme scores. See Fig. 1 for an example.

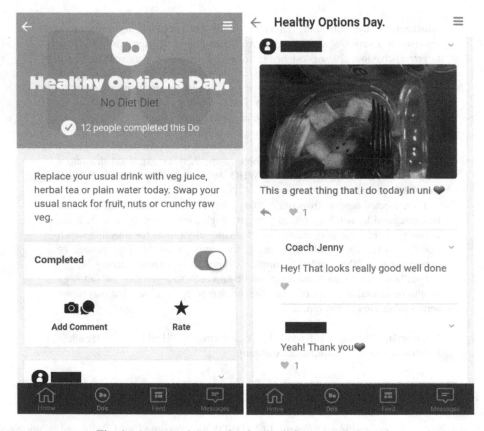

Fig. 1. An example Do, plus feedback from user and coach.

While many of the "Dos" in a DSD intervention are directly related to the objective of the programme, interventions also aim to promote behavioural flexibility in general. This aspect of the interventions helps people practice behaving in ways they currently do not, or that are outside their comfort zone, such as assertively, proactively or spontaneously. A person who answered that they do not behave assertively might receive a prompt, *"Be a bit more assertive today: Speak up when you would normally hold back. Be direct in asking for what you want."*

DSD's behaviour model was originally based on findings from a series of papers and books by psychologists Fletcher, Pine and others (e.g. [2, 5]) which listed 30 behaviours and aimed to promote them all, on the grounds that the more behaviours a person has to choose from, the more behaviourally flexible they were. Subsequent analysis (reported in [4]) found that while most of those 30 behaviours are associated with better wellbeing (in self-report data), not all of them are; thus the DSD model currently promotes twenty-one of the original behaviours (the 21 nearest to the right in Fig. 2).

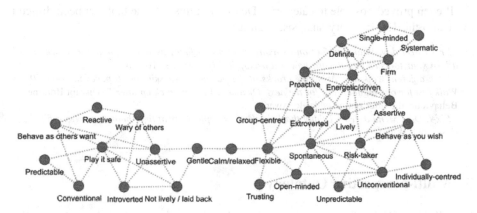

Fig. 2. A correlation network showing co-occurrence of the 30 behaviours, from [2].

2 Ontology

Not all the Dos in DSD's database are explicitly targeted at modifying one of the twenty-one behaviours directly. A first attempt to categorise the Dos produced a list of 130 different categories, such as "Spend time in nature", "Cut out moaning/complaining" or "Take Risks". The latter is directly related to one of the 21 behaviours ('risk-taker') but the other two are not.

If the majority of the 130 categories of Dos are not directly promoting one of the twenty-one behaviours, then how can they be classified? A further analysis grouped most of the 130 categories into eight top level categories:

1. Actions that directly express one of the 21 behaviours.
2. Actions that disrupt the user's general routine behaviours.
3. Actions that require physical exercise.
4. Actions that make user of the person's skills or talents.
5. Actions that express kindness to others.
6. Being social; connecting or sharing with other people.
7. Being aware; noticing things around you that might normally be ignored.
8. Being organised.

Some of these top level categories have subcategories; we were pleased to find that the subcategories predicted by literature or common sense fitted the collection of available Dos. For example, "being kind" can be broken down according to the five typical "love languages" [6]: expressing words of affection; offering someone quality time; giving gifts; performing acts of service; and offering affectionate physical contact. The "being aware" category also breaks down into five obvious groups corresponding to the five senses, although a 'General' subcategory was also needed to accommodate Dos such as:

> *"Tourist Day. Be a tourist in your local town, send postcards, browse souvenirs, take photos, visit at least one attraction you've never been to before."*

It even proved possible to categorise Dos within this scheme that had been difficult to fit into the 130 category analysis, such as:

> *"Fresh Feet day. Walk barefoot on as many different surfaces as you can today. Feel free to adorn your tootsies too. Record how it looked/felt."* (Be Aware: Touch)
> *"Do a different walk day. Avoid the cracks in the pavement, or skip for 10 paces in every 50. Walk fast for one minute, slow for the next. Or take a bag and pick up litter."* (Disrupt Routine Behaviour; the litter option adds Be Aware)
> *"Fix-It Day. Mend at least 1 thing that's broken, or replace spent light bulbs/batteries/refills."* (Use your Skills)

3   Multi-perspective Ontology

Not all of the 130 subcategories fitted into the above eight top level categories. For example, there is a subcategory that has been loosely named "Smoking related", consisting of 'Dos' designed for people on smoking cessation programmes. Some of them are *disruptor* Dos, provided for people who find themselves desperate for a cigarette and want to be distracted quickly. These Dos are therefore obtainable on demand, reasonably brief to complete, and can be performed immediately. However, the "Smoking related" Dos range across several of the top level categories, particularly those involving exercise, disrupting routines, or being organised.

It is not a problem in principle for Dos to appear in more than one category. However, what is happening here is that Dos are being categorised according to their purpose – to distract people from smoking in the short term – rather than their function (awareness, socialising, exercise, etc.).

Kingston [7] refers to this as a multi-perspective approach to classification. He proposes that a complete classification for any knowledge management application can be obtained by classifying according to five or six different perspective – WHO, WHAT, HOW, WHEN, WHERE and (sometimes) WHY.

If we apply this analysis to the 130 categories of Dos, we observe the following:

- The eight-way classification described in the previous section describes the function of the various Dos. This can be seen as the HOW perspective.
- There are categories of Dos that are deemed relevant only to a single DSD programme – stress reduction, weight loss, smoking cessation or diabetes self-management. Since these are categorised according to the goal that is being aimed for, which is the purpose of the programme, these can be considered to be the WHY perspective.

- Some categories relate to objects (or groups of objects) in the world. There are food-related Dos; alcohol-related Dos; business-related Dos; environment-related Dos; and digital-related Dos. These constitute the WHAT perspective.

We can also see that some or all Dos could benefit from having some attributes defined:

- The disruptor Dos are designed to be brief and able to be performed immediately. These are two key features of the WHEN perspective: start time (which can be at various levels of detail, from minutes to months) and duration of an activity or event.
  Another Do that has a key WHEN attribute is:

  "Be more spontaneous today. Do something on the spur of the moment without too much deliberation. Surprise someone by doing something different."

- The WHO perspective has a similar duality. Some Dos (particularly those related to socialising or kindness) may specify who should be an appropriate target of the Do. Also, some Dos are not appropriate for certain users to perform – strenuous physical exercise should probably be avoided for patients on a weight loss programme, for example.
- Some Dos specify WHERE they should take place, either generally or specifically. For example,

  "Be unpredictable today! Wave at a stranger on a passing bus, or out of your window."

In addition to all the above, it is also possible in theory to record who, what, how, when, where and why the user actually performed the Do, if the user comments on their Do in sufficient detail. Some of this information is automatically available: for example, if a Do is sent out on a Monday and the user reports completing it on a Thursday, the time when the Do was performed is known to an accuracy of 1–2 days.

The thesis of this paper is that applying a multi-perspective ontology to the Dos (i.e. populating six attributes that represent WHO, WHAT, HOW, WHEN, WHERE and WHY) will offer significant benefits for DSD's management of their behaviour change programmes.

4 Knowledge Management Benefits of a Multi-perspective Approach

A multi-perspective categorisation like this one should enable targeting of Dos to particular users; automating the selection of Dos; and creation of further Dos.

4.1 Targeting Dos to Particular Users

The Holy Grail for an organization offering behaviour change programmes is to select interventions that will have the maximum effect for a particular user to achieve a particular goal. Having a multi-perspective ontology can help significantly with such selections. The reason is that the various attributes of Dos can be mapped against results of the behaviour change programmes and also between themselves, making it possible to determine if (for example) exercise-related Dos have more effect in the summer months, or social-related Dos are more effective if they take place outside work rather than inside work.

4.2   Automating Selection of Dos

DSD is currently testing a change where users are offered a choice of three Dos instead of being sent just one. The rationale behind this change is that certain users like some Dos better than others.

Using a multi-perspective ontology, it would be possible to ensure that the three Dos offered are significantly different from each other. This would be done by making sure the three Dos all had different values on each one of the different attributes.

Another approach would be to combine automated selection with targeting of Dos by supplying Dos that are similar to ones that the user has previously liked. It is important to select Dos that the user is going to enjoy, as assuring engagement with the programme is one of the biggest hurdles that DSD faces. This could be done using a simple case based reasoning approach.

This approach would appear even more intelligent if an extra layer of dimensionality was given to the attributes. For example, all attributes could be given dimensions of "safe" through to "extreme". For exercise, walking would be "safe", sprinting or wrestling would be "extreme". For kindness-related Dos, physical affection might be considered "extreme". For socializing Dos, casual contacts would be "safe" while making a long-term commitment to a group that required significant amounts of time (a drama production, perhaps) might be "extreme".

If the user selects "extreme" Dos two or three times in a row and/or indicates that s/he enjoyed them, then it would be a good idea to include in the next choice of three a Do that is "extreme" on a different attribute.

4.3   Creating New Dos

Finding the inspiration to expand an already extensive set of Dos is a difficult task. After a while, duplication of existing Dos is a significant risk; indeed, DSD's database already contains some Dos that are virtually duplicates of others.

However, with a multi-perspective categorization, it is possible to list Dos according to all their categories. If some categories have few or no Dos, it is a much easier task to think of new Dos for those categories, because the categories themselves act as priming information. For example, one category would be: being kind to someone by spending quality time with them – related to food – at work – WHO and WHEN are left to the user's discretion. This might lead to a new Do of "*Buy lunch for someone at work today who you don't normally talk to. Eat your lunch with them and do your best to listen more than you talk.*" The WHY perspective would be the goal of the programme; this Do might not be appropriate for a diabetes self-management programme.

Another method to create new Dos is crowd-sourcing i.e. allowing users who have experience of the programme to create their own Dos by simply deciding that they will do something different, of their own choosing. Users are encouraged to feed back their new Dos to the development team, who can decide whether to add them to their database of Dos.

Deciding whether the new Do is truly new or is a duplication or instance of an existing Do is a large task when there are 2500 Dos. However, if the new Do can be classified according to the multi-perspective ontology, the number of existing Dos to compare for duplication falls to a much more manageable number.

In theory, a language processing application might be developed to help in automatic classification of these potential new Dos. In practice, the volume of new Dos is expected to be no higher than 10 per week, and the effort required to add six attributes to each of 10 or fewer Dos is insufficient to justify the development of intelligent supporting software.

5   A Perspective from Ontology Theory

The development of ontologies has frequently been proposed as an aid to knowledge management but much less frequently implemented. The reasons are usually to do with issues that relate to the theory of ontologies.

5.1   Reusability Versus Specificity

Ontologies were once touted as the next big thing in knowledge management [8, 9] because they were supposed to be re-usable. The idea was that a knowledge categorization would be defined once and could then be re-used by multiple applications.

It turned out that this did not work well. Categorisations were often domain-specific. Sometimes this was because there was no underlying real-world categorisation, and so arbitrary categories had to be invented; Wielinga [10] gave an example from the Rijksmuseum in Amsterdam of experts in paintings using a completely different classification of colour from experts in ceramics. Colour does not have fundamental categories in the real world; rather, it is formed by the perception of three wavelengths of light. So only a handful of colour categories can be unambiguously defined (the eight categories that involve all or none of each wavelength); other categories must be agreed.

There were other reasons too. Sometimes the parties creating the classification had a vested interest in seeing their area of interest classified as high up the tree as possible [11]. Sometimes the issue was the lack of a multi-perspective classification, particularly relating to purposes, leading one ontology to classify a strut (within a building) as a "beam" while another might classify it as a "support" [12].

When we apply these insights to our multi-perspective ontology based on behaviour change, new opportunities can be identified. Our ontology is really an ontology of activities that happen to be directed towards goals in healthcare and wellbeing; so the attributes and (perhaps) range of values for at least two of the six perspectives (WHEN and WHERE) can be re-used directly from other activity-based ontologies. Reuse may be possible for the WHO perspective as well.

The perspectives that are directly related to healthcare are HOW (the eight categories identified in Sect. 2) and WHY (the goal of each programme). The WHY perspective is uncontroversial; it is an (uncategorized) list of health benefits that are commonly sought by large groups of people. So the key ontological benefit for healthcare from this project are the eight categories of the HOW perspective.

Are these re-usable? It seems likely that they will be re-usable in other behaviour change programmes. It is unclear whether it might be of benefit in programmes such as cognitive therapy, which focus on modifying thinking and beliefs rather than on changing behaviours. We claim that our ontology is likely to be re-usable for similar types of application but make no further commitment.

5.2   Mixing of Perspectives Within Classifications

A second problem is that many ontologies mix up taxonomies, mereonomies and other relation-based structures. [13] reviewed the ACM Digital Classification and showed how the subcategories mixed categories based on programming techniques; categories based on applications of programming; and, in the case of the Hardware category, subcategories based on parts.

The ontology presented in this paper largely avoids mixed perspectives; its breakdowns are heavily based on methods for achieving the top level goal (i.e. they all follow the HOW perspective). The 'five love languages'; the five senses (for Awareness interventions); different types of exercise; different ways of using skills and talents; different ways to be organized; and different ways of disrupting routines are all method-based breakdowns. This increases the possibility that the different categories can each support knowledge management in the same way, making the ontology easier for DSD to apply. It also suggests that overarching dimensions (such as "safe" versus "extreme") might be developed that apply across all categories.

5.3   Level of Abstraction

A third problem that arises with ontologies is that the level of interest that an application took in a particular category affected how it was classified within the ontology. To quote [7], a car salesman may view 'colour' as merely an attribute of the concept 'car', while a photographer might view 'colour' as a concept in its own right with attributes including 'hue' and 'saturation'.

When something is a concept in one ontology but a property in another, this implies that the two ontologies are one level of abstraction apart regarding this thing. Guarino [14] identifies no fewer than nine levels at which an ontology may exist, ranging from the atomic and static levels (where 'wavelengths of light' belong) right up to intentional and social levels (at the latter of which social rules and conventions apply). These are shown in Fig. 3.

The Dos can all be said to exist at the intentional level since they require intentional behaviour, although few refer directly to social rules or conventions. However, some social rules need to be applied on a day when a user is expected to choose someone to whom to show physical affection. So our ontology is at least internally consistent in terms of abstraction.

```
Atomic
   Individuation: minimal size
   Persistence: spatio-temporal continuity
Static
   Individuation: mereological sum of atoms
   Persistence: same properties
Mereological
   Individuation: mereological sum of entities
   Persistence: same parts
Topological
   Individuation: self-connection
   Persistence: similar topology
Morphological
   Individuation: proximity
   Persistence: similar shape
Functional
   Individuation: purpose
   Persistence: persistence of functionality
Biological
   Individuation: presence of life
   Persistence: persistence of life
Intentional
   Individuation: intentional behavior
   Persistence: persistence of intentional behavior
Social
   Individuation: inter-agent connections
   Persistence: persistence of inter-agent connections
```

Fig. 3. Guarino's nine ontological levels.

Is our ontology re-usable? The answer is that it should be re-usable for other behaviour change programmes because such programmes (by definition) require intentional behaviour. However, it is probably not that helpful for an application at a much lower level of abstraction, such as a natural language analysis application that determines the parts of speech present in a typical 'Do' or other instructed activity.

6   Conclusions and Future Work

We have shown how a multi-perspective ontology can provide significant knowledge management benefits to an organisation that offers healthcare through behaviour change. It can help generate new interventions and select interventions that are appropriate for a particular user to achieve a particular goal. We believe that it can also help improve engagement with the programme.

We believe that our ontology is re-usable across other behaviour change applications but we will not commit to it being useful for other types of application.

In future work we hope to report on interaction and outcome data from newly revised programmes, making use of our ontology, to test our beliefs empirically.

Acknowledgements. The authors were supported by Innovate UK via Knowledge Transfer Partnership 10152. Thanks are due to Professor Ben (C) Fletcher for comments on this paper.

References

1. Pine, K., Fletcher, B.: Shifting brain channels to change health behaviour. Perspect. Public Health. **134**(1), 16–17 (2014). https://doi.org/10.1177/1757913913514705
2. Fletcher, B., Hanson, J., Pine, K., Page, N.: FIT – Do something different: A new psychological intervention tool for facilitating weight loss. Swiss J. Psychol. **70**(1), 25–34 (2011)
3. Pine, K., Fletcher, B.: Changing people's habits is associated with reductions in stress, anxiety and depression levels. Technical report, Do Something Different Ltd. (2016)
4. Charlton, N., Kingston, J., Petridis, M., Fletcher, B.: Using data mining to refine digital behaviour change interventions. In: Proceedings of 7th International Conference on Digital Health 2017, London, United Kingdom, pp. 90–98. ACM (2017)
5. Fletcher, B., Pine, K.: Flex: Do Something Different. University of Hertfordshire Press, Hertfordshire (1999)
6. Chapman, G.: The Five Love Languages: How to Express Heartfelt Commitment to Your Mate. Northfield, Chicago (1995)
7. Kingston, J.: Multi-Perspective Modelling for Knowledge Management and Knowledge Engineering: Practical Applications of Artificial Intelligence. CreateSpace (2017). ISBN 978-1539048343
8. Brandt, S., Morbach, J., Miatidis, M., Marquardt, W.: An ontology-based approach to knowledge management in design processes. Comput. Chem. Eng. **32**(1), 320–342 (2008)
9. Abecker, A., van Elst, L.: Ontologies for knowledge management. In: Staab, S., Studer, R. (eds.) Handbook on Ontologies. International Handbooks on Information Systems, pp. 435–454. Springer, Heidelberg (2004). https://doi.org/10.1007/978-3-540-24750-0_22
10. Wielinga, R.: Personal communication to the first author of this paper. University of Amsterdam (1997)
11. Kingston, J.: Merging top level ontologies for scientific knowledge management. In: Proceedings of the AAAI Workshop on Ontologies and the Semantic Web, pp. 147–154 (2002)
12. Kingston, J.: Multi-perspective ontologies: Resolving common ontology development problems. Expert Syst. Appl. **34**(1), 541–550 (2008)
13. Kingston, J.: Ontology, knowledge management, knowledge engineering and the ACM classification scheme. In: Bramer, M., Preece, A., Coenen, F. (eds.) Research and Development in Intelligent Systems, pp. 207–220. Springer, London (2003). https://doi.org/10.1007/978-1-4471-0651-7_15
14. Guarino, N.: Some ontological principles for designing upper level lexical resources. In: Rubio, G., Castro, T. (eds.) Proceedings of First International Conference on Language Resources and Evaluation, Granada, Spain, pp. 527–534 (1998)

Using Semantic Web Technologies to Underpin the SNOMED CT Query Language

Mercedes Arguello Casteleiro[✉], Dmitry Tsarkov, Bijan Parsia, and Ulrike Sattler

School of Computer Science, The University of Manchester, Manchester, UK
{m.arguello,bijan.parsia,
uli.sattler}@manchester.ac.uk,
dmitry.tsarkov@gmail.com

Abstract. SNOMED International is working on a query language specification for SNOMED CT, which we call here SCTQL. SNOMED CT is the leading terminology for use in Electronic Health Records (EHRs). SCTQL can contribute to effective retrieval and reuse of clinical information within EHRs. This paper analyses the functional capabilities needed for SCTQL and proposes two implementations that rely on ontological representations of SNOMED CT: one based on the W3C SPARQL 1.1 query language and another based on the OWL API. The paper reports the performance and correctness of both implementations as well as highlights their benefits and drawbacks.

Keywords: SNOMED CT · Reference sets · Ontology · SPARQL · OWL API

1 Introduction

SNOMED Clinical Terms (SNOMED CT) is a semantically rich and clinically validated terminology maintained and distributed by SNOMED International [1], the new trading name for International Health Terminology Standard Development Organization (IHTSDO). SNOMED CT stands as the leading global clinical terminology for use in Electronic Health Records (EHRs) [1]. In the UK, the National Health Service (NHS) in England intends to adopt SNOMED CT across all care settings by 2020 [2]. In the US, SNOMED CT is a key clinical terminology for EHR Certification and Meaningful Use [3]. It has been acknowledge that worldwide, despite the reported use of SNOMED CT in over 50 countries; there are few production systems [4]. Although recent examples of successful implementations of SNOMED CT have been published, such as an EHR system from NHS Wales [2].

SNOMED CT constantly grows and the January 2017 release contained 326,734 active concepts [5] and more than 1.6 million synonyms [2]. SNOMED CT size and scope bring challenges when making SNOMED CT usable in practice. To tackle

---

D. Tsarkov—Now at Google International GmbH, Brandschenkestrasse 110, 8002 Zürich, Switzerland.

© Springer International Publishing AG 2017
M. Bramer and M. Petridis (Eds.): SGAI-AI 2017, LNAI 10630, pp. 217–231, 2017.
https://doi.org/10.1007/978-3-319-71078-5_20

SNOMED CT size and make it customizable to specific applications, the reference set mechanism is one method for filtering and arranging SNOMED CT concepts for specific domains or use cases [6]. SNOMED CT concepts belonging to a reference set (*Refset* for short) are portable and can be distributed to other organisations with similar needs. Three examples of well-known SNOMED CT *Refsets* are the following: (1) Clinical Observations Recording and Encoding (CORE) Problem List Subset of SNOMED CT [7]; (2) SNOMED CT Nursing Problem List Subset [8]; (3) the Veterans Health Administration and Kaiser Permanente (VA/KP) Problem List subset [9]. In the UK, specific *Refsets* are included in the release of SNOMED Clinical Terms UK Edition [10]. However, current tools for building *Refsets* tend to be ad-hoc use of browsers and spreadsheets or in-house developments [11].

SNOMED CT *Refsets* may be specified statically, by enumeration, or dynamically, by means some some query mechanism, such as custom code. Current tools for building *Refsets* tend to be ad-hoc use of browsers and spreadsheets or in-house developments [9]. The IHTSDO Workbench [12] is a set of open-source software tools that includes a complex rule-based *Refset* builder, which requires a detailed technical knowledge of the inner workings of SNOMED CT. Furthermore; the specification of the *Refset* is tool bound and not portable. Thus, systems share enumerations of terms, rather than the criteria for being in that *Refset*.

SNOMED CT can support data analytics in three broad healthcare areas [13]: point-of care analytics; population-based analytics; and clinical research. Big data analytics in healthcare can facilitate the discovery of associations and the understanding of patterns and trends within massive amounts of healthcare data. As Raghupathi and Raghupathi [14] emphasise *"big data analytics has the potential to improve care, save lives and lower costs"*. As the content for data elements in an EHR can be a concept-based *Refsets*, the capability of writing machine processable queries that identifies the valid values for EHR data elements is another step toward effective retrieval and reuse of clinical information. Hence, SNOMED International is working on a formal language for representing computable queries over SNOMED CT content [15], and a new specification will be released by December 2017. SCTQL is a superset of the SNOMED CT Expression Constraint Language [16].

To enable clinical queries over SNOMED CT content and more particularly the creation of *simple Refsets* (i.e. just a collection of concepts [6]), an early draft of the SNOMED CT query language - we call it here SCTQL for short – was released [17] and an early implementation was made available [18]. Neither of them (i.e. SCTQL specification [17] nor its implementation [18]) builds on formal knowledge representations like the W3C Web Ontology Language (OWL) [19]. However, each new international release of SNOMED CT (two per year) allows the transformation of SNOMED CT into OWL by means of a script written in the Perl language [12].

This paper investigates the use of the W3C SPARQL 1.1 query language [20] along with the OWL API [21] for implementing SCTQL. The OWL API is an Application Programming Interface (API) based on Java language for working with OWL ontologies [21]. Hence, this paper draws upon Semantic Web technologies to support SCTQL and seeks to enhance SCTQL by providing implementations that rely on ontological representations. As SNOMED CT is a large biomedical ontology in OWL, it is feasible to envision the development of query language functions specific for other ontologies while taking into account the prototypical implementations presented here. It should be noted "*description logic based ontology languages like OWL carry a clear-cut semantics*" [22].

This paper belongs to knowledge representation and reasoning, a field within Artificial Intelligence. As it has been acknowledged by Baader et al. [23], the Semantic Web "*greatly depends on the availability of well-defined semantics and powerful reasoning tools*". For an overview of the Semantic Web and its supporting technologies, we refer the reader respectively to [24, 25]. For an introduction to description logics (DLs) and the relationship between DLs and OWL, we refer the reader to [26]. The two implementations for SCTQL presented in this paper require the reader to be familiarised with OWL [19], OWL API [21], and SPARQL [20].

2 Preliminaries: SNOMED CT and *simple Refsets* in OWL

The OWL 2 Web Ontology Language (informally OWL 2) [19] is the most recent update of the W3C OWL and has three profiles: OWL EL; OWL RL; and OWL QL. Each profile can be seen as a sublanguage that "*restricts the available modelling features in order to simplify reasoning*" [27]. Large biomedical ontologies like SNOMED CT are typically modeled in OWL EL. For OWL EL, classification is the most important inference task [27], where the hierarchical structure (a.k.a. taxonomy) of SNOMED CT terms in OWL can be computed automatically.

Each SNOMED CT release contains three components: concepts, description and relationships. As Wang et al. [28] emphasise the fundamental construct used in the definition of concepts is the SNOMED CT linkage concept 246061005|Attribute (attribute)|, its subtypes serve to connect one concept to another. Indeed, the biomedical concepts in SNOMED CT are grouped into 19 (subsumption) hierarchies by using the SNOMED CT linkage concept 116680003|Is a (attribute)| as the taxonomy relation.

Most of the SNOMED CT biomedical concepts correspond to OWL Classes, for example 3415004|Cyanosis|. However, SNOMED CT biomedical concepts from the Linkage concept hierarchy correspond to OWL ObjectProperties, for example 246075003|Causitive agent|.

According to the latest SNOMED Technical Implementation Guide [12]: "*A Concept is considered to be fully defined if its defining characteristics are sufficient to define it relative to its immediate supertype(s). A Concept which is not fully defined is Primitive*". In the language of description logics, according to Jiang and Chute [29]: "*the asserted conditions of a primitive concept are necessary but not sufficient, and the asserted conditions of a fully defined concept are both necessary and sufficient*". Table 1 provide an example of how a primitive and a fully defined SNOMED CT concept are represented in the Manchester OWL Syntax [30].

The 116680003|Is a (attribute)|, in OWL 2 [19] corresponds to the so-called sub-class axiom, which is the SubClassOf in the Manchester OWL Syntax. Most of the subtypes of the 246061005|Attribute (attribute)| correspond in OWL to Object Properties [19] and are represented as sub-property axioms. These Object Properties are used within Role groups as DL existential restrictions (limited existential quantification) to formalised fully defined concepts. Role groups were designed as an extension

Table 1. Exemplifying primitive and fully defined SNOMED CT concepts in OWL.

SNOMED CT	Manchester OWL syntax
Primitive concept	Class: SCT_275521001 Annotations: rdfs:label "Blue baby (disorder)" SubClassOf: SCT_95617006
Fully defined concept	Class: SCT_206324006 Annotations: rdfs:label "Neonatal acrocyanosis (finding)" EquivalentTo: SCT_25003006 and (RoleGroup some (SCT_246454002 some SCT_255407002))

to the Ontylog description logic [31] to represent the (potential) grouping of SNOMED CT's attributes. Typically a fully defined concept may have one or more Role groups.

Figure 1 illustrates the correspondence between SNOMED CT concepts and OWL Classes and OWL ObjectProperties above-mentioned. In SNOMED CT a *simple Refset* is a set of SNOMED CT biomedical concepts. In OWL, a *simple Refset* is a set of OWL class names.

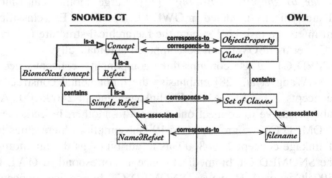

Fig. 1. The correspondence between SNOMED CT concepts and OWL classes and OWL ObjectProperties.

We have provided an overview of SNOMED CT in OWL and also proposed a semantically meaningful representation for *simple Refsets*. Next section presents an analysis of the different functions, i.e. SCTQL queries.

3 Analysis of the SNOMED CT Query Language Specification

After examining the early draft of the specifications for SCTQL [17], we observe that SCTQL provide different kinds of functions (SCTQL queries). Therefore, we have organised SCTQL functions into five categories, i.e. query types that we have introduced:

- α category for functions that define a set of operations.
- β category for functions that involve reasoning. It is possible to distinguish:
  - β1 category for functions that perform a selection based on concept hierarchy, i.e. is-a relationships.
  - β2 category for functions that perform a selection based on relationships other than is-a.
- ζ category for functions that do not involve reasoning, i.e. syntactic queries. It is possible to distinguish:
  - ζ1 category for functions that perform a selection based on relationships.
  - ζ2 category for functions that perform filter operations. These are easy queries.
  - ζ3 category for functions that perform string-matching operations. These are easy queries.
- δ category for functions that can be expressed as a combination of other functions. Their meaning is fully determined via the meaning of other queries.
- ψ category for functions that depend on the native translation of SNOMED CT into OWL. Initially, only the active SNOMED CT concepts are included in the OWL file generated with the Perl script [12], and therefore, to retrieve All SNOMED CT concepts, it is necessary to create a *simple Refset* with the non-active ones. It should be noted that when a concept becomes inactive this is indicated by the value of the active field [12] in the concept text file of the SNOMED CT Release Format 2.

Table 2 contains the above-mentioned category functions (right-hand side column) and the SCTQL queries (left-hand side column) as they appear in the specifications draft for SCTQL [17]. We have modified the input parameter notation of the functions slightly: letters in bold and lowercase means relationships or string literals, while letters in uppercase means a *Refset*. It should be noted that *simple Refsets* in SCTQL are only handled by name, i.e. *NameRefset*.

In Table 2, each function has as output a *simple Refset*, and can have zero or more input parameters. From our examination of the early draft of the specifications for SCTQL [17], we realise that there are four different types of input parameters:

- SNOMED CT *simple Refsets*, i.e. set of OWL class names, we refer to these as A, B and C.
- SNOMED CT biomedical concepts that correspond to OWL class names, we also refer to these as A, B and C.
- SNOMED CT biomedical concepts that correspond to OWL ObjectProperty names, we refer to these as **p**, **p1**, and **p2**. This notation differs from the one that appears in the specification draft of SCTQL [17]. We write them lowercase to distinguish clearly between these and the two above mentioned, which appear written with capital letters.
- String literals, we refer to these as **s**.

We also notice that some functions from Table 2 are not atomic, in the sense that they can be expressed as a combination of other functions. Table 3 shows the equivalences found for four SCTQL functions.

The basic query functions (i.e., simple SCTQL queries) from Table 2 can be nested to produce complex query expressions. According to the early specification draft for

Table 2. SNOMED CT query language functions and the categories assigned.

SCTQL function	Function category assigned
MembersOf(**NamedRefset**) Intersection(A, B) Union(A, B) Excludes(A, B)	α
All	ζ2, ψ
FilterOnFullyDefined(A)	ζ2
FilterOnPrimitive(A)	ζ2, δ
FilterOnActive(A)	ζ2, ψ
FilterOnNoMatch(**s**, A)	ζ3, δ
FilterOnMatch(**s**, A)	ζ3
FilterOnLeaf(A)	β1
ChildrenAndSelf(A)	β1, δ
Children(A)	β1
DescendantsAndSelf(A)	β1, δ
Descendants(A)	β1
HasDirectRel(**p**, B)	β2
HasRel(**p**, B)	β2
HasGroupedRels(**p1**, B, **p2**, C)	ζ1

Table 3. Equivalences found for SCTQL functions from Table 2.

Function	Equivalent query expression
FilterOnPrimitive(A)	Exclude(A,FilterOnFullyDefined(A))
FilterOnNoMatch(**s**, A)	Exclude(A,FilterOnMatch(**s**,A))
ChildrenAndSelf(A)	Union(A,Children(A))
DescendantsAndSelf(A)	Union(A,Descendants(A))
FilterOnActive(A)	Intersection(A,All)

SCTQL [17]: "*Where functions are nested, the innermost functions should be evaluated first, before passing the resulting reference set members to the functions they are nested in*". For example, the following SCTQL query expression returns all fully defined concepts in the Clinical finding hierarchy.

FilterOnFullyDefined(DescendantsAndSelf(404684003|Clinical finding|))

4   Translation of SCTQL into SPARQL and Implementations

We now provide the details of the translation of the SCTQL queries into SPARQL as well as an overview of the two alternative implementations for SCTQL.

By translating the function definitions from Table 2 (simple SCTQL queries) into SPARQL 1.1 [20], it is feasible to provide a more formal semantic definition for the

SCTQL queries, which is profitable for the two implementations for SCTQL that we propose. For simplicity, we treat a single SNOMED CT biomedical concept – which is represented as an OWL Class name – as a *simple Refset* with one element. Thus, all arguments to all SCTQL query functions are *simple Refsets*.

Let's start with a simple example of a simple SCTQL query, like the following: *Children(3415004|Cyanosis|)*. This simple SCTQL query returns concepts in the Clinical finding hierarchy that are direct sub-types (i.e. children) of the SNOMED CT concept 3415004|Cyanosis|. This simple SCTQL query can be translated into SPARQL 1.1 as it follows:

SELECT DISTINCT ?x
FROM <file:./src/data/Snomed_2017.owl>
FROM NAMED <file:./src/data/RefsetA.owl>
WHERE {   GRAPH <file:./src/data/RefsetA.owl>
{?y rdfs:subClassOf owl:Thing .}
?x rdfs:subClassOf ?y . }

The SPARQL 1.1 SELECT queries for the simple SCTQL queries, as the one detailed above, consist of four parts:

1. The Dataset clause – This contains one default graph clause and zero or more named graphs. The default graph does not have a name, while each named graph corresponds to an input *simple Refset* and has an Internationalized Resource Identifier (IRI).
2. The SELECT clause – This clause identifies the variables that appear in the query results. In this translation, there is always one variable in the head of the SELECT, as the query result is always a result set or RDF graph, i.e. a *simple Refset*.
3. The WHERE clause – This clause provides the basic graph pattern to match against the data graph [20].
4. The Solution modifier – Like the DISTINCT solution modifier, which eliminates duplicate solutions.

Typically, there is a list of PREFIX that appears before the SELECT clause. For the SPARQL 1.1 queries created for SCTQL, the same list of PREFIX (i.e. owl; rdf; rdfs; xsd; and SCT) appears repeatedly. To further illustrate this: the PREFIX owl corresponds to http://www.w3.org/2002/07/owl and the PREFIX SCT corresponds to http://www.ihtsdo.org/. To make the SPARQL 1.1 SELECT queries more readable in this paper, we omit the PREFIX statements and the Dataset Clauses.

4.1   Introducing the Translation Function

Table 4 specifies the translation of the functions (SCTQL queries) from Table 2 into SPARQL 1.1 [20]. Due to the limitation of space only some of the functions from Table 2 are shown in Table 4.

Table 4. Translation of SCTQL queries to SPARQL 1.1 SELECT queries.

SCTQL query q()	SPARQL 1.1 SELECT query translate(q,?x)
MembersOf(**NameRefset**)	SELECT ?x FROM IRI(Snomed_2017.owl) FROM NAMED IRI(SimpleRefsetA) WHERE {GRAPH IRI(SimpleRefsetA) {?x a owl:Class . } . }
Intersection(A, B)	SELECT ?x WHERE { Translate(A, ?x) . Translate(B, ?x) . }
Union(A, B)	SELECT ?x WHERE { { Translate(A, ?x) . } UNION { Translate(B, ?x) . } }
Excludes(A, B)	SELECT ?x WHERE { Translate(A, ?x) . MINUS { Translate(B, ?x) . } }

FilterOnLeaf(A)	SELECT ?x
	WHERE { Translate(A, ?x)
	      FILTER NOT EXISTS
	   {?y rdfs:subClassOf+ ?x .
	      FILTER (?y != owl:Nothing) } }

Children(A)	SELECT DISTINCT ?x WHERE { Translate(A, ?y) ?x rdfs:subClassOf ?y . }
Descendants(A)	SELECT DISTINCT ?x WHERE { Translate(A, ?y) ?x rdfs:subClassOf+ ?y . }

HasDirectRel(**p1**, B)	SELECT DISTINCT ?x
	WHERE { Translate(B, ?C) .
	{{ ?x rdf:type owl:Class;
	          ?t ?y .
	   FILTER (?t = rdfs:subClassOf || ?t = owl:equivalentClass)
	      ?y rdf:type owl:Class;
	      owl:intersectionOf [list:member ?e] .
	      ?e rdf:type owl:Restriction ;
	      owl:onProperty ?p ;
	      owl:someValuesFrom ?C .
	          FILTER (?p = SCT:ObjPropA)
	} UNION { ?x rdf:type owl:Class;
	          ?t ?y .
	   FILTER (?t = rdfs:subClassOf || ?t = owl:equivalentClass)
	      ?y rdf:type owl:Class;
	      owl:intersectionOf [list:member ?el]
	      ?el owl:onProperty SCT:RoleGroup ;
	         owl:someValuesFrom ?e .
	      ?e rdf:type owl:Restriction ;
	      owl:onProperty ?p ;
	      owl:someValuesFrom ?C .
	          FILTER (?p = **p1**) }
	} }

The translation function **translate(q,?x)** takes two arguments: the query **q** and a name of a variable **?x**. The introduction of the translation function simplifies significantly the rewriting of SCTQL functions (or queries) into SPARQL 1.1.

A SCTQL query expression is a possibly nested expression build from the functions defined in Table 2, where each parameter is either: a *NameRefset* (used in the MembersOf function), or a string, or a SCTQL query expression. It should be noted that *simple Refsets* in a SCTQL query expression are only handled by name, i.e. *NameRefset*.

4.2   Overview of the Two Alternative Implementations for SCTQL

There are three options for the formulation, and further implementation, of the SCTQL queries and query expressions:

1. SPARQL 1.1 under the OWL entailment regime – the main drawback of this option is the lack of query engines that support SPARQL 1.1 OWL entailment regime.
2. SPARQL 1.1 under the RDF entailment regime – the main drawback of this option is the number of additional pre-computed files that are needed to provide the inferred model when reasoning is required.
3. Change between SPARQL 1.1 entailment regimes according to the query at hand.

We generally prefer the third option above-mentioned as the queries tend to be more natural, i.e., "syntactic" queries can use a "more syntactic" entailment regime instead of requiring complex workarounds. In Table 4, the last SPARQL SELECT query requires SPARQL 1.1 under the RDF entailment regime.

Despite the desirability of the third option mentioned, there are relatively few SPARQL 1.1 engines that support the OWL entailment regime, which limits the utility of the translation as an implementation technique. For example, our preferred SPARQL engine, Jena ARQ [32], only supports the SPARQL 1.1 RDF query language [33]. To a certain extend the second option mentioned is already favoured by the SNOMED Technical Implementation Guide [12]: *"Experience suggests that a pre-computed transitive closure table out-performs other options and is robust, flexible and easy to implement. Therefore, unless storage capacity is significant concern, this approach is recommended"*. Therefore, and in the same vein as [34], this study pre-computes the transitive closure of rdfs:subClassOf for the SNOMED CT biomedical concepts and used it in some queries as the default graph.

A second implementation is based on the Java OWL API [21]. The OWL API implementation for SCTQL, called it here OWL API++, makes use of the OWLReasoner interface to ask for inferred information, and therefore, it does not need to use pre-computed files when reasoning is provided. Table 5 exemplifies some of the SCTQL queries from Table 4 in OWL API++.

Table 5. Exemplifying the OWL API implementation of SCTQL queries from Table 4.

SCTQL query	OWL API ++
MembersOf(NamedRefset)	OWLOntology o = manager.loadOntologyFromOntologyDocument(new File(NamedRefset)); return new ReferenceSet(o.getClassesInSignature());

Intersection(A, B)	Set<OWLClass> toReturn =
	new HashSet<OWLClass>(referenceSets[0].asSet());
	for (ReferenceSet refSet : referenceSets)
	        toReturn.retainAll(refSet.asSet());
	return new ReferenceSet(toReturn);

Union(A, B)	Set<OWLClass> toReturn =
	new HashSet<OWLClass>();
	for (ReferenceSet refSet : referenceSets)
	        toReturn.addAll(refSet.asSet());
	return new ReferenceSet(toReturn);

Excludes(A, B)	Set<OWLClass> toReturn =
	new HashSet<OWLClass>(A.asSet());
	toReturn.removeAll(B.asSet());
	return new ReferenceSet(toReturn);

Children(A)	Set<OWLClass> toReturn =
	new HashSet<OWLClass>();
	for (OWLClass C : A.asSet())
	toReturn.addAll(reasoner.getSubClasses(C,true).getFlattened());
	return new ReferenceSet(toReturn);

Descendants(A)	Set<OWLClass> toReturn =
	new HashSet<OWLClass>();
	for (OWLClass C : A.asSet())
	toReturn.addAll(reasoner.getSubClasses(C,false).getFlattened());
	return new ReferenceSet(toReturn);

5   Cross-Comparing Both Implementations: Test Suite Results

One of the difficulties to provide an implementation for SCTQL is to preserve the semantics that appears in the specification draft of SCTQL [17]. It is not only necessary to check that both implementations will give the same results, but also that the results provided is what a clinician expects.

As there is not yet a reference test suite for SCTQL, we developed a small initial test suite of queries to test and compare both implementations (SPARQL 1.1 and OWL API++). This test suite is formed by creating a set of *simple Refsets* by expert selection [4] and a set of SCTQL queries that are representative of the basic features of the SCTQL specification. The set of *simple Refsets* created will be parameters for the SCTQL queries. Figure 2 shows the hierarchical arrangement of the SNOMED CT concepts considered for the test suite, which are clinical findings.

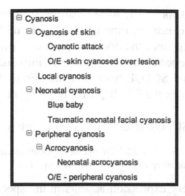

Fig. 2. Hierarchical overview of the SNOMED CT concepts included in the test suite.

All the SCTQL queries have been run in a MacBook Pro with a processor 2.7 GHz Intel Core i7 and 16 GB of RAM. Four *simple Refsets* were defined. *Simple Refset A* only contains the SNOMED CT clinical finding 3415004|Cyanosis|, and thus, it is a *simple Refset* with only one OWL class name that is represented in the Manchester OWL Syntax as follows:

Class: <http://www.ihtsdo.org/SCT_3415004>
SubClassOf: Thing

Simple Refset B (also called *Cyanosis Refset* here) contains all the SNOMED CT concepts that appear in Fig. 2. Table 6 contains some examples of the SCTQL queries ran. For each SCTQL query, Table 6 shows N, which is the number of SNOMED CT concepts retrieved for the resulting *simple Refset*, as well as the execution time taken for the two implementations – one based on the query engine ARQ for Jena [32] and the other one based on OWL API [21]. As the implementation based on the OWL API can use different reasoners, we use FaCT++ [35] and ELK [36].

Table 6. Exemplifying the run times of SCTQL queries with both implementations.

SCTQL query	N	OWL API++		SPARQL 1.1 Jena ARQ
		FaCT++	ELK	
Intersection (A, B)	1	778 s	68 s	34 s
Excludes (B, A)	11	778 s	68 s	34 s
Children (A)	4	778 s	68 s	38 s
Descendants (A)	11	778 s	68 s	38 s

Although Table 6 only contains some of the SCTQL queries ran for the test suite, the number of SNOMED CT concepts retrieved for the resulting *simple Refset* (denoted as N in Table 6) is the same for both implementations. Furthermore, the *simple Refsets* obtained are in agreement with expected result for two clinicians, who provide feedback of the outcome for each SCTQL query within the test suite.

The run times obtained for OWL API++ can be split into initialisation time and execution time, where the execution time is almost cero milliseconds for the SCTQL queries from Table 6. Hence, once the first SCTQL query is made with the OWL API++, the subsequent SCTQL queries are much faster as initialisation happens only at the beginning, i.e. when the first SCTQL query is made. From Table 6, it is also easy to assume that the more complex the SPARQL 1.1 queries, the longer it takes to execute them.

We also ran complex SCTQL query expressions such as the following one:

Intersection(DescendantsAndSelf(418925002|Immune hypersensitivity reaction|), HasDirectRel(246075003|Causitive agent|, FilterOnActive(All)))

The above SCTQL query expression appears in the specification draft of SCTQL [17], and it returns all concepts in the "*Immune hypersensitivity reaction hierarchy that have an explicit ungrouped 'Causative agent' relationship defined to any [active] target concept*". This SCTQL query expression yields 63 SNOMED CT concepts for the resulting *simple Refset*. The execution time was 308 ms in the implementation based on the OWL API using ELK as reasoner (disregarding the initialisation time), and 50 s using the query engine ARQ for Jena.

Most of the SCTQL queries and query expressions for the test suite are from the examples in [17]. The full test suite consists of 48 simple queries (3 variants of each construct) and 12 compound queries. Both implementations gave exactly the same answers for all SCTQL queries.

6 Discussion

SCTQL aims at computable queries over SNOMED CT content, and therefore, a major application is in data analytics (i.e. performing queries). For example, find all EHRs of patients with clinical statements coded with concepts in the *Cyanosis Refset*.

Other authors have investigated the use of SPARQL queries over SNOMED CT content. To illustrate some of the existing work: (a) Kim and Cohen [37] developed a prototype system that generates SPARQL queries from natural language that works on SNOMED CT; and (b) Alonso-Calvo et al. [38] presented a query abstraction mechanism that allows the creation of complex SPARQL queries over a core dataset, which integrates terminologies such as SNOMED CT. However, to the best of our knowledge, the use of the W3C SPARQL 1.1 query language [20] or the OWL API [21] for implementing SCTQL has not been attempted before.

By translating the function definitions for SCTQL into SPARQL 1.1, we demonstrate that the current state of the art of Semantic Web technologies can provide a formal semantic definition for the SCTQL queries. This formal representation is profitable for the two implementations for SCTQL that we propose, which are radically different and yet their results converge. In this paper, we also introduced a semantically meaningful representation for *simple Refsets*.

While it is impossible to show that our formalization captures the intended semantics of SCTQL (which is not fully specified), we believe that it is a reasonable semantics and fairly close to the intended. We also acknowledge that SPARQL 1.1 is a rich query language, although syntactically too complex for daily use as a *simple Refset* description language. Hence, providing a java interface can ease the adoption of both implementations.

We developed a test suite to corroborate that the number of SNOMED CT concepts obtained for the SCTQL queries executed (the resulting *simple Refset*) were in agreement with the expectations of two clinicians. This initial success encourages further experimentation with NHS Refsets as well as well-known Refsets, such as the CORE Problem List Subset of SNOMED CT [7]. Indeed, we intend to radically expand the set of queries tested with a particular focus on compound complex queries to fully exercise the implementations.

There are at least three areas of improvement. Firstly, it is necessary to conduct more experiments involving more clinicians to demonstrate that the implementations provided obtain the results (*simple Refsets*) expected by clinicians. Secondly, usability tests are needed to check if the java interface that we develop for both implementations of SCTQL is easy to use for technical professionals. Finally, although we identify three options for the formulation, and further implementation, of the SCTQL queries and query expressions, only one was adopted for the practical implementation (see Subsect. 4.2 for details).

7   Conclusion

SNOMED CT has the potential to provide the core general terminology for EHRs. The availability of implementations for SCTQL can be a significant contribution for real-time querying and retrieval of information from EHRs. This paper demonstrates the viability of using Semantic Web technologies to produce implementations for SCTQL that rely on ontological representations of SNOMED CT. The paper also hints at benefits and drawbacks of the two implementations presented: one based on the W3C SPARQL 1.1 query language and another based on the OWL API.

References

1. SNOMED International. http://www.snomed.org
2. Wardle, M., Spencer, A.: Implementation of SNOMED CT in an online clinical database. Future Hosp. J. **4**, 126–130 (2017)
3. NLM Tools for EHR Certification and Meaningful Use. http://www.nlm.nih.gov/healthit/meaningful_use.html
4. Lee, D., Cornet, R., Lau, F., de Keizer, N.: A survey of SNOMED CT implementations. J. Biomed. Inform. **46**, 87–96 (2013)
5. SNOMED CT Worldwide. http://www.snomed.org/snomed-ct/snomed-ct-worldwide
6. Lee, D.H., Lau, F.Y., Quan, H.: A method for encoding clinical datasets with SNOMED CT. BMC Med. Inf. Decis. Making **10**, 53 (2010)
7. Clinical Observations Recording and Encoding (CORE) Problem List Subset of SNOMED CT. http://www.nlm.nih.gov/research/umls/Snomed/core_subset.html
8. SNOMED CT Nursing Problem List Subset. http://www.nlm.nih.gov/research/umls/Snomed/nursing_problemlist_subset.html

9. Veterans Health Administration and Kaiser Permanente (VA/KP) Problem List subset. http://www.nlm.nih.gov/research/umls/Snomed/snomed_problem_list.html

10. UK SNOMED CT subsets. http://isd.digital.nhs.uk/trud3/user/guest/group/0/pack/40

11. Hansen, D.P., Giermanski, M., Dujmovic, M., Passenger, J., Lawley, M.J.: Building SNOMED CT reference sets for use as interface terminologies. Electron. J. Health Inf. **6**, 1 (2011)

12. SNOMED Technical Implementation Guide. http://confluence.ihtsdotools.org/display/DOCTIG/Technical+Implementation+Guide

13. Data Analytics with SNOMED CT. http://snomed.org/analytics

14. Raghupathi, W., Raghupathi, V.: Big data analytics in healthcare: promise and potential. Health Inf. Sci. Syst. **2**, 3 (2014)

15. SNOMED CT Query Language. http://confluence.ihtsdotools.org/display/SLPG/SNOMED+CT+Query+Language

16. SNOMED CT Expression Constraint Language. http://confluence.ihtsdotools.org/display/DOCECL/Expression+Constraint+Language+-+Specification+and+Guide

17. SNOMED CT Query Language Specification version 0.8 draft. http://www.cs.man.ac.uk/~rector/temp/SNOMED_TQL_for_comment.doc

18. SNOMED CT Query Service. http://github.com/IHTSDO/snomed-query-service

19. OWL 2. http://www.w3.org/TR/owl2-overview/

20. SPARQL 1.1 query language. http://www.w3.org/TR/sparql11-query/

21. Horridge, M., Bechhofer, S.: The OWL API: A Java API for OWL ontologies. Seman. Web **2**, 11–21 (2011)

22. Schulz, S., Jansen, L.: Formal ontologies in biomedical knowledge representation. Yearb Med Inform **8**, 132–146 (2013)

23. Baader, F., Horrocks, I., Sattler, U.: Description logics as ontology languages for the semantic web. In: Hutter, D., Stephan, W. (eds.) Mechanizing Mathematical Reasoning. LNCS, vol. 2605, pp. 228–248. Springer, Heidelberg (2005). https://doi.org/10.1007/978-3-540-32254-2_14

24. Berners-Lee, T., Hendler, J., Lassila, O.: The semantic web. Sci. Am. **284**, 28–37 (2001)

25. Antoniou, G., Van Harmelen, F.: A Semantic Web Primer. MIT Press, Cambridge (2004)

26. Baader, F., Horrocks, I., Lutz, C., Sattler, U.: An Introduction to Description Logic. Cambridge University Press, Cambridge (2017)

27. Krötzsch, M.: OWL 2 profiles: an introduction to lightweight ontology languages. In: Eiter, T., Krennwallner, T. (eds.) Reasoning Web 2012. LNCS, vol. 7487, pp. 112–183. Springer, Heidelberg (2012). https://doi.org/10.1007/978-3-642-33158-9_4

28. Wang, Y., Halper, M., Wei, D., Gu, H., Perl, Y., Xu, J., Elhanan, G., Chen, Y., Spackman, K.A., Case, J.T., Hripcsak, G.: Auditing complex concepts of SNOMED using a refined hierarchical abstraction network. J. Biomed. Inform. **45**, 1–14 (2012)

29. Jiang, G., Chute, C.G.: Auditing the semantic completeness of SNOMED CT using formal concept analysis. J. Am. Med. Inform. Assoc. **16**, 89–102 (2009)

30. Horridge, M., Drummond, N., Goodwin, J., Rector, A.L., Stevens, R., Wang, H.: The manchester OWL syntax. In: OWLed, vol. 216 (2006)

31. Hartel, F.W., de Coronado, S., Dionne, R., Fragoso, G., Golbeck, J.: Modeling a description logic vocabulary for cancer research. J. Biomed. Inform. **38**, 114–129 (2005)

32. Jena ARQ. http://jena.apache.org/documentation/query/

33. SPARQL 1.1 Entailment Regimes. http://www.w3.org/TR/sparql11-entailment/

34. Zhang, G.-Q., Bodenreider, O.: Using SPARQL to test for lattices: application to quality assurance in biomedical ontologies. In: Patel-Schneider, P.F., Pan, Y., Hitzler, P., Mika, P., Zhang, L., Pan, J.Z., Horrocks, I., Glimm, B. (eds.) ISWC 2010. LNCS, vol. 6497, pp. 273–288. Springer, Heidelberg (2010). https://doi.org/10.1007/978-3-642-17749-1_18

35. FaCT++. http://owl.man.ac.uk/factplusplus/
36. ELK. http://www.cs.ox.ac.uk/isg/tools/ELK/
37. Kim, J.D., Cohen, K.B.: Natural language query processing for SPARQL generation: a prototype system for SNOMED CT. In: BioLINK, pp. 32–38 (2013)
38. Alonso-Calvo, R., Paraiso-Medina, S., Perez-Rey, D., Alonso-Oset, E., van Stiphout, R., Yu, S., Taylor, M., Buffa, F., Fernandez-Lozano, C., Pazos, A., Maojo, V.: A semantic interoperability approach to support integration of gene expression and clinical data in breast cancer. Comput. Biol. Med. (2017)

Applications of Machine Learning

Feature Level Ensemble Method for Classifying Multi-media Data

Saleh Alyahyan[✉] and Wenjia Wang

School of Computing Sciences, University of East Anglia, Norwich, UK
{s.alyahyan,Wenjia.Wang}@uea.ac.uk

Abstract. Multimedia data consists of several different types of data, such as numbers, text, images, audio etc. and they usually need to be fused or integrated before analysis. This study investigates a feature-level aggregation approach to combine multimedia datasets for building heterogeneous ensembles for classification. It firstly aggregates multimedia datasets at feature level to form a normalised big dataset, then uses some parts of it to generate classifiers with different learning algorithms. Finally, it applies three rules to select appropriate classifiers based on their accuracy and/or diversity to build heterogeneous ensembles. The method is tested on a multimedia dataset and the results show that the heterogeneous ensembles outperform the individual classifiers as well as homogeneous ensembles. However, it should be noted that, it is possible in some cases that the combined dataset does not produce better results than using single media data.

Keywords: Multimedia data mining · Feature level data aggregation · Diversity · Heterogeneous ensemble · Classification

1 Introduction

There has been a rapid rise in the generation of multimedia data, not merely in terms of quantity, but also in the level of complexity as well as variety. Dealing with a vast volume and variety of multimedia data presents a considerable challenge to the existing techniques in machine learning and data mining. Therefore it is necessary to develop new techniques and methods that are capable of dealing with multimedia data more effectively and efficiently for various data mining tasks, e.g. classification. Classification of multimedia data has numerous important applications in a wide range of fields, including crime detection, healthcare and business, etc. Two phases are usually needed for classifying multimedia data: first, features need to be extracted from various media datasets and aggregated; second, suitable machine learning algorithms need to be applied [1] to generate classifiers.

In general, multimedia data are characterised by some kinds of heterogeneity, as they often contain different types of data, such as text, images [2], video and audio. These characteristics present an opportunity to apply machine learning

© Springer International Publishing AG 2017
M. Bramer and M. Petridis (Eds.): SGAI-AI 2017, LNAI 10630, pp. 235–249, 2017.
https://doi.org/10.1007/978-3-319-71078-5_21

methods with two different strategies. The first is to combine the multiple media datasets with their features, which is usually called as feature level data fusion. It involves extracting the features from different types of data, from all the data sources, and combining or merging all the features in order to generate just one dataset, which is sometimes referred as a single flat dataset. The second strategy is called decision-level data fusion. Instead of fusing all the subsets into one big set in feature-level fusion, this strategy uses each subset separately to generate models, and then combines the output decision of the models to produce a final decision [3]. This study will focus on the former strategy, as it is commonly used in data mining practice to investigate how ensemble methods and feature-level fusion could be used more effectively, to improve the accuracy of classification.

An ensemble combines multiple models using a grating technique with an aim of improving results [4], which has been demonstrated to be beneficial in the machine learning field for the problems with single media data. However, for multimedia data, there are various factors, including the individual model accuracy, diversity among member models, the number of member models and the decision fusion function used in the ensemble [5–9], which need to be taken into consideration in order to build an effective ensemble.

This research investigates the methods for building effective ensembles for feature-level fused multimedia data, particularly the heterogeneous ensembles, which are composed of different types, such as decision trees, Bayesian networks and neural networks etc., of classifiers, to examine if an heterogeneous ensemble is more accurate and reliable than homogeneous ensembles – composed of classifiers of the same type, e.g. decision trees only.

The rest of the paper is organized as follows. Section 2 briefly reviews some related previous studies. Section 3 describes our proposed methods in detail, including the tools and programs used in the research. Section 4 provides details of the experiment conducted and our results. Section 5 gives conclusions and suggestions for further work.

2   Related Work

There are several studies that have applied machine learning methods to multimedia data. Mojahed et al. [10] applied the machine learning clustering method to heterogeneous (not necessarily multimedia though) datasets. Due to the fact that there were not many heterogeneous datasets publicly available, they created their own heterogeneous datasets, which contained different types of media. Their combined data achieved a significant advantage on clustering performance over that of using only one type of data.

Tuarob et al. [11] applied the machine learning heterogeneous ensemble approach to classify social media datasets. They conducted their experiments using three datasets: two datasets collected from Twitter and one from Facebook. They used five different feature extraction methods to generate the data needed for machine learning algorithms. Each of them created a subset of all the combined data. Five base classifiers were used in their experiments, and the classifiers' results were combined using different methods, including majority voting and weighted voting. They suggested that the additional features may increase the accuracy of classifiers. However, strictly speaking, in this study, the datasets are not of multimedia, but a single media of multiple textual datasets.

Mehmood and Rasheed [12] managed to classify microbial habitat preferences, based on codon/bi-codon usage. They attained a high dimensional dataset by combining different datasets from different data sources. They showed that the combination, on the feature level, leads to a high dimensional dataset. Thus, they focused on feature selection to reduce the dimensionality of the combined dataset. They reduced a huge number of variables with accepted classification accuracy.

Chen et al. [13] also conducted an experiment on combining heterogeneous datasets to a single dataset, and applied homogeneous ensemble classification methods upon it. They used support vector machine as base classifier. In addition, they used real-word microblog datasets, provided by Tencent Weibo. Their results show that the aggregated dataset outperforms any single dataset. Nevertheless, the datasets they used are not of multimedia either. Hence, the level of effectiveness of these ensemble methods on multimedia data is unknown.

In summary, previous studies have used feature-level combination methods and different machine learning approaches to analyse so-called heterogeneous datasets, whilst in fact their datasets mostly come from different data sources of the same type. Thus, these studies were limited by their single medial of data and how their methods may perform on multimedia datasets is unknown.

3   The Feature Level Ensemble Method

3.1   The Framework of the Feature Level Ensemble Method

The proposed feature-level ensemble method (FLEM), as illustrated in Fig. 1, consists of four modules/stages: multimedia data aggregation module, modelling module, model selection module and combination module.

In general, a multimedia dataset (MMD) should consist of several subsets of various media, e.g. text, images, audio, etc. The FLEM starts with extracting D_i's features $(1 \leq i \leq n)$, from each subset of the MMD by using appropriate feature extraction methods. Then, all features are normalised and aggregated to form one big dataset, i.e., $D = N(D_1 \cup D_2 \cup D_3 \cup \ldots \cup D_n)$. These operations are usually called feature aggregation, which is why our approach is named as Feature-Level Ensemble Method, or FLEM in short.

The second stage is to generate various types of individual models, m_i $(1 \leq i \leq n)$, to create a pool of models, $PM = \{m_1, m_2, \ldots, m_n\}$ as the member candidates of ensemble. The models are called homogeneous models if they are generated by using the same learning algorithm with variations on its parameters and/or data partitions, or called heterogeneous models if they are generated by using different algorithms. A homogeneous ensemble is built with just homogeneous models, whilst a heterogeneous ensemble is constructed with heterogeneous models. In this study, over 10 different base learning algorithms have been selected to generate homogeneous and heterogeneous individual models.

The third stage involves model selection based on a set of defined criteria and rules. In this study, *accuracy* and *diversity* are used as selection criteria either separately or jointly. Three different rules for model selection are devised explained in the next section. Finally, the selected models are combined into one ensemble and their classification decisions are aggregated using a combination method to reach the final form of the ensemble.

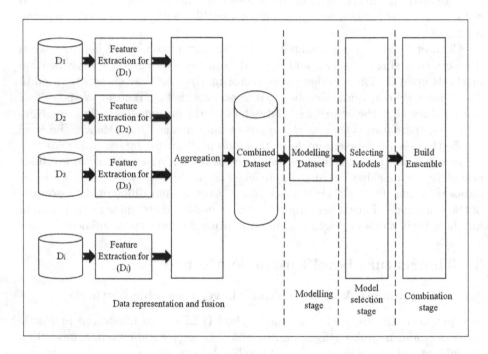

Fig. 1. A general framework for the feature-level ensemble method (FLEM).

3.2   Rules for Selecting Models

Three rules, $R0, R1$ and $R2$, as illustrated by Fig. 2, were devised for selecting models based on various criteria.

R0: This rule uses *accuracy* of classifiers as the criterion for selection. The FLEM firstly computes the accuracy, $(Acc(m_i))$, for each of the n models in the model pool PM and sorts them in a descending order based on the accuracy of the models $(Acc(m_i))$. Then the FLEM selects the N most accurate models from the PM using Eq. 1 and adds them to the ensemble, Φ, as shown in Fig. 2(a).

$$m_i = max\left\{Acc(m_j), m_j \in PM\right\} i = 1\dots N. \tag{1}$$

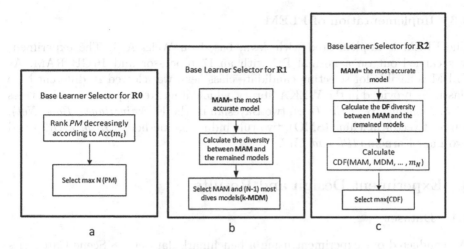

Fig. 2. Main steps for R0, R1 and R2 in HES [14]

R1: This rule uses both *accuracy* and *diversity* in sequence for model selection. FLEM first removes the most accurate model (MAM), $m_1 = max\{Acc(m_j), m_j \in PM\}$, from PM and adds it to ensemble Φ.

Then the pairwise diversity between MAM and remaining models in PM, are calculated with the Double Fault (DF) measure [15]. Then FLEM sorts the models in PM in a decreasing order based on the magnitude of the DF's. The $(N-1)$ most diverse models from the sorted PM are selected (Eq. 2) and added to the ensemble, Φ. Therefore Φ now contains MAM and the (N − 1) most diverse models from PM.

$$m_i = max\{DF(m_1, m_j), m_j \in PM\}\, i = 2\ldots N \tag{2}$$

R2: This rule uses both *accuracy* and two types of *diversity* measures, namely the *DF* diversity and the *Coincident Failure Diversity* (CFD) method [16]. Firstly, MAM is selected and removed from PM and added to Φ. Then the most diverse model (MDM) is determined from PM using $MDM = max\{DF(m_1, m_j), m_j \in PM\}$ and added to Φ, which now contains both the MAM and MDM models. From this point on, the CFD diversity measure is used to select further models with the aim of maximising the CFD diversity of the ensemble if they are included in Φ. The ensemble with the maximum CFD diversity is selected as the final ensemble, Φ using $\Phi = max\{CFD(\Phi \Leftarrow m_j), m_j \in PM\}$.

Rule $R2$ may be time consuming if the size of the model pool PM is large and all the possible combinations between Φ and the remaining members of PM are considered.

3.3   Implementation of FLEM

The FLEM is implemented with Java, based on Weka API. The experiment was carried out on a normal PC with an I7 processor and 16 GB RAM. As FLEM is flexible for selecting candidate classifiers, we selected 10 different base classifiers provided in the WEKA library, which are: three types of decision trees (*J48, RandomTree, REP-Tree*), two Bayesian methods (*NaiveBayes, BayesNet*), Support vector machine (SMO), two rule induction methods (*JRip, PART*) and two Lazy learners (*IBk and LWL*).

4   Experiment Design and Results

4.1   Dataset

We conducted our experiment using a benchmark dataset – 8 Scene Categories Dataset [17], which contains two parts in different media: 2688 images and their annotations represented by XML files. The images are categorized into eight

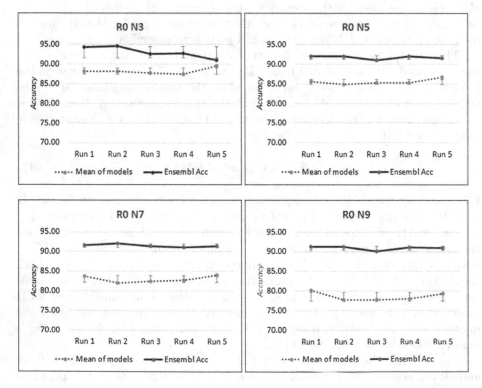

Fig. 3. The results of FLEMs built with rule R0. Each sub-graph shows the ensembles with different sizes 3, or 5, or 7 or 9. The solid and dashed lines are the mean accuracy of FLEMs and the mean accuracy of the models in the FLEMs respectively, with their standard deviations as error bars.

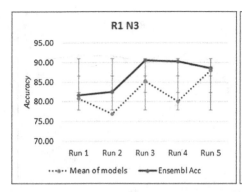
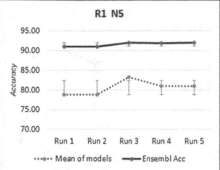

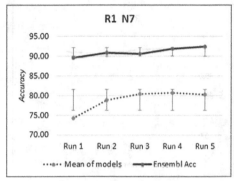
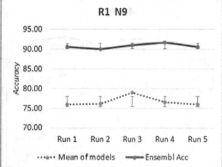

Fig. 4. The mean test accuracy of FLEMs built with rule R1. Four sub-graphs show the ensembles with different size of 3, 5, 7 and 9.

classes in according to their scenes and objects captured by the images. Each XML file contained a number of tags that describe an image. The annotations were dealt with as text and 782 textual features were extracted from the texts to form a data subset D_t. For the imagery data, 567 features were extracted from the images using Histograms of Oriented Gradients (HOG) [18] to form another data subset, i.e. imagery data D_g.

The textual and imagery features from these two data subsets were aggregated to form a single dataset, $D = N(D_t \cup D_g)$, which contains 2688 instances and each has 1358 features in total, as inputs and one classification output of 8 classes.

4.2 Experiment Design and Results

We conducted a series of experiments to investigate the performance of the FLEM working, with three selection rules separately, on the multimedia data. The factors that were investigated include (1) the performance measures and criteria for selecting classifiers, which are represented by the three rules: R0, R1 and R2, (2) the size of ensemble – varied from 3, 5, 7 to 9, and (3) the salience of multimedia data, i.e. if the combined multimedia data D can produce better

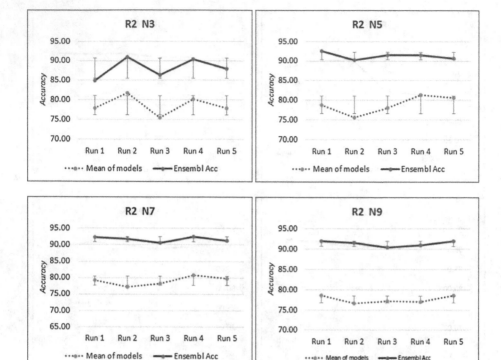

Fig. 5. The mean test accuracy of FLEMS built with rule R2. Four sub-graphs show the ensembles with different size of 3, 5, 7 and 9.

results, compared with each of the single-media data subsets: D_t and D_g. For each specific set-up, the experiment was repeated 5 times with different data partitions to check consistency.

In addition, for comparison with heterogeneous ensembles, homogeneous ensembles were built with the classifiers selected only from the same type. As ten different types of base learning algorithms were used for generating classifiers, ten homogeneous ensembles were constructed for each set-up of above listed factors.

Therefore, for all possible combinations of these parameters, over 200 sets of experiments were conducted in total.

Results of FLEMs Built with Three Rules and Variable Sizes: Figures 3, 4 and 5 show some results (means and standard deviations) obtained from these experiments of FLEMs constructed with three rules and different sizes. These figures show clearly that FLEMs built with the three rules are generally much better than individual classifiers on average because the mean accuracies (solid lines on the figures) of FLEMs are about 10% higher than the mean accuracies (dashed lines) of the individual classifiers in the FLEMs.

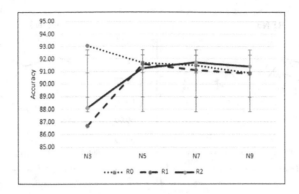

Fig. 6. Comparison of three rules as the size of FLEM varies.

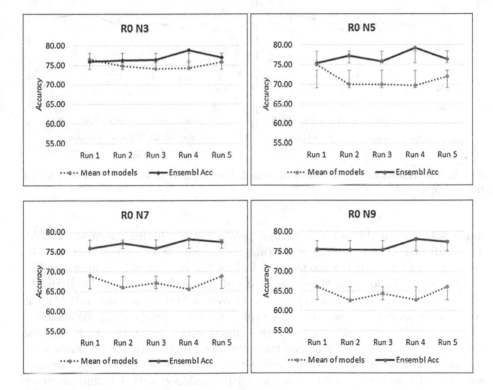

Fig. 7. The results of HESs built with rule R0 and different sizes (3, 5, 7 and 9) for the image dataset. The solid and dashed lines are the mean accuracy of HESs and the models of the HESs, with standard deviations as error bars, respectively.

Figure 6 compares the results of FLEMs built with the three rules and variable sizes from 3 to 9 on the test data. As can be seen, there is not much difference in overall classification accuracy between the three rules when the ensemble sizes are equal to 5 and more. But when the size of ensembles is small, i.e. 3, R0 did

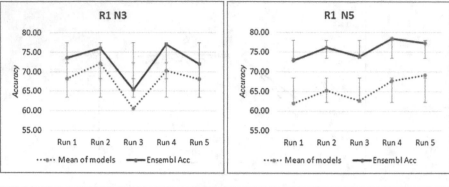

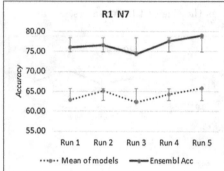
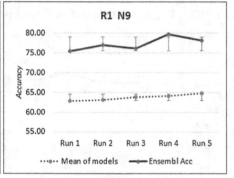

Fig. 8. The results of HESs built with rule R1 and different sizes (3, 5, 7 and 9) for the image dataset.

much better than the other two rules, producing the highest accuracy (93%). This indicates that it is very important to choose the classifiers that are the most accurate ones in the model pool PM as the core models in an ensemble, which is what R0 does. So, that those best individual classifiers can dominate the performance of the ensemble to produce the overall best classification. When the size of an ensemble increases the three rules appear to produce similar accuracy consistently. However, R2 possesses the largest mean accuracies with smallest standard deviations, which means the ensembles built with R2 are more consistent or reliable, as well as more accurate. So, we conclude that the ensemble with model selection criteria using the CFD combined with DF and accuracy measures (R2), provides a superior result to that of either pair-wise diversity (R1) or accuracy (R0) alone. Diversity and accuracy must both be taken into consideration when constructing large ensembles for classification.

Results of Using Text, Images and Combined Datasets: As designed, further experiments were conducted by separately using three sets of data: text, imagery and combined, in order to investigate if the aggregation of subsets of multimedia data gives better results. The experiments on the textual dataset D_t

alone were conducted with our Heterogeneous Ensemble System, called HES_T, and their results were reported in our earlier paper [14]. The experiments on the image dataset D_g, called HES_G, were conducted in this study in the same way as the one used for the text experiments. The results of HES_G, obtained in these experiments, are shown in Figs. 7, 8 and 9.

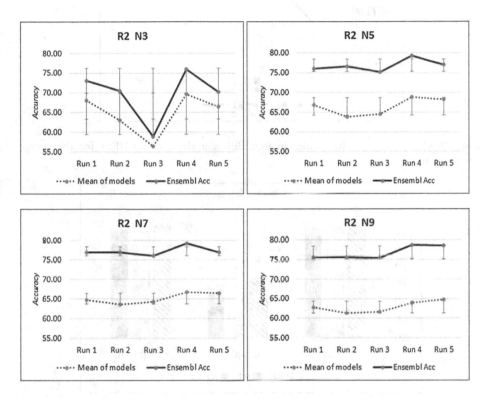

Fig. 9. The results of HESs built with rule R2 and different sizes (3, 5, 7 and 9) for the image dataset.

The summary of the results of varying the ensemble size from 3 to 9 on the test dataset for each of the three rules is shown by Fig. 10.

A further observation from these results is that, using FLEM, the accuracy of the combined text and imagery datasets was lower than that of using the text dataset alone. Furthermore, the accuracy of the image dataset alone was lower than that of the text dataset, as shown in Fig. 11. A plausible explanation for these differences is that the features extracted from the imagery dataset did not very well represent the information associated with the underlying classification knowledge of the problem, or even worse brought in some noises, and hence confused the learning algorithms resulting in quite weak or bad models, which in turn resulted in weak ensembles. On the other hand, the text data, or more precisely speaking, the features extracted from the text data, are more

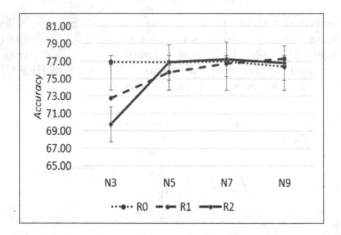

Fig. 10. Comparing all three rules in four different sizes of the HESs for the image dataset only.

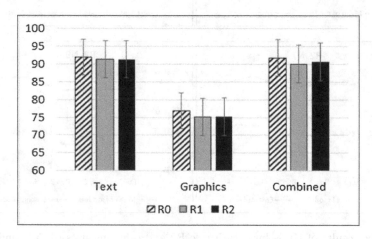

Fig. 11. Comparison of all the ensembles built with three rules for text dataset, image dataset and the combined multimedia dataset respectively.

representative or salient as the ensembles built with the models trained with the text data are more accurate, about 15% higher than those of ensembles built with the image data.

With the combined dataset, the ensembles produced good results, which are comparable to those obtained by the text data only. But on the whole, in this application, the aggregation of multimedia datasets did not offer much additional benefit in terms of improving classification accuracy.

Comparison with Homogeneous Ensembles: Another set of experiments was conducted to compare the performance between heterogeneous and various homogeneous ensembles, built using all the three model selection rules that have been implemented in FLEMs.

Table 1 shows the mean accuracies for the feature level heterogeneous ensembles and all homogeneous ensembles built with rules R0, R1 and R2. It is very clear that, on average the heterogeneous ensembles are much better, about 10% higher, than the homogeneous ensembles constructed using the same rules.

Table 1. The comparison results between the heterogeneous ensemble and the homogeneous ensemble for FLEM for all the three rules

	Heterogeneous		Homogeneous	
	Mean	SD	Mean	SD
R0	91.79	0.92	80.05	0.78
R1	90.05	2.26	80.04	0.99
R2	90.63	1.70	80.01	0.97

5   Conclusion and Future Work

Aggregating and mining multi-media datasets effectively is a challenge task in machine learning and data mining fields. In this work, we developed a feature-level ensemble method (FLEM) with an aim of achieving better classification of multimedia data. Our FLEM consists of four stages: extracting features from multimedia subsets and aggregating them into a single dataset, modelling the combined dataset, selecting models with different rules based on various criteria, and building heterogeneous ensembles. The experimental results have demonstrated our FLEM is capable of handling multimedia datasets – unstructured text data and imagery data, simultaneously and builds the best ensembles with appropriate datasets, with either combined multi-media data or single-media data. In general, the heterogeneous ensembles are much better than homogeneous ensembles in terms of accuracy and consistency.

Another point drawn from the results of this study, is that it is necessary to be cautious when combining multiple data subsets of a problem because the aggregated data may not produce a better result than that of using data subsets of single-media. Possible reasons include poor features extracted from each subset, which capture more noise rather than useful information; and/or inappropriate aggregation, which may introduce some inconsistency or even contradictions into the final dataset and therefore cause a great deal of difficulty and/or confusion in learning.

Some further work can be done in our approach on various aspects. For example, firstly, it could be useful to apply some feature selection methods on each of data subsets before aggregation, to eliminate irrelevant or redundant features, which in turn can reduce the dimensionality of the data and simplify learning. Secondly, more rules could be devised to select the models to increase overall accuracy levels. Thirdly, it would prove useful to analyse multi-media datasets which contain other, different types of media, which have not yet been the subject of this research. Finally, instead of aggregating multiple data sets at feature-level, it appears more promising to apply decision-level aggregation strategy, which is to generate the models independently from each of data subsets and then combine them to form an ensemble.

References

1. Zhang, Z., Zhang, R.: Multimedia data mining. In: Data Mining and Knowledge Discovery Handbook, pp. 1081–1109 (2010)
2. Wu, X., Zhu, X., Wu, G.-Q., Ding, W.: Data mining with big data. IEEE Trans. Knowl. Data Eng. **26**(1), 97–107 (2014)
3. Ballard, C., Wang, W.: Dynamic ensemble selection methods for heterogeneous data mining. In: 2016 12th World Congress on Intelligent Control and Automation (WCICA), pp. 1021–1026. IEEE (2016)
4. Dietterich, T.G.: Ensemble methods in machine learning. In: Kittler, J., Roli, F. (eds.) MCS 2000. LNCS, vol. 1857, pp. 1–15. Springer, Heidelberg (2000). https://doi.org/10.1007/3-540-45014-9_1
5. Wang, W.: Some fundamental issues in ensemble methods. In: IEEE International Joint Conference on Neural Networks, IJCNN 2008 (IEEE World Congress on Computational Intelligence), pp. 2243–2250. IEEE (2008)
6. Caruana, R., Niculescu-Mizil, A., Crew, G., Ksikes, A.: Ensemble selection from libraries of models. In: Proceedings of 21st International Conference on Machine Learning, p. 18. ACM (2004)
7. Zhang, S., Cohen, I., Goldszmidt, M., Symons, J., Fox, A.: Ensembles of models for automated diagnosis of system performance problems. In: Proceedings of International Conference on Dependable Systems and Networks, DSN 2005, pp. 644–653. IEEE (2005)
8. Zenobi, G., Cunningham, P.: Using diversity in preparing ensembles of classifiers based on different feature subsets to minimize generalization error. In: De Raedt, L., Flach, P. (eds.) ECML 2001. LNCS, vol. 2167, pp. 576–587. Springer, Heidelberg (2001). https://doi.org/10.1007/3-540-44795-4_49
9. Liu, Y., Yao, X., Higuchi, T.: Evolutionary ensembles with negative correlation learning. IEEE Trans. Evol. Comput. **4**(4), 380–387 (2000)
10. Mojahed, A., Bettencourt-Silva, J.H., Wang, W., de la Iglesia, B.: Applying clustering analysis to heterogeneous data using similarity matrix fusion (SMF). In: Perner, P. (ed.) MLDM 2015. LNCS, vol. 9166, pp. 251–265. Springer, Cham (2015). https://doi.org/10.1007/978-3-319-21024-7_17
11. Tuarob, S., Tucker, C.S., Salathe, M., Ram, N.: An ensemble heterogeneous classification methodology for discovering health-related knowledge in social media messages. J. Biomed. Inform. **49**, 255–268 (2014)
12. Mehmood, T., Rasheed, Z.: Multivariate procedure for variable selection and classification of high dimensional heterogeneous data. Commun. Stat. Appl. Methods **22**(6), 575–587 (2015)
13. Chen, Z.-Y., Fan, Z.-P., Sun, M.: Behavior-aware user response modeling in social media: learning from diverse heterogeneous data. Eur. J. Oper. Res. **241**(2), 422–434 (2015)

14. Alyahyan, S., Farrash, M., Wang, W.: Heterogeneous ensemble for imaginary scene classification. In: Proceedings of 8th International Joint Conference on Knowledge Discovery, Knowledge Engineering and Knowledge Management (IC3K 2016), KDIR, Porto, Portugal, 9–11 November 2016, vol. 1, pp. 197–204 (2016)
15. Giacinto, G., Roli, F.: Design of effective neural network ensembles for image classification purposes. Image Vis. Comput. **19**(9), 699–707 (2001)
16. Partridge, D., Krzanowski, W.: Software diversity: practical statistics for its measurement and exploitation. Inf. Softw. Technol. **39**(10), 707–717 (1997)
17. Oliva, A., Torralba, A.: Modeling the shape of the scene: a holistic representation of the spatial envelope. Int. J. Comput. Vis. **42**(3), 145–175 (2001)
18. Dalal, N., Triggs, B.: Histograms of oriented gradients for human detection. In: IEEE Computer Society Conference on Computer Vision and Pattern Recognition, CVPR 2005, vol. 1, pp. 886–893. IEEE (2005)

Reliability Based Bayesian Inference for Probabilistic Classification: An Overview of Sampling Schemes

P.G. Byrnes[✉] [iD] and F.A. DiazDelaO

Institute for Risk and Uncertainty, University of Liverpool, Liverpool, UK
{paul.byrnes,f.a.diazdelao}@liverpool.ac.uk

Abstract. As physical systems have become more complex, the demand for models which incorporate uncertainties in the systems behavior has grown. Bayesian updating is a powerful method which allows models to be learned as new information and data becomes available. In a high dimensional setting, Bayesian updating requires the computation of an integral which is analytically intractable. Markov Chain Monte Carlo (MCMC) techniques include a popular class of methods to solve such an integral. A disadvantage of MCMC however, is its low computational efficiency for problems with many uncertain parameters. Accordingly, a relation between the Bayesian updating problem and the engineering reliability problem has been established. The BUS (Bayesian Updating with Structural Reliability Methods) approach enables reliability methods which are efficient in high dimensions, but retain the advantages of MCMC, to be applied to Bayesian updating problems. Subset Simulation (SuS) is an efficient Monte Carlo technique suitable for such tasks. The BUS algorithm requires a likelihood multiplier to be calculated prior to implementation of SuS. The issue of correctly choosing a suitable multiplier value has gathered much interest. Consequently, a modified BUS framework has been developed which computes the multiplier automatically. The choice of MCMC algorithm within SuS greatly affects sample quality, model efficiency and sample acceptance rate. A low sample acceptance rate results in many repeated samples and thus low efficiency. As such this research investigates the effect of different sampling schemes within the SuS algorithm on the performance of the modified BUS framework for binary probabilistic classification models.

Keywords: Machine learning · Classification · Bayesian updating · Reliability analysis · MCMC · Subset Simulation

1 Introduction

A Bayesian classification framework requires the computation of a posterior probability distribution of a class given a data observation. Markov Chain Monte Carlo (MCMC) [1] techniques include a popular class of methods to directly generate samples from such a posterior distribution. An issue which stems from standard MCMC implementation is its inability to efficiently generate samples for problems with a large

© Springer International Publishing AG 2017
M. Bramer and M. Petridis (Eds.): SGAI-AI 2017, LNAI 10630, pp. 250–263, 2017.
https://doi.org/10.1007/978-3-319-71078-5_22

number of uncertain parameters. As such, maintaining the advantages of MCMC based methods whilst greatly improving efficiency is highly desirable.

Viewed as an extension of rejection sampling [2], BUS (Bayesian Updating with Structural reliability methods) [3] suggests the application of reliability methods to Bayesian updating problems. Subset Simulation (SuS) [4] is an adaptive Monte Carlo simulation method used in reliability engineering which is extremely efficient in estimating rare events. Through the expression of the (rare) failure event F as contained in a nested sequence of more frequent events, SuS is enabled to calculate the probability of failure. Prior to the implementation of SuS under the BUS framework, a constant referred to as the likelihood multiplier is required to be chosen. However, correctly choosing the value of this multiplier has in general remained an open question. A modified BUS [5] algorithm has been proposed which learns the multiplier automatically allowing SuS to generate posterior samples.

The choice of MCMC algorithm applied within SuS is an important factor as it dictates the models efficiency, sample quality and sample acceptance rate. Consequently, the objective of this paper is to investigate the effect of different sampling schemes within the SuS algorithm on the performance of the modified BUS framework in a classification setting. A binary Gaussian Process (GP) classification model is implemented on the 'USPS' data set [6]. The remainder of this paper is organized as follows: Engineering reliability analysis and MCMC sampling schemes are introduced in Sect. 2. Section 3 briefly presents the modified BUS framework. Gaussian Process classification is received in Sect. 4 followed by numerical experiments in Sect. 5.

2 Engineering Reliability Analysis

A response variable Y which is dependent on input variables $x = (x_1, \ldots, x_d)$ may represent the behavior of a system

$$Y = h(x_1, \ldots, x_d) \tag{1}$$

where d represents the dimension of the problem and $h(x)$ the performance function. One of the most computationally challenging problems in reliability engineering is calculating the probability of failure. In this setting, the failure domain F is populated by the output of Y which exceeds a critical threshold b.

$$F = \{x : h(x) > b\} \tag{2}$$

Let $\psi(x)$ denote the joint probability density function (PDF) for a continuous random variable x. The engineering reliability problem is to compute the probability of failure $P(F)$ given by

$$P(F) = P(x \in F) = \int_F \psi(x) dx \tag{3}$$

In a well-designed system $P(F)$ is extremely small and thus may be viewed as a rare event. Additionally, in a high dimensional setting it is often the case that the failure domain is disjoint and thus sampling may prove challenging. Consequently, rare event simulation techniques have been developed.

SuS is such a rare event simulation technique which expresses F as an intersection of nested events. Through the expression of $P(F)$ as

$$P(F) = P(F_1) \prod_{i=1}^{m} P(F_i \mid F_{i-1}) \tag{4}$$

where F_0 is a rather frequent event and F_i extremely rare. Providing that the conditional probabilities are chosen in the correct manner, they may be made large enough so as to be estimated by simulation means. Hence, the original rare event problem is broken down into a series of intermediate sub-problems which define a series of intermediate thresholds. The algorithm proceeds as follows:

1. *Define N and p_0*
   Initialize $m=0$
   Generate samples $\{X_i^0 : 1, \dots, N\}$ from the input PDF π
   Calculate $Y_i^0(x_i)$ for $\{x_1, \dots, x_N\}$
   Set $n_F(0) = \sum_{i=1}^{N}(Y_i^0 > b)$
2. **while** $p_0 > n_F(m)/N$ **do**
   $m = m + 1$
   Sort Y in descending order
   Store N_s samples as 'seeds' for F_m
   Calculate b_m
   Populate F_m by MCMC
   Calculate $n_F(m)$
   end while
3. *Calculate $P_F \approx p^m \frac{n_F^m}{N}$*

where m represents the current threshold level. Let $p_0 \in [0, 1]$ be the level probability which in essence governs how many intermediate failure thresholds are required to reach the failure domain F and $N \in \mathbb{N}$ be the total number of generated samples. While $n_s = p_0 N \in \mathbb{N}$ governs the required number of accepted samples at each level.

SuS requires the parameters p_0 and N be determined before beginning the simulation. Beginning at $level_0$, the algorithm probes the input space generating N independent and identically distributed (i.i.d) samples by direct Monte Carlo methods. Based on the values of Y computed by $h(x)$, the first intermediate failure threshold b_1 is calculated. The n_s samples which exceed b_1 from $level_0$ are stored as seeds for generating additional samples conditional on $F_1 = \{Y > b_1\}$ at $level_1$. For $level_1$ a MCMC sampling scheme is utilized to populate F_1. Similar to $level_0$ the samples which exceed b_2 are used as seeds for the next level. The generation of intermediate levels is continued in the same manner until the above stopping condition is met. The importance of the choice of MCMC algorithm chosen will be addressed in the following section. For more details on the implementation of SuS, refer to [4].

2.1   MCMC Sampling Schemes

As a Markov Chain progresses, the correlation between samples increases and thus less information may be extracted from the generated posterior samples. Consequently, with respect to SuS, a MCMC algorithm which efficiently explores each intermediate failure domain is highly desirable. The Metropolis-Hastings (M-H) [7] algorithm is the most widely used MCMC approach for sampling from distributions which are difficult to sample from directly. Although it can be extremely effective, M-H becomes inefficient in high dimensions resulting in a low sample acceptance rate. Accordingly, numerous alternative methods have been developed. The Modified Metropolis [4] (MM) allows for the generation of samples from high dimensional conditional distributions by assigning a one-dimensional proposal PDF to each proposed sample. The algorithm proceeds as follows:

1. *For each $i = 1, \dots, n$, generate candidate sample $x_i' = (x_1', \dots, x_n')$.*
   a) *Generate a pre-candidate u_i' by sampling from the PDF $q_i(\cdot \mid x_i)$*
   b) *Accept or reject u_i'*

$$
x_i' = \begin{cases} u_i', & \text{with prob } a_i \\ \\ x_0, & \text{with prob } 1 - a_i \end{cases}
$$

$$
, \text{where } a_i = min\left\{\frac{\phi(u_i')}{\phi(x)}\right\}
$$

2. *Accept or reject x'*

$$
x_1 = \begin{cases} x', & x' \in F \\ \\ x_0, & x' \notin F \end{cases}
$$

where $q_i(\cdot \mid x_i)$ is a one-dimensional proposal PDF, ϕ the one dimensional standard Gaussian PDF and x_0 the current sample state. A sample x' is generated from $q_i(\cdot \mid x_i)$ and is either accepted or rejected based on the above criteria. This is repeated until the stationary distribution has been reached. Stemming from MM a Delayed Rejection Modified Metropolis (DRMM) [8] has been proposed which introduces a second proposal distribution at the pre-candidate state. In the event that the initial pre-candidate sample is rejected, a new candidate is generated from a proposal which is dependent on the rejected sample. As a result, the number of repeated samples is reduced.

An input which greatly effects the efficiency and chain correlation of both MM and DRMM algorithms is the choice of proposal distribution. The proposal distribution effects both the sample acceptance rate and the transition of the Markov Chain from one state to another. To nullify the importance of proposal choice, Subset Infinity (SuSInf) [9] has been developed. SuSInf allows for the generated samples to be dependent on the statistics of the current sample only. The algorithm proceeds as follows:

1. *For* $i = 1, ..., n$ *generate candidate sample* $x'_i = (x'_1, ..., x'_n)$ *from a Gaussian PDF with mean* g_i *and variance* s_i.
2. *Accept or reject* x'

$$x_1 = \begin{cases} x', & x' \in F \\ x_0, & x' \notin F \end{cases}$$

where s_i is the standard deviation of the candidate x'_i from the current sample x_0 and $g_i = \sqrt{1 - s_i^2}$. For further details refer to [9]. This study investigates the performance of MM, DRMM and SuSInf within the modified BUS framework for a classification problem.

3 Modified BUS Formulation

For the sake of brevity for the remainder of this paper let the posterior distribution be expressed as follows:

$$P(x) = P_D^{-1} L(x) q(x) \tag{5}$$

where $L(x)$ denotes the likelihood function, $q(x)$ the prior PDF and P_D^{-1} the normalizing constant $\int L(x)q(x)dx$. The modified BUS formulation [5] is an extension of the original BUS [2] algorithm and interprets the Bayesian Updating problem as rare event simulation. It recognizes that the probability of acceptance (P_A) in Rejection sampling is equivalent to the probability of failure (P_F) in reliability analysis when a uniform random variable on $[0, 1]$ is added to the sample space of the uncertain parameter which in this case is represented by x. The Rejection sampling algorithm generates a sample from $P(x)$ as follows:

1. *Generate U uniformly distributed on* $[0, 1]$ *and x with the prior PDF* $q(x)$.
2. *If* $U < cL(x)$, *return x as the sample. Otherwise repeat step 1.*

where c is a constant such that the rejection principle inequality $(cL(x) \leq 1)$ holds. However, given that $q(x)$ is from the entire sample space, P_A is extremely small and thus may be viewed as a rare event. Therefore, the modified BUS allows the application of SuS to sample from P_A where the failure domain now takes the form of a posterior distribution. Let the failure domain of interest be defined as

$$F = \{Y > -ln(c)\} \tag{6}$$

such that

$$Y = ln\left(\frac{L(x)}{u}\right) \tag{7}$$

where u is a standard uniform random variable on $[0, 1]$. For a choice of c such that the rejection principle inequality holds the distribution of the samples conditional on $\{Y > b\}$ will remain unchanged for a sufficiently large b.

The natural logarithm is introduced to Y, for two main reasons. Firstly, it ensures that Y is a well defined random variable. Secondly it allows the model evidence to be expressed as

$$P_D = e^b P(Y > b) \qquad \text{for any} \qquad b > b_{min} \qquad (8)$$

This form of the model evidence results in both P_D and $P(Y > b)$ exhibiting characteristic trends as b increases and surpasses b_{min}. Thus, allowing the identification of the level at which generated samples are distributed per the posterior.

Regarding $P(Y > b)$, as the threshold levels increase $P(Y > b)$ goes from a slowly decreasing function through a transition stage to an exponentially decaying function. Where this transition takes place at b_{min}. Similarly, lnP_D goes from a linearly increasing function as b increases through a transition stage to remaining constant equal to lnP_D. For the sake of simplicity let $V(b)$ represent lnP_D. Figure 1 contains a graphical representation of how $lnP(Y > b)$ and $V(b)$ change when SuS has surpassed b_{min}.

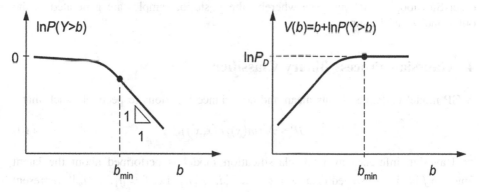

Fig. 1. Theoretical characteristic trends of $lnP(Y > b)$ and $V(b)$.

Based on the above characteristic trends an automatic stopping condition may be implemented once the algorithm detects that the transition has occurred. As SuS progresses, the number of samples generated from the prior distribution at each level decreases before converging to zero once the posterior has been reached. Through the expression of the probability of a sample being generated from the prior as

$$a_m = P_x\left(L(x) > e^{b_m}\right) \qquad (9)$$

the stopping condition takes the form of a reliability problem that in turn may also be solved by SuS. Seeing as a_m tends to zero as m increases, in reality a tolerance must be chosen whereby once a_m is less than the chosen value, the simulation stops. A flowchart of the proposed algorithm is presented in Fig. 2. Both an inner-SuS and

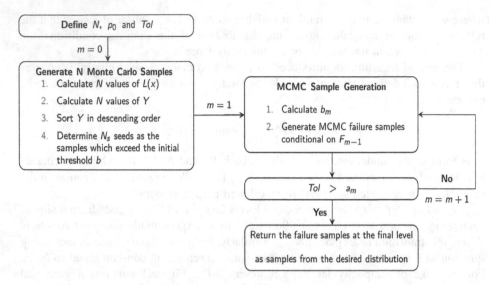

Fig. 2. Flowchart for the modified BUS algorithm.

outer-SuS loop are taking place whereby the posterior samples are generated in the outer and a_m in the inner.

4 Gaussian Process Binary Classifier

A GP model is defined by its mean and covariance functions respectively such that

$$GP \sim \mathcal{N}(m(x), k(x, x')) \tag{10}$$

Bayesian inference in a GP classification model is performed about the latent function f having observed data $D = \{(y_i, x_i) \mid i, \ldots, n\}$. Let $f = [f_1, \ldots, f_m]^T$ represent the values of the latent function, $d = [d_1, \ldots, d_m]^T$ the model inputs and $y = [y_1, \ldots, y_m]^T$ the class labels where $y \in \{-1, 1\}$. Often in a binary setting since neither of the class labels is more probable the mean of the prior over f is set to zero. A covariance function of the form $k(x, x' \mid \theta)$, where θ represents the functions hyperparameters is combined with the zero-mean function to define the GP. Through the application of Bayes rule the posterior distribution over the latent function f for given hyperparameters θ is expressed as

$$p(f \mid D, \theta) = \frac{p(y \mid f) p(f \mid X, \theta)}{p(D \mid \theta)} = \frac{\mathcal{N}(f \mid 0, K)}{p(D \mid \theta)} \prod_{i=1}^{m} \Phi(y_i f_i) \tag{11}$$

where Φ represents the continuous density function (CDF) of the standard Gaussian distribution. Marginalizing the distribution of the latent function to predict y^* from d^*

$$p(f_* \mid D, \theta, d) = \int p(f_* \mid f, X, \theta, d) p(f \mid D, \theta) df \tag{12}$$

in turn allows the predictive distribution to be obtained by taking the expectation of the marginal

$$p(y_* \mid D, \theta, d_*) = \int p(y_* \mid f_*) p(f_* \mid D, \theta, d_*) df_* \tag{13}$$

This study computes the above posterior through the modified BUS framework utilizing each of the MCMC sampling schemes previously mentioned.

5   Numerical Experiments

The USPS database presented in Fig. 3, is the digital recognition of digits on hand written envelopes [6]. The data set consists of 10 individual classes in 256 dimensions. A binary sub-problem from the USPS digit data is defined by considering the problem of discriminating images showing the digits 3 and 5. The data is split randomly into 767 training cases and 773 test cases. The digit 3 is assigned the label $y = 1$ and 5 $y = -1$. The inputs are standardized to a zero mean and unit variance.

Fig. 3. USPS hand written digit data base [10].

The covariance function chosen is the squared exponential

$$k(x, x' \mid \theta) = \sigma^2 \, exp \left(\frac{\|x - x'\|^2}{-2l^2} \right) \tag{14}$$

where $\theta = [\sigma, l]$, σ^2 refers to the signal variance and l is the characteristic length scale. The likelihood function used is the CDF of the standard Gaussian distribution

$$\Phi(x) = \int_{-\infty}^{x} \mathcal{N}(x \mid 0, 1)dx \tag{15}$$

The modified BUS framework was implemented using the three MCMC approaches which will be referred to as BUS_{MM}, BUS_{DRMM} and BUS_{SuSInf} respectively for the remainder of this study. Each algorithm was run 1,000 times independently with $N = 1,000$ and $p_0 = 0.1$. A one-dimensional proposal PDF was chosen to be uniform on [0,1]. From Fig. 4 it is evident that there is an overall agreement between characteristic trends produced. The general nature of the curves follows that predicted in Fig. 1.

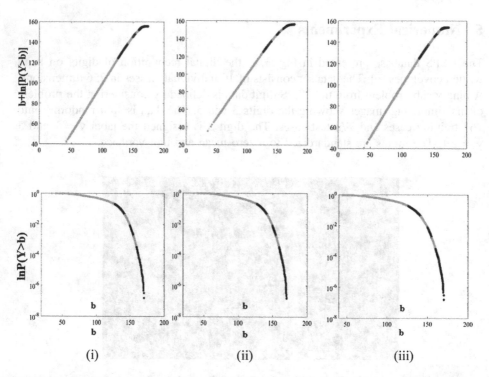

Fig. 4. Log-evidence of characteristic trends for 1000 samples per level using (i) BUS_{MM}, (ii) BUS_{DRMM} and (iii) BUS_{SuSInf}. Both $V(b) = b + lnP(Y > b)$ (Top) and $lnP(Y > b)$ (Bottom) exhibit behavior which coincides with the theory. The transition in color represents each intermediate threshold value.

For the automatic stopping condition a tolerance of $a_m = 10^{-6}$ was set as the threshold for the probability of inadmissibility in Eq. (9). Table 1 reveals that each modified BUS implementation has converged to a value smaller than a_m at $level_5$. Thus, the samples generated after $level_5$ may be assumed to be drawn from the desired posterior. The probability of sample acceptance (P_{ACC}) at the termination level is also

Table 1. MCMC algorithm diagnostics

	a_5	P_{ACC}	TME	Error %
Modified BUS$_{MM}$	$4.21e^{-08}$	$1.1e^{-03}$	$18.1 \cdot 10^3$	7.4%
Modified BUS$_{DRMM}$	$3.23e^{-08}$	$1.31e^{-03}$	$18.1 \cdot 10^3$	8.3%
Modified BUS$_{SuSInf}$	$1.97e^{-07}$	$5.65e^{-04}$	$17.4 \cdot 10^3$	7.6%

included. The computational demand is measured by Total Model Evaluations (TME) which is the number of $L(x)$ calls required to draw 1000 samples from the posterior. As expected, BUS$_{MM}$ and BUS$_{DRMM}$ produce the same number of TME. This stems from the repeated sample generation in DRMM occurring at the pre-candidate state resulting in no additional calls of $L(x)$. However, they do differ in running time as is discussed later. It is evident that BUS$_{SuSInf}$ has the fewest number of TME. Regarding classification test error percentage, BUS$_{MM}$ has slightly outperformed the other sampling schemes.

An interval of potential hyperparameter values was chosen for the implementation of each sampling scheme using the GP classifier. Given that GP classifiers require a prudent choice of hyperparameters for optimal test performance, an optimized classifier using the modified BUS$_{MM}$ was also implemented using Expectation Propagation [11] as a benchmark comparison. The parameters for SuS were set to $N = 5,000$ and $p_0 = 0.2$ respectively. The probability of inadmissibility converged to a value smaller than a_m at $level_6$. Thus, the samples generated after this level may be used to produce predictive latent function values f^*. A contour plot of the log marginal likelihood for both BUS$_{MM}$ and EP is presented in Fig. 5. It is evident that the posterior is skewed and

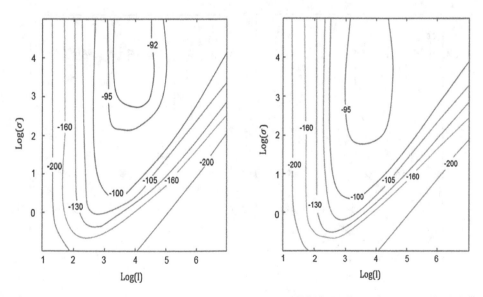

Fig. 5. Log marginal likelihoods produced by the modified BUS (Left) and Expectation Propagation (EP) (Right).

the marginal contour plots are well peaked in both cases, whilst both marginals are producing maximums at similar locations in the posterior. In general, we would expect log hyperparameter values which produce a high marginal value to perform relatively well in a predictive setting.

The scaled information score, given by

$$I = H + \frac{1}{2n} \sum_{i=1}^{n} (1 + y_i) \, log_2(p_i) + (1 - y_i) \, log_2(1 - p_i) \qquad (16)$$

where n is the number of test observations, is a measure of classification performance on the test data. The value of I may range from 0 to 1 where 1 bit indicates perfect prediction and 0 bits random guessing. The entropy for the training set labels is given by

$$H = -\sum_{y=\pm 1} \frac{n_{test}^y}{n_{test}} \, log_2 \frac{n_{train}^y}{n_{train}} \leq 1 \qquad (17)$$

where n_{test}^y and n_{train}^y denote the number of observations in the test and training data sets repetitively with the given target class label. In this case $y = 1$. Figure 6 contains a contour plot for the modified BUS$_{MM}$ and EP. As suggested by the log marginals it is apparent that the optimal log hyperparameters have resulted in the highest information scores being produced. The maximum values being 0.91 and 0.89 for the modified BUS$_{MM}$ and EP respectively.

Aside from the scaled information score, box plots for the misclassification rate for 1000 independent runs of both the modified BUS$_{MM}$ algorithm and EP using their

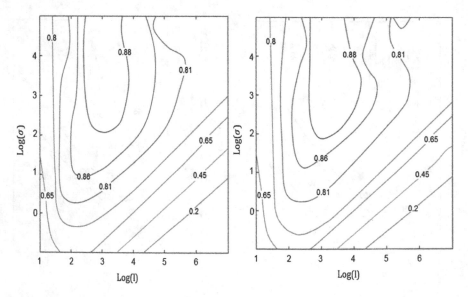

Fig. 6. Information scores produced by the modified BUS$_{MM}$ (Left) and Expectation Propagation (EP) (Right).

respective optimal log hyperparameter values are presented in Fig. 7. The error threshold used for each test point was 0.5. It is evident that the modified BUS_{MM} has produced a smaller spread and an average error rate of 2.8%, whilst the average error rate for EP was 3.3%. The decrease in error % for BUS_{MM} stems from the hyperparameter optimization and the greater number of samples generated at each level. It is worth noting the SuS parameters were varied. However, the degree of increased accuracy did not justify the additional computational expense.

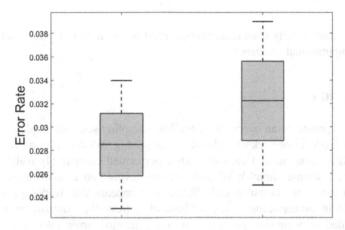

Fig. 7. Misclassification of GP model based on 1000 independent runs of the modified BUS_{MM} framework (Left) and EP (Right).

In addition to the two algorithms discussed thus far, both Laplace approximation and standard MCMC were also applied to the USPS data set. Given that the posterior appears to be skewed, the Laplace approach performed extremely poorly in terms of prediction whilst as expected MCMC proved to be extremely expensive in terms of computational time. It is worth noting that all methods were applied to an additional data set, namely the Ionosphere which occurs in 34 dimensions. Results obtained coincided with those presented above, however they are not included in this paper [12].

Regarding computational efficiency, each algorithm was run 1000 times independently using their respective optimal log hyperparameter values. The mean running time on each data set was recorded ± the time variance. The results are presented in Table 2. It is evident that in both instances EP runs quicker than the modified BUS framework. As expected both running times increase in the higher dimensional example, however, the extent of this increase may be worth noting. EP increases by over 400% whereas the average increase across each modified BUS approach is 66%. As previously discussed, the difference between the running times for BUS_{MM} and BUS_{DRMM} stems from the additional pre-candidate step in DRMM. Whilst we acknowledge that this computational efficiency comparison is heavily dependent on the computer used and the extent to which the code is optimized, this result may justify future research into whether the general modified BUS framework is a viable

Table 2. Average running time for 1000 simulations

Method	Ionosphere Time (Seconds)	USPS Time (Seconds)
Laplace	$0.05 \pm 8e^{-05}$	0.15 ± 0.001
EP	$1.04 \pm 9e^{-05}$	5.61 ± 0.69
Modified BUS$_{MM}$	6.75 ± 0.76	11.24 ± 0.95
Modified BUS$_{DRMM}$	6.94 ± 0.29	12.04 ± 0.81
Modified BUS$_{SuSInf}$	6.24 ± 0.81	9.24 ± 0.32
MCMC	124.35 ± 2.3	372.43 ± 762

alternative to traditionally used deterministic methods in a high dimensional setting in terms of computational efficiency.

6 Conclusion

This paper has presented an overview of MCMC sampling schemes implemented under the modified BUS framework in a classification setting. Whilst differing in theoretical groundings it is apparent that each algorithm performed comparably well in terms of computational expense, number of intermediate levels and classification error rate. However, in terms of computational efficiency it appears that BUS$_{SuSInf}$ may prove most suitable in higher dimensions. Additionally, from the comparison with EP in terms of scaled information scores and misclassification error rates, the framework appears to produce similar results. The difference in increased computational times may justify future research into whether the general modified BUS framework is a viable alternative to deterministic methods in high dimensional settings in terms of computational expense.

References

1. Neal, R.M.: Probabilistic inference using Markov chain Monte Carlo methods. Technical report CRG-TR-93-1, Department of Computer Science, University of Toronto (1993)
2. Smith, A., Gelfand, A.: Bayesian statistics without tears: a sampling-resampling perspective. Am. Stat. Assoc. **46**(2), 84–88 (1992)
3. Straub, D., Papaioannou, I.: Bayesian updating with structural reliability methods. J. Eng. Mech. **141**(3), 04014134 (2015)
4. Au, S.K., Beck, J.: Estimation of small probabilities in high dimensions by subset simulation. Probab. Eng. Mech. **16**, 263–277 (2001)
5. DiazDelaO, F.A., Garbuno-Indigo, A., Au, S.K., Yoshida, I.: Bayesian updating and model class selection with subset simulation. Comput. Methods Appl. Mech. Eng. **317**, 1102–1221 (2017)
6. Le Chun, Y., Boser, B., Denker, J., Henderson, D.: USPS data set, handwritten digit recognition with back propagation network (1990)
7. Hastings, W.: Monte Carlo sampling methods using Markov chains and their application. Biometrika **57**, 97–109 (1970)

8. Miao, F., Ghosn, M.: Modified subset simulation method for reliability analysis of structural systems. Struct. Saf. **33**, 251–260 (2011)
9. Au, S.K., Patelli, E.: Rare event simulation in finite-infinite dimensional space. Reliab. Eng. Syst. Saf. **148**, 67–77 (2016)
10. Liu, C., Yan, T., Zhao, W.: Incremental tensor principal component analysis for handwritten digit recognition. Math. Probl. Eng. **2014**, 1–10 (2014)
11. Minka, T.: A family of algorithms for approximate Bayesian inference. PhD thesis, Department of Electrical Engineering and Computer Science, MIT (2001)
12. Byrnes, P., DiazDelaO, F.A.: Bayesian updating for probabilistic classification using reliability methods. In: UNCECOMP, Rhodes, Greece (2017)

Algorithms and Architecture for Real-Time Recommendations at News UK

Dion Bailey[1], Tom Pajak[1], Daoud Clarke[2(✉)], and Carlos Rodriguez[3]

[1] News UK, London, UK
{dion.bailey,tom.pajak}@news.co.uk
[2] Hyperparameter Ltd., London, UK
daoud@hyperparameter.com
[3] Kainano Ltd., London, UK
carlos.rodriguez@kainano.com

Abstract. Recommendation systems are recognised as being hugely important in industry as shown by Amazon and Netflix, and the area is now well understood. However, most recommendation systems are not optimised for the news room environment. At News UK, there is a requirement to be able to quickly generate recommendations for users on news items as they are published. However, little has been published about systems that can generate recommendations in response to changes in recommendable items and user behaviour in a very short space of time. In this paper we describe a new algorithm for updating collaborative filtering models incrementally, and demonstrate its effectiveness on clickstream data from *The Times*. We also describe the architecture that allows recommendations to be generated on the fly, now used in production for *The Times* and *The Sun*, and how we have made each component scalable.

Keywords: Recommendation systems · Real-time · Text mining

1 Introduction

In 2014 News UK completed a refresh of its data platforms and brought this process in-house. Now that we had greater access to our data we wanted to provide our customers with a premium digital experience based on their individual habits and behaviours. Other competitors in the market offer this, and we believe it will help us improve engagement and reduce churn. There are a number of products in the market that attempt to achieve this, however, we required a platform that was able to adapt to the constant changing news cycle and not centred around evergreen or e-commerce data. The decision was made to develop a platform tailored to our unique business models. We have two major News Titles with two different business models, *The Times & The Sunday Times* and *The Sun*. On the Times, we are in the unique position of knowing a lot about our users, their behaviours, their preferences and their level of engagement with our products due to the digital product suite being behind a paywall. *The Times &*

© Springer International Publishing AG 2017
M. Bramer and M. Petridis (Eds.): SGAI-AI 2017, LNAI 10630, pp. 264–277, 2017.
https://doi.org/10.1007/978-3-319-71078-5_23

The Sunday Times currently has over 400,000 subscribers. *The Sun* is a brand that is going for major reach across all of its products; since removing its paywall last year it has become the second largest UK newspaper [8].

The platform we designed is intended to improve the numbers above and increase retention by employing personalization techniques where it makes sense for users. We want to maintain the current editorial package, but use the information we have at our disposal to present content relevant to the user, which provides a more engaging product experience.

Our paper is structured as follows. In the remainder of this section we outline related work, our approach and the datasets used. In Sect. 2 we describe the algorithms we used and the offline evaluations we performed. This includes the major contribution of this paper, a novel algorithm for updating collaborative filtering models incrementally. In Sect. 3 we describe our evaluation, and in Sect. 4 we give our results. We show that the incremental approach works as well as non-incremental under the right conditions. In Sect. 5 we describe the architecture of our system, concluding in Sect. 6.

1.1 Related Work

Diaz-Aviles et al. [3] describe an algorithm for real-time recommendations called Stream-Ranking Matrix Factorization (RMFX) in the context of recommending for social media. This performs matrix factorization and ranking of recommendations on streaming data. However their system requires specifying the set of users and items in advance, which is not appropriate in our setting where we must handle new users and items (in our case new articles) all the time.

The xStreams system of Siddiqui et al. [9] does handle new users and items, however it does not incorporate the matrix factorization algorithms which provide the current state-of-the art recommendations.

The system used for real-time recommendations on YouTube is described by Covington et al. [2], which uses a sophisticated deep-learning model built on TensorFlow [1]. However the focus of the paper is on the deep learning model used rather than the real-time aspect of the system.

1.2 Approach

Our approach has been a pragmatic one. We performed an offline evaluation of a number of standard approaches to recommendation generation. We then chose the best performing systems to implement in production. Whilst the only way to be confident that a recommendation is providing the desired benefit is to measure its impact on relevant metrics in on online test, the advantage of an offline experiment is to gain confidence that the algorithms being used are likely to do better than the baselines, and to allow us to iterate quickly. The initial requirement for recommendations was to send an email to users once a day with personalised recommendations. Our first implementation precomputed recommendations for all users. These were then sent to users via email at a preconfigured time. We found that it took a long time to precompute and store the recommendations for all users: with a Spark cluster of forty machines, the recommendations could take up to half an hour to generate.

We decided to re-architect our system when we were tasked with building a system to serve recommendations on demand for *The Times* and *The Sun* websites. In particular, for *The Sun*, new content is generated throughout the day, and we wanted that content to be recommendable as soon as possible. In our new architecture, we no longer precompute recommendations. Instead, models are updated continuously as new information about users is received. The models are stored in a database that allows them to be very quickly retrieved, and recommendations are generated at the point that they are needed via an HTTP request to our API.

This approach not only means that recommendations are always up-to-date, but also means that we do not need to generate and store recommendations for all users, a process which is both time and space intensive.

1.3   Datasets

We collected ten days' worth of *Times* user behaviour from web logs. For each pair of user and item, we collated the user events as follows:

- **Dwell time:** this was estimated based on time between subsequent clicks. If the time between subsequent clicks by the same user was less than 30 min, it was assumed that the user spent that time on the first item clicked on. Thus the last item clicked on by a user would never receive a dwell time event. In the long term, we plan to have more accurate measures of dwell time.
- **Shares:** the number of times that the user shared the item.
- **Comments:** the number of times the user commented on the item.

These data were translated using a simple rule to determine whether or not there was an implicit expression of interest in the item by the user. We call such interactions "significant". We defined a significant interaction to be a dwell time of more than ten seconds, or any positive number of shares or comments. Reducing the data to this simple binary signal simplified the choices we had to make in designing and evaluating the algorithms. We plan to investigate more sophisticated possibilities in future work, for example, determining what is a significant action differently for each user.

2   Algorithms

We evaluated two recommendation algorithms, one collaborative in nature and one content based, and two baselines that we wished to improve upon: global popularity ranking and randomly chosen articles. The first chooses the articles that have the highest number of significant actions in the training set, and the second chooses from articles seen in the training set at random.

```
users ← empty dictionary;
items ← empty dictionary;
ratings ← empty dictionary;
while more batches exist do
    read new batch with n_u users and n_i items;
    foreach user u in batch do
        // initialise unseen user vectors to a new random vector:
        if u not in users then
            | users[u] ← new initial user vector;
        end
        // keep track of all user ratings so far:
        if u not in ratings then
            | ratings[u] ← empty set;
        else
            | ratings[u] ←
            | ratings[u] ∪ new items with significant actions for u in this batch;
        end
    end
    // initialise unseen item vectors to a new random vector:
    foreach item i in batch do
        if i not in items then
            | items[i] ← new initial item vector;
        end
    end
    // perform a learning iteration:
    R ← matrix of shape n_u × n_i with values from ratings;
    X ← matrix of shape n_u × k with values from users;
    Y ← matrix of shape n_i × k with values from items;
    LatentFactorUpdate(R, X, Y);
    update ratings, users and items with values from R, X and Y;
end
```

Fig. 1. Incrementally updating a collaborative filtering model. Each batch is a streamed collection of user actions. The positive integer k is a parameter of the underlying collaborative filtering algorithm specifying the dimensionality of the factorization. The matrices X, Y and R are built from dictionaries of ratings, users and items by defining an order on users and items and iterating the maps in that order. The function LatentFactorUpdate updates X and Y from R using the underlying collaborative filtering algorithm.

2.1 Incremental Updates for Collaborative Recommendations

Our main contribution is an algorithm for updating collaborative models incrementally, described in Fig. 1. In theory, the model could work with any collaborative filtering algorithm that allows user and item vectors to be updated from some initial state.

The algorithm is based on the observation that in collaborative filtering algorithms that decompose a matrix into products of latent factors, the set of users

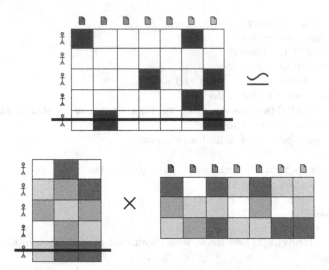

Fig. 2. Depiction of the matrix factorization algorithm, and how a user can be added or removed by adjusting the matrices. The matrix at the top depicts the matrix of user preferences, with users in rows and items in columns. This is approximately factored into two matrices, one for items and one for users. Removing a user from the preference matrix results in removing the corresponding row in the users matrix. In our algorithm we do the converse by adding a randomly initialised vector to the users matrix along with the user's actions to the preference matrix.

and items under consideration can easily be altered by adding or removing rows or columns from the matrices (see Fig. 2). It works by processing batches of user actions, updating the vectors only for users in each batch. We found that it was necessary to keep track of all user actions performed to date; for each user in the batch, we retrieve these actions and perform a model update using the underlying collaborative algorithm.

Some concerns when implementing this algorithm are:

- determining the size of the batch: if batches are too small, the algorithm does not work reliably. This was mitigated by adding in some randomly chosen users if there were not enough in the batch. The number of users needed in the batch was determined empirically.
- processing batches in parallel: if the level of parallelism is too high, the algorithm does not converge to an optimal solution.

Storing and retrieving user actions and user and item vectors becomes a major concern when implementing this algorithm at scale. Most of our effort has been around designing an architecture to do this reliably, described in Sect. 5.

2.2 Algorithmic Complexity

Keeping the model constantly up-to-date comes with an associated computational cost. Let $f(n)$ be a function describing the time complexity of the underlying matrix factorization algorithm, where n is the number of user-article pairs in the dataset, i.e. the number of non-zero entries in the matrix. Our algorithm splits the n datapoints into batches of size b. In the worst case (when there is a very small number of users), all the data from the previous batches needs to be included in each batch. Thus the complexity is

$$O(\sum_{i=1}^{n/b} f(ib))$$

In the case where f is linear, this becomes $O(n/2 + n^2/2b) = O(n^2/b)$. Making b bigger mitigates the additional cost, and if $b = n$ we recover $O(n)$ complexity.

2.3 Collaborative System

The collaborative filtering algorithm we use for the latent factor update step is based on an approach to implicit feedback datasets [5]. This suggests an alternative to treating a rating matrix R as a set of explicit ratings given by the user. Each value is considered as a rating together with a confidence in that rating. In their scheme, items with a low rating are given a low confidence.

The implementation we use makes use of conjugate gradient descent to perform the updates [10]. This is a faster algorithm with time complexity $O(nEk^2)$ where E is the number of iterations and k the number of latent factors. The original algorithm has cubic time complexity with respect to k [7].

Intuitively, it makes sense to consider algorithms for implicit feedback. This approach is in theory perfectly suited to our case, since we have only implicit signals of interest in articles from users and no reliable signal that the user is not interested in an article. Thus, if we know that a user has shared an article or read it for five minutes, we can be fairly confident that the user is interested in it. However, if the user did not read the article we can be much less certain that the user is not interested in it. In order to verify this hypothesis, we performed some initial experiments in which we found that algorithms designed for implicit signals gave much higher accuracy on our datasets than those designed for explicit signals.

We used Ben Frederickson's open source implementation[1] which is written in Python and Cython, which compiles to C. The library makes use of the low-level BLAS library for vector operations, which makes it very fast.

On top of this, we implemented the weighted regularization scheme described in [11] in the Cython version of the library, which we found provided a modest improvement in accuracy in our preliminary experiments.

The algorithm assumes that for each user u and item i we have values $p_{ui} \in \{0, 1\}$ which describes whether or not the user has implicitly expressed a preference for the item and $c_{ui} \in \mathbb{R}$ that expresses our confidence in the user's preference for that item [5]. These values are assumed to be derived from the implicit rating r_{ui} given by the user for the item in such a way that $p_{ui} = 1$

---

[1] https://github.com/benfred/implicit.

if and only if $r_{ui} > 0$, and $c_{ui} = 1$ if and only if $r_{ui} = 0$, with $c_{ui} > 1$ otherwise. One suggestion is that $c_{ui} = 1 + \alpha r_{ui}$ for some parameter α to be tuned. The intuition behind this is that items for which we have no information from a user are treated as a negative signal with low confidence, while implicit signals from a user are treated as a positive signal with higher confidence. In practice, the values are chosen to have this form to make the vectors in the intermediate computations sparse.

Given these matrices, the goal is to learn vectors x_u for each user and y_i for each item such that we minimize the following:

$$\min_{x_*, y_*} \sum_{u,i} c_{ui}(p_{ui} - x_u^T y_i)^2 + \lambda \left(\sum_u n_{x_u} \|x_u\|^2 + \sum_i n_{y_i} \|y_i\|^2 \right)$$

where λ is a regularization constant and n_{x_u} and n_{y_i} are the number of non-zero entries in the vectors x_u and y_i respectively. This is solved using the conjugate-gradient approach described in [10].

In the experiments we report here we used a dimensionality of 50 for the factor vectors; we found this worked well in initial experiments.

2.4 Content-Based Learning to Rank

The content-based system is based on the Learning to Rank model [6], which treats the task of ranking pages as a supervised learning problem. We consider two "classes" of articles: those that interest the user and those that do not. Since we do not make use of any explicit signals from users, for the purpose of training a model, we identify these two classes with the following sets of articles:

- The "positive" articles are those that the user has had a significant interaction with.
- The "negative" articles are a random sample of articles that the user has not interacted with at all.

For each user, we train a logistic regression model on this data and use it to rank articles as to their likelihood of being of interest to the user.

Implementation Details. We use the Liblinear implementation [4] of the logistic regression algorithm, and perform a search on the cost parameter for each user, considering costs of 10, 20 and 50, having found that costs below this range are rarely optimal. We perform cross validation on the training set, choosing the value that gives the highest F1 score.

Features. We use the following features (see Fig. 3):

- The name of the article section,
- Each term in the "author" text,
- Each term in the article title and body.

Fig. 3. A *Times* article showing the features used for training the content-based system (outlined).

All text is tokenized and lower-cased and a simple stop-word list is applied, but no stemming or lemmatization is performed. Tokens from each type of feature (section name, author text and title and body text) are distinguished by adding a unique prefix for each type. Features are treated as binary variables as is typical in document classification. This means we look only at the presence or absence of a feature, rather than counting occurrences.

Feature Selection. We experimented with a variety of feature selection methods, but found the following simple approach worked the best. We train a logistic regression model using all features, then take the top 2,500 and bottom 2,500 features (those with the highest and lowest coefficients) from the learnt model, and set the remaining coefficients to zero. This has the advantage of giving us a sparse model, which helps to generate recommendations quickly since the model is smaller, but also seems to provide a marginal improvement in recommendation quality.

Selecting Random Articles. We found that when the ratio of irrelevant to relevant articles was too high, the learning algorithm became unreliable. Restricting the number of negative articles to at most five times the number of positive ones provided a good compromise, representing the underlying imbalance in the dataset whilst still keeping learning reliable.

Boosting Popular Articles. We found that the content-based system alone performed poorly compared to the global top items baseline. Boosting the ranking of popular items lead to a significant increase in our evaluation metric. To do this, we computed a score

$$s_{ui} = p_{ui}(f_i + \beta)$$

where p_{ui} is the probability output by the logistic regression model for user u and item i, f_i is the number of users that have a significant action for item i and β is a smoothing value which we set at 10. The smoothing value allows for items that have no significant actions to still be recommended.

3   Evaluation

3.1   Evaluation Metrics

The offline evaluation method we have been using has been designed with the following in mind:

- Make the evaluation representative of how the system will be used in practice
- Design the evaluation so that all types of algorithm can be compared
- Make the evaluation metric intuitively simple

These considerations rule out the normal metrics that are used for example in evaluating matrix factorisation algorithms, since we also want to be able to evaluate classification based approaches. In our first application, we send out an email containing 10 recommendations to users. For this reason we have opted for the "precision at 10" metric.

3.2   Evaluation Procedure

The data consists of (user, article, interactions) tuples, where "interactions" consists of all interactions that a user has had with that article, including dwell time, comments and shares. We split these data randomly into a training set consisting of 80% of the data, and the remaining 20% is held out as a test set. We then train a model on the training set, generating recommendations for each user from articles seen in the training set. For each user we take the top ten recommendations excluding items that occur in the training set for that user, and count the proportion of them that occur for that user in the test set. This is averaged over all users to get the mean precision at 10 score.

4   Results

Results for the systems we evaluated are shown in Table 1. Only the collaborative system was significantly better than the Global Top Items baseline. Figure 4 shows how the precision at 10 score varies with batch size. For batch sizes over 10,000 there is no significant increase in the score. Using a single batch is equivalent to training using the underlying collaborative filtering model; since the score is not significantly different to training with batches of 10,000, it is clear that our incremental approach works, at least with the set-up we have chosen. In initial experiments, we also found that the batch size needed is dependent on the dimensionality of the learnt factors: the higher the dimensionality, the larger the batch size needed to avoid harming the score. One limitation of our approach is that the batch size will need to be tuned for each dataset once an appropriate dimensionality has been chosen.

Figure 5 shows how the score is affected by processing multiple batches in parallel. As long as the total number of data points being trained simultaneously (the batch size times the number trained in parallel) is much less than the total dataset size, the score is not significantly affected.

Table 1. Precision at 10 on the held out test set for the systems and baselines we considered.

System	Precision at 10	Standard error
Random baseline	0.0056	0.0008
Global top items	0.0276	0.0021
Content	0.0281	0.0021
Collaborative	0.0750	0.0043

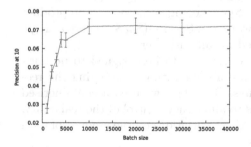

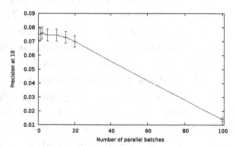

Fig. 4. Precision at 10 with batch size.

Fig. 5. How precision at 10 is affected by the number of batches that are processed in parallel, for a batch size of 100,000.

4.1 Performance

Tests were created to verify the different performance levels of the Recommendation Engine in terms of the number of concurrent clients, how old the recommended assets could be and how many containers were deployed at the same time (horizontal scalability). We selected Jmeter as the tool to run these tests given its simplicity for creating different scenarios.

Table 2. Real-time performance results for our system using eight containers for each recommendation algorithm and thirty concurrent clients.

System	Users/sec	Average latency (ms)
Collaborative	663	382
Content	412	690
Top articles	305	86

Results are shown in Table 2. Latency for content-based recommendations is higher because the model size (sparse vectors with up to 5000 non-zero dimensions) is much greater than for the collaborative system (in this test the vectors were 200 dimensional dense vectors); the majority of the time is spent transferring the model from Bigtable to the cluster. Top article latency is low because the top articles can be cached between subsequent requests, and all that is needed is to retrieve and exclude seen items for the user.

5 Architecture

Our focus on the architecture was to provide a base structure where the collaborative and content based algorithms had enough resources to ingest and train the data with minimum delay and maximum scalability. Although intended to be used initially on *The Times* and *The Sun*, the engine needed to be product agnostic and with delivery model of Software as a Service (SaaS), where a single deployed version of the application is used for all customers.

Given these requirements, each component had to be designed to be horizontally scalable to support huge amounts of data without increasing the recommendation serving latency and freshness. For that, we used a containerised architecture with Docker and Kubernetes to allow easy control of the scalability. Data stores would also have to cope with these variations on the amount of data and be able to scale up and down.

PubSub was used for data ingestion since we can guarantee that all messages are processed using its acknowledgment model and we can configure its bandwidth quota as needed, although the default of 100 mb/s should be sufficient. Bigtable was selected as the main storage for being a massively scalable NoSQL database with low latency and high throughput. It stores all the user actions, user models and asset models.

Clients of the engine typically will query for the latest recommendations, including the last few hours or days, but we also wanted to support cases where they would need recommendations for much longer periods. Because of that, it was not feasible to load thousands of models from Bigtable, which sits outside the cluster and has much more limited bandwidth compared with the cluster's internal speed. We created a cache component that would run inside the cluster and initialise all existing recommendable assets models from Bigtable. Each serving API also had its own short-lived in-memory cache for further optimisation.

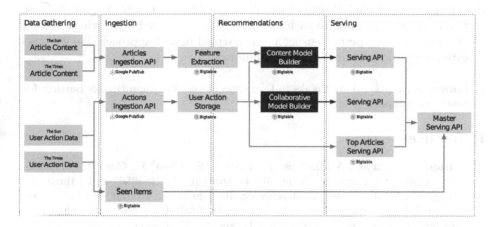

Fig. 6. The major components of our real-time architecture.

All the components of the Recommendation Engine can be divided into four layers (see Fig. 6):

- Data gathering: collection of user actions and content from our online publications to send to PubSub.
- Data ingestion: messages from PubSub are processed and stored in the engine. User actions are stored in Bigtable and feature extraction is performed on article content.
- Data training: use collaborative and content based algorithms to train the ingested data and store the resulting models.
- Recommendation serving: APIs to generate recommendations using query parameters and previously generated assets models and user models.

New algorithms can be incorporated into the Recommendation Engine by creating components fitting into the training and recommendation serving layers.

6 Conclusion

We have described a novel algorithm for incrementally updating collaborative filtering models. We demonstrated its effectiveness in an offline evaluation and described the conditions under which the incremental update works reliably for our dataset. We also described the architecture which allows us to perform real-time recommendations. This system is in use in production for *The Times* and *The Sun*, increasing user retention and opening up a world of possibilities for product enhancements.

In future work, we hope to combine our content-based and collaborative systems. In our ongoing online tests measuring click-through rates on recommendations, we have found that for some users, content-based recommendations seem to be more effective, while for others, the collaborative filtering recommendations give higher click-through rates. We would like to be able to give the best recommendations possible to each user, so we may try and learn which system works best for users, perhaps using a multi-armed bandit approach. We will also investigate hybrid recommendation techniques.

Acknowledgments. Many thanks to Dan Gilbert and Jonathan Brooks-Bartlett for feedback and support.

References

1. Abadi, M., Agarwal, A., Barham, P., Brevdo, E., Chen, Z., Citro, C., Corrado, G.S., Davis, A., Dean, J., Devin, M., Ghemawat, S., Goodfellow, I., Harp, A., Irving, G., Isard, M., Jia, Y., Jozefowicz, R., Kaiser, L., Kudlur, M., Levenberg, J., Mané, D., Monga, R., Moore, S., Murray, D., Olah, C., Schuster, M., Shlens, J., Steiner, B., Sutskever, I., Talwar, K., Tucker, P., Vanhoucke, V., Vasudevan, V., Viégas, F., Vinyals, O., Warden, P., Wattenberg, M., Wicke, M., Yu, Y., Zheng, X.: TensorFlow: large-scale machine learning on heterogeneous systems (2015). Software available: https://www.tensorflow.org/
2. Covington, P., Adams, J., Sargin, E.: Deep neural networks for Youtube recommendations. In: Proceedings of 10th ACM Conference on Recommender Systems, New York, NY, USA (2016)
3. Diaz-Aviles, E., Drumond, L., Schmidt-Thieme, L., Nejdl, W.: Real-time top-n recommendation in social streams. In: Proceedings of 6th ACM Conference on Recommender Systems, pp. 59–66. ACM (2012)
4. Fan, R.E., Chang, K.W., Hsieh, C.J., Wang, X.R., Lin, C.J.: Liblinear: a library for large linear classification. J. Mach. Learn. Res. **9**(August), 1871–1874 (2008)
5. Hu, Y., Koren, Y., Volinsky, C.: Collaborative filtering for implicit feedback datasets. In: 8th IEEE International Conference on Data Mining, ICDM 2008, pp. 263–272. IEEE (2008)
6. Liu, T.Y., et al.: Learning to rank for information retrieval. Found. Trends® Inf. Retr. **3**(3), 225–331 (2009)
7. Pilászy, I., Zibriczky, D., Tikk, D.: Fast ALS-based matrix factorization for explicit and implicit feedback datasets. In: Proceedings of 4th ACM Conference on Recommender Systems, pp. 71–78. ACM (2010)
8. Ponsford, D.: NRS national press readership data: telegraph overtakes Guardian as most-read 'quality' title in print/online. Press Gazette, 26 June 2017
9. Siddiqui, Z.F., Tiakas, E., Symeonidis, P., Spiliopoulou, M., Manolopoulos, Y.: xStreams: recommending items to users with time-evolving preferences. In: Proceedings of 4th International Conference on Web Intelligence, Mining and Semantics (WIMS 2014, p. 22. ACM (2014)

10. Takács, G., Pilászy, I., Tikk, D.: Applications of the conjugate gradient method for implicit feedback collaborative filtering. In: Proceedings of 5h ACM Conference on Recommender Systems, pp. 297–300. ACM (2011)

11. Zhou, Y., Wilkinson, D., Schreiber, R., Pan, R.: Large-scale parallel collaborative filtering for the Netflix prize. In: Fleischer, R., Xu, J. (eds.) AAIM 2008. LNCS, vol. 5034, pp. 337–348. Springer, Heidelberg (2008). https://doi.org/10. 1007/978-3-540-68880-8_32

Customer Contact Journey Prediction

Paul N. Taylor[✉][iD]

BT Research and Innovation, Ipswich, UK
paul.n.taylor@bt.com

Abstract. Complex businesses often have complex interactions with their customers. In this paper we describe the customer contact journey method of analysing these interactions. We introduce a predictive model created by BT that is able to predict with high accuracy the potential outcomes of customer journeys. A method to use a predictive model to streamline customer interactions using case management techniques and issues relating to the implementation of that model into production are discussed.

Keywords: Customer journey · Prediction · Case study · Machine learning

1 Introduction

It is inevitable in a large and complex organisation that sometimes business processes will not complete as expected. The causes of such failures are not always foreseeable. In these cases it is incumbent on the organisation to proactively resolve each issue, or for the customer to contact the organisation if the issue becomes evident to them. Dealing with customer issues can be a complex and time consuming endeavour which is compounded by potential organisational and infrastructural barriers.

In this paper a model for reasoning about the effort required by customers and organisations to resolve issues is discussed, and a predictive model which is used to improve the customer experience in these cases is introduced. The performance of the predictions produced by the model is then examined from both a scientific and business perspective.

1.1 Background

BT is a very large organisation. Hundreds of thousands of people interact with the organisation to a greater or lesser degree each month. These interactions can take on many forms from calls into contact centres to automated SMS messaging. For the purposes of this paper the definition of an interaction is as follows:

Definition 1. *An interaction is defined as one instance of a human agent being deployed to work on behalf of a customer of the organisation. eg. a contact centre agent taking an inbound call.*

© Springer International Publishing AG 2017
M. Bramer and M. Petridis (Eds.): SGAI-AI 2017, LNAI 10630, pp. 278–290, 2017.
https://doi.org/10.1007/978-3-319-71078-5_24

There are many types of interactions that are possible for an organisation to undertake given this definition. For example:

- Telephone Calls
- E-mail
- SMS
- Online chat (aka. eChat)
- Offline.

Each of these types of interaction requires effort, both effort expended by the customer and effort expended by the organisation. Offline interactions are particularly noteworthy as they involve effort on behalf of the organisation but do not involve the customer directly, so no customer effort is accumulated.

1.2   Customer Contact Journeys

Interactions with an organisation can be observed and analysed individually, but can also be grouped together in what is known as a customer journey. A customer journey can be defined as:

Definition 2. *A customer contact journey is defined as the sequence of interactions undertaken by the customer in a coherent sequence. The contact journey begins with the first interaction (if the customer does not currently have an active journey) and closes when the customer has not needed to interact with the organisation for 28 days.*

Examining the customer experience in terms of an entire customer contact journey can be very helpful when looking for opportunities to improve. It is sometimes the case that customer interactions do not occur in isolation. For example, a customer placing an order would receive two or three follow up SMS messages regarding order status which form part of the same journey. A further example of a customer contact journey can be seen in Table 1.

Table 1. An example customer contact journey

Seq. no.	Day no.	Contact type	Customer effort	Org. effort
1	1	Inbound call	400	300
2	5	Inbound call	100	300
3	6	SMS	60	60
Total			560	660

There are a number of metrics can be calculated using the customer contact journey methodology to report on the performance of the organisation. One might calculate the average number of contacts in a journey, the average amount of effort expended on journeys, or the number of calendar days between the start and end of the journey.

One metric used inside the organisation is the cumulative effort expended on the journeys. An example of this calculation for one journey is included in the journey example in Table 1. This metric is used to measure organisational efficiency. If the amount of effort in customer journeys is low, then the organisation is easy to do business with, if high then the opposite is true.

1.3   Identifying Sub-optimal Journeys

Unfortunately not all customer contact journeys flow as smoothly as the organisation would like. It is sometimes necessary for multiple interactions over a number of days or weeks to be required to fully resolve an issue. Extended customer journeys are a key cause of customer dissatisfaction.

One tactic that can be used to streamline these customer contact journeys is that of case management. A case management process removes customers from the usual process after some trigger and assigns them to a specialist case management team for investigation by experts. Identifying the trigger at which to move customers into case management is now a key issue. If customers are moved too early then the case management team would become overwhelmed, if the customers are moved too late then potentially avoidable dissatisfaction remains.

A simple strategy would be to define an effort threshold at which journeys would be assigned to a case manager. It may be difficult however to find the appropriate point at which customers should be moved into case management. Using a fixed threshold also does not account for the actual state of any journey. For example, a customer falling 30 seconds shy of the threshold would not be case managed even though any subsequent contact would almost certainly put them over the threshold.

Using machine learning, it is possible to improve process of selecting customers for case management by predicting the likelihood of a customer exceeding the threshold after (or during) each interaction. Rather than using a fixed effort threshold, instead the organisation can use a confidence threshold. This means that customers that are more likely to exceed the threshold are treated immediately rather than waiting for a threshold breach. Moving the customers into case management earlier would improve the customer experience by giving them the support they require earlier, and would improve operational efficiency by deploying customer service agents more effectively.

Specifying the confidence threshold at which to treat customers is underpinned by business strategy. The key balance is between the relative importance of customer experience, cost control and operational capacity. In order to guide the operational managers in selecting an appropriate decision threshold, an interactive tool was built. Further detail on this is given in Sect. 5.1.

2   Data

Given the objective of this modelling exercise is to be able to predict when a customer is likely to breach the case management threshold, data specifying the current state of a customers contact journey is needed. There is a wide variety of such data available concerning both individual interactions, and the current state of the journey. This includes items such as:

- The employee details of the contact handler.
- The date/time the interaction started and ended.
- The number of interactions so far in the contact journey.
- The customer effort associated with the interaction (seconds).
- The organisations effort associated with the interaction (seconds).
- The cumulative effort so far in the contact journey.

The interaction data can be further augmented using additional information that is known about the customer and their account. Further, it is possible to compute fields that relate to the history of this customer. Historical fields are particularly interesting when examining the links between particular behaviour patterns and the resulting customer experience. Examples of these more general fields might be:

Which services are currently active on the customers account?
- How many service requests has the customer raised within the last x days?
- Has the customer had an open order in the last x days?
- What was the value of the customers most recent bill?
- How long since the customer last raised a complaint?

The challenge, given the wide variety of data available, was to discover the particular combination that produced the best performing classifier. The production of the classifier itself is discussed in the following section (Sect. 3).

A number of the fields required preprocessing to be suitable for the classifiers in SciKit Learn [4], in particular the classifiers in SciKit require numeric input so categorical variables must be converted into an appropriate representation (in this case One-Hot Encoding was used).

For date fields, such as date of the customers last order, the situation is less straightforward. As we are looking for a situational prediction, data specifying the date relative to the current position is relevant in addition to data about the absolute date. Therefore date fields, where included, were decomposed into the following fields:

- Day of the week (One-Hot encoded)
- Hour of the day
- Days since the start of the journey
- Days since the previous contact

It was also vital to sanity check the availability of the attributes. For example, it would not have been possible to make predictions based on the customers current service mix, if that service mix was only updated weekly. The list of attributes used in the final model are given in the following section (Sect. 3).

An additional complication in this case was that the input data was not evenly split between the two classes. Those journeys that exceed the threshold for case management are a very small percentage of the overall volume. This complicates the modelling process as small increases in the false-positive rate would have a very large impact in the number of cases being unnecessarily sent into case management (therefore increasing cost). In this case, a model with a low false-positive rate but a lower true-positive rate was to be preferred, to one with higher values for the false positive and true positive rates.

3   Learning the Model

The broad aim for this modelling process was to keep the resulting model as simple as possible to ease deployment. Therefore the modelling process started with logistic regression as the technique of choice. Logistic regression allows the resulting model to be easily expressed as a single formula. If no appropriate logistic regression model were found then more complex techniques would have been considered, however this was not necessary. Jupyter notebooks [2] were used to record and perform the analysis. The use of notebooks allowed the code performing the analysis and the explanatory rationale to be kept together and stored for later reference.

The modelling process itself was conducted by first considering what pieces of data were hypothesised to have a predictive benefit. Next, each set of possible predictive attributes were tested and the resulting model evaluated. Finally, combinations of the best performing attribute sets were considered to see if higher performance could be achieved. Ensemble techniques were not considered for this modelling task.

For each group of attributes the modelling process was as follows:

1. Run SQL queries that extract the customer contact journeys from the warehouse
2. Run SQL queries to extract the additional data required by the current hypothesis
3. Process the categorical and data fields into encodings appropriate for SciKit [4] (using Pandas [3])
4. Join the results of the SQL and preprocessing into an input set for SciKit (using Pandas)
5. Run `cross_val_predict` with a `LogisticRegression` classifier from SciKit for initial results using 3-fold cross validation
6. If promising, train the model of data from the first week of data and test against following weeks to ensure the model is stable over time
7. Evaluate the model performance.

After the hypotheses were tested a suitable model was found. The performance of this model is discussed in Sect. 4. The attributes of the selected model were as follows:

- Organisational effort on this interaction (scaled 0–1 as 0-threshold)
- Index of the interaction in the journey (indexed from 1)
- The running sum of the organisational effort to this point in the journey (similarly scaled)
- A 0/1 flag indicating if the customer had a telephone service at the start of the journey
- The age of the telephone service at the start of the journey (or zero if none)
- A 0/1 flag indicating if the customer had a broadband service at the start of the journey
- The age of the broadband service at the start of the journey (or zero if none)
- A 0/1 flag indicating if the customer had a TV service at the start of the journey
- The age of the TV service at the start of the journey (or zero if none).

All of the other hypotheses or combinations thereof produced a weaker model and so were discarded in favour of the model produced by the above listed attributes. This has the advantage of being relatively small, and therefore easy to encode in a formula. An additional advantage is that is depends on information which is easily available in production with no complex preprocessing necessary.

4   Evaluating the Model

The modelling process continued until a suitable set of attributes were discovered. Evaluating the model to determine suitability involved examining the model performance from two sides. First, the performance of the model on each interaction and second the performance of the model in terms of the each customer journey. Considering the performance of the model on overall journey was essential as that maps directly to key organisational performance metrics.

4.1   Performance on Interactions

The SciKit Learn classification report showing the classification performance for the model considering each interaction independently is shown in Table 2. An Receiver Operating Characteristic (ROC) curve and a Precision-Recall curve are shown in Figs. 1 and 2 respectively. The Area Under Curve (AUC) value is 0.79.

4.2   Performance on Journeys

In terms of the organisational context for this model, performance at the journey level was more important than performance at the interaction level because that is where the business benefit would be accrued. The performance of the model

Table 2. Classification report for journey level predictions

	Precision	Recall	F1-score	Support
Under threshold	0.82	0.95	0.88	583358
Over threshold	0.62	0.26	0.37	170702
Avg/total	0.77	0.80	0.76	754060

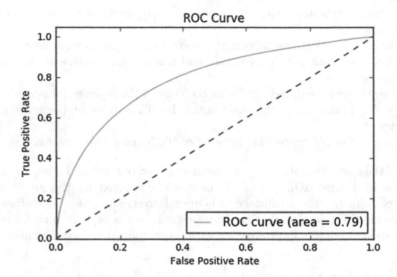

Fig. 1. AOC curve for the prediction results on individual interactions.

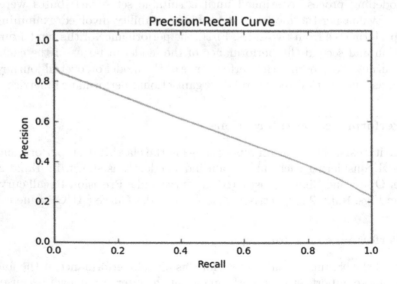

Fig. 2. Precision-Recall curve for the prediction results on individual interactions.

at the journey level was calculated by aggregating a data frame using pandas which contained the input data and the predicted class.

For example, if a journey which exceeds the threshold (Class 1) has the confidence for Class 1 after each interaction of 0.1, 0.2, 0.6 & 0.8 and the decision threshold is set at 0.5 the predictions are 0, 0, 1, 1. Considered at the interaction level, the accuracy of the model is 50%. To calculate the performance of the model at the journey level we need only a single value, this is calculated as 1 if any of the interactions are predicted as Class 1, or 0 otherwise. Therefore in this example, the actual class is 1 and the predicted class is 1, so the model is accurate for this journey.

Once all journeys have been aggregated similarly the result was a pandas data frame containing the following:

- The ID of the journey (used for grouping only)
- The effort incurred at the point of the first Class 1 prediction
- The total effort in the journey
- The index of the interaction at which the first Class 1 prediction was made
- The total number of interactions in the journey
- The aggregated prediction
- The actual class

Table 3. Classification report for journey level predictions

	Precision	Recall	F1-score	Support
Under threshold	0.98	0.94	0.96	1006410
Over threshold	0.58	0.84	0.69	97690
Avg/total	0.95	0.93	0.94	1104100

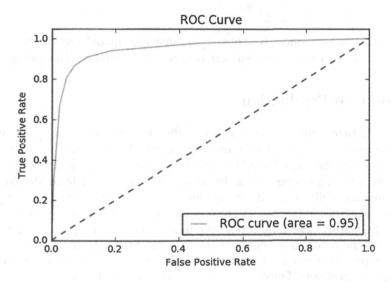

Fig. 3. AOC curve for the prediction results on complete customer journeys

Using the aggregated prediction and actuals from the data frame produces the classification report shown in Table 3. ROC and Precision-Recall curves for the model are shown in Figs. 3 and 4. The Area Under the Curve value is 0.95. In addition, the potential effort and interaction savings can be calculated by summing the difference between the first-prediction value and total values for the respective columns. How the business chooses to operate the predictive model will limit how much of that benefit may be achieved.

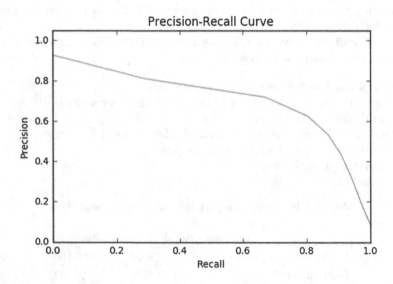

Fig. 4. Precision-Recall curve for the prediction results on complete customer journeys.

The estimated business benefits of running this model are substantial but unfortunately cannot be reported here due to commercial confidentiality.

5   Route to Production

Extensive change control processes surrounding key systems used by the organisation for customer interactions presents a key challenge to putting models into production. Methods which could provide a prediction on top of existing warehouse and reporting systems would be present an easier route to production than those requiring additional software or changes to strategic systems.

Logistic regression techniques are very amenable to such an approach because a simple SQL statement that applies the model to an input set can be produced easily from the model intercept and co-efficients. SciKit Learn allows access to the intercept and coefficients of a fitted model using the attributes `intercept_` and `coef_` respectively. Once the intercept and coefficients are known the well-known function for calculating probability in logistic regression models can be coded into the language of choice. In this case SQL was used, and an example is shown in Fig. 5.

The SQL statement utilises a WITH clause to encapsulate the data preparation steps. The remainder of the query utilises the columns from the prepared data and multiplies them in turn by the appropriate coefficient. These values are then used standard formula to calculate the confidence value which an in turn be used by the organisation as appropriate.

```sql
with data_prep as (
  -- SQL that prepares the input data into the format
  -- expected by the model
)
select
  journey_id, contact_idx,
  1/(1+exp(-(
  (-2.5486990334429844) +
  (age_bb * -0.003298131521577589) +
  (age_pstn * -0.0038478418659244548) +
  (age_vision * -0.0070566297725420859) +
  (bt_effort * 0.12713923867080948) +
  (had_bb * 0.15155429739903176) +
  (had_pstn * -0.33435063478186056) +
  (had_vision * 0.10245808942853511) +
  (journey_contact_seq * 0.025388945948437547) +
  (rsum * 3.9524758462289142)))) as confidence
from data_prep;
```

Fig. 5. Example code listing showing how SQL can be used to calculate a logistic regression model

Once the implementation of the model is available, then it needs to be inserted into the workflow appropriately. Initial implementation for this model comprises the delivery of a list of customers likely to require treatment in the near future to the team managers responsible for case management. The managers will then be able to allocate likely customers from this list to case managers for proactive treatment. The list will be presented as a report in the usual management information system lowering the barriers to successful use.

For an initial period the model will be used on an experimental basis. The list of customers presented to the case managers for treatment will comprise only part of the customer base, with a percentage of randomly selected customers omitted from treatment. This will allow accurate statistics to be gathered on the observed impact of the proactive case management versus the control group who will have an unmodified experience. Performing a trial in this way will allow the impacts of the predictive case management approach to be robustly calculated.

The data regarding each run of the predictive model will also be archived into the appropriate data warehouse. This will allow extended analysis in the coming months to discover what long-term impacts on customer satisfaction and on customer retention can be attributed to proactive case management.

5.1   Impact Dashboard

A further key challenge to implementing the model in production is a non-technical one. The gatekeepers for change in the customer service part of the organisation are not typically specialist modellers or data scientists. These stake-holders are not used to dealing with systemic uncertainty or the trade-offs

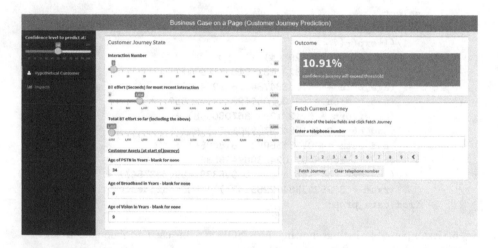

Fig. 6. Screenshot of the first page of the impact dashboard

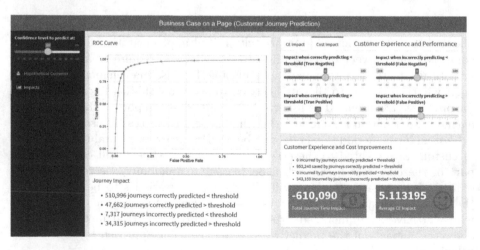

Fig. 7. Screenshot of the second page of the impact dashboard

inherent in the use of a predictive model. To attempt to ease this difficulty an interactive dashboard was constructed using R [5] and Shiny [1]. The dashboard used the model and statistics produced by the modelling process to present outcomes calculated from historical data in business terms rather than in the usual classification metrics.

The first part of the dashboard (Fig. 6) allows the users to investigate the relationships between the input parameters of the model and the confidence value that is produced. In addition the users were able to load details of recent customer contact journeys, have the model applied, and see the output value. This helps the users gain confidence the model is behaving in a way that is intuitively understandable.

The second part of the dashboard (Fig. 7) allowed the users to set an expected impact for customer experience and cost for each possible predictive outcome (True Positive, False Positive, True Negative and False Negative). An historic data set is provided along with the dashboard. Once the user has specified their impact values and a decision threshold, the model is applied across the historical data and the impacts calculated. The business user can then see the expected business impact of operating the model in terms of measures they understand. The expected outputs of the model were presented as the net cost impact (negative for an overall saving, positive for an overall cost), and the expected percentage change in customer experience (positive for improvement, negative for deterioration).

Producing such an interactive dashboard eased the process of getting the predictive model into production because it gives the business users who need to provide resource or approvals the confidence to do so. Giving the stakeholders confidence that they understand the likely impacts of the model significantly reduces non-technical barriers to implementing the model in production.

6   Conclusions and Future Work

This paper has presented an application of a logistic regression model to the task of improving customer contact journeys by using a machine learnt model to make predictions about those journeys. The data and methods used for the machine learning process were discussed as was the approach taken to move the model into production. The performance of the model resulting from cross-validation testing on historical data was also presented.

Many organisations have customer interface functions where customer issues are raised and treated. Similar data to that discussed here is also often available in those organisations. Whilst the specific case discussed within the paper and the latter half of the attributes used in the model are BT specific, the initial few have a very broad applicability and should be of use to other organisations attempting similar modelling.

At the time of writing the trial mentioned in Sect. 5 has not currently started although it will do so shortly. It is hoped that the actual results of running the model in production can be communicated at a later date.

References

1. Chang, W., Cheng, J., Allaire, J., Xie, Y., McPherson, J.: shiny: Web Application Framework for R (2017). R package version 1.0.3. https://cran.r-project.org/package=shiny
2. Kluyver, T., Ragan-Kelley, B., Pérez, F., Granger, B., Bussonnier, M., Frederic, J., Kelley, K., Hamrick, J., Grout, J., Corlay, S., Ivanov, P., Avila, D., Abdalla, S., Willing, C.: Jupyter notebooks – a publishing format for reproducible computational workflows. In: Proceedings of the 20th International Conference on Electronic Publishing, pp. 87–90. IOS Press (2016)
3. McKinney, W.: Data structures for statistical computing in python. In: van der Walt, S., Millman, J. (eds.) Proceedings of the 9th Python in Science Conference, pp. 51–56 (2010)
4. Pedregosa, F., Varoquaux, G., Gramfort, A., Michel, V., Thirion, B., Grisel, O., Blondel, M., Prettenhofer, P., Weiss, R., Dubourg, V., Vanderplas, J., Passos, A., Cournapeau, D., Brucher, M., Perrot, M., Duchesnay, E.: Scikit-learn: machine learning in python. J. Mach. Learn. Res. **12**, 2825–2830 (2011)
5. R Core Team: R: A Language and Environment for Statistical Computing. R Foundation for Statistical Computing, Vienna, Austria (2017). https://www.R-project.org/

Applications of Neural Networks
and Fuzzy Logic

A Better Predictor of Marathon Race Times Based on Neural Networks

Dimitris C. Dracopoulos$^{(\boxtimes)}$

University of Westminster, London, UK
d.dracopoulos@westminster.ac.uk

Abstract. A novel application of artificial neural networks is presented for the prediction of marathon race times based on performances in races of other distances. For many years Riegel's formula was used for the prediction of time in running races, given the race time of a person in a different distance. Recently, two different models which perform better than the classic formula in the prediction of marathon times were published in the literature. This work shows how a new approach based on artificial neural networks outperforms significantly these recently published models for marathon time prediction.

Keywords: Marathon time race prediction · Neural networks · Prediction · Running

1 Introduction

During the last decade, the sport of long distance running has become popular for amateur runners. It is common for many millions of such runners to participate in race events from 5K to a marathon each year.

Predicting how fast one can go in a future race based on performances in recent races of other distances is important for recreational runners (but also for elite athletes). Besides curiosity, the two main crucial reasons for the prediction are:

- how to design a training plan (training which takes several months before a race) based on the target race time
- what pace to follow during the race.

The latter is essential not only for achieving the desired time but also a pace which is too quick in the beginning of a race can lead to "catastrophic" results, especially in longer distances such as the marathon.

2 Current Approaches for Race Time Prediction

For many years the Riegel formula [1] has been used to predict race times based on a recent race time in a different shorter distance. There are many time predictors available on the Web, e.g. the web page of the well known to runners

© Springer International Publishing AG 2017
M. Bramer and M. Petridis (Eds.): SGAI-AI 2017, LNAI 10630, pp. 293–299, 2017.
https://doi.org/10.1007/978-3-319-71078-5_25

Runner's World magazine [2]. Most of these predictors have implemented the Riegel formula which was considered the most accurate until very recently:

$$time_{race2} = time_{race1} \cdot \left(\frac{distance_{race2}}{distance_{race1}}\right)^k \tag{1}$$

where $race1$ is the shorter recent race, $race2$ is the race for which the prediction is made and k is the "fatigue factor" typically set in the range of values of $k = 1.05$ to $k = 1.07$, while in the case of world-class runners its value is set to $k = 1.08$ [1].

Recently, two new models were published by Vickers and Vertosick [3] which perform significantly better than the classic Riegel formula in the prediction of marathon race times. The formulas were adopted by *Runner's World* to implement a new predictor in the case of the marathon distance [4,5]. The two models implementing the formulas are based on the prediction of a marathon race time either using one shorter distance race time or two shorter distance race times respectively.

In their work, Vickers and Vertosick [3], collected data for 2303 recreational endurance runners via a questionnaire published in the news website *Slate.com*. Although other studies exist for elite runners [6], the performance and race time prediction for the recreational runners have been poorly addressed [3]. After the validation of data from the questionnaires, there were only 493 runners who ran a marathon and two other races of different distances (after dropping the very fast and the very difficult races reported by the users) and these were the data used for reporting their published results for the marathon race time prediction. All the data are available to the public via [3] (additional File 2). The 493 runners data include:

- $N = 337$ data used for training, i.e. from the overall dataset in the aforementioned file, the runners who were in *group 1* or *group 2* and where *cohort3* was 1 (ran a marathon and two other races of different distances).
- $N = 156$ data used for testing, i.e. from the overall dataset in the aforementioned file, the runners from *group 3* and where *cohort3* was 1.

Some times reported by people answering the questionnaire were associated with "difficult" and "fast" races. These times were adjusted in order to be more representative of a runner's time for an "average" difficulty race of that distance. To do so, Vickers and Vertosick created a model to predict race velocity in *meters/sec* for each race distance separately, adjusted for race difficulty (difficult, average or fast). Based on the differences in speed between average and difficult races and average and fast races, some velocity coefficients were calculated for each race distance (marathon, half marathon, 10 miles, 10K, 5 miles, 5K). These coefficients were added to the true velocity reported by each runner, in order to calculate the adjusted times (for more details of this see [3] and their additional File 1 which contains the values of the coefficients). Both original and adjusted times are included in the full dataset in the aforementioned dataset file (additional File 2).

The analysis in [3] showed that from all the collected data, the independent variables which are required to predict a longer distance race time are:

1. the time(s) of recent shorter distance race(s)
2. the typical weekly mileage while training for the longer distance race.

The two models that were developed by Vickers and Vertosick for the marathon race prediction which performed significantly better than Riegel's formula were:

Model 1

Predict the marathon race time based on a single recent race of a shorter distance:

$$v_{Riegel} = \frac{42195}{time_{race1} \cdot (\frac{42195}{distance_{race1}})^{1.07}} \tag{2}$$

where $time_{race1}$ is the adjusted time for the shorter race in the case of a difficult or a fast shorter race.

$$velocity_1 = 0.16018617 + 0.83076202 \cdot v_{Riegel} + 0.06423826 \cdot \frac{typical\_mileage}{10}) \tag{3}$$

$$time_{marathon} = \frac{42195}{60 \cdot velocity_1} \tag{4}$$

where $time_{marathon}$ is the predicted time (in minutes) for the marathon race.

Model 2

Predict the marathon race time based on two recent races r_1, r_2 of shorter distances (where the distance for r_2 is longer than the distance of r_1:

$$k_{\frac{r_2}{r_1}} = \frac{\ln(\frac{time_{r_2}}{time_{r_1}})}{\ln(\frac{distance_{r_2}}{distance_{r_1}})} \tag{5}$$

where $time_{r_1}, time_{r_2}$ are the adjusted times for the shorter races in the case of a difficult or a fast shorter race.

$$k_{marathon} = 1.4510756 - 0.23797948 \cdot k_{\frac{r_2}{r_1}} - 0.01410023 \cdot \frac{typical\_mileage}{10} \tag{6}$$

$$time_{marathon} = \frac{time_{r_2} \cdot (\frac{42195}{distance_{r_2}})^{k_{marathon}}}{60} \tag{7}$$

where $distance_{r_2}$ is the distance of race r_2 the longer of the two shorter distance races and $time_{marathon}$ is the predicted time (in minutes) for the marathon race.

3   Neural Implementation and Results

The aim of the work described here is to develop models for the prediction of marathon race times based on neural networks and compare them with the current state of the art predictors described in the previous section.

The standard multilayer perceptron was used for the development of two different predictor models in alignment with the two Vickers-Vertosick models [3]:

- **Neuromodel 1**: Marathon time predictor given a recent race time of a shorter distance
- **Neuromodel 2**: Marathon time predictor given two recent race times in shorter distances.

Two different feedforward neural networks were trained based on backprop-agation, for each of the two model cases above. In both cases, the Levenberg-Marquardt method was used for the optimisation of the weights of the networks.

Both the training and the testing of the networks was done using the same datasets as the ones used in [3], in order to compare the neural networks performances directly with the Vickers-Vertosick and Riegel predictors. Thus, from the 493 data described in the previous section, the first 337 were used for training purposes and the last 156 data for testing. In the case of the neural networks approach, the 337 data were further divided into 294 data (the first of the 337) for training and 43 (the last of the 337) for validation. The 294 data are used for training which is stopped when the error on the validation set (43 data) starts increasing.

Different topologies were tried with both 1 and 2 hidden layers with a variable number of neurons in each, in order to determine the optimal topology for each of the two neuromodels. The optimum topologies reported below were decided after training all combinations of neural networks with 1 and 2 hidden layers with 5–20 neurons in each layer. Thus $16 \times 16 = 256$ neural networks were trained with 2 hidden layers and 16 neural networks were trained with a single hidden layer. Each of these networks were trained separately for 10000 times, i.e. each of the 10000 times the network was initialised with different initial weights. The training time for each network took only up to a few seconds on a Quad-Core AMD Opteron 2.2 GHz machine. This iterative procedure gave the optimum topologies described next.

3.1   Neuromodel 1

The neural network consisted of 3 inputs. The first two are the distance $distance_{r_1}$ and the adjusted time $time_{r_1}$ for the shorter race $r1$. The third input was the typical weekly mileage while training for the marathon race.

The optimised trained network used two hidden layers with 7 and 12 neurons respectively. The prediction was the marathon race time in minutes.

3.2 Neuromodel 2

The neural network consisted of 5 inputs. The first two are the distance $distance_{r_1}$ and the adjusted time $time_{r_1}$ for the shorter race $r1$. The third and fourth inputs are the distance $distance_{r_2}$ and the adjusted time $time_{r_2}$ for the second shorter race $r2$, where $distance_{r_2} > distance_{r_1}$. The fifth input was the typical weekly mileage while training for the marathon race.

The optimised trained network used two hidden layers with 5 and 12 neurons respectively. The prediction was the marathon race time in minutes.

3.3 Results

The same metrics that were used in [3] were calculated for the same test data (156 data), in order to have a direct comparison of the neural approach with the improved Vickers-Vertosick predictors (improved in terms of performance compared with the Riegel formula). These metrics were the mean square error and the penalised mean square error. Since overestimation of a runner's velocity is more detrimental than underestimation (a runner who starts too slow can speed up during a race whereas a runner who starts too fast will usually slow dramatically) the penalised mean squared error is calculated so that an overestimate of velocity has double the weight of an underestimate [3]. The two errors are shown below:

$$mse = \sum_{i=1}^{N}[target_{time}(i) - predicted_{time}(i)]^2 \tag{8}$$

$$penalised\ mse = \sum_{i \in target_{time} > predicted_{time}}^{N} [2 \cdot (target_{time}(i) - predicted_{time}(i))]^2$$

$$+ \sum_{i \in target_{time} \leq predicted_{time}}^{N} [target_{time}(i) - predicted_{time}(i)]^2 \tag{9}$$

where $N = 156$ the size of the test data and all times are in minutes. In (9), the first summation term corresponds to the overestimate of the prediction (the time of the prediction is faster than the actual target) and thus it has the double weight of the second summation term (the predicted time is slower than the actual target).

Table 1 contains the errors for both the MSE and the penalised MSE for the three approaches, i.e. the Riegel formula, the Vickers-Vertosick (V-V) with one shorter race (model 1) and two shorter races (model 2) and the Neuromodel 1 (one shorter race) and Neuromodel 2 (two shorter races). The Riegel errors were calculated based on the longest race time available which was shorter than the marathon distance. A value of $k = 1.07$ was used for the Riegel formula. All errors are calculated for the test data $N = 156$.

Table 1. Comparison results among the Riegel formula, the two Vickers-Vertosick (V-V) models and the two Neuromodels for marathon race time prediction (Neuro 1 and Neuro 2 corresponding to Neuromodel 1 and Neuromodel 2 respectively).

	Riegel	V-V 1-input	Neuro 1	V-V 2-inputs	Neuro 2
MSE	354.7152	227.593808	172.065806	208.289713	159.457859
Penalised MSE	1318.625974	646.096737	454.432942	524.977394	394.612895

It is clear that both the Neuromodel 1 and the Neuromodel 2 perform significantly better than the two models recently introduced in [3], for the task of marathon race time prediction.

4   Conclusions

The task of long distance race time prediction based on performances in races of shorter distances is important both to recreational and elite runners. This is because the design of an individual training plan is largely based (among other factors) on the target race time and also because the pace which a runner follows during a race depends on the predicted time. Given the fact that many millions of runners participate in races every year gives extra motivation and importance to tackle this problem by making the prediction as accurate as possible.

For many years the same formula was used for this prediction task and only recently two new models were introduced which outperform the classic formula previously used for marathon time prediction.

The work here shows that approaches based on feedforward neural networks perform significantly better than these two newly introduced models.

The derived neural networks (neuromodel 1 and neuromodel 2) together with other Matlab code and files which can be used to reproduce the results of this paper can be found in: https://github.com/ddracopo/race-prediction.

Acknowledgements. The author would like to thank Andrew J. Vickers and Emily A. Vertosick for making available to the public the data collected for the derivations of their models and also for answering questions regarding their usage of the data to derive their published results.

References

1. Riegel, P.S.: Athletic records and human endurance: a time-vs.-distance equation describing world-record performances may be used to compare the relative endurance capabilities of various groups of people. Am. Sci. **69**(3), 285–290 (1981). http://www.jstor.org/stable/27850427
2. Runner's World race time predictor. https://www.runnersworld.co.uk/health/rws-race-time-predictor
3. Vickers, A.J., Vertosick, E.A.: An empirical study of race times in recreational endurance runners. BMC Sports Sci. Med. Rehabil. **8**, 26 (2016)

4. Here's a better marathon time predictor: your old calculator was doing it wrong. Runner's World. https://www.runnersworld.com/marathon-training/heres-a-better-marathon-time-predictor

5. Race time predictor. http://www.runnersworld.com/tools/race-time-predictor

6. Karp, J.R.: Training characteristics of qualifiers for the U.S. Olympic marathon trials. Int. J. Sports Physiol. Perform. **2**(1), 72–92 (2007)

Fuzzy Logic Based Personalized Task Recommendation System for Field Services

Ahmed Mohamed[1], Aysenur Bilgin[2], Anne Liret[3](✉),
and Gilbert Owusu[1]

[1] Business Modelling and Operational Transformation Practice,
British Telecom, Ipswich, UK
[2] ILLC, University of Amsterdam, Amsterdam, Netherlands
[3] BMOT Research, BT France, Paris, France
anne.liret@bt.com

Abstract. Within service providing industries, field service resources often follow a schedule that is produced centrally by a scheduling system. The main objective of such systems is to fully utilize the resources by increasing the number of completed tasks while reducing operational costs. Existing off the shelf scheduling systems started to incorporate the resources' preferences and experience which although being implicit knowledge, are recognized as important drivers for service delivery efficiency. One of the scheduling systems that currently operates at BT allocates tasks interactively with a subset of empowered engineers. These engineers can select the tasks they think relevant for them to address along the working period. In this paper, we propose a fuzzy logic based personalized recommendation system that recommends tasks to the engineers based on their history of completed tasks. By analyzing the past data, we observe that the engineers indeed have distinguishable preferences that can be identified and exploited using the proposed system. We introduce a new evaluation measure for evaluating the proposed recommendations. Experiments show that the recommended tasks have up to 100% similarity to the previous tasks chosen by the engineers. Personalized recommendation systems for field service engineers have the potential to help understand how the field engineers react as the workstack evolves and new tasks come in, and to ultimately improve the robustness of service delivery.

Keywords: Fuzzy logic · Similarity · Recommendation system

1 Introduction

Resource planning is an integral component of service chain management as it ensures that customer commitments are met, a high quality service is maintained and that operational costs are kept as low as possible. Increasing complexity of IT (Information Technology), telecom and network services lead to the requirement for service organizations to operate with a large and diverse multi-skilled workforce. Such requirements, which occur frequently in real world, make the resource planning scenarios challenging as the different types of services may require individual planning approaches. However, all the approaches aim at providing a resource plan for the entire

© Springer International Publishing AG 2017
M. Bramer and M. Petridis (Eds.): SGAI-AI 2017, LNAI 10630, pp. 300–312, 2017.
https://doi.org/10.1007/978-3-319-71078-5_26

workforce to guarantee an optimal overall balance [1]. The challenge is twofold: firstly, to find the right balance between the service levels delivered to the customers, and the resource costs incurred by the business [1], secondly to find an adaptable approach to handle the dynamic aspect of tasks plan and workforce in real world [2]. To achieve high quality of service as well as reduce the company's expenses, efficient resource allocation is essential [3]. Traditional scheduling systems use all the available measures in order to optimize resource allocation against cost and quality of service; however, they neglect the experience and preferences of the resources [4–6].

Employee empowerment is a powerful management concept that helps improve morale and productivity [7]. At BT, this concept has been introduced and applied to a subset of engineers by giving them the power to choose their own tasks based on a mix of organizations and engineers criteria using a set of real time tools. Records state that after the introduction of these set of empowerment tools, the overall travel has been reduced by 17% and the engineers' utilization has increased by 10%.

Inspired by this success, we hereby introduce a fuzzy logic based personalized task recommendation system that learns implicitly from the completed task history of individual engineers and recommends tasks similar to their previous choices. The proposed system tries to tackle several challenges. Firstly, it should be emphasized that the process of recommending tasks has a different nature compared to the process recommending products such as consumer goods, books, movies, music, restaurants, etc. all of which can be recommended to other users. The context for task recommendation is different because once a task is completed, it cannot be recommended to other engineers. Furthermore, the evaluation of the success of product recommendation systems differs from the evaluation of the success of the proposed task recommendation system. The former usually rely on the available information such as ratings, feedback or reviews explicitly given by the users. However, in our case study, we do not have such information available to assess the success accuracy of the recommendations. In order to overcome this shortcoming, we propose an evaluation metric along with the proposed system.

Due to the challenging nature of the task recommendation criteria and to the lack of available ratings/feedback data, we have chosen to exploit the linguistic advantage of fuzzy logic systems (FLSs) that allow expert knowledge to be transparently incorporated in the design process. Furthermore, there exists a great deal of uncertainty with regards to the diversity of the completed tasks including the duration of the task and the location of the task as well as the frequency of the prevailing skills used by the resources. By using an expert knowledge based FLS to calculate similarity between the newly available tasks and the preferred completed tasks retrieved from the historical data, it is possible to assist the task selection process of the engineers in the field and hence improve the experience of the diverse workforce in service-based organizations.

The remaining part of the paper is organized as follows: Sect. 2 presents an overview on recommendation systems, the usage of fuzzy logic in recommendation systems, and existing evaluation techniques. We give the details of the proposed fuzzy logic based personalized recommendation system as well as the proposed evaluation metrics in Sect. 3. The experiments and results are explained in Sect. 4. Finally, Sect. 5 presents the conclusions and future work.

2 Related Work

With the increase in the number of diverse users of the internet as well as the amount of digital data published online, having access to relevant information content for the individuals has become a desired, yet, challenging priority. As noted by Babodilla et al. [8], recommender systems have been developed in parallel with the web and the consequent need for fast and accurate search engine. The following section gives an overview of the various approaches to the recommendation systems.

2.1 Overview of Recommendation Systems

Information filtering algorithms are amongst the various fundamental considerations in order to generate recommendations [8]. Nevertheless the approaches and taxonomies used to design recommendation systems are numeral and continuously improving since the suitability of one or the other turns to depend on the utilization context and the quality of available data. Commonly referred as traditional methods include collaborative filtering-based, content-based, and knowledge-based approaches [9, 10]. Recently other recommendation methods have been developed such as fuzzy set-based, social network-based, trust-based, context awareness-based, and grouped recommendation approaches [9]. Furthermore, there are hybrid approaches that employ a combination of the aforementioned methods.

In the content-based approach, recommendations are generated from the features associated with products and the given user ratings [11]. In the collaborative filtering approach, the recommendations are generated using only information about rating profiles for different users [11]. The objective of content-based approaches is to find similarity between objects, whereas the goal of collaborative approaches is to find similarity between users.

In the knowledge-based approach, the system generates recommendations based on inferences about a user's needs and preferences [11]. It has been observed that case-based approaches notably contribute to the success of knowledge-based recommendation systems. Essential to these systems is a similarity score, which represents how much the user preferences (problem description) match the recommendations (solutions to the problem). Mostly, the similarity score is interpreted as the utility of the recommendation for the user [10]. There exists another type of knowledge-based systems that are known as constraint-based systems. Both approaches utilize similar piece of knowledge, but they differ in the way solutions are calculated. Specifically, case-based recommenders generate recommendations on the basis of similarity metrics (that help identifying *hidden* relationship between items and users), whereas constraint-based recommenders mainly exploit predefined knowledge bases that contain *explicit* rules about how to relate user requirements with item features [10]. For a personalized task recommendation system for the field service engineers, we will employ a knowledge-based approach where the cases will be consisting of the previously completed tasks from the historical data and the constraints will be inherent in the task specification with regards to the required skills and importance of the tasks, which are considered to be above user preferences.

The commonly known challenges of various techniques used in recommendation systems are sparsity, cold-start problem, scalability, and over specialization problem [12]. Collaborative filtering suffers from scalability, sparsity and cold-start problems because the approach depends on the (user-item) rating matrix for generating recommendations, on the one hand, and on the other hand, the lack of data for new items or new users will cause accuracy issues, while the growing amount of information where several new items or new users may be added each day, would cause scalability problems [9, 12]. Lastly, over specialization problem prevents a user from discovering new items and other available options [12]. Especially, content-based methods suffer from over specialization problem as they cannot predict user's new behavior such as having a new interest. Compared to collaborative and content-based approaches, knowledge-based recommenders avoid some of the common drawbacks, such as the cold-start problem, since recommendations do not depend on a base of user ratings [13] and requirements are directly elicited within a recommendation session [14]. These characteristics make knowledge-based recommenders not only valuable systems on their own, but also highly complementary to other types of recommender systems [13].

In order to tackle the aforementioned problems, many advanced recommendation approaches have been proposed, such as social network-based recommender systems, fuzzy recommender systems, context awareness-based recommender systems and group recommender systems.

2.2   Overview of Fuzzy Logic in Recommendation Systems

Fuzzy logic allows for the management of non-stochastic uncertainty induced from subjectivity, vagueness and imprecision in the data, as well as the domain knowledge and the objects (tasks in our case) under consideration; hence, this approach is applied with a certain success to problems requiring to handle subjective user behaviors, imprecise information in real situations and the gradualness of preference profiles that are essential to recommendation systems [9, 15, 16].

Fuzzy logic has been successfully employed in recommendation systems where user preferences and item features have been represented as fuzzy sets [17], as well as where the most suitable items are selected using incomplete and uncertain information [15].

To the best of our knowledge, the existing fuzzy logic based recommendation systems tend to be utilized in entertainment, content and e-commerce [18] domains where products of interest contain books, music, movies and news, which can be frequently consumed; or other consumer goods/services [19] such as mobile phones, tablets, laptops, cars, etc. which can be considered to be less frequently bought or consumed. In our case, although tasks can be represented using features as in the aforementioned products, they cannot be recommended to another field service engineer. Therefore, we focus on approaches that model user preferences.

The design process of a recommender system strongly relies on the right understanding of the user preferences. A recent study on comparative preference elicitation [20] suggests that most of the approaches for understanding user preferences are based on having *explicit* feedback from the users. As a matter of fact, Fuzzy logic based recommendation systems can be found in various domains that model user preferences using explicit information such as user ratings/feedback [15, 21, 22]. However, in many real-life situations, we need to rely on *implicit* feedback. With regards to the personalized support in the selection of a task (piece of work) for the field engineers, the proposed system depends on implicit feedbacks, which in our case are deduced from the closed tasks history for each engineer. The proposed system is detailed in Sect. 3.

2.3   Evaluation Metrics

The commonly used evaluation metrics for the recommendation systems can be categorized under 4 categories, which are prediction metrics (e.g. Mean Absolute Error (MAE), Root of Mean Square Error (RMSE), etc.), set recommendation metrics (e.g. precision, recall, etc.), rank recommendation metrics (e.g. the discounted cumulative gain), and diversity metrics (e.g. the novelty of the recommended items) [8]. Del Olma and Gaudioso [23] differentiate between interactive and non-interactive systems in recommendation systems and propose a general framework that considers each recommender as being composed of a guide subsystem and a filter subsystem. For task recommendation, which can be referred to be a solely filtering subsystem, none of the existing measures are appropriate for evaluation as we do not have predictions, user ratings, or enough feedbacks about the adherence or not to the recommended tasks, at that stage. Therefore, we propose a new evaluation measure in Sect. 3.3.

3   The Proposed Fuzzy Logic Based Personalized Recommendation System

The proposed fuzzy logic based recommendation system employs a hybrid approach combining content-based and knowledge-based methods, which is described in this section. Since we represent the tasks to be recommended using their features such as duration, skill needed, and location etc., we take advantage of a content-based method. In addition, we embed knowledge-based approaches as we make use of constraints in the task selection process to recommend tasks that are compatible with the engineer (e.g. matching skills, co-located areas) as well as using rule-based expert knowledge in order to overcome the cold-start problem. Regarding over-specialization problem inherent to content-based methods, we propose to use a time-window for the past data to be able to learn from suitable task history (e.g. if the engineer acquired a new skill, or moved to another home location). The following sections explain the data, the design of the proposed system as well as the proposed evaluation measure in detail.

3.1 Features Used as Inputs

Three months of historical task completion data has been used in building and evaluating the proposed system. Table 1 presents an example of the data and the features used. Table 1 shows sample examples of the features we identified as key for users to distinguish relevance of work. Note these features may change when the task related to the work is amended (duration of appointment visit, extra access right required for instance). These features are defined in Table 2 and are used as inputs for the proposed system. Features can be of Numerical or Categorical types. The approach we will propose in next section is able to handle these two types of features. This is an improvement compared to approaches treating only one type of information because it allows combining qualitative and quantitative dimension in a single approach.

Table 1. Example of the data and the features used in the proposed system.

Task id	PWA	Primary skill	Duration (mins)	Customer type	Exchange	Business priority (1 = highest)	Root skill	Parent skill
Task 1	Area 1	PS 1	31	PA 1	E_1	3	RS 1	S 10
Task 2	Area 1	PS 2	47	TA 1	E_2	10	RS 1	S 10
Task 3	Area 1	PS 5	47	TA 2	E_2	10	RS 2	S 20
Task 4	Area 1	PS 2	50	TA 1	E_2	2	RS 1	S 10
Task 5	Area 1	PS 1	19	WD 5	E_5	15	RS 1	S 10
Task 6	Area 1	PS 5	55	TA 2	E_4	3	RS 2	S 20
Task 7	Area 2	PS 4	19	WD 2	E_1	15	RS 1	S 10

Table 2. Definition of the features.

Feature	Type	Definition
Working area	Categorical	A geographical area of exchanges
Exchange	Categorical	A specific geographical location
Root skill	Categorical	The highest level of skill
Parent skill	Categorical	One of the children skills of a specific root skill
Primary skill	Categorical	One of the children skill of a specific parent skill
Estimated duration	Numerical	The estimated task duration in minutes
Response code	Categorical	A code that indicates how urgent is the task
Business priority	Categorical	A priority that indicates the importance of a task (The lower the number, the higher the priority)

3.2 Design of the Proposed System

The proposed recommendation system is sketched in Fig. 1. The content of the recommended items is personalized thanks to a computation of similarity with past working experience of users, which accuracy is evolving thanks to a learning phase. The output of the learning phase is then used to refine the similarity criteria involved in the fuzzy rules set for task recommendation.

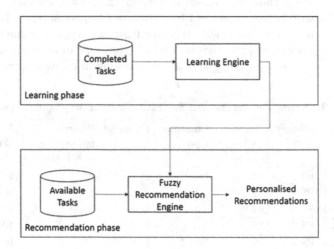

Fig. 1. Overview of the proposed fuzzy logic based personalized recommendation system.

As shown in the Fig. 1, the proposed system is divided into two phases:

- Learning phase
- Recommendation phase

Learning phase. In the learning phase, the features seven categorical features and one numerical feature defined in Table 2 have been used. As the system is personalized for an individual engineer, the learning engine component receives the completed tasks for that engineer, to be processed. The objective of the learning engine is to build frequency tables for categorical inputs and to calculate several statistics (i.e. minimum, maximum, mean) for the numerical input. The underlying idea is that the more frequent a feature (e.g. skills, locations) is present in the work previously completed by the engineer, the more knowledgeable the engineer would become. In a context of service delivery, such measure of the frequency of "success utilization of given knowledge" turn to indicate a form of implicit preference for the engineer. Figure 2(a–c) shows a visualization of some of the frequency information that belongs to an engineer's history of completed tasks. It can be observed that the engineer has a preferred working location or PWA (i.e. Aberdeen Denburn), a preferred parent skill (i.e. Power Medium), which is an abstract level above a set of knowledge-related operational skills, and a preferred primary skill (i.e. PLR81). Similar patterns have been noted for the other features in Table 2 but not visualized here due to space limitations.

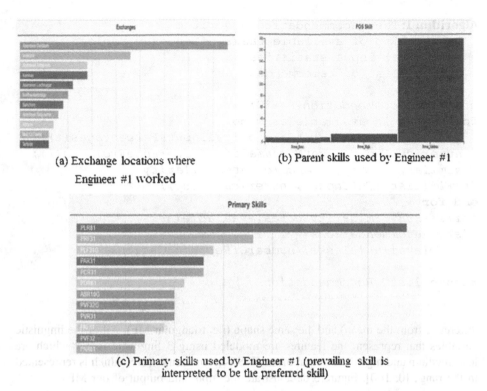

(a) Exchange locations where Engineer #1 worked

(b) Parent skills used by Engineer #1

(c) Primary skills used by Engineer #1 (prevailing skill is interpreted to be the preferred skill)

Fig. 2. Visualization of some of the frequency information for Engineer #1's completed task history.

Recommendation phase. In the recommendation phase, the frequency tables and the statistical information calculated in the learning phase are used to build the inputs for the fuzzy logic based recommendation engine. The output of the proposed system is a ranked list of recommendations that is sorted based on the similarity score calculated by the FLS. Each recommendation takes the form of a task recommended from the newly available tasks.

The fuzzy recommendation engine component takes each of the available tasks and for each feature of the newly available task, it makes use of the frequency tables and statistics that have been created/calculated in the learning phase. For the seven categorical features, these frequency tables are used as look-up tables from which the numerical inputs (*i.e.* the normalized percentage) are retrieved as inputs to the FLS. For the numerical feature, the statistics (*i.e.* the mean, the maximum and the minimum) are used to calculate a normalized difference from the mean. The FLS takes the aforementioned height inputs and calculates a similarity score for the new task. The same steps are iterated over the whole list of potential candidate tasks given as input to the algorithm. The tasks are then ranked as per decreasing similarity score. The algorithm employed by the fuzzy recommendation engine component is presented in Algorithm 1.

The membership functions (MFs) for all of the inputs are designed to have the same universe of discourse (*i.e.* normalized percentage in the unit interval and normalized

Algorithm 1: The recommendation algorithm
  Input: List of available tasks, frequency tables,
   numerical input statistics
  Output: List of recommended tasks

numberOfRecommendations ← 30;
for task *t* in *availableTasks* **do**
  listOfCatInputs ← *getCategoricalInputsPercentages(t);*
  numericalInput ← *getNornamalisedDifferenceFromMean(t);*
  similarityScore(t) ← *calculateSimilarityUs-*
ingFLS(listOfCatInputs, numericalInput);
end for
sortTasksBySimilarityScores(availableTasks);
listOfRecommendations = limitRecommenda-
tionTo(availableTasks, numberOfRecommendations);

return *listOfRecommendations;*

difference from the mean) and the same shape (i.e. triangular MF). All of the linguistic variables that represent the features are modeled using 3 linguistic terms, which are low, medium and high. The output of the FLS is a similarity score, which is represented in the range [0, 100]. Figure 3 demonstrate the input and output of our MFs.

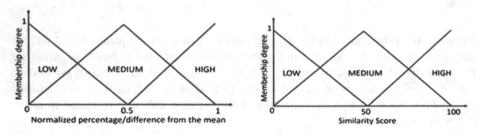

Fig. 3. Visualization of the shape of our input membership functions (*left*) and output of membership functions (*right*).

In Fig. 3 the input is the normalized variant of the difference between the feature value and the mean computed from historical data; the output is the similarity score related to this feature.

The rule-base of the FLS is designed to consist of incomplete (i.e. using one antecedent) IF-THEN fuzzy rules, as shown in Table 3 for categorical features as well as the numerical feature, respectively. It should be noted that the rules can be easily modified to incorporate expert knowledge for special cases. For example, some rules can be set to follow the expert preference (e.g. business priority) while complying with the engineer's learned preferences about the other features. The proposed system will adjust the ranked list of recommendations accordingly and automatically at each run.

Table 3. Fuzzy logic system Rules for the categorical inputs and the numerical input.

Antecedent (IN)	Consequence (THEN)	Antecedent (IN)	Consequence (THEN)
Categorical input	Similarity score	Numerical input	Similarity score
LOW	LOW	LOW	HIGH
MEDIUM	MEDIUM	MEDIUM	MEDIUM
HIGH	HIGH	HIGH	LOW

The choice of using three fuzzy rules items has been made because of the need to be scalable and comprehensively configurable by end users. Each new feature will be represented by three additional rules (linear growth of complexity), so this will bind the impact of dimensionality which in recommendation system can be a blocker to real time execution in real world. Moreover only the type of knowledge preferences for each feature needs to be set up.

3.3   Proposed Evaluation Measure

As the existing evaluation metrics are not applicable for the proposed task recommendation system, we have developed a new measure to evaluate the quality of the recommended tasks. The underlying procedure is detailed as follows:

1. Identify the prevailing (*i.e.* the most preferred) category for each of the categorical features and keep it as the reference recommendation for the engineer.
2. Retrieve the top N tasks from the ranked list of recommendations presented to the engineer.
3. For each task T within the top N tasks, calculate one-to-one matching similarity between the reference recommendation and the task T. The similarity score for the task T is the ratio (*i.e.* the percentage) of the correctly matched categories to the number of categories (*i.e.* seven for the proposed system).
4. Take the average similarity score for all top N tasks and this is the final evaluation measure score.

The evaluation process is based on the categorical features and excludes the numerical feature. This is because we believe that the numerical feature would not contribute to a reliable evaluation metric due to the fact that the mean is calculated using all of the skills during the learning phase. Although this evaluation process meets the nature of task recommendation in a better way compared to the existing measures, the outcome of the evaluation depends on the availability of tasks that would be similar to the reference recommendation for the engineer based on his completed task history. Another evaluation technique would be to run a pilot study, however, this is considered to be out of scope for this paper.

4 Experiments and Results

The experiments have been conducted using 13 randomly selected field engineers having different geographical home locations and various skills. The size of the historical data (i.e. the number of completed tasks) for each engineer was diverse with a minimum of 34 tasks, a maximum of 577 tasks and a mean of 441 tasks. For the number of newly available tasks, the size of the data ranged from 17429 tasks to 20726 tasks with a mean of 19175 tasks. We have performed comparison between 2 FLSs using type-1 and linear general type-2 fuzzy sets [24] for the proposed algorithm detailed in Algorithm 1. The results, which employ the proposed evaluation measure presented in Sect. 3.3, are reported in Table 4.

Table 4. Similarity score results of type-1 (T1) and linear general type-2 (LGT2) based FLSs for different number of recommended tasks (N)

Engineer ID	N = 5		N = 10		N = 20		N = 40	
	T1	LGT2	T1	LGT2	T1	LGT2	T1	LGT2
Engineer #1	100.0	100.0	100.0	100.0	100.0	100.0	100.0	100.0
Engineer #2	68.57	62.85	65.7	60.0	61.4	60.0	57.1	56.8
Engineer #3	85.7	85.7	81.4	81.4	79.3	79.3	77.5	77.5
Engineer #4	85.7	85.7	87.1	91.4	88.6	88.6	85.4	87.1
Engineer #5	74.3	74.3	72.9	72.9	70.7	70.7	71.8	71.8
Engineer #6	54.3	54.3	48.6	48.6	47.9	47.9	52.1	52.1
Engineer #7	85.7	85.7	85.7	85.7	82.1	82.1	76.8	76.8
Engineer #8	71.4	71.4	71.4	71.4	71.4	71.4	65.0	65.0
Engineer #9	77.1	77.1	74.3	74.3	72.9	72.9	72.1	72.1
Engineer #10	57.1	57.1	64.3	64.3	65.0	65.0	61.4	61.4
Engineer #11	57.1	57.1	57.1	57.1	52.9	52.9	48.9	48.9
Engineer #12	100.0	100.0	100.0	100.0	99.3	99.3	92.5	92.5
Engineer #13	60.0	60.0	58.6	58.6	57.9	57.9	53.6	51.8
Average	**75.2**	**74.7**	**74.4**	**74.3**	**73.0**	**72.9**	**70.3**	**70.3**

Based on the results shown in the last row of Table 4, the type-1 FLS is performing slightly better on average. We have observed that the additional parameters for the LGT2 FLS (i.e. footprint of uncertainty parameters) need to be tuned separately for each engineer. Furthermore, as the number of recommended tasks increase, the average similarity score decreases.

As mentioned previously, the proposed evaluation measure highly depends on the newly available tasks to recommend from. It should be noted that the proposed fuzzy logic based personalized task recommendation system managed to achieve 100% similarity score when identical tasks exist in the newly available task dataset. This indicates its calibration has reach a good accuracy level.

5   Conclusions and Future Work

In this paper, we proposed a fuzzy logic based personalized task recommendation system for field service engineers. The system combines content-based and knowledge based recommendation methods and uses seven categorical and one numerical feature in the proposed case study. To the knowledge of the authors, the novelty relies in the simplicity and scalability of the approach for a recommendation system: (a) The choice of using three fuzzy rules per feature allows a linear growth of the system along the number of features; (b) the recommendation drivers exposed by the system are comprehensively configurable by end users, who only have to set up the type of knowledge preferences for each feature; (c) To calculate the relevance of tasks, the system accepts numerical and categorical features and is able to combine them into a uniform reference. This is all the more important for a real time recommendation system that the confidence into the result strongly depends on the ability for explaining in a human comprehensive manner.

Another advantage is that the proposed system is able to tackle the curse of dimensionality problem inherent to rule-based fuzzy logic systems, which is caused by the number of antecedents in a fuzzy rule. Indeed, by using incomplete fuzzy rules, the rule-base of the proposed system would grow linearly rather than exponentially when the number of features increases. Hence, it can be deduced that the proposed system is scalable.

The experiments were based on real world data consisting of tasks for field engineers. Two FLSs based on type-1 and linear general type-2 fuzzy logic were compared. The results suggest that the type-1 FLS outperformed the linear general type-2 system due to the fact that the former does not require tuning for each engineer. We intend to run a controlled trial as another evaluation technique for the future work.

Acknowledgments. This study is partially supported by the Marie Curie Initial Training Network (ITN) ESSENCE, grant agreement no. 607062.

References

1. Kern, M., Shakya, S., Owusu, G.: Integrated resource planning for diverse workforces. In: 2009 International Conference on Computers & Industrial Engineering CIE, pp. 1169–1173. IEEE (2009)
2. Mohamed, A., Hagras, H., Shakya, S., Liret, A., Dorne, R., Owusu, G.: Hierarchical type-2 fuzzy logic based real time dynamic operational planning system. In: Bramer, M., Petridis, M. (eds.) Research and Development in Intelligent Systems XXXI, pp. 255–267. Springer, Cham (2014). https://doi.org/10.1007/978-3-319-12069-0_19
3. Voudouris, C., Owusu, G., Dorne, R., Lesaint, D.: Service Chain Management: Technology Innovation For The Service Business. Springer Science & Business Media, Heidelberg (2007). https://doi.org/10.1007/978-3-540-75504-3
4. Haugen, D.L., Hill, A.V.: Scheduling to improve field service quality. Decis. Sci. **30**(3), 783–804 (1999)
5. Petrakis, I., Hass, C., Bichler, M.: On the impact of real-time information on field service scheduling. Decis. Support Syst. **53**(2), 282–293 (2012)

6. Collins, J.E., Sisley, E.M.: Automated assignment and scheduling of service personnel. IEEE Expert 9(2), 33–39 (1994)
7. Alsheddy, A., Tsang, E.P.: Empowerment scheduling for a field workforce. J. Sched. 14(6), 639–654 (2011)
8. Bobadilla, J., Ortega, F., Hernando, A., Gutirrez, A.: Recommender systems survey. Knowl.-Based Syst. 46, 109–132 (2013). http://www.sciencedirect.com/science/article/pii/S0950705113001044
9. Lu, J., Wu, D., Mao, M., Wang, W., Zhang, G.: Recommender system application developments: a survey. Decis. Support Syst. 74, 12–32 (2015)
10. Ricci, F., Rokach, L., Shapira, B.: Introduction to recommender systems handbook. In: Ricci, F., Rokach, L., Shapira, B., Kantor, P.B. (eds.) Recommender Systems Handbook. Springer, Heidelberg (2011)
11. Burke, R.: Hybrid web recommender systems. In: Brusilovsky, P., Kobsa, A., Nejdl, W. (eds.) The Adaptive Web. LNCS, vol. 4321, pp. 377–408. Springer, Heidelberg (2007). https://doi.org/10.1007/978-3-540-72079-9_12
12. Sharma, L., Gera, A.: A survey of recommendation system: research challenges. Int. J. Eng. Trends Technol. (IJETT) 4(5), 1989–1992 (2013)
13. Trewin, S.: Knowledge-based recommender systems. Encycl. Libr. Inf. Sci. 69(32), 180–200 (2000)
14. Felfernig, A., Friedrich, G., Jannach, D., Zanker, M.: Developing constraint based recommenders. In: Ricci, F., Rokach, L., Shapira, B., Kantor, P.B. (eds.) Recommender Systems Handbook, pp. 187–215. Springer, Heidelberg (2011). https://doi.org/10.1007/978-0-387-85820-3_6
15. Wu, D., Zhang, G., Lu, J.: A fuzzy preference tree-based recommender system for personalized business-to-business e-services. IEEE Trans. Fuzzy Syst. 23(1), 29–43 (2015)
16. Zenebe, A., Norcio, A.F.: Representation, similarity measures and aggregation methods using fuzzy sets for content-based recommender systems. Fuzzy Sets Syst. 160(1), 76–94 (2009)
17. Yager, R.R.: Fuzzy logic methods in recommender systems. Fuzzy Sets Syst. 136(2), 133–149 (2003)
18. Martinez, L., Barranco, M.J., Perez, L.G., Espinilla, M.: A knowledge based recommender system with multi granular linguistic information. Int. J. Comput. Intell. Syst. 1(3), 225–236 (2008)
19. Ojokoh, B., Omisore, M., Samuel, O., Ogunniyi, T.: A fuzzy logic based personalized recommender system. Int. J. Comput. Sci. Inf. Technol. Secur. 2(5), 1008–1015 (2012)
20. Parra, D., Amatriain, X.: Walk the talk. In: Konstan, Joseph A., Conejo, R., Marzo, José L., Oliver, N. (eds.) UMAP 2011. LNCS, vol. 6787, pp. 255–268. Springer, Heidelberg (2011). https://doi.org/10.1007/978-3-642-22362-4_22. http://dl.acm.org/citation.cfm?id=2021855.2021878
21. Zhang, Z., Lin, H., Liu, K., Wu, D., Zhang, G., Lu, J.: A hybrid fuzzy-based personalized recommender system for telecom products/services. Inf. Sci. 235, 117–129 (2013)
22. Herrera-Viedma, E., Porcel, C., Lopez-Herrera, A.G., Alonso, S.: A fuzzy linguistic recommender system to advice research resources in university digital libraries. In: Bustince, H., Herrera, F., Montero, J. (eds.) Fuzzy Sets and Their Extensions: Representation, Aggregation and Models, vol. 220, pp. 567–585. Springer, Heidelberg (2008)
23. Del Olmo, F.H., Gaudioso, E.: Evaluation of recommender systems: a new approach. Expert Syst. Appl. 35(3), 790–804 (2008)
24. Bilgin, A., Hagras, H., Van Helvert, J., Alghazzawi, D.: A linear general type-2 fuzzy-logic-based computing with words approach for realizing an ambient intelligent platform for cooking recipe recommendation. IEEE Trans. Fuzzy Syst. 24(2), 306–329 (2016)

Application of Neural Network in Modeling Commuter Choice Behavior with a Novel Fuzzy Access Measure

Dewal Mishra$^{(\boxtimes)}$ and A.K. Sarkar

Birla Institute of Technology and Science, Pilani, Rajasthan, India
`dewal.mishra@gmail.com`

Abstract. Public transit systems (PTS) in major cities of developing countries are under immense pressure due to the rising populations. Most city dwellers in these countries depend on PTS for their daily commute and are highly sensitive to shifting to private vehicles when utility of the PTS decreases for them. Accessibility to PTS is an aspect of transport planning which impacts the shifting behavior of the commuters to a large extent. For assessing the impact of access to PTS on commuter choice behavior; binary logistic regression and neural network (NN) models were developed using socio demographic and commute related data collected through a revealed preference (RP) survey experiment in Indore city in India. Accessibility to the PTS was quantified using a fuzzy weighted average (FWA) measure employing temporal impedances experienced by the commuters and the value they associate with each of the impedance. Both models show significant correlation between quantified accessibility and choice behavior. The neural network model developed for this study shows better predictive powers as the apparent validity of the model was found to be 0.883 (area under curve for the receiver's operational characteristic curve) which was greater as compared to apparent validity for regression model, 0.753. Predictions made by the models for shifting behavior were validated using data from a stated preference (SP) survey experiment for the same sample set. The NN model performed better in this scenario as well with 68.34% correct predictions as opposed to 65.96% correct predictions from the regression model.

Keywords: Accessibility · Fuzzy weighted average · Neural network

1 Introduction

Accessibility of a public transit system (PTS) as a concept has been a subject of debate in urban planning sphere for a long period of time. The research on the topic has been extensive, but a consensus on how to define accessibility has not been reached in academic circles. Consequently, multiple definitions of accessibility can be found in the literature. Geurs and van Eck [1] define accessibility as, *"the extent to which the land use-transport system enables (groups of) individuals or goods to reach activities or destinations by means of a (combination of) transport mode(s)"*. Bhat et al. [2] on the other hand define accessibility as, *"accessibility is a measure of the ease of an individual to pursue an activity of a desired type, at a desired location, by a desired mode,*

© Springer International Publishing AG 2017
M. Bramer and M. Petridis (Eds.): SGAI-AI 2017, LNAI 10630, pp. 313–321, 2017.
https://doi.org/10.1007/978-3-319-71078-5_27

and at a desired time". Bertolini et al. [3] in their study define accessibility as *"the amount and diversity of places that can be reached within a given travel time and/or cost"*. Many more definitions that contemplate different possible dimensions of accessibility can be found in the literature [4–6]. These different explanations of accessibility have led to formulation of numerous measures that can be broadly categorized as infrastructure based, activity based and utility based. A much comprehensive account of different accessibility measures, their formulation and use can be found in the literature [2, 4, 7–10]. The measures found in literature quantify and explain how effectively the PTS serve the commuter in reaching opportunities or destinations but the ease with which the commuters can reach the PTS itself has not been studied sufficiently. Another aspect of the accessibility definitions and measures is that they are objective in nature, the subjectivity of the decision making process of the commuter hasn't been addressed properly [11, 12].

This study uses a fuzzy weighted average (FWA) approach for quantifying accessibility to a PTS. This approach utilizes the temporal impedances experienced by commuters while accessing the PTS and the value that every commuter imparts to these specific impedances in creating a subjective measure for calculating accessibility to their nearest PTS station. To assess the impact of the defined accessibility on the overall choice behaviour of the commuter a binary logistic regression model (BLM) was developed. BLM have been used for choice modelling in numerous studies [13–18] and have been a part of planning efforts. But with the advancements in machine learning and predictive model building techniques such as NN and genetic algorithms the possibilities of developing better performing modeling techniques have increased. This study compares the performance of the BLM and NN model developed from a single data set to ascertain the possibility of use of these new advancements in transport planning context.

2 Study Area

The data for performing this study were gathered from the commuters of a bus rapid transit (BRT) system which was introduced in Indore city in India in the year 2013 by replacing two intra-city bus service (IBS) routes. Indore is the largest city in the state of Madhya Pradesh both in size and population. It is the industrial and educational hub for the central region of India with an average 85.18% literacy rate. With a healthy amount of job opportunities, a significant education infrastructure boom and a sturdy economic backbone due to a thriving trading scene; Indore is a strong, attractive force for residents of underdeveloped villages and small cities surrounding it.

Table 1 shows Indore city's decadal growth in various aspects. A private vehicle ownership increase of 11.56% over the decade is a significant rise when compared to a total population rise of 3.96%. Such increase in vehicle ownership is a cause of concern especially when the city has had an annual growth in the size of 5.67% indicating higher congestion rates on the city roads. An annual rise of 6.92% in fatalities is also alarming. The BRT system in Indore was planned to be a network of corridors approximately 100 km in length however as of yet only a 11.5 km long pilot corridor has been put into operation. The corridor is separated from general traffic with permanent barricades and cuts through the Central Business District (CBD) of the city.

Table 1. Indore city decadal growth.

Parameter	Year 2000–01	Year 2010–11	Year 2015	Annual growth rate (%)
Population	1.64 million	1.9 million	3.4 million	3.96
Private vehicle ownership	0.45 million	0.97 million	N.A	11.56
Traffic accidents	2,617	3,473	5,873	3.27
Fatalities	130	220	444	6.92
City extent	110 sq.km	172.4 sq.km	N.A	5.67

BRT system in Indore was an instant success as the exclusive bus lanes drastically reduced end to end travel times without any rise in fares (fares were kept the same as IBS). Coupled with these two big incentives was the attraction of the buses being air conditioned and run on headways of 5 min throughout the operation period providing more comfort, reliability and reduced waiting times. An analysis of the ticketing data revealed that over the years, the BRT has witnessed a substantial rise in average daily ridership which sits at 48000 passengers per day. From the same ticketing analysis, the peak hours were observed to be 10–11 am and 6–7 pm (3400 and 3800 average passengers respectively) during the operating times of 6 am to 10 pm. The continued increase in ridership is one major reason for choosing Indore and BRT as the study area. Also, since the BRT system is to be expanded significantly, the results from this study will help guide the planning efforts. More importantly, the results from this study will prove to be a guiding tool for similar such endeavours in cities and countries resembling the study area.

3 Data Collection

Data used for performing this study was collected from all the BRT stations in July 2016. The survey questionnaires were distributed over the period of one week (Monday through Sunday) throughout the operation times. To increase variance in the data, questionnaires were distributed arbitrarily. The designed survey gathered data pertaining to commuters' travel details prior to and after introduction of the BRT.

A study [13] conducted in Malaysia has shown that age, gender, car ownership, travel time, travel cost, household size and income are significant parameters while modelling modal shift from private car to public transportation. Conclusions drawn in other studies [13, 15, 19–21] also support including socio-economic demographics like age, income, gender, household size and vehicle ownership while developing a mode choice model. Therefore, age, gender, household income, vehicle ownership and occupation were the socio-economic variables included in the analysis. For transit related data, waiting times at feeder stops as well as BRT stations, in-vehicle travel times in feeder and BRT and time taken to reach the destination after alighting from the service were chosen. Two pilot survey exercises were performed because sometimes a large number of predictor variables in an analysis can yield an inelegant and complex model and may present the problem of over fitting the data [23]. The final survey was defined after acquiring critical inputs from operating authorities of BRT, planning experts and taking into account the learnings from the pilot surveys.

The required sample size for the ridership was calculated assuming a confidence level of 99% and a confidence interval of 5% [24]. After the data collection, refinement and weeding out outliers, the final sample size obtained was 802 samples which was found to be sufficient for performing the analysis.

4 Model Development and Validation

The response variable for both of the developed models was dichotomous in nature. Since the BRT was introduced by replacement of IBS routes, the passengers shifting from the now defunct IBS were deemed as "retained" users while the rest were deemed as "choice" users. IBM SPSS 22.0 package was used for developing the models.

4.1 Binary Logistic Regression Model

BLM is based on the utility theory which hypothesizes that an individual will likely shift to BRT if it's utility is more than the utility of the mode they are using. Without loss of generality, it can be said that the utility of shifting is the difference between utilities of the two alternatives.

The model coefficients obtained are presented in Table 2 below.

The analysis was performed on the 802 respondent sample set. Column 1 in Table 2 shows the explanatory variables considered for constructing the model and Column 2 shows the categories in which the explanatory variables were divided. Column 3 shows the coefficient estimates for the model. These estimates tell the amount of increase (or decrease, if the sign of the coefficient is negative) in the predicted log odds that would be predicted by a 1-unit increase (or decrease) in the predictor, holding all other predictors constant. Column 4 provides the result of the 2-tailed p-value used in testing the null hypothesis. Coefficients having p-values less than alpha (0.05) are statistically significant i.e. they bear a significant effect on the dependent variable. Column 6 presents the odds ratio for the categories which are the exponentiation of the coefficients. Odds ratios are used to compare the relative odds of the occurrence of the outcome of interest (shifting modes), given exposure to the variable of interest (Age, Gender, Access etc.) [25, 26].

The accessibility measure (denoted as "Access" in the output table) has a positive coefficient. Theoretically, the measure values range from 1 to 5, where 1 denotes the best possible access one can experience (least amount of time taken when highest weight is imparted to it) and vice versa for a "Access" value of 5. Therefore, a high value of access measure will indicate a higher probability of shifting from BRT to other modes. These results substantiate the hypothesis of this study that access plays an important role in choice modelling since an individual with poor access to BRT is

Table 2. BLM model details.

Explanatory variables (1)	Categories (2)	Coefficients (3)	p-value (4)	Odds ratio (5)
Age	Less than 18 years	1.22	0.005	3.386
	18 to 30 years	0.74	0.002	2.096
	More than 30 years*	1		
Occupation	Student	0.548	0.037	1.731
	Working professional	1.21	0.001	2.252
	Other*	1		
Income	Less than INR 1 LPA	0.674	0.046	1.961
	INR 1LPA to INR 3 LPA	1.21	0.001	3.355
	More than INR 3 LPA*	1		
Gender	Male	0.502	0.001	1.643
	Female*	1		
Vehicle owned	Two wheeler	0.465	0.046	1.592
	Four wheeler	−0.741	0.032	0.477
	Bicycle	0.515	0.115	1.674
	None*	1		
Waiting time	Less than 10 min	1.889	0.000	6.615
	10 to 20 min	2.237	0.000	9.361
	More than 20 min*	1		
In-vehicle travelling time	Less than 15 min	1.788	0.000	5.978
	15 to 30 min	1.742	0.000	5.711
	More than 30 min*	1		
Time to reach destination after egress from mode	Less than 10 min	1.448	0.000	4.253
	10 to 15 min	1.533	0.000	4.634
	More than 15 min*	1		
Access		0.652	0.000	1.918
Constant		−7.709	0.000	0.000

likely to shift to some other mode (Odds ratio for "Access" = 1.198). For determining the goodness of fit, Hosmer and Lemenshow test was performed. The results of the test are insignificant (p-value >0.05), therefore it can be concluded that the model fits the data well [27].

A receiver's operational characteristic (ROC) curves were also plotted for the BLM model for testing its performance. The optimism in apparent performance for the model was found to be 0.01. This test shows that the model developed is able to differentiate between the choice and retained users and is making predictions based on the attribute measures used in making the model.

4.2   Neural Network Model

NN differs from discrete choice methods in its use of pattern association and error correction as the underlying mechanisms to represent a problem in contrast to the random utility maximization rule [28]. The utilization of NN enables the user to represent human perception relating to a problem as a network of neurons. Table 3 presents the network architecture information. Hyperbolic tangent function was used as the activation function in the hidden layer because it converges faster than the standard logistic function (a non-symmetric sigmoid function) [29]. Sigmoid function was chosen as the activation function for the output layer over the much used softmax function.

Table 3. NN model details.

Input layer	Factors	1	Age
		2	Occupation
		3	Income
		4	Gender
		5	IVTT
		6	Vehicle
		7	T.Wait
		8	T.Des
	Covariates	1	Access
	Number of units[a]		25
	Rescaling method for COVARIATES		Standardized
Hidden layer(s)	Number of hidden layers		1
	Number of units in Hidden layer 1[a]		9
	Activation function		Hyperbolic tangent
Output layer	Dependent variables	1	Choice
	Number of units		2
	Activation function		Sigmoid
	Error function		Sum of squares

[a]Excluding the bias unit.

The data used for developing the NN model was the same data used for generating the BLM, from which 553 samples (70%) were used for training and the rest 249 samples (30%) were used for testing the network. Also, all the same predictors were used in both the analyses (Input Layer-Factors and Covariates, Table 3). Although the predictive powers of the network decrease if two or more hidden layers are used [30] two architectures (one and two hidden layers keeping other characteristics constant) were used to generate networks for a better understanding of the impact of hidden layers. Percentage incorrect predictions reported during testing were 12.0% and

11.98% (one and two hidden layers respectively) therefore it can be said that increasing the number of hidden layers does not improve the predictive capability. Thus, single hidden layer was used in order to avoid complexity in results. The AUC of the ROC curve obtained for the model is 0.898 which implies that the discriminatory power of the network is very good [31].

The importance of any attribute used to construct the model is a measure of change in the network's prediction for different inputs to the said attribute. Normalized importance is simply the ratio of attribute importance value to largest importance value assigned to the attributes in ANN modelling process and it is expressed as a percentage (%). From Fig. 1 it can be stated that the accessibility measure introduced in this study ("Access") has the highest impact on overall choice model performance. Vehicle ownership and time taken to reach destination after egress from the mode were found to be the next most influential variables for the model. Gender was found to be the least influencing factor amongst the other predictor variables.

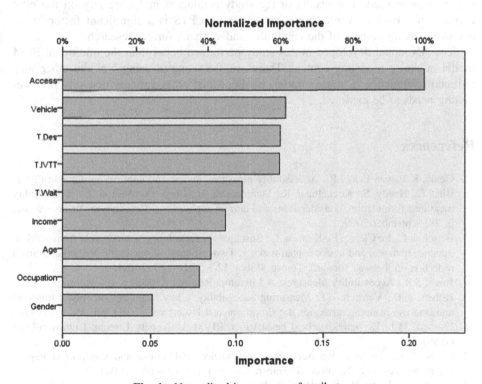

Fig. 1. Normalized importance of attributes.

4.3   Model Validation

For validating the models, data from a stated preference (SP) survey experiment were used. In this experiment the commuters were asked if they would switch modes from BRT if their access times were increased by 5, 10 and 15 min. Access to the PTS was then calculated for these commuters using the defined measure and shifting probability calculated using both the models for every commuter. The BLM model made 65.96% correct predictions whereas the NN model made 68.34% correct predictions. Therefore, it is safe to say that the NN model is a better alternative to the BLM when modelling choice.

5 Conclusion

This study introduces a basic fuzzy tool as a quantifying measure for access to a PTS. The measure collates the temporal aspects of the journey to the nearest transit station with the value that the individuals associate with the journey enabling the user to add another dimension to the planning process which was missing in traditional techniques. This measure also enables the planner/operator to identify the importance of individual attributes on the overall choice of mode which wasn't possible when traditional access measures were used. The results of the study conducted in Indore city on the pilot corridor of a BRT network show that access to a PTS is a significant factor in the decision-making process of the commuter and warrants further research.

The NN model developed in this study performed better than the traditional BLM model in choice modeling context. Therefore, the scope of using NN and other such artificial intelligence in transportation planning and other spheres that rely on forecasting needs to be explored.

References

1. Geurs, K.T., van Eck, J.R.: Accessibility measures: review and application, Utrecht (2001)
2. Bhat, C., Handy, S., Kockelman, K., Mahmassani, H., Chen, Q., Weston, L.: Accessibility measures: formulation, considerations and current applications. Research report no. 4938-2, p. 28, September 2000
3. Bertolini, L., Le Clercq, F., Kapoen, L.: Sustainable accessibility: a conceptual framework to integrate transport and land use plan-making. Two test-applications in the Netherlands and a reflection on the way forward. Transp. Policy 12(3), 207–220 (2005)
4. Jones, S.R.: Accessibility Measures: A Literature Review. Berkshire, Crawthorne (1981)
5. Hilbers, H.D., Verroen, E.J.: Measuring accessibility, a key factor for successful transport and land-use planning strategies. In: Environmental Issues, vol. P 363, pp. 25–36 (1993)
6. Hagoort, M.J.: De bereikbaarheid bestaat niet. RIVM, University Utrecht, Bilthoven/UTR (1999)
7. Geurs, K.T., van Wee, B.: Accessibility evaluation of land-use and transport strategies: review and research directions. J. Transp. Geogr. 12(2), 127–140 (2004)
8. Geurs, K.T., Boon, W., Van Wee, B., F. Ltd. TTRV: Social impacts of transport: literature review and the state of the practice of transport appraisal in the Netherlands and the United Kingdom. Transp. Rev. 29(1), 69–90 (2009)
9. Baradaran, S., Ramjerdi, F.: Performance of accessibility measures in Europe. J. Transp. Stat. 4(2/3), 31–48 (2001)
10. Vandenbulcke, G., Steenberghen, T., Thomas, I.: Mapping accessibility in Belgium: a tool for land-use and transport planning? J. Transp. Geogr. 17, 39–53 (2009)

11. Budd, J.W., Mumford, K.A.: Family-friendly work practices in Britain: availability and perceived accessibility. Hum. Resour. Manag. **45**(1), 23–42 (2006)
12. Curl, A., Nelson, J.D., Anable, J.: Does accessibility planning address what matters? A review of current practice and practitioner perspectives. Res. Transp. Bus. Manag. **2**, 3–11 (2011)
13. Nurdden, A., Atiq Rahmat, R.O., Ismail, A.: Effect of transportation policies on modal shift from private car to public transport in Malaysia. J. Appl. Sci. **7**(7), 1013–1018 (2007)
14. Khan, O.: Modelling passenger mode choice behaviour using computer aided stated preference data. Queensland University of Technology (2007)
15. Jin, X.: Impacts of accessibility, connectivity and mode captivity on transit choice. Transit **200**, 145 (2005)
16. Kedia, A.S., Dhulipala, S., Salini, P.S., Jabeena, M., Katti, B.K.: Transit shift response analysis through fuzzy rule based – choice model: a case study of Indian metropolitan city. Transp. Dev. Econ. **3**(1), 1–13 (2017)
17. Park, H.M.: Regression models for binary dependent variables using Stata, SAS, R, LIMDEP and SPSS, vol. 4724, no. 812 (2010)
18. Chaudhary, N.: Analysing Modal Shift: Case of BRTS Jaipur, CEPT (2009)
19. Cerdá, A.: Accessibility: a performance measure for land-use and transportation planning in the Montréal metropolitan region (2009)
20. Dissanayake, D., Morikawa, T.: Investigating household vehicle ownership, mode choice and trip sharing decisions using a combined revealed preference/stated preference nested logit model: case study in Bangkok metropolitan region. J. Transp. Geogr. **18**(3), 402–410 (2010)
21. Maunganidze, L., Del Mistro, R.: The role of bus rapid transit in improving public transport levels of service, particularly for the urban poor users of public transport: a case of Cape Town, South Africa. In: South African Transport Conference (2012)
22. Nurdden, A., Rahmat, R., Ismail, A.: Effect of transportation policies on modal shift from private car to public transport in Malaysia. J. Appl. Sci. **7**(7), 1013–1018 (2007)
23. Sanche, R., Lonergan, K.: Variable reduction for predictive modeling with clustering. In: Casualty Actuarial Society Forum, pp. 89–100 (2006)
24. Hsieh, F.Y., Bloch, D.A., Larsen, M.D.: A simple method of sample size calculation for linear and logistic regression. Stat. Med. Stat. Med. **17**, 1623–1634 (1998)
25. Smith, G.C.S., Seaman, S.R., Wood, A.M., Royston, P., White, I.R.: Correcting for optimistic prediction in small data sets. Am. J. Epidemiol. **180**(3), 318–324 (2014)
26. Szumilas, M.: Information management for the busy practitioner explaining odds ratios. J. Can. Acad. Child Adolesc. Psychiatry **19**(3), 227–229 (2010)
27. East Carolina University: Binary Logistic Regression with SPSS. http://core.ecu.edu/psyc/wuenschk/MV/Multreg/Logistic-SPSS.PDF. Accessed 16 Feb 2017
28. Hensher, D.A., Ton, T.T.: A comparison of the predictive potential of artificial neural networks and nested logit models for commuter mode choice. Transp. Res. Part E Logist. Transp. Rev. **36**(3), 155–172 (2000)
29. LeCun, Y., Bottou, L., Orr, G.B., Müller, K.-R.: Efficient BackProp. In: Orr, G.B., Müller, K.-R. (eds.) Neural Networks: Tricks of the Trade. LNCS, vol. 1524, pp. 9–50. Springer, Heidelberg (1998). https://doi.org/10.1007/3-540-49430-8_2
30. Shaft, I., Ahmad, J., Shah, S.I., Kashif, F.M.: Impact of varying neurons and hidden layers in neural network architecture for a time frequency application. In: 10th IEEE International Multitopic Conference 2006, INMIC, pp. 188–193 (2006)
31. Hosmer, W.D., Lemeshow, S.: Applied Logistic Regression, 2nd edn. Wiley-Interscience Publication, New York (2000)

Case-Based Reasoning

Predicting Fraud in Mobile Money Transfer Using Case-Based Reasoning

Adeyinka Adedoyin[1], Stelios Kapetanakis[1(✉)], Georgios Samakovitis[2],
and Miltos Petridis[3]

[1] University of Brighton, Brighton, UK
{A.Adedoyin,S.Kapetanakis}@brighton.ac.uk
[2] University of Greenwich, London, UK
G.Samakovitis@gre.ac.uk
[3] Middlesex University, London, UK
M.Petridis@mdx.ac.uk

Abstract. This paper proposes an improved CBR approach for the identification of money transfer fraud in Mobile Money Transfer (MMT) environments. Standard CBR capability is augmented by machine learning techniques to assign parameter weights in the sample dataset and automate k-value random selection in k-NN classification to improve CBR performance. The CBR system observes users' transaction behaviour within the MMT service and tries to detect abnormal patterns in the transaction flows. To capture user behaviour effectively, the CBR system classifies the log information into five contexts and then combines them into a single dimension, instead of using the conventional approach where the transaction amount, time dimensions or features dimension are used individually. The applicability of the proposed augmented CBR system is evaluated using simulation data. From the results, both dimensions show good performance with the context of information weighted CBR system outperforming the individual features approach.

Keywords: Money transfer fraud · Case-based reasoning · Genetic algorithm · Simulation data · Mobile money

1 Introduction

Mobile Money Transfer (MMT) services are financial services provided by a Mobile Network Operator (MNO) that enable transfer of funds using a digital equivalent of cash (electronic money) between service subscribers through mobile channels [1]. While in developed countries MMT is merely seen as an extension to existing banking services, several developing countries, where access to banking is often challenging for individuals and businesses, tend to view mobile money transfer technologies as platforms with significant strategic and societal value in supporting financial inclusion to unbanked and under-banked populations. More than 2.5 billion adults globally lack a formal bank account, with the majority in developing countries. However, approximately 68% of that population have

© Springer International Publishing AG 2017
M. Bramer and M. Petridis (Eds.): SGAI-AI 2017, LNAI 10630, pp. 325–337, 2017.
https://doi.org/10.1007/978-3-319-71078-5_28

access to a mobile phone [2]. In a 2013 Gartner report [3], the worldwide market for MMT was estimated to reach over 450 million subscribers in 2017, with a mobile transaction value of more than $721 billion. The main drives behind the success of mobile money are the explosive growth in the number of mobile devices and the drop in computing power cost, which has made mobile phones more accessible [4].

The ability of MMT to handle large numbers of small value payments, its suitability for transferring funds worldwide in digital currencies, and the current absence of robust regulatory oversight, makes it both an attractive target for attackers and fraudsters, and an equally attractive vehicle for money laundering [5]. While in most countries Anti-Money Laundering (AML) and transaction fraud reporting is compulsory for service providers and financial institutions [1], in many of them, existing ML legislation is not presently fit to fully accommodate the relatively young m-money markets. This absence of suitable oversight intensifies the risk exposure of MMT to fraud, money laundering and other financial misuse. For example, where proper controls are not deployed, fraudsters can get access to MMT services without disclosing their identity to the MNO, by taking advantage of prepaid phones, pooling and delegation of mobile devices [1,6].

A crucial observation is made at this point to distinguish between capabilities for investigating transaction fraud, as opposed to these addressing the identification of money laundering; while transaction fraud is typically recognised as most commonly associated with money laundering [1], money laundering activity itself may technically exist in the absence of transaction fraud (e.g. through the use of mule accounts [1]). Even more crucially, money laundering is $process - driven$, as opposed to transaction fraud, which is $event - driven$. As a consequence, AML predictive modelling is far more complex and computationally demanding than fraud monitoring, while selection of suitable Artificial Intelligence approaches becomes significantly more challenging for AML. In the context of this work we are considering the development of monitoring and predictive models for transaction fraud, and with view to merely supporting AML indirectly.

Different types of monitoring and predictive models have been proposed for identifying fraud in financial transactions streams [1]. Most are based on data-driven (machine learning) methods, typically requiring a significant amount of financial transaction historical data [7]. The challenges in obtaining real life financial transaction data sets for research purposes are well-known [8] including data protection and confidentiality, ethical issues, time, and the cost associated with collecting multiple instances of a diverse set of data sources. In addition, when real life data sets are available, these may be small in size and lack information on confirmed fraud cases and their possible taxonomies [9]. A case-based reasoning approach offers an alternative that is commensurate with the limited datasets described above. It is more transparent than black-box models, such as neural networks and has the ability to operate with limited experience, learn and improve predictive accuracy as more data becomes available [7,10]. To the best of our knowledge, there is relatively limited literature on applying CBR to the field of financial transaction fraud detection.

In this paper, we propose an improved CBR approach by complementing standard CBR methods with machine learning capabilities for assigning parameter weights and automating the random selection of k-value in order to detect financial transaction fraud. Both the standard and proposed CBR approach were analysed using simulation dataset. We motivate the use of the proposed CBR approach by comparing it's results with that of the standard CBR.

The remaining parts of this paper are organized as follows: Sect. 2 presents a short overview of related work on financial fraud detection using Case-based reasoning. Section 3 discusses our CBR system approach. In Sect. 4, our experiment data and implementation are presented, and in Sect. 5 this approach is empirically evaluated using simulated data generated with Multi-agent based simulator in [11]. Finally, Sect. 6 concludes the paper and outlines future works.

2   Background

Research from the literature on predicting fraud in financial transaction services has focused on statistical, machine learning and other classification techniques and they all provide effective results. However, the design of statistical and rule-based system requires a significant amount of expert knowledge which, in turn, makes the process costly and time-consuming.

As an alternative, machine learning methods such as Artificial Neural Networks (ANN), Support Vector Machines (SVM) and Bayesian belief network have been widely used to predict different types of financial transaction fraud following a data-driven approach (i.e. on the basis of past observations of fraudulent/genuine transactions). For example, Bekirev et al. [12] and Mohamed et al. [13] used a feedforward approach to detect payment card fraud and telecommunication fraud respectively. In addition, the literature reports hybrid approaches, where statistical techniques are combined with neural networks to predict financial fraud. Ravisankar et al. [14] used a probabilistic neural network to identify companies that resort to financial statement fraud. Examples of prediction methods based on neural network and SVMs include [15]. However in the absence of significant size of historical data, they tend not to perform well. A detailed review of machine learning applications in solving financial fraud problems is provided by Albashrawi in [16].

Case-based Reasoning method as an alternative to standard machine learning methods, comes with a number of advantages when applied to the field of financial transaction fraud. For example, Case-based Reasoning features has the ability to (i) learn in the absence of historical consumption data, while continuously improving when more data becomes available over time, (ii) realize knowledge transfer as spending habits evolve; as is the case where information on one transaction is exploited to improve predictions for different yet similar transactions, and (iii) provide precedent-based justification instead of justifying a solution by showing a trace of the rules that led to decision [17,18]. One of the initial works where CBR approach was applied to the field of financial transaction fraud was published by Park and Han [19]. They used multi-agent

Case-based reasoning approach to reduce the number of final-line fraud investigation in credit approval process, achieving precise results.

In [20] and [21], promising results were produced with a simplified CBR model for monitoring and predicting financial transaction fraud. However, the predictive accuracy of that model was lower than that of a neural network of similar complexity and featured a relatively high false positive rate. As discussed in [22], this identified weakness is considered as damaging as high false negative rates for customer trust, acutely reflecting why precision requirements for operational fraud detection systems are high, and partly explaining current reluctance to adopt unified industry-wide approaches. This paper therefore seeks to deliver improved performance by supplementing the standard CBR capabilities by using a machine learning technique to assign parameter weights in the sample dataset and automate k-value random selection in k-NN classification between the range 3,5,7 or 9.

3   CBR Model

This section describes our CBR system and the feature weights optimization, followed by a brief outline of the dataset used. The section concludes with a discussion of the experiments and their results.

3.1   Case Representation

The use of mobile money transfer varies widely across households due to a number of aspects of consumer behaviour like the product and brand choice, purchase amount, and income group [23]. This indicates that consumer purchase behaviour is temporal in nature. Thus, as the spending behaviour of customers is temporal in nature and most of the individuals exhibit consistent spending behaviour, an event-driven process chain of transactions can be a robust representation of the spending behaviour. Therefore, in order to represent the behavioural pattern of users, it is necessary to define events that model the MMT process. However, according to [24], it is challenging to derive a workflow of transactions from the control flow of mobile money systems, because every user is free to use the system as they wish (for instance, the user can choose their own amounts, frequencies, communities of interests, etc.). For this reason our events representation was generated from the users behaviour in the mobile money system. For each process instance, there is pair of active users and type of transaction (i.e., (user1,CASHIN)), making the assumption that the amounts in transactions of the same type (i.e., only CASHIN, only TRANSFER, etc.) are similar, while amounts of different types of transaction are not [24,25]. For the needs of event representation and case construction in the transaction streams, five different types of mobile-enabled financial operations available in the sample data were used, namely: Money Deposit (A), Money Withdrawal (B), Merchant Payment (C), Person-to-person transfer (D), and Airtime Recharge (E). A possible graphical representation of user's behaviour in the log trace can be seen in Fig. 1.

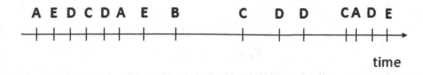

Fig. 1. Possible representation of user's behaviour

In mobile money transfer transaction processing, the spending behaviour contains information about the transaction amount, time gap since last transaction, day of the week, etc. The transaction amount, frequency, and time are closely related to spending behaviour of a person which are actually influenced by income, resource availability, and lifestyle of the person. In most conventional fraud detection system (FDS), the transaction amount is considered as the most important parameter for fraud detection. Also, previous research work has shown that efficiency of any FDS is associated with the amount and time dimensions separately [26]. However, we propose the classification of information into five contexts and combine them into a single dimension to capture user behaviour effectively. This gives significant improvement in accuracy over a system that considers each feature dimension individually [26]. Below are the five types of information context used:

1. **Transaction type:** Transaction type entities
2. **Client:** Features of entities (client ID, Profile e.g. savings or current account, account balance, spending habit category)
3. **Interval:** Features of entities (Month of the year, Day of the Week).
4. **Location:** Location entities
5. **Amount:** Quantization of amount entities into finite levels up to maximum daily spending limit.

For the CBR system process representation, we start with a simple definition. Consider the total set of events E in the log file, each event is a quintuple $(\overline{v}_i)$ representing the different contexts of information for the events.

$$\overline{v}_i = [\, c_1, c_2, \ldots, c_n \,] \tag{1}$$

where (c_n) is the context of type n, $(n = 1 \ldots 5)$

Each instance of query (Z_m) can be defined as:

$$Z_m = [\, \overline{v_1^z}, \ldots, \overline{v_m^z} \,] \tag{2}$$

where m is the length of the event query Z_m.

For the Case base representation, each case (X) contains a description (D) with the corresponding solutions (S), i.e. an outcome tag (y) associated to each event or transaction type. That is,

$$X = [\, D_x, S_x \,] \tag{3}$$

where

$$D_x = [\,\overline{v_1^x}, \ldots, \overline{v_5^x}\,]$$ (4)

$$S_x = y_1, \ldots, y_n$$ (5)

However, to classify the transaction outcome our system uses a binary classification (safe, and fraudulent), therefore $n = 2$.

3.2   Case Similarity

For the needs of similarity measure, the similarity between two cases is defined as a weighted average of the vector similarities. In previous work, the flexibility of weighting was not exploited, i.e. all weights were simply set to the same value. However, since different vectors are obviously of different importance, we decided to take advantage of the capability of genetic algorithms to determine the optimal weights for each vector. During the retrieval process, an ordered list of k most similar cases to the query were retrieved and returned. This was implemented using a k-Nearest Neighbour algorithm. The overall similarity value was computed by weighting the local similarity of each vector $(\overline{v}_i)$. The resulting value is weighted with a value (w_i) that represents the relevance of the corresponding transaction in the global similarity computation:

$$Sim(Z_m, D_x) = \sum_{j=1}^{m} w_j * \sigma(\overline{v_j^z}, \overline{v_j^x})$$ (6)

where m is the length of the event query and $\sigma(\overline{v_j^z}, \overline{v_j^x})$ is the similarity between the jth events in the target query and source case in the case base respectively.

3.3   CBR Model Weights

In order to exploit the flexibility of weighting all the input vectors, a Genetic Algorithm (henceforth GA) was used to calculate their weight so as to reflect the significance of each vector as determined by the GA procedure. Optimal weighting of variables using GA was extensively used in the literature, as for instance in [27–29]. The method in [27] was adapted for the configuration of GA in obtaining the optimal weights for each of the vectors. In the experiment, the GA uses a population of individuals representing the different weights, and the generation of the population evolves until the individual weights with the best performance is returned. Each individual weight contains both the vector weight and k parameter of the k-Nearest Neighbour algorithm to estimate the best number of cases that must be retrieved to classify new transactions. For the needs of configuration, the genetic algorithm was run with an initial population of 1000 individuals. Each individual contains the weights of each vector and the value of k (a random value 3, 5, 7 or 9) that the CBR model uses in the retrieval stage. Also, at the initial stage a random value was assigned to each weight, then later normalised to sum of 1. The following cycle is repeated until there is no more improvement in the performance of the best individual population:

1. Fitness Evaluation: At this stage the genetic algorithm executes a cross-validation of the weights and k value for each individual population to generate the fitness performance.
2. Remove: After the evaluation of all the individual population, 25% of the population with the worst fitness performance was removed.
3. Cross-over: To reproduce the population that was removed (i.e. 25% individual removed after the fitness evaluation), the genetic algorithm combines the individual population with the best performance. During the cross-over process, the parent individuals are taken in pairs and then combined together to form a new individual called child. The weight of each child individual contains the average weights of the parents (normalised weight) and the value of k is computed analogously.
4. Mutation: During the implementation of the mutation function, the Individuals along with their weights are chosen randomly for modification, using 5% of the population. These modification prevents local maximum values.

4 Experiment

4.1 Data

Obtaining transaction data from financial institutions can be difficult due to a number of reasons, such as ethical limitations, privacy issues and government or corporate policies. In addition, when such data are made available they may be small in quantity, lack information on confirmed fraud cases, or carry limited features information. Therefore, for the evaluation of our suggested approach we simulated transactions using a Multi-Agent Simulation Tool-kit (MASON) [30] that combines the behaviour and habits of several users within a Mobile money environment. Multi-agent based simulators have been extensively used in the literature to represent agents with different behaviours in a swarm, as in [11,31–33]. In this paper, the simulator was built according to the methodology proposed in [34] and implemented using adapted multi-agent based simulator (MABS) developed by Lopez-rojas and Axelsson [11].

Simulation walk-through: The first step of the simulation was to set up agents and their locations. Then different clients that will be present in the simulation were randomly generated, and each client is assigned an ID. A client state at each time depends on a Markov transition matrix that assigns when to change from Active to Inactive and from savings to current account, with higher limits on daily transaction. The clients in this simulation have basic operations; they can either make a deposit, withdrawal, person-to-person transfer, pay a merchant, buy airtime or decide not to perform any transaction. If a client needs to perform an action, it conducts a local search within its network to see which of its neighbours are in active state. If the search is successful, then it places a request for a type of operation using a probabilistic transition function. The request placed depends on the transition function from client account balance, daily limits on each clients account type, and user spending habits category. When the balance is high the

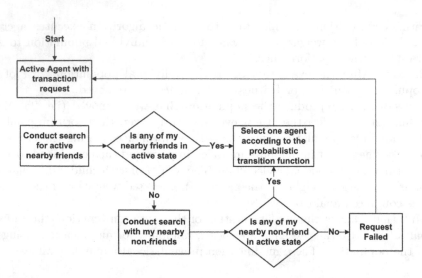

Fig. 2. A flowchart representing the simulation Walk-through

agent has a higher probability to make a withdrawal, transfer, pay a merchant, or airtime recharge, rather than a deposit. Figure 2 outlines these activities.

However, if the search is unsuccessful, the client can delegate a request to an inactive client to conduct a local search within its own neighbourhood for a mediator. Once this is achieved a routing record is created with information about the originator of the request. At each pass, the routing record is updated with information about the intermediate requestor. At some point, if the search is successful then the delegated client places a request to perform an operation on behalf of the initial requesting client. The delegation of request stops after a search is conducted in the neighbourhood a level above the requesting clients level. For each simulation the input parameters values were modified in order the improve the quality of the simulation. A total of 2000 end users were created from different cities performing several transactions with partners either inside or outside of their network. The simulator stores transactions details in a log file and each entry contains informations such as the transaction type, amount, sender and receiver profile (Id, account type), time-stamp etc. The simulation was run for six months between 1st of September 2013 and 28th of February 2014. At the end of the data preparation phase a total of 141,556 transactions were generated with 282 transactions (0.2%) labelled as suspicious. The data generated by the simulation represent a realistic situation of common class imbalance problem in financial transaction dataset, where one of the classes is very large in comparison to the other one.

4.2   Experiment Implementation

The CBR approach was implemented as described in the previous section using jCOLIBRI framework [35]; a Java framework that allows rapid prototyping of a CBR system, the development and deployment of the CBR system in real scenarios. For the needs of experiment evaluation, we compared our approach with the conventional individual feature similarity dimension as the baseline. In order to achieve this, two experiments were performed:

In the first experiment, labelled StdCBR (Standard CBR), the flexibility of weighting individual features was not exploited. All weights were assumed to be normalized and of equal importance for both feature dimensions i.e. equal for individual feature dimension and classification of features in to five contexts. The global similarity measure was computed using Euclidean distance:

$$d = |Z - X| = \sqrt{\sum_{i=1}^{m} w_i |Z_i - X_i|^2} \tag{7}$$

where w_i is the weight of vector (attribute) i, Z is the query (new case), X is the source (retrieved case), m is the number of vectors in each case, and i is an individual vector from 1 to m.

As a potential improvement in the second experiment a featured weighted CBR system was carried out (FWCBR); relevant optimal weights for the features were assigned using a genetic algorithm and the value of k was computed analogously for both feature dimensions. The similarity function was computed by optimally combining the individual local similarity of $(\overline{v}_i)$ into a global similarity as discussed in Sect. 3.2. For the needs of experiment evaluation due to the computational cost of genetic algorithm, the number of transaction data used from the simulation dataset were limited to 2000 out of which 0.084% were labelled as fraudulent. Only 25 users who had done more than 60 transactions (average transaction generated by the end users) were randomly selected. The experiments were ran for 10 iterations and the average was taken for the final classification result. For better precision, 5-fold cross validation was used.

5   Experimental Results (Evaluation)

In this section we present prediction performance results for both models FWCBR and StdCBR with K= 3. Use of larger values of k in the experiment did not present any significantly different results. The results associated to each model are shown in Tables 1, 2, 3 and 4. The standard CBR model (StdCBR) without weight optimization is used as a baseline for understanding the ground necessary for a conventional CBR system to solve the classification problem. The model shows extremely good results for a weighted context of information dimension (Table 3) with recall and precision levels of approximately 93% and 86% respectively. Although the standard CBR model with individual feature dimension shows the capability of detecting the positive class (78%), it features a low recall value (0.46%).

Table 1. Combined confusion matrix of the models from Individual feature dimension

Individual-dimension				
	Fraud		Normal	
Prediction	Std-CBR	FW-CBR	Std-CBR	FW-CBR
Fraud	77	124	90	43
Normal	22	19	1811	1814

Table 2. Combined confusion matrix of the models from Context of information dimension

Context-dimension				
	Fraud		Normal	
Prediction	Std-CBR	FW-CBR	Std-CBR	FW-CBR
Fraud	130	155	37	12
Normal	14	25	1819	1808

Table 3. Model comparison based on Recall and Precision in alignment with context

Model	Individual-dimension		Context-dimension	
	Recall	Precision	Recall	Precision
Std-CBR	0.46	0.78	0.74	0.87
FW-CBR	0.78	0.90	0.93	0.86

Table 4. Average prediction accuracy of the models

Model	Individual dimension	Context dimension
StdCBR	0.94	0.96
FWCBR	0.97	0.98

Table 4 describes the average accuracy for both models using the two different feature dimensions. The performance of all the four models exceeds 90%, with the weighted CBR system (FW-CBR) based on the context of information perspective leading (98%), as shown in Table 4.

Figure 3 shows results from the developed CBR system. From the interface, 3 nearest neighbours can be seen for each new case, classification score (fraud as 1 and non-fruad as 0), as well as their similarity performance. This can provide a good insight into a number of final line case investigation for experts after the existing detection system has been utilised.

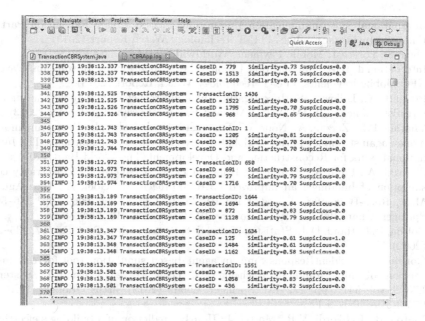

Fig. 3. Transaction neighbours summary

6   Conclusions

In this paper, an enhanced CBR model is proposed with the aim of improving the performance of standard CBR systems for fraud identification in Mobile Money Transfer (MMT). The enhanced system uses a combination of CBR and GA as a tool to optimize the significance level (weights) of the features. For the evaluation, instead of using the conventional approach where the transaction amount, time dimensions or features dimension are used individually, we classify the log information from the simulation data into five contexts and then combine them into a single dimension. Results demonstrate that the classification of log information into five contexts improves the performance of our proposed weighted CBR system with prediction accuracy of 0.97% and 0.98% for the two feature dimension perspectives. In addition, the ranking of clusters of transaction neighbours for new cases in the summary window may operate as an effective tool for experts to develop preliminary insight into suspicious transactions which can then be investigated in more detail. The computational complexity associated with the use of genetic algorithms is seen as one of the major challenges in our approach and more emphasis is placed in future work on reducing computation cost to improve the scalability of our proposed system.

References

1. Zhdanova, M., Repp, J., Rieke, R., Gaber, C., Hemery, B.: No smurfs: revealing fraud chains in mobile money transfers. In: 9th International Conference on Availability, Reliability and Security, ARES 2014 (2014)

2. International Telecommunication Union: The Mobile Money Revolution Part 2: Financial Inclusion Enabler. ITU-T Technology Watch Report (2013)
3. Shen, S.: Forecast: Mobile Payment, Worldwide, 2013 Update (2013)
4. International Telecommunication Union: The Mobile Money Revolution. Part 1: NFC Mobile Payments. ITU-T Technology Watch Report (2013)
5. Bennett, N., Dilloway, S.: Investigating the convergence of money laundering and terrorist financing. In: ACAMS AML and Financial Crime Conference (2013)
6. Chatain, P.L., Zerzan, A., Noor, W., Dannaoui, N., de Koker, L.: Protecting mobile money against financial crimes: global policy challenges and solutions. The International Bank for Reconstruction and Development/The World Bank (2011)
7. Shabani, A., Paul, A., Platon, R., Hüllermeier, E.: Predicting the electricity consumption of buildings: an improved CBR approach. In: Goel, A., Díaz-Agudo, M.B., Roth-Berghofer, T. (eds.) ICCBR 2016. LNCS, vol. 9969, pp. 356–369. Springer, Cham (2016). https://doi.org/10.1007/978-3-319-47096-2_24
8. Bolton, R.J., Hand, D.J.: Statistical fraud detection a review. Stat. Sci. **17**, 235–249 (2002)
9. Gorton, D.: IncidentResponseSim: an agent based simulation tool for risk management of online fraud. In: Buchegger, S., Dam, M. (eds.) Secure IT Systems. LNCS, vol. 9417, pp. 172–187. Springer, Cham (2015). https://doi.org/10.1007/978-3-319-26502-5_12
10. Platon, R., Dehkordi, V.R., Martel, J.: Hourly prediction of a building's electricity consumption using case-based reasoning, artificial neural networks and principal component analysis. Energy Build. **92**, 10–18 (2015). Elsevier
11. Lopez-Rojas, E.A., Axelsson, S.: Multi agent based simulation (MABS) of financial transactions for anti money laundering (AML). In: 17th Nordic Conference on Secure IT (2012)
12. Bekirev, A.S., Klimov, V.V., Kuzin, M.V., Shchukin, B.A.: Payment card fraud detection using neural network committee and clustering. Optical Memory and Neural Networks (Information Optics) (2015)
13. Mohamed, A., Bandi, A.F.M., Tamrin, A.R., Jaafar, M.D., Hasan, S., Jusof, F.: Telecommunication fraud prediction using backpropagation neural network (SoC-PaR). In: International Conference of Soft Computing and Pattern Recognition, Malaysia (2009)
14. Ravisankar, P., Ravi, V., Raghava Rao, G., Bose, I.: Detection of financial statement fraud and feature selection using data mining techniques. Decis. Support Syst. **50**, 491–500 (2011). ScienceDirect
15. Roselina, S., Subariah, I., Azlan, M.Z., Abdikarim, H.E.: Detecting SIM box fraud by using support vector machine and artificial neural network. J. Teknol. **74**, 131–143 (2015)
16. Albashrawi, M., Lowell, M.: Detecting financial fraud using data mining techniques: a decade review from 2004 to 2015. J. Data Sci. **14**, 553–569 (2016)
17. Chi, R.T., Kiang, M.Y.: An integrated approach of rule-based and case-based reasoning for decision support. In: Proceedings of the 19th Annual Conference on Computer Science, CSC 1991 (1991)
18. Watson, I.: Case-based reasoning is a methodology not a technology. Knowl.-Based Syst. **12**, 303–308 (1999). Elsevier
19. Park, C.S., Han, I.: A case-based reasoning with the feature weights derived by analytic hierarchy process for bankruptcy prediction. Expert Syst. Appl. **23**, 255–264 (2002). Elsevier

20. Adedoyin, A., Kapetanakis, S., Petridis, M., Panaousis, E.: Evaluating case-based reasoning knowledge discovery in fraud detection. In: 24th Workshop on Case Based Reasoning (ICCBR2016): Synergies Between CBR and Knowledge Discovery (2016)

21. Kapetanakis, S., Samakovitis, G., Gunasekera, P.V.G.B., Petridis, M.: Monitoring financial transaction fraud with the use of case-based reasoning. In: Seventeenth UK Workshop on Case-Based Reasoning (2012)

22. Samakovitis, G., Kapetanakis, S.: Computer-aided financial fraud detection: promise and applicability in monitoring financial transaction fraud. In: Proceedings of International Conference on Business Management and IS, Dubai, United Arab Emirates (2013)

23. Slocum, J.W., Mathews, H.L.: Social class and income as indicators of consumer credit behavior. J. Mark. **34**, 69–74 (1970)

24. Rieke, R., Zhdanova, M., Repp, J., Giot, R., Gaber, C.: Fraud detection in mobile payments utilizing process behavior analysis. In: International Conference on Availability, Reliability and Security (ARES) (2013)

25. Giot, R., Gaber, C.: Predictive Security Analysis - Concepts, Implementation, first Results in Industrial Scenario (2013)

26. Kundu, A., Panigrahi, S., Sural, S., Majumdar, A.: BLAST-SSAHA hybridization for credit card fraud detection. In: IEEE Transactions on Dependable and Secure Computing (2009)

27. Lopez-de-Arenosa, P., Díaz-Agudo, B., Recio-García, J.A.: CBR tagging of emotions from facial expressions. In: Lamontagne, L., Plaza, E. (eds.) ICCBR 2014. LNCS, vol. 8765, pp. 245–259. Springer, Cham (2014). https://doi.org/10.1007/978-3-319-11209-1_18

28. Manzoor, J., Asif, S., Masud, M., Khan, M.J.: Automatic case generation for case-based reasoning systems using genetic algorithms. In: Third Global Congress on Intelligent Systems (2012)

29. Ahn, H., Kim, K., Han, I.: Hybrid genetic algorithms and case-based reasoning systems. In: Zhang, J., He, J.-H., Fu, Y. (eds.) CIS 2004. LNCS, vol. 3314, pp. 922–927. Springer, Heidelberg (2004). https://doi.org/10.1007/978-3-540-30497-5_142

30. Luke, S., Cioffi-Reevilla, C., Panait, L., Sullivan, K., Cioffi-Revilla, C., Sullivan, K., Panait, L., Balan, G.: Mason: a multiagent simulation environment. Simulation **81**, 517–527 (2005)

31. Tahir, A., Adeyinka, A.: Autonomic service management in mobile cloud infrastructures. Int. J. New Comput. Archit. Appl. **4**, 91–107 (2014)

32. Gaber, C., Hemery, B., Achemlal, M., Pasquet, M., Urien, P.: Synthetic logs generator for fraud detection in mobile transfer services. In: Sadeghi, A.-R. (ed.) FC 2013. LNCS, vol. 7859, pp. 397–398. Springer, Heidelberg (2013). https://doi.org/10.1007/978-3-642-39884-1_35

33. Luke, S., Ziparo, V.A.: Learn to behave! rapid training of behavior automata. In: Proceedings of Adaptive and Learning Agents Workshop at AAMAS (2010)

34. Lundin, E., Kvarnström, H., Jonsson, E.: A synthetic fraud data generation methodology. In: Deng, R., Bao, F., Zhou, J., Qing, S. (eds.) ICICS 2002. LNCS, vol. 2513, pp. 265–277. Springer, Heidelberg (2002). https://doi.org/10.1007/3-540-36159-6_23

35. Recio-Garcia, J.A., Gonzalez-Calero, P.A., Diaz-Agudo, B.: jcolibri2: a framework for building Case-based reasoning systems. Sci. Comput. Program. **79**, 126–145 (2014)

Predicting Dust Storms Using Hybrid Intelligence System

Tariq Saad Al Murayziq[1], Stelios Kapetanakis[1(✉)],
and Miltos Petridis[2]

[1] School of Computing, Engineering and Mathematics,
University of Brighton, Brighton, UK
{tsal0, s.kapetanakis}@brighton.ac.uk
[2] Department of Computer Science, Middlesex University, London, UK
M.Petridis@mdx.ac.uk

Abstract. Global dust storm events seem to increase and become more severe year over year. Thus, dust storm event understanding in terms of causes, pre-ignition signals, generation processes, and procedures can be of great significance due to the impact they can have to the society. Dust storm behaviours is usually based on five attributes mainly. These are wind speed, pressure, temperature, humidity and surface condition. Dust storm may affect both rural and urban life conditions since they can cause significant difficulties to outdoor activities in low visibility – high degree of danger weather. However, dust storm predictions using historical storm data has not been used yet effectively. This study examines the process of predicting and identifying dust storms using past storm events through a novel combination of Bayesian networks (BNs), case-based reasoning (CBR) approach and rule based system (RBS) techniques.

Keywords: Case-based reasoning · Bayesian network · Dust storm prediction · Weather forecast prediction · Artificial intelligence · Rule-based systems

1 Introduction

Dust storms are caused by strong blowing winds over loose sand or soil. Since deserts contain an extensive abundance of loose sand they are the common sites for dust storm formulation. Studies have indicated that desert dust storms become more common due to the strong air heating waves causing instability to the lower atmosphere at certain times of the year. This instability combined with strong winds in the internal troposphere downward to the surface, generate stronger air-streams at the surface [22, 23]. Dust storms can have a severe impact to urban life due to particle pollution. Dust impacts severely humans as compared to any other pollutant, as there is no safe threshold to gratify safe exposure. Dust comprises mixtures of inorganic and organic substances, and has been linked to cardiovascular dieses, Asthma and eye and skin infection to cities that have frequent dust events [3].

Efficient dust storm prediction can be of great benefit to both citizens and government units since an "on-time" warning regarding a forthcoming storm event can trigger the application of measures and strategies to prepare a city and avoid negative

© Springer International Publishing AG 2017
M. Bramer and M. Petridis (Eds.): SGAI-AI 2017, LNAI 10630, pp. 338–351, 2017.
https://doi.org/10.1007/978-3-319-71078-5_29

consequences [4]. Limited ability to predict prohibits the authorities, e.g. the National Centre of Meteorology and Seismology in the United Arab Emirates, to give early enough warnings thus citizens can have severe effects in their normal everyday routine. Government units monitor closely any available weather signals and can raise warnings every three hours e.g. giving information regarding dust conditions as well as visibility to the local media sources and the public. However, due to the current lack of effective prediction mechanisms, citizens usually are informed too late and they may already face the severity of weather conditions.

Research in the area has shown that Case-based Reasoning (CBR) can be effective in predicting dust storm events. This work extends CBR prediction further by combining prediction with effective sets of actions that can assist in taking decisions and actions according to the severity of the experienced weather phenomenon. This work is structured as follows: Sect. 2 presents the relevant research in CBR, Rule-based systems and Machine learning in dust storm prediction, Sect. 3 presents our Research Methodology, Sect. 4 presents the prediction results whereas Sect. 5 concludes this work and discusses future areas of work and application.

2 Empirical Literature

There are mainly two methods for detecting dust storm currently used categorised as either passive or active. Passive methods are divided into two sub methods: (M1 and M2). M1 relates to Visible and Infrared Method (VIM) containing satellite-derived IR imagery and contrast decrease in visible imagery to recover desert aerosol optical thickness over land. M1 is used from Meteosat to compute aerosol optical depth over the sea. Based on a desert model of aerosol and a method for earth-atmosphere radiative transfer, it utilizes a combination of visible as well as mid-IR solar channels to identify dust over the desert [11]. M2 pertains to: Thermal Infrared Method (TIM), identifies soil-derived and volcanic aerosols by utilising infrared observations only at the estimated wave-lengths of 12.0, 11.0 and 12 μm, taking advantage of the good dust detection over bright surfaces and during the night as compared with VIM [11].

Passive methods can be of help, however active methods may also be utilised, such as the Active Lidar Method (ALM) of remote sensing. ALM-based techniques might be divided into two parts: The Scene Classification Algorithm (SCA) and the Selective Iterated-boundary Locator Algorithm (SILA). It is noted that SILA can be adapted to identify a feature by utilising dynamic threshold scheme(s). SCA can classify a feature as either aerosol or cloud based on two wavelength backscatter lidar profiles. SCA is frequently utilised as an operational algorithm based on either multiple facets or on a single one utilising a confidence function constructed from multiple-dimensional or one-dimensional PDFs to differentiate among aerosols and clouds [11].

Satellite and statistical image processing methods for dust storm prediction can be of help, however the sheer mechanism for detecting the outbreak of dust storms is not yet completely understood. Therefore, traditional methods for local dust storm prediction seem susceptible to further improvement. New techniques for prediction may pertain to Artificial Intelligence (AI) techniques since it has proven effective in similar fields: According to Houeland et al. (2010) an integration of Bayesian Networks (BNs) and Case-based Reasoning (CBR) can provide effective prediction outputs. The benefit of integrating BN and CBR is the dynamic adaption of computations. This means that weather experts could empirically identify when there is sufficient representative training information for a BN to generally generate better results as compared to the expert-modified CBR cases, and identify the best-performing technique to resolve the following problem query. A BN and CBR integration can be even more advantageous since it can offer extended functionality apart from solving problems. The integration of ensemble CBR technique can help dealing with exceptions that might be applied to recover short-cut solutions rather than performing normal reasoning [12]. It is also noted that ensemble AI can satisfy numerous queries regarding the statistical charac-teristics of the domain, including the probability for each possible grouping as a solution, or the chance of a problem having specific attributes provided the observed outcome. This can lead to easier and simpler solution to the problem and increase the accuracy of the classification [12].

Rule-based systems (RBS) have been a successful enabler to expert system such as PrismTCS [13], allowing a stable operation in cases where performance has to be standardised. AI complements RBSs since it applies a "cause to impact" technique whereas Prism apply an "impact to cause" technique. RBSs in the form of PRISM or the Information Entropy Based Rule Generation can reduce uncertainty while increasing accuracy, efficiency and interpretability of a target class. One of the major interests in this area is the construction of systems that could be founded on both expert data and knowledge [14]. Therefore, the construction methods may be divided into two main classes: data based construction and knowledge based construction. RBSs can be classified in the following elements: number of outputs and inputs, type of output and input values, the structure type, logic type, rule bases type, number of machine learners as well as computing environment type. For RBSs both outputs and inputs could be multiple or single [14]. RBSs can be complemented and enhanced with AI as it has been shown in forecasting of visibility, precipitation, marine fog, severe weather as well as other climatological conditions [14] as well as in the prediction of dust events [1, 2]. Our work aims to extend this further and propose an end to end framework for severe weather phenomena prediction to policy formulation and their latter application.

3   Research Methodology

Artificial intelligence techniques have been applied successfully in a number of domains [15]. In this paper we present an AI methodology for dust storms prediction, based on historical data. We use data collected from meteorological stations in Riyadh, Saudi Arabia. CBR networks can reason against present cases based on historical data whereas BNs can reduce uncertainty factors within the dataset. A combined BN-CBR technique can be effective on a historical data case base and with a pipeline of rules it could be able to generate action policies for government units against a range of possible severe weather phenomena. In our proposed approach, rules are being gen-erated with the aim to reduce unwanted implications stemming from dust events and generating sets of applicable safety actions. A simplified version of our approach can be seen in Fig. 1.

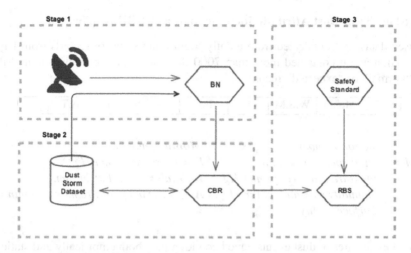

Fig. 1. Hybrid SBR-BN approach for dust storm prediction.

3.1 Stage One: Data Acquisition

Riyadh, the capital city of Saudi Arabia has frequent exposure to dust events [16]. Specifically stations on the north of Riyadh have a variety of cases due to their co-location with the capital's desert, usually the starting point of regional storms. Weather storm cases are classified using BN algorithms (1) and Weka toolbox, based on the probability to solve the uncertainty within the existing dataset and future cases to reduce ambiguity. An example of such is that: some cases may contain all the relevant dust characteristics but in reality they are not related to storms for a number of reasons. Such cases will not be classified as storm ones, to help the latter CBR processing and prediction. Studies have indicated that the Bayesian networks (BNs) belong to the probabilistic graphical models family. It is noted that their graphical structures can represent knowledge pertaining to domain of uncertainty. In particular, every node in the graph shows a random variable, whilst the edges amid the nodes show probabilistic dependencies upon the equivalent random variables [17]. Deficiency of knowledge is taken into consideration in the network by the Bayesian probability theory's application. This enables subjective evaluations of the likelihood that a specific outcome will happen to be combined with more impartial data quantifying the occurrence's frequency in determining conditional probabilistic correlations. Since uncertainty is taken into consideration in the model itself, the Bayesian networks can be a suitable technique for handling the system's uncertainty which is usually a main issue in ecological systems [17, 18].

$$P\,(E|F) = \frac{P(F|E)P(E)}{P(F)} \tag{1}$$

where two event E and F as such that P(E) ≠ 0 and P(F) ≠ 0.

3.2   Stage Two: Dust Attribute Identification and CBR Application

Our used dataset was collected from a daily monitoring series of records from Riyadh radar station and it contained more than 7000 dust cases among a few hundred thousand "normal" or "expected" records

S.N	Month	W.S.M	P	P.S	Rainfall	H	A.T	S

S.N = station number.   **Month** = month.
W.S.M = wind speed max km/h.   **P** = pressure in mm Hg.
P.S = pressure sea level in mm Hg.   **Rainfall** = Rain fall in mm.
H = Humidity max and min in H.   **A.T** = Air temperature max and min in C.
S = Surface ability.

The key features of dust events have been identified both empirically and statically: At first weather experts from Meteorology department in Saudi Arabia have ranked and explained the key characteristics that usually lead to dust events in the region of Middle East. From their experience key characteristics were the:

- **W.S.M** = wind speed max.
- **P.MIN** = pressure min.
- **H.M** = humidity min.
- **A.T** = air temperature max.
- **S** = surface ability.
- **Rainfall** = no rain.

Secondly, we have used the attribute ranker in the Weka tool and its information gain algorithm (2) to calculates information relative to the stated class. The results were in accordance with the ranking of the meteorological professionals.

$$\text{InfoGain(Class, Attribute)} = H(\text{Class}) - H(\text{Class} \mid \text{Attribute}). \tag{2}$$

After the successful acquisition and identification of case characteristics using BNs, CBR had a solid case base for imminent operation. Its similarity calculation made sure that any retrieved weather data were parsed to detect attribute values from historical data. CBR revision phase was applied afterwards to ensure that phrases conform to writing conventions in the domain.

Finally, the CBR Retain step was attributing the most relevant solution to the investigated case and added it to the case-base. Studies have indicated that a retention step may be undertaken in the Case Based reasoning whereby novel cases consisting of the output and input are added to the case-base after an expert review. In cases where CBR was not able to reason were also subjected to expert review or were red-flagged for further investigation.

We have used the Weighted Euclidean Distance (WED) (3) as a base for our CBR similarity scores. WED is based on the location of objects in the Euclidean space, which is an ordered set of real numbers. According to Pal and Shiu, the distance between any two cases is calculated as the root of the sum of the square of the arithmetical differences between two corresponding objects [19]. The 3-nearest neighbour (3NN) was applied after the similarity calculation, to vote on the conclusive results of the nearest solution, that matched to incoming dust cases.

$$D(x, y) = \sqrt{\sum_{i=0}^{n} wi(xi - yi)^2}$$

(3)

3.3   Stage Three: RBS Safety Actions Generation

RBSs can apply knowledge from an expert system as well as to encode it into the set of rules and be able to reuse it as advice along with the logic behind it [14]. Further reiterations indicate that RBSs comprise sets of rules of IF-THEN, a set of facts and several controllers to reason upon facts. When coning across to similar data, an expert system will be consistent in generating an action since they tend to be rather simple models but robustly implemented, suitable for a ranger of challenges.

RBSs can relate to either forward-chaining and backward-chaining [20] techniques. A forward-chaining, data-driven case is a system that compares its input data in its working memory over the states of the weather parameters (IF parts) and identifies the relevant rules to activate. If all actions are already well known, and the aim of the system is to get to know where that data heads to, forward-chaining seems the most applicable RBS method. In our work, almost all actions are "well known" since all the primary objectives are collected from the metcorology department and its weather experts.

To apply RBS, we need to identify the relevant rules and evaluate them. To do so we have selected CHAID algorithm. CHAID belongs to the family of Decision Trees (DTs) and it is stands for Chi-squared Automatic Interaction Detector. It is used widely to classification problems and decision support [21]. We have selected CHAID among others since it can generate more expressive rules than other classification and association rule algorithms such as Apriori, C5.0 and C&R tree and were confirmed by our weather experts. The CHAID generated rules based on historical weather data and the weather experts have assessed and evaluated them based on their experience. RBS rules and their relevant actions have been coded in C# language as a forward chain RBS. Such implementation allowed a dust storm prediction and could generate follow-up actions to mitigate severe weather events. Such prediction could be used in parallel with a BN-CBR prediction result, to increase the accuracy of the final prediction. In addition, all the produced RBS actions can be stored in the case base, building up an action-set for future use from the BN-CBR process or for any other study purpose.

4   Results and Discussion

Based on the available past data, the following variables were identified as being the key features of dust storms:

- **Month** = *month of the recorded dust case*
- **Rainfall** = *how many mm its rain in that day*

- **W.S.M** = *wind speed max*
- **P.M** = *pressure max*
- **P.MIN** = *pressure min*
- **P.S.M** = *pressure sea level max*
- **P.S.MIN** = *pressure sea level min*
- **H.M** = *humidity max*
- **H.MIN** = *humidity min*
- **A.T.M** = *air temperature max*
- **A.T.MIN** = *air temperature min*
- **Surface** = *Surface ability*

```
=== Attribute Selection on all input data ===

Search Method:
Attribute ranking

Attribute Evaluator (supervised, Class (nominal): 14 Dust ):
Information Gain Ranking Filter

Ranked attributes:
0.25602  2 WIND_MAX_SPEED
0.04106  1 MONTH
0.03267  4 PRESSURE_MIN_STATION_LEVEL
0.02964  6 PRESSURE_MIN_SEA_LEVEL
0.02408  8 AIR_TEMPERATURE_MIN_DB
0.02406  9 RELATIVE_HUMIDITY_MAX
0.01976  5 PRESSURE_MAX_SEA_LEVEL
0.0189   3 PRESSURE_MAX_STATION_LEVEL
0.01823  10 RELATIVE_HUMIDITY_MIN
0.01258  7 AIR_TEMPERATURE_MAX_DB
0.00997  11 RAINFALL_TOTAL
0        12 Surface ability

Selected attributes: 2,1,4,6,8,9,5,3,10,7,11,12: 12
```

Fig. 2. Dust storm attribute ranking

Figure 2 shows the ranking of our identified dust storm features. An information gain algorithm was applied which calculated the information gain relative to the stated class. The results are in accordance with the ranking of the meteorology experts. Such ranking allows to determine the optimal weight of each component.

Figure 3 illustrates how air pressure and wind speed are correlated. Dust storms are significantly more likely to arise when there is low air pressure and the wind speed is high.

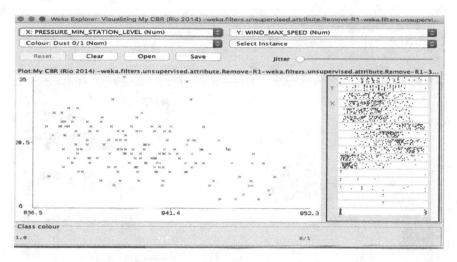

Fig. 3. The correlation between pressure and wind.

Figure 4 illustrates how humidity and air pressure are correlated. Dust storms are significantly more likely to arise when there is low humidity and low air pressure.

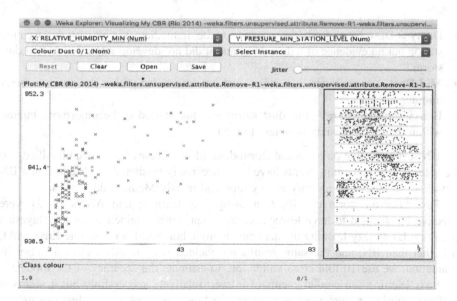

Fig. 4. The correlation between pressure and humidity.

A Bayesian network is employed to classify historical dust storms and group these cases into various categories to depict their severity, and classify unclassified cases, based on probability:

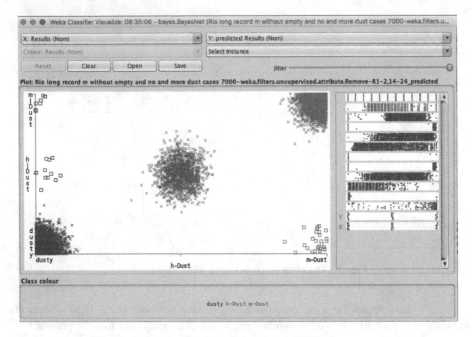

Fig. 5. Using the Bayesian network to classify dust events.

- **Dusty** = Dust lifted from the ground in the immediate vicinity of the weather station but no evidence of a dust whirl and it did not develop into a full-blown dust storm.
- **Mid-Dust** = A moderate dust storm that has intensified within the previous sixty minutes.
- **Heavy dust storm** = A full dust storm that has started or become more intense within the previous sixty minutes (Fig. 5).

BN seem effective on historical storm data. Most of cases have been classified and the categories of uncertain events have been accurately predicted. It observed that BN classifier can efficiently identify Heavy dust and mostly Medium dust cases.

Past work on storm classification using lazy learning and ANNs [1, 2] were effective but seemed to have lower accuracy than those obtained using the Bayesian classifier. Using lazy learning the accuracy is high, but the Mean Absolute Error MAE is higher than BN, and the same results are yielded with an ANN classifier. For its evaluation, we use 10-fold cross validation, to estimate the accuracy of the model.

Lazy learning can predict events of interest relatively successfully but it seems to perform with less accuracy when categorising 'mid-dust' and 'heavy dust storms'.

Bayesian Network with Case-Based Reasoning. CBR cycle utilises the BN outcomes with old and new cases in the database matched using case-based reasoning. By doing so, it will be possible to forecast dust storms. The selected methodology uses historical examples to set a benchmark so that dust storms can be more clearly understood.

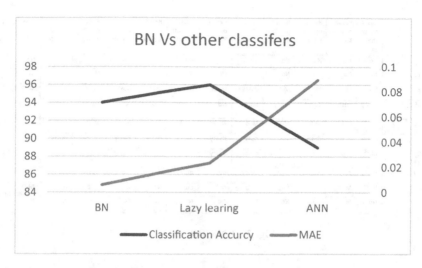

Fig. 6. Bayesian network (BN) vs other classifiers.

The cases are classified using a Bayesian network and the following processes are followed:

1. A Euclidean distance equation is employed to identify similarities among database cases and the case under investigation. The Euclidean distance equation is applied separately for each case variable with different variable weights (based on each feature's ranking). The next step is to aggregate the equation results for each of the cases, thereby calculating a similarity score. These values are then sorted according to their numerical value(s) in descending order. The equation above is used to calculate the degree of similarity between a new case and the database of old cases. It also gives a collection of cases that are like the specific case being studied at present.

2. Data are imported into the MyCBR tool. By doing so it is possible to establish the similarity between cases by applying weighted Euclidean distance equation measurements. It will be necessary to amend the weight values for some of the variables to reflect the main characteristics of the dust storm. Case-based reasoning was employed to classify a randomly chosen subsets from the database. These samples were typically 10–12% of the database and the classification of these samples remained unknown. Instead, they were classified using case-based reasoning by means of similarity measures and 3NN classification. A total of ten experiments were carried out for each case and averages were taken of these results. Based on these results, the accuracy of case-based reasoning is found to be within the range of 60–80%. However, the results are significantly more accurate when case-based reasoning is combined with a Bayesian network classifier as in Fig. 6. Indeed, combining these two yields accuracy results of between 80% and 90% when forecasting 'no dust', 'dusty' and 'mid-dust' storms. It is believed that this method would also perform well when forecasting 'heavy dust storms' but more samples would be required to test this reliably.

ID	Result of the case	Result of 1st 3-KNN	Result of 2nd 3-KNN	Result of 3rd 3-KNN	Result of 4th 3-KNN	Result of 5th 3-KNN	Result of 6th 3-KNN	Result of 7th 3-KNN	Result of 8th 3-KNN	Result of 9th 3-KNN	Result of 10th 3-KNN	Final result
5-2546	No	No	No	No	No	No	No	No	No	No	No	No
3-1910	No	No	No	No	No	No	No	No	No	No	No	No
3-1787	M-D	M-D	M-D	M-D	dusty	M-D	M-D	dusty	dusty	M-D	M-D	M-D
7-2555	dusty	dusty	dusty	dusty	dusty	No	dusty	dusty	No	dusty	dusty	dusty
4-1023	M-D	M-D	M-D	M-D	M-D	M-D	M-D	M-D	M-D	M-D	M-D	M-D
5-255	dusty	dusty	dusty	dusty	dusty	dusty	dusty	dusty	dusty	dusty	dusty	dusty
8-2557	M-D	H-D	H-D	H-D	dusty	dusty	dusty	No	dusty	No	No	Not Good results
4-1299	dusty	dusty	dusty	dusty	dusty	dusty	dusty	dusty	No	dusty	No	dusty
2-510	M-D	M-D	M-D	M-D	M-D	M-D	dusty	No	M-D	M-D	dusty	M-D
2-453	No	No	No	No	No	No	No	No	No	No	No	No

Fig. 7. BN-CBR result.

Rule based System and Safety Actions. Rule based systems might be divided into four main types in relation to number of outputs and inputs: multiple-output-multiple-input, single-output-multiple-input, multiple-output-single-input, and single-output-single-input. It should be noted that all the above four types might fit the features of association rules. This is since the relation rules reflect the correlation between the attributes. A relation rule might have multiple or single rule terms in both the antecedent and consequential (right hand side) of the rule. In this study single-output-multiple-input was applied, to get proper actions. CHAID algorithm also has been chosen among other algorithms to identify the rules (see Fig. 7), and applied using SPSS modeler program. CHAID has been success in generating more real rules with good accuracy, while in Quest and C.50 the rules were scarce.

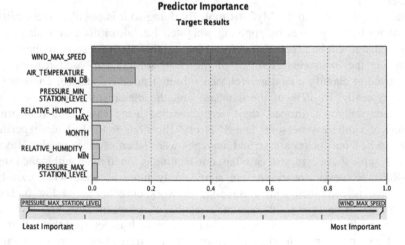

Fig. 8. CHAID predictor importance.

Rules and Actions. After the rules generating by CHAID algorithm, the rules have been evaluated by weather experts and were highly recommended (see Figs. 8 and 9). To set the proper actions, safety standards are taken into consideration to come up with more effective safety strategies. For example, if the wind speed exceeds 30 km/h and the condition is medium dust, then the action is informing the health and education sectors to take their steps. In C# code, it's required to enter the day weather record or the coming dust case that predict form BN-CBR, then the program will run until it identifies the most appropriate rule to activate and match it with actions (Figs. 10 and 11).

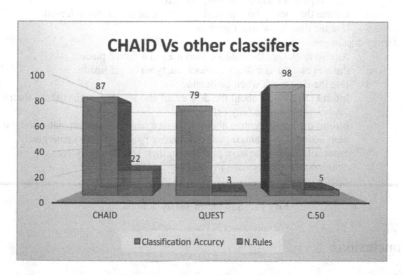

Fig. 9. CHAID predictor importance.

```
WIND_MAX_SPEED > 19 and WIND_MAX_SPEED <= 22 [ Mode: dusty ]
    PRESSURE_MIN_STATION_LEVEL <= 937.600 [ Mode: dusty ] => dusty
    PRESSURE_MIN_STATION_LEVEL > 937.600 and
    PRESSURE_MIN_STATION_LEVEL <= 938.400 [ Mode: m-Dust ] => m-Dust
    PRESSURE_MIN_STATION_LEVEL > 938.400 and
    PRESSURE_MIN_STATION_LEVEL <= 939.800 [ Mode: h-Dust ] => h-Dust
    PRESSURE_MIN_STATION_LEVEL > 939.800 [ Mode: dusty ] => dusty
WIND_MAX_SPEED > 42 [ Mode: m-Dust ]
    RELATIVE_HUMIDITY_MAX <= 37 [ Mode: h-Dust ] => h-Dust
    RELATIVE_HUMIDITY_MAX > 37 and RELATIVE_HUMIDITY_MAX <= 43
    [ Mode: m-Dust ] => m-Dust
    RELATIVE_HUMIDITY_MAX > 43 [ Mode: m-Dust ] => m-Dust
WIND_MAX_SPEED > 32 and WIND_MAX_SPEED <= 35 [ Mode: m-Dust ]
    AIR_TEMPERATURE_MIN_DB <= 28.100 [ Mode: m-Dust ]
    RELATIVE_HUMIDITY_MIN <= 15 [ Mode: h-Dust ] => h-Dust
    RELATIVE_HUMIDITY_MIN > 15 [ Mode: m-Dust ] => m-Dust
    AIR_TEMPERATURE_MIN_DB > 28.100 [ Mode: m-Dust ] => m-Dust
```

Fig. 10. Sample of generating rules by CHAID.

- Dusty: Be Aware
    - o   Inform the community that the Dusty weather could lead your vison and health.
    - o   Monitor next hours forecast.
    - o   Dusty places may decrease the vison, especially in the night.
- Medium dust storm: Get prepare.
    - o   Monitor next hours forecast.
    - o   Inform the schools and health's centres about the dust event and weather status.
    - o   Get prepare for any traffic conjunction.
    - o   Inform the society how to deal with the dust storm through media.
    - o   Use the dust mask when go outside.
- Heavy dust storm: Take action
    - o   Advise to change the outdoor activities in affected places.
    - o   Put wet cloth under doors to block dusty air to get inside.
    - o   Use the dust mask when go outside.
    - o   Inform the schools about the dust event and weather status to take their actions for example "day off".
    - o   Inform the health centres about the dust event and weather status to take their actions for example "expected more patient visit the emergency, especially those who have problem in their respiratory system.
    - o   Announce the dust events in local media.

Fig. 11. Sample of safety actions.

5   Conclusions

Dust storms is a severe weather phenomenon, capable of causing citizen disturbance, spread disease, cause environmental damage and adversely affect economic output. This paper has demonstrated how case-based reasoning can be used to forecast the magnitude of dust storms before they occur. Case-based reasoning draws on historical experience to solve future problems that are expected to be similar in nature. Therefore, in such cases, the strategy proposed to mitigate future dust storms is likely to be like those that have been deployed in the past. It has been demonstrated that combining case-based reasoning with a Bayesian network can yield effective results; case-based reasoning is known to offer a viable method for solving current problems based on historical experience, while Bayesian networks have been shown to offer a suitable method for classifying historical episodes of dust storms. In addition, a rule-based system used to develop a bid to enhance safety and reduce the economic harm that is caused by dust storms. From the results above BN-CBR could effectually predict dust storm, and RBS manage as well in producing proper safety actions. In future work we plan to confirm the effectiveness of this combined case-based and Bayesian approach for forecasting heavy dust storms will require an improved dataset to be hourly dataset, instead of daily.

References

1. Al Murayziq, T.S., Kapetanakis, S., Petridis, M.: Using case-based reasoning and artificial neural networks for the efficient prediction of dust storms. J. Expert Update 16(1), 39–48 (2016)
2. Al Murayziq, T.S., Kapetanakis, S., Petridis, M.: Towards successful dust storm prediction using Bayesian networks and case-based reasoning. In: Petridis, M. (ed.) Proceedings of the 21st UK CBR Workshop, Peterhouse. Brighton Press, pp. 34–43, December 2016
3. UNEP, WMO, UNCCD: Global Assessment of Sand and Dust Storms (2016)
4. Global, U., Alert, E., Geas, S.: Forecasting and early warning of dust storms. Environ. Dev. 6, 117–129 (2013)
5. Study, A.C., City, Z.: Dust storm prediction using ANNs technique. 2, 512–520 (2008)
6. Aprendizagem Simbólica e Sub-Simbólica – 2010 Samuel Mascarenhas (2010)
7. Kolodner, J.L.: An introduction to case-based reasoning. Artif. Intell. Rev. 6, 3–34 (1992)
8. Kiskac, B.: Weather prediction expert system approaches (Ceng-568 Literature Survey). Middle East, pp. 1–14 (2004)
9. Ahn, H., Kim, K.: Bankruptcy prediction modeling with hybrid case-based reasoning and genetic algorithms approach. Appl. Soft Comput. 9, 599–607 (2009)
10. Ceccaroni, L.: Integration of a rule-based expert system, a case-based reasoner and an ontological knowledge-base in the wastewater domain. 8, 1–10 (2000)
11. Overview, A., Dust, A., Methods, D., Satellite, U.: An overview of passive and active dust detection methods using satellite measurements. J. Meteorol. Res. 28, 1029–1040 (2014)
12. Houeland, T.G., Bruland, T., Aamodt, A., Langseth, H.: A hybrid metareasoning architecture combining case-based reasoning and Bayesian networks (extended version). IDI.NTNU. No (2011)
13. Liu, H., Gegov, A., Stahl, F.: Categorization and construction of rule based systems. In: Mladenov, V., Jayne, C., Iliadis, L. (eds.) EANN 2014. CCIS, vol. 459, pp. 183–194. Springer, Cham (2014). https://doi.org/10.1007/978-3-319-11071-4_18
14. Alsaiari, N.O.: An expert system for weather prediction based on animal behaviour
15. Chen, S.H., Jakeman, A.J., Norton, J.P.: Artificial intelligence techniques: an introduction to their use for modelling environmental systems. Math. Comput. Simul. 78, 379–400 (2008)
16. Park, S.U., Choe, A., Park, M.S.: Asian dust depositions over the Asian region during March 2010 estimated by ADAM2. Theor. Appl. Climatol. 105, 129–142 (2011)
17. Pearl, J.: Bayesian networks (2011)
18. Cofino, A.S., Cano, R., Sordo, C., Gutierrez, J.M.: Bayesian networks for probabilistic weather prediction. In: Proceedings of the 15th European conference on Artificial Intelligence, vol. 700, pp. 695–700 (2002)
19. Shiu, S.C.K., Pal, S.K.: Case-based reasoning: concepts, features and soft computing. Appl. Intell. 21, 233–238 (2004)
20. Cahn, R.S.: Introduction to rule-based systems theory of rule-based systems. 41(3), 116 (2014)
21. Wilkinson, L.: Tree structured data analysis: AID, CHAID and CART. In: Proceedings of Sawtooth Software, pp. 1–10 (1992)
22. Sissakian, V.K., Al-Ansari, N., Knutsson, S.: Sand and dust storm events in Iraq. Nat. Sci. 5, 1084–1094 (2013)
23. Stefanski, R., Sivakumar, M.V.K.: Impacts of sand and dust storms on agriculture and potential agricultural applications of a SDSWS. In: IOP Conference Series: Earth and Environmental Science, vol. 7, p. 12016 (2009)

AI Techniques

Decision Support System for Green Real-Life Field Scheduling Problems

Yizi Zhou[1]([⊠])(iD), Anne Liret[2](iD), Jiyin Liu[1](iD), Emmanuel Ferreyra[3](iD),
Rupal Rana[1](iD), and Mathias Kern[2](iD)

[1] Loughborough University, Loughborough, UK
y.zhou2@lboro.ac.uk
[2] British Telecommunications plc, Ipswich, UK
[3] University of Essex, Colchester, UK

Abstract. A decision support system is designed in this paper for supporting the adoption of green logistics within scheduling problems, and applied to real-life services cases. In comparison to other green logistics models, this system deploys time-varying travel speeds instead of a constant speed, which is important for calculating the CO_2 emission accurately. This system adopts widely used instantaneous emission models in literature which can predict second-by-second emissions. The factors influencing emissions in these models are vehicle types, vehicle load and traffic conditions. As vehicle types play an important role in computing the amount of emissions, engineers' vehicles' number plates are mapped to specified emission formulas. This feature currently is not offered by any commercial software. To visualise the emissions of a planned route, a Heat Map view is proposed. Furthermore, the differences between minimising CO_2 emission compared to minimising travel time are discussed under different scenarios. The field scheduling problem is formulated as a vehicle routing and scheduling problem, which considers CO_2 emissions in the objective function, heterogeneous fleet, time window constraints and skill matching constraints, different from the traditional time-dependent VSRP formulation. In the scheduler, this problem is solved by metaheuristic methods. Three different metaheuristics are compared. They are Tabu search algorithms with random neighbourhood generators and two variants of Variable Neighbourhood search algorithms: variable neighbourhood descent (VND) and reduced variable neighbourhood search (RVNS). Results suggest that RVNS is a good trade-off between solution qualities and computational time for industrial application.

Keywords: Green logistic scheduling system · Speed profile · Metaheuristics comparison · Heat map

1 Introduction

Green logistics has gained increasing awareness from the governments and service provisioning companies, recognizing that the traditional distribution and

© Springer International Publishing AG 2017
M. Bramer and M. Petridis (Eds.): SGAI-AI 2017, LNAI 10630, pp. 355–369, 2017.
https://doi.org/10.1007/978-3-319-71078-5_30

production logistics is not sustainable in the long term. However challenges in such transformation are firstly the design of operationally efficient and accurate approach of CO_2 emissions calculation and secondly the smooth adoption of CO_2 awareness in planning decisions across actors. Transportation is a major source of carbon emissions, and the main task in this paper is to design a decision support system that provides engineers guidance on their daily schedule and routine based on the lowest emission or fuel consumption efficient routes. Field scheduling problems aim at scheduling field tasks to the right mobile engineers at the right time. An integrated system of a scheduling and routing engine and a vehicle specified instantaneous emission model is developed. The unique features of the system are: (1) Automated vehicles' details mapping to emission formula, which is not provided in any commercial emissions software; (2) tailored speed profiles for different regions in UK, based on real-world traffic data and driving behaviours of engineers' data from a field service provider; (3) computing emissions data for every granularity like road segment level, task level, engineer level, day level and so on. Although fuel consumption data gives company an idea of the overall emissions associated with each vehicle and engineer, the emission data gives more detailed information on fuel consumption e.g. per task; (4) Switchable green scheduling and routing simulation engines depending on the users need: a faster solution algorithm (reduced variable neighbourhood search) and another algorithm runs longer but yields better solutions (random neighbourhood Tabu search); (5) Map visualizing (Heat map): the emissions on travels are colored and benchmarked against different levels of CO_2 emissions.

1.1   Green Vehicle Routing Problem

Green vehicle routing is one of the subjects of study. Initial works in this area have primarily focused on reducing the total distance travelled to reduce the total emissions. [1] took a distance-based emission model when solving a green capacitated vehicle routing problem. They used average fuel consumption data per 100 Km for a heavy-duty truck with various states of load. Fuel consumption is directly related to CO_2 emissions as the fixed carbon content in chemical compound of fuel. A fuel conversion factor (converting to CO_2 emissions) was derived to be 2.61 kg CO_2/litre. A linear programming model with CO_2 emission minimisation objective function was built and solved by a Tabu search algorithm. CO_2 emissions are not only influenced by travel distance, but by many other factors, such as road characteristics, vehicle speed and load. According to [2], speed is more important than distance travelled when estimating emissions. During times of congestion, vehicles generate much more emissions than when travelling at free flow speed. It is important to measure time varying travel speed to capture congestion situations. Therefore, time-dependent vehicle routing and scheduling problem (VRSP) emerges. This problem is alike traditional vehicle routing problems (VRP), but with the travelling times between nodes depend on the time of the day, such as peak and off-peak times with different traffic flow speeds. [3] studied a CO_2 emission minimisation vehicle routing problem with fluctuating travel speed. Test cases were generated on a London road map with real traffic data, including speed data for each road. Also, there are multiple possible road links that connect two customers' sites like in real life, so path selection will be part of the decision problem. They treated travel speed as a decision variable, ranging up to the current maximum traffic flow speed on the link travelled. They showed that with path selection and speed optimisation, 2–3% emissions are saved comparing with always using fastest path and traffic flow speed. However, if the speed range emissions level is not very sensitive to speed change, setting travel speed to traffic flow speed will give a good solution as well.

1.2 CO_2 Emission Models

As emissions is affected by travel speed, vehicle types and many other factors, the shortest or quickest route may not be optimal with respect to carbon emissions or fuel consumptions. In this case, green vehicle routing depends on accurate computation of the carbon emissions to generate a route plan that is truly greener than the distance or travel time minimisation [4]. There are various emission models that differ in nature of estimating emission levels and fuel consumptions. They are either a macroscale model that aggregate total emissions and works as a rough estimate or a microscale model that can predict a relatively more accurate second-by-second emission level. A detailed review of existing emission models can be found in [5]. Regardless of emission models applied, CO_2 emissions could be 15–20% higher in real traffic conditions as quoted in [6]. One possible reason is most emission models predict emissions based on hot stabilised engine conditions and do not consider cold engine starts when emissions will be 10% higher. Two emissions models are frequently used in the literature of green vehicle routing problem. The MEET project funded by the European Union aimed to provide a basic, Europe-wide procedure for evaluating the impacts of transport on air pollution [7]. Several models were developed for different types of vehicles with various weight ranges. Those models are microscale level models, which are able to predict second-by-second emission levels. Vehicle emission levels are calculated based on travel speed, vehicle mass and vehicle type, and can be adjusted to road gradient as well as vehicle load. The MEET model is an average of various speed-emission curves of a range of driving cycles. A driving cycle means a specific pattern of driving behaviour containing a different combination of stops, starts, accelerations and decelerations. So, the effect of acceleration is implicitly included. Similar models can be found in [8], developed in the UK by TRL (transportation research lab) and named NAEI. NAEI database are based on many measurements from various programs conducted over year. The database complied as part of MEET project, also included data from TRL.

1.3   Time-Dependent Speed Profile

Both MEET and NAEI models take speed as an input to calculate emissions. According to [4], using fixed speed to compute emissions in emission model can sometimes give less than half of those computed under realistic driving conditions with fluctuating speed. The author demonstrated the effect of fluctuating speed on the accuracy of carbon emission computations in green vehicle routing. The time-dependent travel speed is necessary. It is modelled by discretizing the day into a number of time buckets (1 h duration or simply morning, midday and afternoon), and then assigned a unique mean speed value to each bucket. [9] divided a day into 24 and 15 time slots respectively, and travel speeds for each time slot for each road segment are estimated using real-life travel data, assuming in each time slot the traffic condition is stable.

2   Problem Statement

The problem studied is new and has some different features compared to the traditional time-dependent vehicle routing problem. As with tradition models the travel speed is time-dependent, and time-window constraints are considered. The new features are (1) the objective of CO_2 emission minimisation; (2) heterogeneous fleet are used; (3) skill matching constraints are propagated. The vehicle scheduling and routing problem of this study involve real life task locations in UK. $V = v_0, v_1, \cdots, v_n$ is a set of nodes representing task locations and v_0 represents the depot, which is the engineers' start work and end work location. $A = \{(v_i, v_j) | v_i, v_j \in V, i \neq j\}$ is the arch set, and we assume engineers will always take the shortest path between two nodes, so there is only one path linking the same pair of nodes. Each arch of A is associated with a non-negative cost C_{ij}, which represents the cost of traveling from v_i to v_j. In this study, this cost is the amount of CO_2 emissions computed using emissions models mentioned previously. The travel speed v_t is a time-dependent speed, derived from our speed profile. Engineers drive different vehicles which have different emission formulas. Each task has a specified skill requirement and each engineer has a set of skills that he/she is capable of conducting. Task can only be scheduled to an engineer with the specified skill. Each task has a time window requirement $[b_i, e_i]$, where b_i is the earliest possible time to start this task and e_i is the latest time. The service start time must fall in to this range. Each vehicle/engineer has a working period, all travels and works can only be scheduled within this working period. In a summary, the problem is a time-dependent green vehicle routing problem with heterogeneous fleet, time window and skill matching constraints. The components of the green scheduling decision support system for this problem are road distance estimation, tailored speed profiles, vehicle specification mapping to emission formula, and scheduling and routing computation engines. Engines consist of different metaheuristics and during the search only feasible solutions satisfying all constraints described (feasible) are evaluated. The engines will be discussed in detail in the next section.

2.1   Travel Distance Estimation

Given locations (longitude and latitude) of two sites, line distance between two sites can be calculated using Haversine formula, which gives the shortest distance over the earth's surface between two sites ignoring terrain. However, in real life vehicles do need to follow the road construction to travel between two sites. 2000 task pairs were randomly selected and the line distance between each pair of tasks was calculated. Then, Google Map Distance API was called to get the road distance estimate between same pairs of tasks. Assuming there is a linear relationship between line distance and road distance, a linear regression analysis was carried out. Assumed that: $RoadDistance = \beta * LineDistance + error$. Linear regression analysis was run to get the estimate value of parameter β. Taking London as an example, the linear model is significant and with a 98.2% R square value, meaning a high goodness of fit value. P-value of F statistic is $0.00 \leq 0.05$, which shows the model is better than the intercept-only model and $\beta = 1.256$.

2.2 Real-Life Travel Speed Profile

Based on the travel journals of engineers from a field service provider, the real travel speed profile was generated for each working area in the UK. Taking London as an example, the profile will capture the average traffic condition throughout the day. It is expected that there will be two peak-hour periods, where the travel speed is low. The travel speed for the hour that the engineer starts to travel to a task is computed. For each task, we will have a speed entry. A day is divided into 24 one-hour-slots, 0:00–24:00. If an engineer travels in a time slot, the travel speed in that slot will be recorded. Then we took the average speed of that slot over 121 days to construct a speed profile. We used speed data entries for 6 months from London. Figure 1 (left) shows two rush hour periods: earlier morning and late afternoon. This advocates expectation of real life traffic conditions. To reduce the total variance of the data, several time slots are grouped together to smooth the data pattern as shown in Fig. 1 (right). The grouping criteria is to group time slots with similar means and hence allocate only one group for the midnight period, as there is less traffic, and therefore travel speeds should be similar. This speed profile will be updated after short period of time by an automated system. Data storage requires the mean value

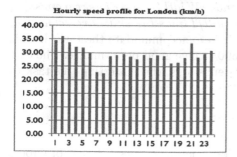 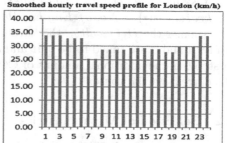

Fig. 1. Speed (km/h) profile for London raw vs. smoothed version

for each hour and the entry number. [9] have carried out similar speed analysis for 24 h in Stuttgart, Germany, with 230 million speed data (3 years).

2.3   Vehicle Details Mapped to Emission Formulas

There are 265 CO_2 emission formulas for different vehicle specification in NAEI project and 33 different emission formulas in MEET project. Both project have formulas for other types of pollutants such as CO, HC and NOx. Given an engineer vehicle's registration number, the information of engineer vehicle's details can be found from TRL website or from company database. Then this vehicle is mapped to one specified formula within the NAEI/MEET formulas set. In NAEI we need vehicle basic types (such as small commercial vehicle or heavy-duty vehicle), fuel type, gross weight, European emission standard and engine capacity, however in MEET, we need basic type, fuel type and gross weight.

3   Solution Engines

3.1   Initial Solution

An initial feasible solution is constructed using an insertion heuristic. This algorithm generates a good quality initial feasible solution, which is important to the success of Tabu search algorithm. RVNS algorithm is more robust to the quality of the initial solution but also requires it to be feasible. Given a list of engineers who are working for a certain period and a list of tasks to be scheduled, a traditional insertion heuristics will randomly choose a task from the task list and insert it into the best and feasible partial route. In vehicle routing problem with time windows and skill matching constraints, this method will lead to problems as it may first insert some tasks that are less difficult to accommodate and leave the tasks which are more difficult to accommodate to be inserted later. In this paper, an extended insertion heuristic is introduced. First, all tasks are ranked in descending order of their difficulties to insert. The difficulty is measured by task time window width and task requested skill's rareness. We want to schedule the most difficult task first. $Difficulty_i = a \cdot TimeWindowWidth(i) + \beta \cdot Taskrareness(i)$, $Taskrareness(i) = No.\ of\ Eng\ has\ the\ skill/Times\ the\ skill\ are\ requested$. The smaller the $Difficulty_i$, the harder it is to accommodate the task. In this study, α and β are tuned to be 0.01 and 300 to give good performance. The cost in step 6 is the additional amount of CO_2 emissions when inserting this task to the current partial route.

3.2   Selection of Metaheuristics

In a survey paper of vehicle routing problem, metaheuristics (71.25% of papers reviewed) are used more often than exact methods and classical heuristics, furthermore simulation and real-time solution methods are rarely applied. Vehicle

---

Algorithm 1. InsertionAlgorithm

1: **Rank** tasks in descending order of $Difficulty_i$
2: **Get** ordered taskList
3: $i \leftarrow 1$
4: **Repeat**
5:     insert $(task_i)$ to lowest cost and feasible position in current partial route
6: $i \leftarrow i + 1$
7: **Until** $i =$ taskList length

---

routing problem is known to be NP-hard, and exact methods are computational costly for industrial sized problems [10]. The state of the art metaheuristics used in green vehicle routing problems are reviewed by [11], and they include: tabu search, simulated annealing, variable neighborhood search, genetic algorithm and ant colony optimization. We will include tabu search and two variants of VNS. We exclude the use of genetic algorithm as its characteristics is not convenient for time-window constrained problems. During the mutate or crossover stage, problem feasibilities are hard to maintain. We tried simulated annealing method but this algorithm depends largely on the decision of parameters and choice of the cooling strategy. We have 5 different test cases, each may have a different set of parameters, SA is not very robust and parameters tuning require extra computational time. Experimental results of SA with different configurations are shown in Fig. 2 showing the solution performance against number of iterations. Among these four configurations, (4) gives the best solution in terms of objective value but computational time is 300 s comparing to 0.06 s in (1).

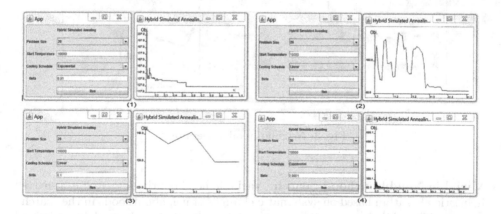

Fig. 2. Simulated annealing results on same data set with different configurations

Neighbourhood Operators. In this paper, 6 different operators are used to enable a wider exploration of solution space as shown in Fig. 3. Those operators are a mix of node, link and chain changes.

1. 2-Opt: this is applied to each single route by breaking two links and reconnect. Before changes the route is A-B-C-D-E-F-G-H and after changes the route is A-B-F-E-D-C-G-H.
2. Swap: this is applied to each single route by swapping the position of two nodes. Before changes the route is A-B-C-D-E and after changes the route is A-D-C-B-E.
3. Exchange: this is applied to a pair of routes by swapping the position of two nodes from each route. Before changes the route is A-B-C and D-E-F and after changes the route is A-B-E and D-C-F.
4. Relocation: this is applied to a pair of routes by taking out one note from one route and insert it into another. Before changes the route is A-B-C-D and E-F-G-H and after changes the route is A-B-D and E-F-C-G-H.
5. 2-Opt*: this is applied to a pair of routes by breaking one link from each route and reconnect two routes. Before changes the route is A-B-C-D and E-F-G-H and after changes the route is A-B-D and E-F-C-G-H.
6. Or-Opt: this is applied to each single route by moving a chain of k nodes to a new position, e.g. chain D-E will be relocated. Before changes the route is A-B-C-D-E-F and after changes the route is A-E-D-B-C-F.

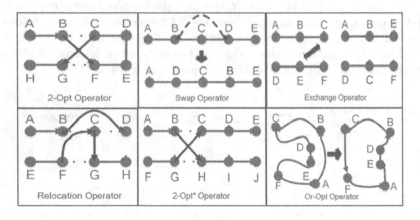

Fig. 3. Neighborhoods' operators

Variable Neighbourhood Search. Variable neighbourhood search is a meta-heuristic algorithm based on systematic changes of neighbourhoods in the search process. The ability of escaping from local optimum is enhanced by starting the search in each neighbourhood from a random neighbour of the incumbent solution. Since it was introduced, this method has developed rapidly and found success in solving combinatorial optimisation problem. The idea of VNS is based on the observation that a local minimum found in one neighbourhood structure is not necessary a local minimum for other neighbourhood structures; A global minimum is a local minimum in the combination of all possible neighbourhood structures; Local minima found by different neighbourhoods are relatively close to each other for many problems. There are several variants of VNS, and in this paper, variable neighbourhood descent and reduced variable neighbourhood search will be studied [12].

Variable Neighbourhood Descent (VND). VND does not involve randomness in the search. Using the current neighbourhood operator k, local search is performed with the best move strategy until no improvement can be found with the current neighbourhood operator. The search then continues using the next neighbourhood operator $k + 1$, or go back to neighbourhood operator 1 if $k = k_{max}$. This searching process will terminate until no improvement is found for all k.

Algorithm 2. VND(x)

1: **repeat**
2:     $k \leftarrow 1$
3:     **repeat**
4:         $x' \leftarrow BestNeighbour(x, k)$
5:         **if then** x' is better than x, $x \leftarrow x'$
6:         **else** $k = k + 1$
7:         **end if**
8:     **until** $k = k_{max}$
9: **until** no improvement could be found

Reduced Variable Neighbourhood Search (RVNS). The problem with descent algorithms is that it can get trapped to the local optima and cannot escape from it even though we use variable neighbourhood operators. RVNS overcomes this by generating all trial solutions through shake, i.e., randomly generating a solution x' from the kth neighbourhood of x. The stopping criterion in this paper is chosen to be a maximum run time.

Algorithm 3. RVNS(x)

1: $Cputime \leftarrow 0$
2: **repeat**
3:     $k \leftarrow 1$
4:     **repeat**
5:         $x' \leftarrow Shake(x, k)$
6:         **if then** x' is better than x, $x \leftarrow x'$
7:         **else** $k = k + 1$
8:         **end if**
9:     **until** $k = k_{max}$
10: **until** $Cputime > time_{max}$

Tabu Search. Tabu search is a metaheuristic search method employing local search methods and have been widely used in vehicle routing problems with time window constraints. Comparing to descent methods, the objective is allowed to deteriorate in order to avoid local minima. To prevent cycling, solutions that are recently visited are prohibited and stored in a tabu list. The stopping criteria is either it reaches the maximum total iterations' numbered *iter_max* or the best solution has not been updated for *iter_cons_max* iterations. Step 6 to 8 perform local search methods within a specified neighbourhood. This neighbourhood is generated at each iteration by a neighbourhood operator which is randomly selected from the previous mentioned six operators. Then the solution that has been previously visited (memorised in tabu list) or violated constraints will be eliminated. The reason for only keeping feasible solutions is once the infeasible solution is accepted, it is hard to regain feasibility using a tabu search algorithm. Then in step 6, local search takes a best improvement strategy, which could be switched to first improvement strategy. The structure of memory is a short-term memory with a fix size of 6, which means the 6 most recent solution will be in the tabu list. $f(x)$ is the fitness score of the solution x, and in this paper it is the total CO_2 emissions amount of the solution.

Algorithm 4. TabuSearch

1: $iter \leftarrow 1, iter\_cons \leftarrow 1; x_{best} \leftarrow x_{initial}, x_{current} \leftarrow x_{initial}$
2: **repeat**
3:      $k = random(1 \cdots 6)$
4:      $k \leftarrow 1, Cputime \leftarrow 0$
5:      **Generate** $neighbour_k(x_{current})$ /* Neighbourhood solutions by kth operator */
6:      Remove tabu and infeasible solution in $neighbour_k(x_{current})$
7:      $x_{current} \leftarrow$ **Best**$(neighbour_k(x_{current}))$
8:      Update TabuList: add $x_{current}$, remove the least recent x
9:      **if then** $f(x_{current}) < f(x_{best}), iter\_cons \leftarrow 1$
10:     **else** $iter\_cons \leftarrow iter\_cons + 1; iter \leftarrow iter + 1$
11:     **end if**
12: **until** $iter = iter\_max$ or $iter\_cons = iter\_cons\_max$

3.3   Real-Life Test Cases and Comparison Between Solution Engines

Five real life data samples were taken from a field service provider with similar problem size (around 100 tasks per sample). The performance measures of the solution are the number of vehicles or engineers scheduled to fulfil all the tasks, total amount of CO_2 emission in grams generated by the final routes planning and number of trips that are bundled together (tasks at the same location). The performance of initial feasible solution by the insertion algorithm are shown in Table 1. Our different test cases have different features. For example, in Fig. 4, comparing test case 1 and test case 3, case 3 has a higher number of wide spread tasks on the map, that is why its initial solution has a higher CO_2 emissions.

Table 1. Initial solution

Text case	No. of task	No. engineer	CO_2 kg	Bundle trip
Case 1	103	19	187.613	46
Case 2	110	18	150.044	51
Case 3	108	20	236.522	46
Case 4	100	17	201.032	42
Case 5	106	24	233.129	41

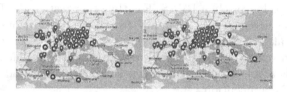

Fig. 4. Test case 1 (left) vs. test case 3 (right)

3.4   Comparison of Metaheuristics on Real-Life Test Cases

VND vs. RVNS. For each test case, we first let VND solve the problem and get the solutions and Cpu times, then we let RVNS run for 100 s which are similar to the Cpu times of VND and compare the results. As RVNS algorithm has a stochastic nature, this algorithm is run for 30 times to conduct statistical analysis. A one-sample t-test is carried out to see if the mean solution of RVNS is significantly different from the VND, and the significance level is set to be 0.1. The results are shown in Table 2 with the best solution. Other than case 2, RVNS yields significantly better solution than VND and it produces the best solution for all 5 cases. Comparing the emissions results, on average RVNS gives 3.7% less emissions with the same computational time. Results suggest that RVNS outperforms VND.

Table 2. Comparison between VND and RVNS

	Emissions kg	Case 1	Case 2	Case 3	Case 4	Case 5
RVNS	Best	148.95	143.32	158.90	130.61	161.95
	Average	160.56	146.74	181.00	165.97	183.73
	S.D	6.28	2.11	14.17	15.14	10.15
VND		171.87	144.34	187.34	170.81	198.52
Cpu time (s)		100	100	150	300	600
p-value		0.000	0.000	0.020	0.091	0.000
Different?		Y	Y	Y	Y	Y

RVNS vs. Tabu. Tabu search algorithm randomly changes neighbourhood, so this algorithm is also run for 30 times for each test cases. The stopping criteria is set to be 15000 maximum evaluations and 300 non-improving evaluations, then the computational time is fluctuating, unlike RVNS which is set to be terminated at a certain maximum run time. Table 3 shows the comparisons of the two engines by the means of average CO_2 emissions and average computational time. The best solution value of CO_2 emissions is highlighted in bold. Among the five test cases, these two engines generated similar solutions for case 3 and case 5 by means of CO_2 emissions, but the computational time of Tabu algorithm is on average 5.37 times longer than RVNS. For the other test cases, Tabu algorithm gave significantly better results than RVNS, the CO_2 emissions is on average 5.35% less, but at an expense of 11.72 times of computational time. Although the best solution was found by the Tabu search algorithm in most cases, results suggest RVNS is a good trade-off between solution quality and computational time for industrial application.

Table 3. Comparison between Tabu and RVNS

	Emissions	Case 1	Case 2	Case 3	Case 4	Case 5
RVNS	Best	148.95	143.32	158.90	**130.61**	**161.95**
	Average	160.56	146.74	181.00	165.97	183.73
	S.D	6.28	2.11	14.17	15.14	10.15
	Cpu Time	100	100	150	300	600
Tabu	Best	**142.52**	**131.57**	**156.31**	140.79	163.24
	Average	156.44	137.83	178.82	153.66	188.73
	S.D	9.00	2.74	7.01	6.15	10.19
	Average time (s)	1642.14	1616.32	1492.69	1668.29	1665.90
	S.D	521.45	503.35	288.39	740.51	457.93
p-value		0.044	0.000	0.454	0.000	0.105
Different?		Y	Y	N	Y	N

4   Heat Map View

The impact of the proposed green logistic engineer scheduling and routing system on the business, can be illustrated graphically. A sample of a scheduling profile of 179 engineers between 01st May and 15th May 2017 is analyzed. This sample resolves 4,173 unique tasks in Colchester and Ipswich domain. It can be noticed from Fig. 5 (left), higher emission from 7 to 9 h. Compared to the picture reported in Fig. 5 (right), which reports the recorded emission from 11 to 13 hrs. Where, roads in shadow represent the transited route with a certain CO_2 emission. Darker colors indicate higher CO_2 emission. The threshold of coloring is adjusted for comparison purposes according to the desired snapshot. Therefore, it is categorized in according to certain ranges, such as: $t_{low} = x[min, \mu - \sigma^2]$, $t_{medium} = x[\mu - \sigma^2, \mu + \sigma^2]$ and $t_{high} = x[\mu + \sigma^2, max]$, where x corresponds to the CO_2 value to be represented, min is the minimum CO_2 value recorded, μ is the mean of the CO_2 emissions after computation, σ^2 is the standard deviation of this CO_2 computation in the specific time window being evaluated and max is the higher recorded value for the CO_2 in the sample in that slot. Therefore, the resulting thresholds are no fixed and correspond to the particular desired granularity. Observing the heat map, we can see that the average level of emissions of 7–9 am is higher comparing to 11–13 h and this is due to the traffic congestions which is as expected.

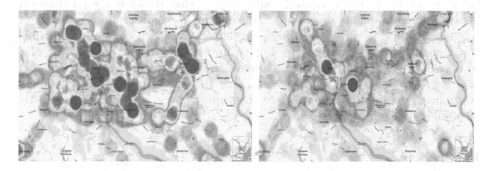

Fig. 5. CO_2 Heat map visualization. (Left) from 7 h to 9 h (Inclusive). (Right) from 11 h to 13 h. (Inclusive).

5   Conclusion

A green logistic constraint satisfaction and optimization based engineer schedul-ing and routing decision support system is designed in this paper, and tested on test cases from a real-life field service provider. Comparing to other green logistics models, this system is more accurate than traditional solutions, as it generates and uses a time-varying travel speed profile instead of a constant speed profile. This speed is then incorporated into the constraint propagation model for the problem together with availability, time window and competences constraints propagation on each engineer and the task potential couple. This proposed sys-tem adapts instantaneous emission models which are widely used in green vehicle logistic studies to the real-world case of heterogeneous vehicle fleet. The factors considered by these models are vehicle types, vehicle load and traffic condi-tions. As vehicle types play an important role in the amount of emissions and as no commercial software maps the two, engineers' vehicles' number plates are mapped to a specified emission formula. These additional factors aim to make the emissions computation more accurate. The vehicle routing problem is solved using three metaheuristics: RVNS, VND and Tabu. Experiments are carried out to compare three different metaheuristics on 5 real-life typical cases. On average

RVNS gives 3.7% less emissions with the same computational time compared to VND, and therefore VND will likely not be included in the final solution engines. For most test cases, Tabu algorithm gave CO_2 related results significantly better than RVNS: the CO_2 emissions is on average 5.35% less, but at an expense of 11.72 times of computational time. Nevertheless, the significantly lower running time cost of RVNS places this algorithm at the top position of industrial operational acceptable algorithm underlying a real-time decision making support solution. The industrial solution relies on fast computations returning a set of time-contextual recommendations about CO_2 impact and feasible time slots regarding a task-engineer assignment decision. Finally we have included both Tabu algorithm and RVNS algorithm in the solution engines, to cope with the variation of the users' needs. Results suggest that RVNS is a good trade-off between solution quality and computational time for industry application, but the users could select Tabu algorithm for better solution if computational time is not a constraint. Finally, to the best of our knowledge this paper is the first to develop a Heat Map view of emissions of schedule plans at different hours of a day: a tool to help managers visualize the emission levels of scheduling and routing plans and graphically see the impact of the proposed green logistic scheduling decision support system.

References

1. Úbeda, S., Faulin, J., Serrano, A., Arcelus, F.: Solving the green capacitated vehicle routing problem using a tabu search algorithm. Lect. Notes Manag. Sci. **6**, 141–149 (2014)
2. Eglese, R., Black, D.: Optimizing the routing of vehicles. In: Green Logistics: Improving the Environmental Sustainability of Logistics, pp. 215–228. KoganPage, London (2010)
3. Qian, J., Eglese, R.: Fuel emissions optimization in vehicle routing problems with time-varying speeds. Eur. J. Oper. Res. **248**(3), 840–848 (2016)
4. Turkensteen, M.: The accuracy of carbon emission and fuel consumption computations in green vehicle routing. Eur. J. Oper. Res. **262**(2), 647–659 (2017)
5. Demir, E., Bektaş, T., Laporte, G.: A comparative analysis of several vehicle emission models for road freight transportation. Transp. Res. Part D: Transp. Environ. **16**(5), 347–357 (2011)
6. Palmer, A.: The development of an integrated routing and carbon dioxide emissions model for goods vehicles (2007)
7. Hickman, J., Hassel, D., Joumard, R., Samaras, Z., Sorenson, S.: Meet-methodology for calculating transport emissions and energy consumption. european commission, dg vii. Technical report, Luxembourg, 362 p. www.inrets.fr/infos/cost319 (1999). ISBN 92-828-6785-4
8. Boulter, P., Barlow, T., McCrae, I.: Emission factors 2009: report 3-exhaust emission factors for road vehicles in the united kingdom. TRL Published Project Report (2009)
9. Ehmke, J., Campbell, A., Thomas, B.: Vehicle routing to minimize time-dependent emissions in urban areas. Eur. J. Oper. Res. **251**(2), 478–494 (2016)

10. Braekers, K., Ramaekers, K., Van Nieuwenhuyse, I.: The vehicle routing problem: state of the art classification and review. Comput. Industr. Eng. **99**, 300–313 (2016)
11. Lin, C., Choy, K., Ho, G., Chung, S., Lam, H.: Survey of green vehicle routing problem: past and future trends. Expert Syst. Appl. **41**(4), 1118–1138 (2014)
12. Hansen, P., Mladenović, N., Pérez, J.: Variable neighbourhood search: methods and applications. Ann. Oper. Res. **175**(1), 367–407 (2010)

Multi-label Classification of Movie Posters into Genres with Rakel Ensemble Method

Marina Ivasic-Kos$^{(\boxtimes)}$ and Miran Pobar

Department of Informatics, University of Rijeka, 51000 Rijeka, Croatia
`{marinai,mpobar}@uniri.hr`

Abstract. Movies can belong to more than one genre, so the problem of determining the genres of a movie from its poster is a multi-label classification problem. To solve the multi-label problem, we have used the RAKEL ensemble method along with three typical single-label base classification methods: Naïve Bayes, C4.5 decision tree, and k-NN. The RAKEL method strives to overcome the problem of computational cost and power set label explosion by breaking the initial set of labels into several small-sized label sets.

The classification performance of base classifiers on different feature sets is evaluated using multi-label evaluation measures on poster dataset containing 6000 posters classified into 18 and 11 genres.

Keeping this in mind, we wanted to examine how different visual feature sets, extracted from poster images, are related to the performance of automatic detection of movie genres, as well as compare it to the performance obtained with the Classeme feature descriptors trained on the datasets of general images.

Keywords: Multi-label classification · RAKEL ensemble method · Movie poster · Classemes · GIST

1 Introduction

Classification of movie posters into genres is a typical multi-label classification problem since a movie can simultaneously belong to more than one genre. Multi-label problems have recently attracted increased attention in the research community. Such problems occur in different domains, from classifying text into categories (e.g. news into local, politics, sports…), image classification, video annotations, to the functional genomics classification (gene and protein function). An overview of various multi-label classification approaches is given in [2].

The early attempts of poster classification into genres took into account only one genre per movie so they have completely avoided the problem of multi-label classification. In [3], 100 movies are classified into four genres (drama, action, comedy, horror) using low-level features extracted from movie trailers. The same features were used in [4] but for three genres (action, drama, and thriller). In [5], GIST, CENTRIST, and W-CENTRIST features are used for classification of genres on 1239 movie trailers.

Later, poster classification was treated as a multi-label problem. In [6], multi-label classification performance was tested for two out of two correct genres and for at least one of two correctly recognized genres. Naïve Bayes, distance-ranking classifiers and

© Springer International Publishing AG 2017
M. Bramer and M. Petridis (Eds.): SGAI-AI 2017, LNAI 10630, pp. 370–383, 2017.
https://doi.org/10.1007/978-3-319-71078-5_31

random k-label sets (RAKEL) have performed similarly. The experiment considered a set of 1500 posters classified into six genres. Color and edge features with the number of faces detected on posters were used for poster representation.

In [7], a 6000 movie poster dataset was used. The best performance was reported for NB with GIST and color-based features. In [8] movies are represented using multiple visual features and the synopsis. A movie is classified by joining the outputs of Support Vector Machine (SVM) classifiers. In [9], different problem transformation methods, binary relevance, RAKEL, and classifier chains with Naïve Bayes as base classifier have been used to deal with the multi-label classification problem. The authors report the best classification results with RAKEL.

Here, we want to automatically classify the movie posters into genres using both the global low-level features extracted from poster images and higher-level image descriptor trained on other datasets. To obtain the global low-level poster features we followed the proposed feature sets in [7] and as higher-level image descriptor, we have used Classemes [10], the classifier-based features that are pre-trained on 2659 real-world object classes.

Apart from examining how is the classification performance related to the different feature sets, we want to investigate the effect of different single-label classification methods used for training the RAKEL [11] ensemble, since RAKEL performed significantly better than other problem transformation methods for the same task in [9].

The rest of this article is organized as follows. Section 2 gives a brief overview of approaches for simplification of the multi-label classification problem into a series of single-label classification problems. RAKEL ensemble method that is used here to deal with poster classification task is described in more detail. Section 3 provides details about the experimental setup, and Sect. 4 explains the metrics for multi-label classification performance. In Sect. 5, the experimental results are presented and discussed. The paper concludes with Sect. 6, where directions for future work are given.

2 Approaches for Simplification of the Multi-label Classification Problem

The movie poster classification task belongs to the class of multi-label classification problems since a movie can simultaneously belong to several genres out of many possible genres. Generally, in multi-label classification, an example can belong to more than one class, while in single-label classification, each example belongs to a single class. There are two common cases in single-label classification, binary classification when there are only two possible classes, and multi-class classification when there are more than two classes. Binary and multi-class classification problems can be considered as special cases of multi-label classification where each sample is associated with only a single label. Therefore, single-label classification is simpler to implement than multi-label classification.

Thus, to deal with the multi-label classification problem, most methods strive to convert it to a series of single-label problems. Therefore, it is understood that they belong to the problem transformation approach. Alternatively, single-label classification methods can be adapted to directly handle the multi-label case, so they belong to algorithm adaptation approach. The way of adaptation depends on the base classification method that is used. Examples of these methods are a Multi-label k-nearest neighbor (ML-kNN) [12] that is derived from a k-nearest neighbor (k-NN) [13], AdaBoost.MH and AdaBoost.MR, derived from the AdaBoost method [14] and various adaptations of the SVM classifier [14].

Finally, approaches that combine several methods to benefit from their individual strengths are developed and referred to as ensemble methods. Some of the widely known ensemble methods are RAKEL [11], and the ensemble of classifier chains (ECC) [15].

Common problem transformation methods include binary relevance (BR) and label power set (LP) methods.

For each possible class label, in the BR method, a binary classifier is trained in 1-vs-all fashion. All binary classifiers are applied to an unknown sample and the classification result consists of all labels assigned by the binary classifiers. The BR method can predict label combinations that are previously unseen. Also, it is computationally simple since it involves only as many classifiers as there are possible classes. On the other hand, it ignores the information about the dependence between labels.

Label powerset (LP) transforms a multi-label problem into a single label problem by forming a new class label from each unique set of labels that exist in a training set. That is, for example, the entire label set (Action, Drama, Science Fiction) of an example poster is replaced with a new class label Action&Drama&ScienceFiction.

The LP method considers label correlations but can only predict label sets observed in the training set. Also, it struggles with the exponential growth of possible label combinations especially in datasets with a large number of training examples or labels.

To overcome the problem of computational cost and power set label explosion, an ensemble method called RAKEL has been recently proposed.

2.1 Rakel Ensemble Method

The aim of RAKEL is to limit the growth of label sets by randomly sampling smaller label sets from the original set of labels. Then, for each of the label sets a multi-label classifier is trained using the LP method. For an unknown example, the decisions of all LP classifiers are gathered and combined to make a multi-label classification result. Thus, RAKEL deals with computationally simpler classification tasks and with the much more balanced distribution of classes than the LP method.

The RAKEL considers m label sets of the same size, k. The label sets can be either disjoint or overlapping, depending on which of the two strategies is used to construct them. In case of disjoint labels sets, the set C of all class labels is partitioned randomly into m disjoint k-size label sets $R_j, j = 1 \ldots m$. In case of overlapping label sets, the m k-size label sets are sampled randomly, without replacement, from all distinct k-label sets of C. The size of label sets k should be small to avoid problems of LP, so it is recommended to use a larger number of classification models (e.g. $m = 2|C|$) to achieve a high level of predictive performance.

Each classifier φ_j solves the single-label classification problem for classes $C_i \in C$ that are the subsets of that label set R_j, and that exist in the training set. Therefore, every single-label classifier can be used as base classifier along with RAKEL. The label set $Y_i = \{C_1, C_m, \ldots, C_r\}$ of each example e_i in the learning set is replaced with a new label that corresponds to the intersection of labels in Y_i and in R_j. For example, if a labelset R_j is defined as $R_j = \{action, comedy, drama\}$ an example-label set pair in the training set $(e_i, \{action, comedy, crime\})$ will be replaced with the pair $(e_i, action\&comedy)$.

For classifying an unknown example e, the results of all classifiers φ_j are joined into final decision using a voting process. As its final prediction is obtained based on predictions that correspond to different overlapping parts of existing label set, RAKEL can predict a label set that is not present in the training set.

3 Experimental Setup

The classification of posters into genres is performed on a dataset obtained from the TMDB [1]. To address this multi-label classification problem, we have used the RAKEL ensemble method along with typical single-label classification methods. The aim was to compare their influence on the classification power and efficiency. The methods have been tested with global low-level features extracted from posters, the GIST structural descriptor and with the Classemes descriptor.

3.1 Data and Step

The poster dataset contains movie posters from 1990–2014 [7]. The dataset includes 6739 movie posters belonging to 18 genres, gathered by taking the top 20 most popular movies in each year in the range (Table 1). The distribution of genres in the dataset was not entirely balanced, as shown in Table 1.

Table 1. Distribution of movies for 18 genres.

C_i	Action	Adventure	Animation	Comedy	Crime	Disaster	Documentary	Drama	Fantasy	History	Horror	Mystery	Romance	SF	Suspense	Thriller	War	Western
$|C_i|$	1815	1081	734	1524	874	64	924	2610	762	675	888	745	934	908	390	1947	527	273

To deal with more balanced data set, we have merged similar genres for which there was insufficient data in the original set of 18 genres, as in [9]. For example, Science Fiction was merged with Fantasy into SF/Fantasy. By merging of genres, 11 genres are created and their distribution is given in Table 2.

Table 2. Distribution of movies for 11 genres.

C_i	Action/Adventure	Animation	Comedy	Drama	Crime/Thriller	Family/Romance	Horror	Western	SF	Documentary	Misc.
$|C_i|$	2597	734	1525	3209	2445	1595	888	279	908	1534	755

3.2   Features

We want to compare the classification performance of single-label classifiers, used along with RAKEL, using different types of features. We used low-level features extracted from a poster image (dominant colors), features based on spatial structure (GIST) and a classifier based features (Classemes).

Dominant color low-level features (referred to as DC) primarily capture information about color that covers most of the poster image. To extract the dominant color features, each poster was converted to HSV color space and proportionally resized so that the width is 100 pixels. Then, the color histogram was calculated on hue (H), saturation (S) and value (V) channels of the whole image, and 12 histogram bins with the highest values for each channel were selected, as in [7]. Additionally, the statistics and color moments (CM), that is the mean, standard deviation, skew, and kurtosis, were computed for each HSV channel. The obtained 48-dimensional DCCM vectors correspond to 12 dominant colors in the poster.

The GIST descriptor [16] captures more information about the poster spatial layout, characterized by properties of its boundaries (e.g., the size, the degree of openness, perspective) and its content (e.g., naturalness, roughness) [16]. The spatial properties are estimated using global features. Global features are computed as a weighted combination of Gabor-like multi scale-oriented filters. The dimension of GIST descriptor is the product of the number of samples used for encoding and the number of different orientations and scales of image components. GIST descriptor of each genre is implemented with 8×8 encoding samples obtained by projecting the averaged output filter frequency within 8 orientations per 8 scales, so the size of GIST feature vector is 500.

Object categories present in posters may correspond to the object classifier-based Classeme features. Classemes [10] are obtained with a linear combination of M non-linear SVM classifiers that are pre-trained on real-world object classes. The SVM classifiers are trained on a different low-level representation of the image in a 1-vs-rest manner. The low-level representation of the image used for the classemes classifiers contains a set of 15 low-level features concatenated into 22860-dimensional vector capturing different visual cues concerning the color distribution, the spatial layout in the image as GIST, oriented and unoriented HOGs, SIFT and SSIM [17].

The size of the classemes feature vector that corresponds to the number of object categories is 2659.

3.3   Configuration of Base Classifiers

For classifying unknown posters into movie genres, we have used three base classification methods along with the RAKEL ensemble method.

We have applied the variant of the RAKEL that randomly selects m distinct label sets R_j of size $k = |R_j| = 3$. The number of label sets m was twice the number of labels in the set C, so for the 11genre task it was $m_{11G} = 22$ and for the 18 genre task it was $m_{18G} = 36$.

To examine the effect of single-level classification method used for training the LP models of RAKEL, we have made experiments using RAKEL along with different single-label classifiers. Using benchmark evaluation metrics, we have compared the performance of three classifiers that belong to different learning paradigms: NB [13] as a probabilistic generative model, the C4.5 decision tree [13] and the k-NN classifier as the lazy learning algorithm.

For the C4.5 tree, the 3-fold reduced error pruning was used with the confidence threshold for pruning of 0.25. The minimum number of instances per leaf was 2. For the k-NN classifier, the 1-NN variant was used. Euclidean distance measure was used in all cases.

4   Evaluation Metrics

The multi-label classification problem requires the use of evaluation metrics that differ from those used in single-label classification and can be grouped into example-based and label based metrics.

To define the evaluation metrics, we assume that an example $e_j \in E, j = 1..N$ has the set of ground truth labels $Y_j = \{C_l, C_m, \ldots, C_r\}$, $Y_j \subseteq C$ where E is a set of feature vectors, and C is a set of all labels. The set of labels for the example e_j that are predicted by a classifier is Z_j.

The example-based metrics are calculated on the average differences between the ground truth and the predicted sets of labels in the test set. We used the following example-based metrics:

Hamming loss is the symmetric difference of the predicted label set and the true label set, i.e. the fraction of the wrong labels to the total number of labels:

$$HammingLoss = \frac{1}{N} \sum_{i=1}^{N} \frac{|(Y_i \setminus Z_i) \cup (Z_i \setminus Y_i)|}{|C|}. \tag{1}$$

In the best case, the value of Hamming loss is zero.

Accuracy is defined as the average ratio of correctly predicted labels and all predicted and true labels for each example:

$$Accuracy = \frac{1}{N} \sum_{i=1}^{N} \frac{|Y_i \cap Z_i|}{|Y_i \cup Z_i|}. \tag{2}$$

Precision is defined as the average ratio of correctly predicted labels and all predicted label for each example.

$$Precision = \frac{1}{N} \sum_{i=1}^{N} \frac{|Y_i \cap Z_i|}{|Z_i|}. \tag{3}$$

Recall is defined as the average ratio of correctly predicted labels classifier and the ground truth labels for each example.

$$Recall = \frac{1}{N} \sum_{i=1}^{N} \frac{|Y_i \cap Z_i|}{|Y_i|}. \tag{4}$$

F-Measure can be interpreted as the harmonic mean of precision and recall.

$$F1 = \frac{1}{N} \sum_{i=1}^{N} \frac{2|Y_i \cap Z_i|}{|Z_i| + |Y_i|}. \tag{5}$$

These measures reach their best value at 1 and the worst at 0.

Label based recall, precision, and F1 measures are calculated for each label separately similarly as in binary classification. For average based results, two kinds of averaging operations called macro-averaging and micro-averaging can be used.

A micro-average evaluation measure gives equal weight to each example and is an average over all the example and label pairs. A macro-average evaluation measure gives equal weight to each label, regardless of its frequency, so is a per-label average [18].

5   Results and Discussion

All experiments were run using 5 runs of 5-fold cross-validation. The following results were obtained as an average of those runs.

We have tested the classification performance on two classification tasks on the transformed data with 11 genres and 18 genres. We have used different feature sets that include GIST features, dominant color features and color moments (DCCM), and Classemes. The size of feature vectors was 500, 48 and 2659, respectively.

The results are obtained with the Naïve Bayes (NB), C4.5 decision tree and k-NN that are used as base classifiers with the RAKEL ensemble method.

Each base classifier has achieved better results for all evaluation measured in the case of a 11G task than 18G tsk for the same set of features which was to be expected because it is a simpler task with fewer classes and with more balanced data set.

For the macro-averaged evaluation measures, the best overall results were achieved with the NB classifier using the Classemes in both 11 genres (F1 = 0.39) and 18 genres classification tasks (F1 = 0.30) (Fig. 1). Similar results (0.37 and 0.29) were achieved with the same classifier using GIST features, in which case the feature vector was 5 times shorter.

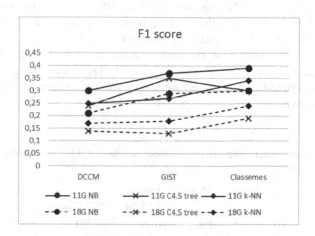

Fig. 1. Macro-averaged F1 scores of NB, C4.5, and kNN for 11G and 18G tasks.

Regarding the F1 and recall scores, the NB classifier performed better than the other tested classifiers for both 11G and 18G tasks and with all features.

The C4.5 tree classifier has performed better than other considered classifiers in terms of precision (Fig. 2), but worse for all other measures, in all cases except for the 11G task with GIST features. All base classifiers achieve better results for the 11G task (Fig. 1 solid line) than for the 18G task (Fig. 1, dashed line), which is expected due to a more complex classification problem in the case of 18 genres.

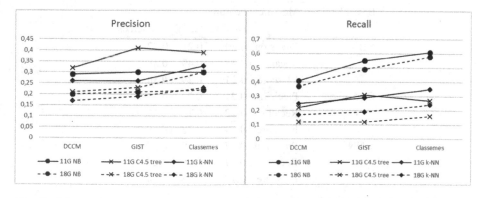

Fig. 2. Macro-averaged precision and recall of NB, C4.5, and kNN for 11G and 18G tasks.

It can be noted that the recall values vary significantly from 0.12 to 0.58 for the 18G task and from 0.22 to 0.61 for the 11G task when all classifiers are considered, but the precision scores are around 0.2 in the case of the 18G task and around 0.3 in the case of the 11G task. The C4.5 has the best results regarding precision, while the significantly highest recall was reached with NB in all cases, Fig. 2.

The feature set for which the base classifiers have the best performance is not the same for all classifiers. The NB and the k-NN classifier achieve the best results with Classemes for both tasks, while the C4.5 decision tree achieves the best results with GIST features for the 11G task and with Classemes for the 18G task (Figs. 1 and 2). Detailed results for all used base classifiers considering different sets of features for label-based measures are given in Tables 3 and 4. The micro-averaged label-based measures and example-based measures were very similar, so here the macro-averaged measures are shown.

Table 3. Label-based macro-averaged evaluation results for 11G task using RAKEL with different base classifiers.

Base classifier	Measure	Features		
		DCCM	GIST	Classemes
NB	Precision	0.29	0.30	0.30
	Recall	0.41	0.55	0.61
	F1 score	**0.30**	**0.37**	*0.39*
C4.5 tree	Precision	0.32	0.41	0.39
	Recall	0.22	0.31	0.27
	F1 score	0.24	*0.35*	0.30
k-NN	Precision	0.26	0.26	0.33
	Recall	0.25	0.29	0.35
	F1 score	0.25	0.27	*0.34*

Table 4. Label-based macro-averaged evaluation results for 18G task using RAKEL with different base classifiers.

Base classifier	Measure	Features		
		DCCM	GIST	Classemes
NB	Precision	0.20	0.21	0.22
	Recall	0.37	0.49	0.58
	F1 score	**0.21**	**0.29**	*0.30*
C4.5 tree	Precision	0.21	0.23	0.30
	Recall	0.12	0.12	0.16
	F1 score	0.14	0.13	*0.19*
k-NN	Precision	0.17	0.19	0.23
	Recall	0.17	0.19	0.24
	F1 score	0.17	0.18	*0.24*

Example-based classification results are presented in Tables 5 and 6 for both 11G and 18G tasks and for different feature sets. All classifiers have obtained better F1 scores on the example-based evaluation level than on label-based level.

Table 5. Example based evaluation results for 11G task, using RAKEL with different base classifiers.

Base classifier	Measure	Features		
		DCCM	GIST	Classemes
NB	Hamming loss	0.33	0.37	0.37
	Accuracy	0.25	0.27	0.29
	Precision	0.32	0.32	0.33
	Recall	0.43	0.56	0.63
	F1 score	**0.34**	**0.39**	*0.41*
C4.5 tree	Hamming loss	0.25	0.25	0.24
	Accuracy	0.24	0.23	0.28
	Precision	0.40	0.38	0.44
	Recall	0.32	0.31	0.37
	F1 score	0.33	0.31	*0.37*
k-NN	Hamming loss	0.30	0.30	0.27
	Accuracy	0.21	0.23	0.29
	Precision	0.31	0.33	0.40
	Recall	0.31	0.34	0.41
	F1 score	0.29	0.32	*0.38*

Table 6. Example based evaluation results for 18G task, using RAKEL with different base classifiers.

Base classifier	Measure	Features		
		DCCM	GIST	Classemes
NB	Hamming loss	0.29	0.32	0.35
	Accuracy	0.18	0.21	0.21
	Precision	0.22	0.24	0.23
	Recall	0.41	0.54	0.59
	F1 score	**0.26**	*0.32*	*0.32*
C4.5 tree	Hamming loss	0.18	0.18	0.17
	Accuracy	0.13	0.13	0.17
	Precision	0.25	0.24	0.30
	Recall	0.17	0.17	0.23
	F1 score	0.19	0.18	*0.24*
k-NN	Hamming loss	0.22	0.22	0.21
	Accuracy	0.15	0.16	0.21
	Precision	0.22	0.24	0.30
	Recall	0.22	0.24	0.30
	F1 score	0.21	0.22	*0.28*

The highest F1 scores have again been achieved with NB for both 11G and 18G tasks, Fig. 3. The F1 scores obtained with NB using GIST and Classemes feature sets are better than with DCCM feature set for both tasks. It is not surprising since DCCM has much smaller feature size.

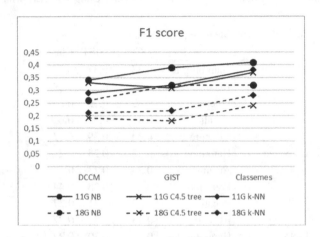

Fig. 3. Example-based average F1 scores of NB, C4.5, and kNN for 11G and 18G tasks.

In fact, every classifier achieved the best results for all evaluation measures when Classemes features were used, Fig. 4. GIST features have performed similarly to Classemes for the F1 score, and only a bit worse than Classemes for other measures, although their dimension is 5 times lower.

For all features, the best F1 score was achieved with NB for both tasks. The NB classifier, that performed the best according to the F1 score, has the highest Hamming loss and the lowest precision, which suggests a larger number of incorrect genre labels are assigned (false positives). On the other hand, the NB classifier has significantly higher recall than other classifiers.

Overall, the best results are obtained using RAKEL with Naive Bayes as a base classifier, with the Classemes features. However, only slightly worse performance of RAKEL with Naive Bayes was observed with GIST features that have much smaller dimensionality. In comparison with published results in [7], for the same classification tasks, we have shown that the introduction of NB as RAKEL base classifier, contributed to the improvement of the classification performance.

The combination of RAKEL and NB has already been proven successful in previous work [9] where RAKEL performed significantly better than other problem transformation methods. A further improvement was achieved by using Classemes features. The use of a more complex model involving C4.5 decision tree and computationally demanding k-NN lazy learning classifier as RAKEL base classifiers provide inferior results and justify the use of combination RAKEL + NB in the multi-label movie genre classification problem.

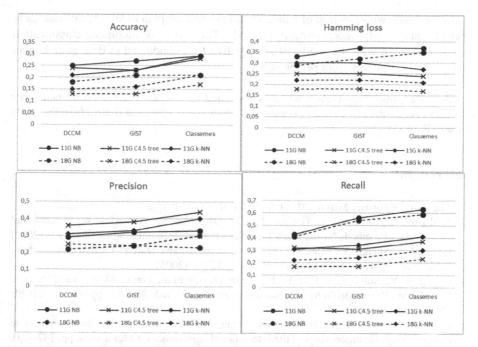

Fig. 4. Example-based average evaluation measures of NB, C4.5 and kNN base classifiers for 11G and 18G tasks.

6 Conclusion and Future Work

In this paper, we present the results of multi-label poster classification into 11 and 18 genres on a dataset containing 6739 movie posters. We have examined the impact of different features extracted from poster images in terms of automatic genre classification. We considered low-level color features comprising dominant colors and color moments, the GIST spatial structure descriptor and classemes classifier-based features.

We have used the RAKEL ensemble method with different single-label classification methods to investigate their influence on the classification performance. The considered classifiers belong to different learning paradigms: NB, a probabilistic generative model, the C4.5 decision tree and the k-NN lazy learning algorithm.

The naive Bayes classifier has shown the best performance in terms of all tested measures except for precision and Hamming loss that is achieved with the C4.5 decision tree, with all features and for both 11 genre and 18 genre tasks. The best results considering the example-based and macro-averaged F1 score were 0.41 and 0.39 for the case of Naive Bayes classifier with classemes for the 11 genres task. For the 18 genre task, the example-based and macro-averaged F1 scores were 0.32 and 0.30 with the same setup.

In our experiments, the Classeme features have shown the best performance overall with most benchmark measures. However, only slightly worse performance was observed with GIST features that have much smaller dimensionality.

In the future work, instead of handcrafted features, we plan to test the automatically learned features using deep learning methods. The results of automatic classification will be compared with the results of a subjective test, conducted to determine human ability to detect genres from poster images.

Acknowledgments. This research was fully supported by Croatian Science Foundation under the project Automatic recognition of actions and activities in multimedia content from the sports domain (RAASS).

References

1. The movie database, March 2014. http://www.themoviedb.org/
2. Madjarov, G., Kocev, D., Gjorgjevikj, D., Džeroski, S.: An extensive experimental comparison of methods for multi-label learning. Pattern Recognit. **45**(9), 3084–3104 (2012)
3. Rasheed, Z., Sheikh, Y., Shah, M.: On the use of computable features for film classification. IEEE Trans. Circ. Syst. Video Technol. **15**(1), 52–64 (2005)
4. Huang, H.-Y., Shih, W.-S., Hsu, W.-H.: A film classifier based on low-level visual features. In: IEEE 9th Workshop on Multimedia Signal Processing, MMSP 2007, pp. 465–468. IEEE (2007)
5. Zhou, H., Hermans, T., Karandikar, A.V., Rehg, J.M.: Movie genre classification via scene categorization. In: Proceedings of the International Conference on Multimedia, pp. 747–750. ACM (2007)
6. Ivašić-Kos, M., Pobar, M., Mikec, L.: Movie posters classification into genres based on low-level features. In: Proceedings of International Conference MIPRO, Opatija (2014)
7. Ivasic-Kos, M., Pobar, M., Ipsic, I.: Automatic movie posters classification into genres. In: Bogdanova, A.M., Gjorgjevikj, D. (eds.) ICT Innovations 2014. AISC, vol. 311, pp. 319–328. Springer, Cham (2015). https://doi.org/10.1007/978-3-319-09879-1_32
8. Fu, Z., Li, B., Li, J., Wei, S.: Fast film genres classification combining poster and synopsis. In: He, X., Gao, X., Zhang, Y., Zhou, Z.-H., Liu, Z.-Y., Fu, B., Hu, F., Zhang, Z. (eds.) IScIDE 2015. LNCS, vol. 9242, pp. 72–81. Springer, Cham (2015). https://doi.org/10.1007/978-3-319-23989-7_8
9. Pobar, M., Ivasic-Kos, M.: Multi-label poster classification into genres using different problem transformation methods. In: Felsberg, M., Heyden, A., Krüger, N. (eds.) CAIP 2017. LNCS, vol. 10425, pp. 367–378. Springer, Cham (2017). https://doi.org/10.1007/978-3-319-64698-5_31
10. Torresani, L., Szummer, M., Fitzgibbon, A.: Efficient object category recognition using classemes. In: Daniilidis, K., Maragos, P., Paragios, N. (eds.) ECCV 2010. LNCS, vol. 6311, pp. 776–789. Springer, Heidelberg (2010). https://doi.org/10.1007/978-3-642-15549-9_56
11. Tsoumakas, G., Vlahavas, I.: Random *k*-labelsets: an ensemble method for multilabel classification. In: Kok, J.N., Koronacki, J., de Mantaras, R.L., Matwin, S., Mladenič, D., Skowron, A. (eds.) ECML 2007. LNCS, vol. 4701, pp. 406–417. Springer, Heidelberg (2007). https://doi.org/10.1007/978-3-540-74958-5_38
12. Zhang, M.-L., Zhou, Z.-H.: A k-nearest neighbor based algorithm for multi-label classification. In: 2005 IEEE International Conference on Granular Computing, vol. 2 (2005)
13. Mitchell, T.M.: Machine Learning. McGraw Hill, Burr Ridge (1997)
14. Tsoumakas, G., Katakis, I.: Multi-label classification: an overview. Int. J. Data Warehoue. Min. **3**(3), 1–13 (2007)

15. Read, J., Pfahringer, B., Holmes, G., Frank, E.: Classifier chains for multi-label classification. Mach. Learn. J. **85**(3), 333–359 (2011). Springer
16. Oliva, A., Torralba, A.: Modeling the shape of the scene: a holistic representation of the spatial envelope. Int. J. Comput. Vis. **42**(3), 145–175 (2001)
17. Shechtman, E., Irani, M.: Matching local self-similarities across images and videos. In: IEEE CVPR 2007, pp. 1–8 (2007)
18. Yang, Y.: An evaluation of statistical approaches to text categorization. Inf. Retrieval **1**(1–2), 69–90 (1999)

Parameter Search for a Small Swarm of AUVs Using Particle Swarm Optimisation

Christoph Tholen[(⊠)] and Lars Nolle

Jade University of Applied Sciences, Wilhelmshaven, Germany
{christoph.tholen,lars.nolle}@jade-hs.de

Abstract. The development of a low cost and intelligent swarm of autonomous underwater vehicles (AUVs) is the long term goal of this research. Such a swarm of AUVs could be used, for example, for locating submarine sources of interest, such as dumped radioactive waste or ammunition. This is a difficult problem for direct search algorithms, because in large areas of the search space, gradient information is not available. The overall search strategy used in the work is based on particle swarm optimisation (PSO). The number of AUVs here is small due to costs and availability. The performance of PSO depends on the right choice of control parameters. Therefore this paper presents an empirical study of the effects of different search parameter settings on the performance of PSO, used with a swarm of three AUVs in a dynamic environment. A simulation of submarine groundwater discharge, based on Cellular Automata, is used as a dynamic test environment. It was shown in this research that PSO in this configuration is robust against control parameter settings.

Keywords: Submarine groundwater discharge · Fluorescent dissolved organic matter · Particle swarm optimisation · Control parameter setting · Cellular automata

1 Introduction

The long-term goal of this research is the development of a flexible and low cost environmental marine observatory. Such an observatory will be based on a swarm of autonomous underwater vehicles (AUVs). AUVs in general are useful for the exploration of intermediate size areas and to locate submarine sources of interest. These could be, for example, dumped waste or ammunition, or environmental parameters, like fluorescent dissolved organic matter (FDOM), salinity or oxygen [1].

The detection of oil or waste using airplanes is one example for the detection of marine hazards with a sensor system [2]. The biggest disadvantage of a sensor system carried by an airplane is, that such a system is only capable of observing the surface of the sea. To examine submarine systems, AUVs could be used instead. Because AUVs have only a limited payload and energy capacity, it is proposed to use a swarm of collaborative AUVs to search larger areas. The number of AUVs is usually small due to costs and availability.

Another possible application for such an observatory is the search for submarine groundwater discharges (SGD) in coastal waters. SGD consist of an inflow of fresh

© Springer International Publishing AG 2017
M. Bramer and M. Petridis (Eds.): SGAI-AI 2017, LNAI 10630, pp. 384–396, 2017.
https://doi.org/10.1007/978-3-319-71078-5_32

groundwater and recirculated seawater from the sea floor into the ocean [3] (Fig. 1). The localisation of SGDs is a technological challenge; however marine scientists are interested in their localisation, because the SGDs discharge continuously nutrients into the coastal environment [4, 5].

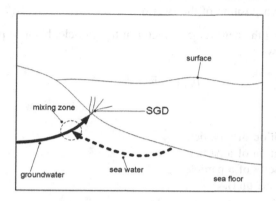

Fig. 1. Submarine groundwater discharge, adapted from [6].

The search of a swarm of collaborating AUVs must be guided by an overall search strategy [7]. In this project particle swarm optimisation (PSO) is used for this task [8].

2 Particle Swarm Optimisation

PSO is modelled on the behaviour of collaborative real world entities (particles), for example fish schools or bird flocks, which work together to achieve a common goal [9, 10]. Each individual of the swarm searches for itself. However, the search behaviour of each individual is also influenced by the other swarm members.

At the beginning of a search, each particle of the swarm starts at a random position and a randomly chosen velocity for each direction of the n-dimensional search space. After initialisation, all particles move through the search space with an adjustable velocity. The velocity of a particle is based on its current fitness value, the best solution found so far by the particle (cognitive knowledge) and the best solution found so far by the whole swarm (social knowledge) (1):

$$\vec{v}_{i+1} = \vec{v}_i \cdot \omega + r_1 \cdot c_1 (\vec{p}_{best} - \vec{p}_i) + r_2 \cdot c_2 (\vec{g}_{best} - \vec{p}_i) \tag{1}$$

Where:

$\vec{v}_{i+1}$: new velocity vector of a particle
$\vec{v}_i$: current velocity vector of a particle
ω: inertia weight
c_1: cognitive scaling factor

c_2: social scaling factor
r_1: random number from range [0,1]
r_2: random number from range [0,1]
$\vec{p}_i$: current position of a particle
$\vec{p}_{best}$: best known position of a particle
$\vec{g}_{best}$: best known position of the swarm.

After calculating the new velocity vector of the particle, his new position $\vec{p}_i$ can be calculated as follows:

$$\vec{p}_{i+1} = \vec{p}_i + \vec{v}_{i+1} \cdot \Delta t \tag{2}$$

Where:

$\vec{p}_{i+1}$: new position of a particle
$\vec{p}_i$: current position of a particle
$\vec{v}_{i+1}$: new velocity of a particle
Δt: time step (one unit).

In (2) Δt, which always has the constant value of one unit, is multiplied to the velocity vector $\vec{v}_{i+1}$ in order to get consistency in the physical units [7].

3   Simulation Based on Cellular Automata

In this research a computer simulation based on a cellular automaton [11] is used, to simulate the distribution of discharged fresh- and recirculating seawater in a coastal environment. To trace the distribution of the discharged water, Fluorescent Dissolved Organic Matter (FDOM) is used. The simulation was developed and tested in recent work [8, 12, 13].

The implemented simulation covers an area of 400 m × 400 m. This area is divided into 160,000 symmetric cells. The edge length of each cell is 1 m. Each cell has an x- and a y-position as well as an FDOM-level. Furthermore, the simulation uses rectangle shaped cells and the von-Neumann neighbourhood [14].

The simulation models the coastal water near the island of Spiekeroog, which is one of the East Frisian Islands, off the North Sea coast of Germany. The dynamic model contains two springs (SGDs) with a constant inflow rate of water and a constant FDOM level. The springs are located at position A = (200 m/200 m) and B = (100 m/300 m) (see Table 1). The parameters of the two springs differ; hence there is a global optimum and a local optimum. Furthermore, the simulation includes an obstacle (sandbank).

Table 1. Parameters of springs.

	Spring A	Spring B
Position	(200 m/200 m)	(100 m/300 m)
Flow rate (m³/iteration)	0.05	0.025
FDOM-level (arbitrary units)	100	50
Comment	Global optimum	Local optimum

The simulation was run for 5000 iterations. Figure 2 shows the distribution of FDOM after different numbers of iterations. As it can be seen, the FDOM distributed symmetrically around the two springs, while the inflow of spring A is significant higher as the inflow of spring B. The FDOM level increases significant only near by the springs, while in the rest of the test environment the FDOM level increase only faintly.

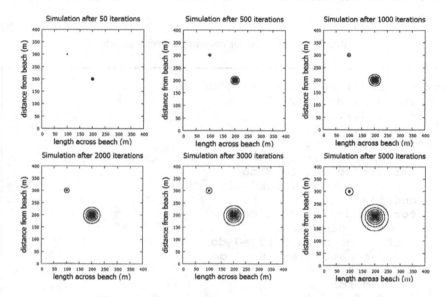

Fig. 2. Dynamic behaviour of the test environment.

The small gradients of FDOM level as well as the dynamic behaviour, makes it a difficult search problem. The simulation is used as a test environment for direct search algorithms. For this research one iteration of the simulation represents a time step of one second.

4 Experiments

In general, the performance of a search algorithm depends heavily on the selection of suitable control parameters. The best parameter setting for a search algorithm depends on the search problem at hand. In this research different strategies of choosing the parameters for a dynamic search problem were tested and compared. Furthermore the performance of the different PSO settings were compared with the performance of an adapted random walk search strategy. The number of particles used here is limited to three, because for this research only three AUVs are available.

4.1 Random Parameter Search

The PSO used in this research has three parameters, ω, c_1 and c_2 (1). The optimal values of this parameters depend on the optimisation problem at hand. In a first step

1000 different parameter settings were chosen randomly. For each of these parameter sets 100 experiments were carried out. Table 2 presents pseudo code for the algorithm used. The parameter values were taken from the range [0.1, 2.1]. This is a common range for the parameter values [15–17]. In addition, 125 experiments were carried out, with all the possible combinations of the parameter values ω, c_1 and $c_2 \in \{0.1, 0.6, 1.1, 1.6, 2.1\}$, for the three control parameters to cover the hole parameter space.

Table 2. Pseudo code for random parameter search.

```
for parameter setting=1 to 1000 do
  omega = rand (0.1,2.1)
  c1=rand(0.1,2.1)
  c1=rand(0.1,2.1)
  for experiment=1 to 100 do
    initialise simulation
    for particle=1 to 3 do
      initialise AUV randomly
    end for
    for round=1 to 5000 do
      update simulation
      if round modulo 10 =0 do
        for particle=1 to 3 do
          move AUV
        end for
      end if
    end for
  end for
end for
```

100 experiments were carried out for each parameter settings and the number of successful searches, i.e. finding the global optimum, were counted. For this research the number of successful searches is defined as fitness.

From Fig. 3 it can be seen that most of the tested parameter settings provide either a poor (fitness between 0 and 10%) or a good (fitness between 60 and 80%) performance, while there are only a few parameter settings that resulted in a fitness between 10–60%.

For the data analysation and visualisation, the factor φ is used in this research, to reduce the number of independent parameters. The factor φ can calculated as follows [18]:

$$\varphi = c_1 + c_2 \tag{3}$$

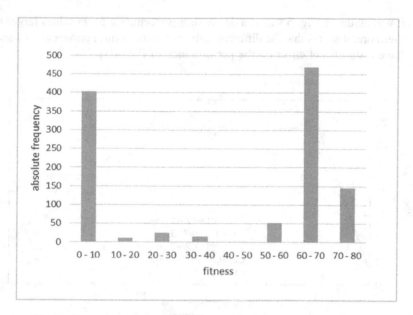

Fig. 3. Frequency of distribution – results of random parameter search.

Figure 4 shows the results of the random parameter search as a three dimensional fitness landscape. It can be observed that the control parameter ω has a much bigger influence on the performance than the control parameters φ. Hence, for parameter sets with ω values lower than one the performance is poor. However, for parameter sets with ω values larger than one the PSO show a good performance.

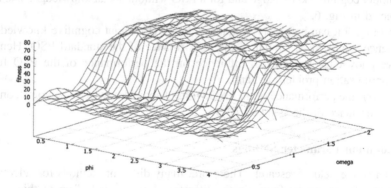

Fig. 4. Fitness landscape as function of φ and ω

From (1) it is presumed that the influence of the cognitive- and the social aspect decrease with higher ω values. If ω increases too much, it might result in a worse performance of the PSO. To review this assumption, more experiments were carried out, using ω values from 0.5 to 60 and constant values for the parameters c_1 and c_2 (Fig. 5).

As it was assumed, Fig. 5 shows a decreasing performance for ω values larger than 10. Furthermore, it seems that the different settings for the control parameters c_1 and c_2 do not have a significant effect on the performance of PSO (Fig. 5).

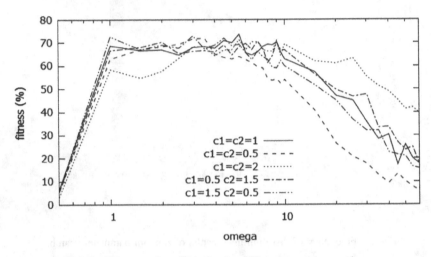

Fig. 5. Fitness as function of ω for different c_1 and c_2 settings.

In addition, it can be observed from Fig. 4 that the performance of PSO is not correlated to the chosen values for c_1 and c_2. In this case, it could be possible to simplify the update rule by removing the cognitive and/or the social knowledge. To test this assumption, more experiments were carried out, using ω values from 0.5 to 60 for a PSO without cognitive knowledge and for a PSO without social knowledge. The results are depicted in Fig. 6.

From Fig. 6 it can be observed that for the PSO without cognitive knowledge the performance seems to be similar to the performance of the standard PSO. Hence the cognitive knowledge has no real influence on the performance of the PSO for this special optimisation problem at hand.

However, the performance of the PSO without social knowledge is worse compared to the performance of the standard PSO.

4.2   Common Parameter Settings

PSO is an active field of research. Therefore, many different methods for selecting the control parameters can be found in the literature [10, 18, 19]. Two of this common settings are used in this research and compared with the results of the random parameter search proposed above.

The first method is known as the Linear Decreasing Inertia Weight setting. For this setting the parameters c_1 and c_2 were set to 1.0 and the value of ω is decreasing linear over the run time as follows [10]:

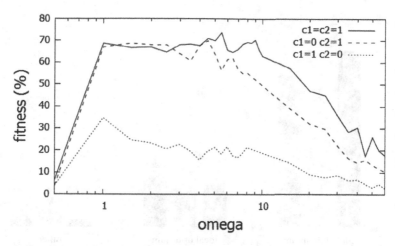

Fig. 6. Fitness as function of ω for a PSO without cognitive knowledge ($c_1 = 0$), for a PSO without social knowledge ($c_2 = 0$) and for a PSO with cognitive and social knowledge ($c_1 = c_2 = 1$)

$$\omega = \omega_{max} \frac{\omega_{max} - \omega_{min}}{n} * i \qquad (4)$$

Where:

ω: inertia weight for the current time step
ω_{max}: start value of inertia weight (10 in this research)
ω_{min}: end value of inertia weight (1 in this research)
n: maximum number of iterations
i: current number of iterations.

The second setting is called the Random Inertia Weight setting. For this setting the parameters c_1 and c_2 were also set to 1.0 and the value of ω is randomly chosen from the range [1.0–10.0] for each iteration [10].

In according to the special search problem the control parameter values differ from the common setting, known from the literature.

For both settings 100 experiments were carried out. As shown in Fig. 7 the performance of the random parameter setting is the best with a success rate of 78% for finding the global optimum. The performance of the other parameter settings is in the same order of magnitude, i.e. in the range of 62–67% for finding the global optimum.

4.3 Adapted Random Walk

To evaluate the performance of methods used above, an adapted random walk was employed in the dynamical test environment. In classical random walk, a new position is chosen randomly from the neighbourhood of the current solution, i.e. the step size is random. However, when using an AUV, different step sizes would lead to acceleration and deceleration. This would consume energy and would reduce the operating time. Ideally, the velocity of an AUV is kept constant and only the heading is changing.

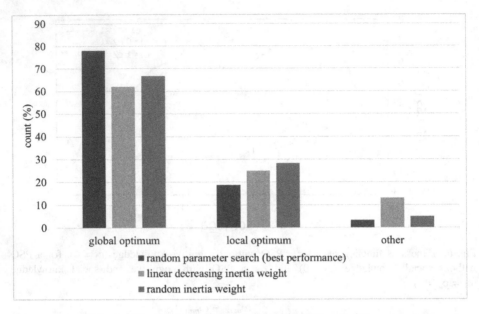

Fig. 7. Clustering of search results for the different settings.

Therefore, in this research an adopted random walk algorithm is introduced. Also, the velocity of an AUV is limited, hence the maximum step size of the particles is limited as well.

In the adopted random walk, the AUVs drive with their maximum speed during the whole search and in each iteration the heading of the AUVs is chosen randomly. With a given heading the velocity in each direction can be calculated as follows:

$$\begin{pmatrix} v_x \\ v_y \end{pmatrix} = v_{max} * \begin{pmatrix} \cos(\alpha) \\ \sin(\alpha) \end{pmatrix} \tag{5}$$

Where:

v_x: speed of the AUV in x-direction
v_y: speed of the AUV in y-direction
v_{max}: maximum possible speed of the AUV
α: current heading of the AUV in degrees (randomly chosen).

100 experiments were carried out for the adapted random walk and the results are compared with the results obtained from PSO.

The convergence speed, i.e. how many iterations the search algorithm needs to find the global optimum, of a search run is another possible indicator for the performance of search algorithms [19]. Figure 8 shows the g_{best} value of the best run for the different parameter settings. In addition, the known maximum value and the best value found so far by the adapted random walk are plotted over time in this figure.

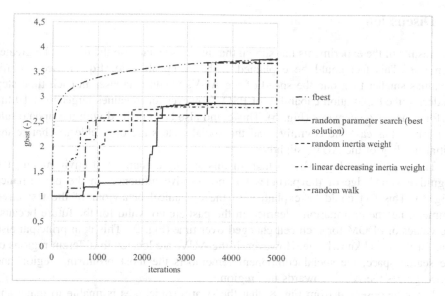

Fig. 8. Best run g_best over iterations for the different parameter settings.

In Fig. 9 the average of the g_{best} values for all 100 experiments is plotted over iterations. The behaviour of the randomly chosen parameters and the common parameter settings seems to be similar. Furthermore, the performances of all the settings are in the same order of magnitude. This results agree with the findings from Fig. 7.

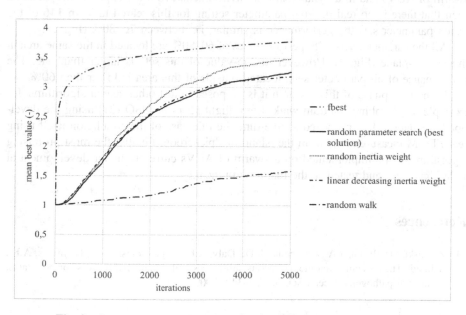

Fig. 9. Average g_best over iterations for the different parameter settings.

5 Discussion

The results of the experiments has shown that in this special case the ω must be greater than one. This fact could be explained with the update rule (Eq. 1); because for ω-values smaller than one the speed of the AUVs would decreases in each time step hindering the exploration capability of PSO. However for ω-values larger than 10 the performance also decreases (Fig. 5). This could also be explained with the update rule (Eq. 1); in this case the cognitive and the social factors are only able to change the initial heading of the AUVs slightly.

The experiments have shown that, in this special dynamic test environment, the cognitive knowledge of the particles has no positive influence on the performance (Fig. 6). This fact could be explain with the dynamical behaviour of the test environment, i.e. the information´s learned in the past are not valid for the future because the values of FDOM for each cell changed over time (Fig. 2). This is in principal also true for the social knowledge. However, if the AUVs are located in different regions of the search space, the social component remembers the most promising region and hence guides the AUVs towards this region.

It can be observed from Fig. 8, that the swarm sometimes is unable to make any improvements for long periods of time. This circumstances might be based on the dynamical behaviour of the test environment.

6 Conclusion and Future Work

The aim of this research was to find optimal parameters for a PSO operating on a small swarm of AUVs and in a dynamical test environment. From the experiments it can be seen that there is no real optimal parameter setting for this search task. In 146 of the tested parameter sets the performance is similar, i.e. between 70–80% (Fig. 3).

All the parameter sets with performances of 60–80% are located in the same area in the $\omega - \varphi$-plane (Fig. 4). However, the ω-value of this sets is larger than one. The performance of all parameter sets, located outside of this area is lower than 60%.

In the next phase of this research it is proposed to test other search algorithms, for example hill climbing, random walk, Lévy flight [20] or APSO [21] using the developed simulation. It is proposed to fine-tune the rule base of the simulation itself using real FDOM measurements from the island of Spiekeroog. Finally, the most promising algorithm will be implemented on a swarm of AUVs currently under development at Jade University and tested in the real environment.

References

1. Zielinski, O., Busch, J.A., Cembella, A.D., Daly, K.L., Engelbrektsson, J., Hannides, A.K., Schmidt, H.: Detecting marine hazardous substances and organisms: sensors for pollutants, toxins and pathogens. Ocean Sci. **5**, 329–349 (2009)

2. Zielinski, O.: Airborne pollution surveillance using multi-sensor systems – new sensors and algorithms for improved oil spill detection and polluter identification. Sea Technol. **44**(10), 28–32 (2003)
3. Moore, W.S.: The effect of submarine groundwater discharge on the ocean. Annu. Rev. Mar. Sci. **2**, 59–88 (2010)
4. Nelson, C.E., Donahue, M.J., Dulaiova, H., Goldberg, S.J., La Valle, F.F., Lubarsky, K., Miyano, J., Richardson, C., Silbiger, N.J., Thomas, F.I.: Fluorescent dissolved organic matter as a multivariate biogeochemical tracer of submarine groundwater discharge in coral reef ecosystems. Mar. Chem. **177**, 232–243 (2015)
5. Beck, M., Reckhardt, A., Amelsberg, J., Bartholomä, A., Brumsack, H.J., Cypionka, H., Dittmar, T., Engelen, B., Greskowiak, J., Hillebrand, H., Holtappels, M., Neuholz, R., Köster, J., Kuypers, M.M.M., Massmann, G., Meier, D., Niggemann, J., Paffrath, R., Pahnke, K., Rovo, S., Striebel, M., Vandieken, V., Wehrmann, A., Zielinski, O.: The drivers of biogeochemistry in beach ecosystems: a crossshore transect from the dunes to the low water line. Mar. Chem. **190**, 35–50 (2017)
6. Evans, T.B., Wilson, A.M.: Groundwater transport and the freshwater–saltwater interface below sandy beaches. J. Hydrol. **538**, 563–573 (2016)
7. Nolle, L.: On a search strategy for collaborating autonomous underwater vehicles. In: Mendel 2015, 21st International Conference on Soft Computing, Brno, CZ, pp. 159–164 (2015)
8. Tholen, C., Nolle, L., Werner, J.: On the influence of localisation and communication error on the behaviour of a swarm of autonomous underwater vehicles. In: Mendel 2017, 23rd International Conference on Soft Computing, Brno, CZ (2017, to appear)
9. Kennedy, J., Eberhart, R.: Particle swarm optimization. In: IEEE International Conference on Neural Networks, vol. 4, pp. 1942–1948 (1995)
10. Bansal, J.C., Singh, P.K., Saraswat, M., Verma, A., Jadon, S.S., Abraham, A.: Inertia weight strategies in particle swarm optimization. In: Third World Congress on Nature and Biologically Inspired Computing, 19–21 October, Salamanca, Spain, pp. 633–640 (2011)
11. Wolfram, S.: Universality and complexity in cellular automata. Physica D: Nonlinear Phenom. **10**(1–2), 1–35 (1984)
12. Tholen, C., Nolle, L., Zielinski, O.: On the effect of neighborhood schemes and cell shape on the behaviour of cellular automata applied to the simulation of submarine groundwater discharge. In: 31th European Conference on Modelling and Simulation, ECMS 2017, pp. 255–261 (2017)
13. Nolle, L., Thormählen, H., Musa, H.: Simulation of submarine groundwater discharge of dissolved organic matter using cellular automata. In: 30st European Conference on Modelling and Simulation, ECMS 2016, pp. 265–269 (2016)
14. Jiménez, A., Posadas, A.M., Marfil, J.M.: A probabilistic seismic hazard model based on cellular automata and information theory. Nonlinear Process. Geophys. **12**(3), 381–396 (2005)
15. Shi, Y., Eberhart, R.: A modified particle swarm optimizer. In: 1998 IEEE International Conference on Evolutionary Computation Proceedings. IEEE World Congress on Computational Intelligence, pp. 69–73 (1998)
16. Faiçal, B.S., Pessin, G., Filho, G.P.R., Carvalho, A.C.P.L.F., Gomes, P.H., Ueyama, J.: Fine-tuning of UAV control rules for spraying pesticides on crop fields: an approach for dynamic environments. Int. J. Artif. Intell. Tools **25**(1), 1660003-1–160003-19 (2016)
17. Družeta, S., Ivić, S.: Examination of benefits of personal fitness improvement dependent inertia for particle swarm optimization. Soft Comput. **21**(12), 3387–3400 (2017)
18. Eberhart, R.C., Shi, Y.: Comparing inertia weights and constriction factors in particle swarm optimization. In: 2000 Congress on Evolutionary Computation, vol. 1, pp. 84–88 (2000)

19. Bratton, D., Kennedy, J.: Defining a standard for particle swarm optimization. In: 2007 IEEE Swarm Intelligence Symposium, pp. 120–127 (2007)
20. Edwards, A.M., Phillips, R.A., Watkins, N.W., Freeman, M.P., Murphy, E.J., Afanasyev, V., Buldyrev, S.V., da Luz, M.G.E., Raposo, E.P., Stanley, H.E., Viswanathan, G.M.: Revisiting levy flight search patterns of wandering albatrosses, bumblebees and deer. Nature **449**, 1044–1049 (2007)
21. Subha, R., Himavathi, S.: Acclerated particle swarm optimization algorithm for maximum power point tracking in partially shaded PV systems. In: 3rd International Conference on Electrical Energy Systems, pp. 232–236 (2016)

Short Application Papers

Deep Learning for Classification of Bi-Lingual Ads in Online Classifieds

Axel Tidemann[✉]

Telenor Research, Trondheim, Norway
axel.tidemann@telenor.com

Abstract. Classification of ads in online classifieds is a domain well suited for applying deep learning for understanding images and text. Since many different items are in the same category, classification based on images alone is hard. Adding the title of the ad increases classification accuracy significantly. This paper describes a system developed for an online classifieds site in Thailand (kaidee.com), where titles are often a mixture of Thai and English. To achieve machine understanding of bi-lingual text, a character-level neural embedding was used. Both 1D convolution and bidirectional long short-term memory (BLSTM) were examined, with convolution being both more accurate and quicker to train. The Inception v3 model was used to extract visual features from images. Visual features and character embeddings are concatenated and fed into a classifier. The results show that this approach is better than classifying based on either image or text alone. A focus of this paper is the simplicity of the solution, yielding an accuracy of 86.0% applied on real-world data.

1 Introduction

Online classifieds is an area where machine understanding of images and text are readily applied. There are primarily two use cases for classifying ads: (1) Customer facing. When a seller is posting an ad, it can be automatically categorized, enhancing the sellers experience of the site/app. (2) Aid the moderation team. All ads need to be approved by a human, and a system that understands ads can make suggestions that speed up the workflow of the moderators.

From a machine learning perspective, ads are a welcoming dataset to work with. Images typically have one object in focus. The title of the ad is a short and concise description. On the other hand, ads in a category might be very different things. Also, the title might contain spelling errors or be a mixture of languages in different alphabets, as is the case in the current domain. This paper describes a system for classifying ads using neural features of images and text, developed for an online classifieds site (kaidee.com) in Thailand.

2 Background

Combining modalities has received increased attention in the literature recently. Audio and video features have been combined to both classify and recreate audio

© Springer International Publishing AG 2017
M. Bramer and M. Petridis (Eds.): SGAI-AI 2017, LNAI 10630, pp. 399–404, 2017.
https://doi.org/10.1007/978-3-319-71078-5_33

and video, by using an autoencoder [8]. The work also investigated how to learn shared representations, e.g. reconstructing audio when given video as input. This was followed by a similar approach [9], where the authors used sparse word count vectors and dense image features instead of audio and video features, employing deep Boltzmann machines.

Combining features from vision, sound and text into a common shared representation, enables both retrieval of similar entities in other domains (e.g. you query the network with an image, and you find related sound and text) as well as classification [1]. The classification rates are not spectacular, but the most interesting result comes from inspecting hidden layer activations, where the authors claim that high-level features have been consolidated across modalities.

This train of thought has been further extended [4], where the authors have different modality networks as well as attention and mixture-of-experts blocks, so the network can perform machine translation as well. What they find is that without much parameter tuning, the network performs surprisingly well, not far from state-of-the-art. After more tuning they expect the network to approach such levels. An interesting find in this paper is that it does not hurt performance to add modules on tasks that normally do not require them, e.g. attention for the ImageNet classification task. However, it is not discussed how much more computational power is required to train such a general model compared to designing specialized modality networks for a given task.

What separates the work presented in this paper from the related work mentioned in this section? It does not deal with content retrieval, nor general-purpose modular architectures. Instead, two tailor-made sub-networks for image and text are combined with a classifier on top, harnessing established practice for understanding images (convolutional neural networks), and evaluating a standard technique for understanding language (BLSTM) versus a novel approach (1-dimensional convolution) to understand bi-lingual text (Thai and English).

3   Materials and Methods

3.1   Data Preparation

The dataset consists of ads in 61 categories. These include cars, motorcycles, hobbies, amulets, apartments, toys, and so on. For each of the categories, 10 000 ads were collected. Ads can have up to 9 images. The first image is selected by the seller to be displayed when browsing and searching, and typically shows the item at its best. Therefore, the first image of an ad is used as input to the system. The size of the images vary, but they are in most cases bigger than the 299×299 size that the Inception model (explained in the following section) automatically scales to. Figure 1 shows some examples of items in different categories.

The text data is a mixture of English, Thai and special characters (including some Chinese and Korean, to a small extent). Thai and English are very different languages. Thai has 44 consonants, 28 vowels and four tone diacritics. Since vowels can be positioned in many configurations based on the following sound, this creates a huge complexity in a Thai corpus compared to English. There are

(a) Food category. Notice how it also includes some kitchen appliances.

(b) Beauty category, containing a variety of different items.

(c) The toy category has items similar to other categories, e.g. cars.

Fig. 1. Examples of variety within a category.

14373 unique characters (more correctly called *graphemes*, but both terms are used interchangeably in this text) in the dataset. The distribution of graphemes is extremely long-tailed. After removing special characters, Latin characters and numbers, 200 graphemes (space included) make up 96.8% of the occurrences in the remaining text corpus. These 200 graphemes plus the characters in the Latin alphabet are one-hot encoded, and used as input to the text embedding layer. The 50 first characters of the title is used; the average length was 24.5 with a standard deviation of 18.6. If shorter than 50, the title is zero-padded.

The data was split into a training set (80%), a validation set to tune the hyperparameters (10%) and the reported accuracy is based on the test set (10%).

3.2 Architecture

The architecture consists of two sub-networks for image and text, see Fig. 2a. The approach of having separate modalities in specific subnetworks is similar to [1,4,8,9]. Deep visual features are extracted from images using the Inception v3 model [10]. A trained instance on ImageNet data is available online[1], which is used in this work. Instead of using the final softmax layer, the layer beneath is used, which contains 2048 non-negative real numbers. The Inception sub-network is fixed throughout the experiments (i.e. not trained further) for two reasons: (1) the ImageNet dataset contains most of the different items encountered for an online classifieds site, (2) fixing the network allows for rapid experimentation, since the deep visual features can be stored in a pre-processing stage.

Since the ad titles are either Thai, English or a mixture of both, it would be beneficial to have a system that can read both languages interchangeably. This is achieved by learning character-level neural embeddings from the data. Two approaches are evaluated: bidirectional LSTM [3] and convolution [6]. Figure 2b shows how the convolution of the text is performed. The neural text embeddings

---

[1] github.com/tensorflow/models/tree/master/inception.

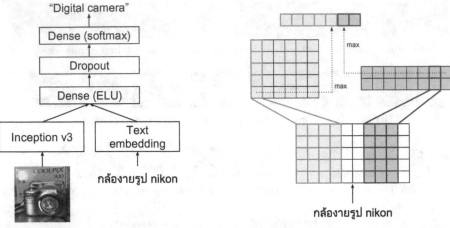

(a) System architecture.   (b) Text embedding using convolution.

Fig. 2. (a) System architecture. When classifying an ad, the image is processed by the Inception v3 framework, reading out the next-to-last layer. The title serves as input to the character-level neural embedding layer, which is either convolution (see (b)) or BLSTM. (b) 1D convolution of characters [6]. The input text is one-hot encoded. Note: on the figure, a simpler 5×10 matrix one-hot encoding is shown, the matrix is actually of size 227×50. The figure shows five filters of width four (orange, to the left), and two filters of width three (red, to the right). The max value is taken for each filter, and is concatenated to form the neural embedding. (Color figure online)

are concatenated with the deep visual features, and used as input to the classifier. The classifier consists of a fully connected (i.e. dense) layer with exponential linear unit activations (ELU) [2]. The ELU has characteristics that alleviate the problem with vanishing gradients, and in addition push the average activation towards zero mean. This removes the need for batch normalization. The activations are fed into a dropout layer, before used as input to another dense softmax layer for classification. The architecture was implemented in Keras.

3.3   Parameter Values

Table 1 describes parameter values. All networks are trained with batch size 1024. Batch sizes in the range [32, 64, 128, 256, 512, 1024] were examined. It has been reported that small batch sizes lead to increased accuracy [5], however this was not observed for the current experiments. This might be due to the fact that each category is quite heterogenous (see Fig. 1), giving large batches the advantage of averaging over the differences. However, this is not examined further. For the hidden layer of the classifier, sizes in the range [64, 128, 256, 512, 1024, 2048] were examined, with 128 turning out to have the best performance.

The parameters for the convolution of text are taken from [6]; filter widths w and number of filters h give an embedding length of 525. f describes the

Table 1. Various parameter settings. See text for details.

ADAM optimizer		CNN		Classifier	
α	0.001	w	$[1, 2, 3, 4, 5, 6]$	n	128
β_1	0.9	h	$[25 \cdot w]$	ELU α	1.0
β_2	0.999	f	tanh	dropout	50%
ϵ	10^{-8}	**BLSTM**		**Other**	
		n	512	batch size	1024
		dropout	50%	epochs	10

activation function of the filters. Due to the convolution embedding length, the number of BLSTM units is $n = 512$. This gives the two text embeddings roughly the same size, for comparison. Dropout rates of 50% are used for the recurrent connections in the BLSTM and the dropout layer. The parameters for the ADAM classifier are those reported as default values in [7]. The α parameter of the ELU is the suggested value in [2]. The system is trained for 10 epochs.

4   Results and Discussion

The fusion of modalities was benchmarked against classifying with either images or text. The results show that combining visual features and character-level neural embedding increases the precision of the classifier, see Table 2. Each configuration was trained and tested 10 times, with random splits for training, testing and validation sets for each iteration. The average testing accuracy for each configuration is shown. For all experiments, the standard deviation was less than 0.005%, and is therefore omitted for legibility.

Table 2. The mean testing accuracy, average of 10. Best result shown in bold.

Modality	Image	Text		Image + text	
Text embedding	N/A	BLSTM	CNN	BLSTM	CNN
Accuracy	66.9%	77.5%	81.5%	83.3%	**86.0%**

An interesting aspect is that the classifier based on just text convolution alone yields very good performance (81.5%). The addition of visual features improves accuracy with 4.5%. Not only does the convolution text embedding yield better performance, it is also the fastest to train - 10 experiments take 140 min on an NVIDIA K40m GPU. Doing the same with BLSTM takes 391 min, almost three times longer.

How is this work different from that of [1,4]? First of all is the simplicity of the solution, where transfer learning and text convolution yield good performance, speeding up training. By fusing modalities, the classifier works better than using either image or text. Secondly, since text is understood on character level, the system is readily applied to any kind of language(s), without having the need to use language-specific word embeddings.

This paper presents a system that facilitates machine understanding of both images and text that is easy to implement, and that provides good accuracy on real-world data. Its application to other domains should be straightforward, since it works on low-level image and text data.

Acknowledgements. The author wishes to thank Cyril Banino-Rokkones for insights and discussions, and Mark Hollow (CTO Kaidee) and his team for data and compute.

References

1. Aytar, Y., Vondrick, C., Torralba, A.: See, hear, and read: deep aligned representations. arXiv (2017)
2. Clevert, D.A., Unterthiner, T., Hochreiter, S.: Fast and accurate deep network learning by exponential linear units (ELUs). arXiv preprint arXiv:1511.07289 (2015)
3. Graves, A., Schmidhuber, J.: Framewise phoneme classification with bidirectional LSTM and other neural network architectures. Neural Netw. **18**(5), 602–610 (2005)
4. Kaiser, L., Gomez, A.N., Shazeer, N., Vaswani, A., Parmar, N., Jones, L., Uszkoreit, J.: One model to learn them all. arXiv (2017)
5. Keskar, N.S., Mudigere, D., Nocedal, J., Smelyanskiy, M., Tang, P.T.P.: On large-batch training for deep learning: generalization gap and sharp minima. arXiv preprint arXiv:1609.04836 (2016)
6. Kim, Y., Jernite, Y., Sontag, D., Rush, A.M.: Character-aware neural language models. In: 30th AAAI Conference on Artificial Intelligence (2016)
7. Kingma, D., Ba, J.: Adam: a method for stochastic optimization. arXiv preprint arXiv:1412.6980 (2014)
8. Ngiam, J., Khosla, A., Kim, M., Nam, J., Lee, H., Ng, A.Y.: Multimodal deep learning. In: Proceedings of 28th International Conference on Machine Learning (ICML-2011), pp. 689–696 (2011)
9. Srivastava, N., Salakhutdinov, R.R.: Multimodal learning with deep Boltzmann machines. In: Advances in Neural Information Processing Systems, pp. 2222–2230 (2012)
10. Szegedy, C., Vanhoucke, V., Ioffe, S., Shlens, J., Wojna, Z.: Rethinking the inception architecture for computer vision. In: Proceedings of IEEE Conference on Computer Vision and Pattern Recognition, pp. 2818–2826 (2016)

Enhancing Symmetry in GAN Generated Fashion Images

Vishnu Makkapati[1]([✉]) and Arun Patro[2]

[1] Myntra Designs Pvt. Ltd., Bengaluru 560068, India
vishnu.makkapati@myntra.com
[2] Department of Electrical Engineering, Indian Institute of Technology Kharagpur,
Kharagpur 721302, India
arun.patro@ee.iitkgp.ernet.in

Abstract. Generative adversarial networks (GANs) are being used in several fields to produce new images that are similar to those in the input set. We train a GAN to generate images of articles pertaining to fashion that have inherent horizontal symmetry in most cases. Variants of GAN proposed so far do not exploit symmetry and hence may or may not produce fashion designs that are realistic. We propose two methods to exploit symmetry, leading to better designs - (a) Introduce a new loss to check if the flipped version of the generated image is equivalently classified by the discriminator (b) Invert the flipped version of the generated image to reconstruct an image with minimal distortions. We present experimental results to show that imposing the new symmetry loss produces better looking images and also reduces the training time.

Keywords: Generative Adversarial Networks · Deep learning · Symmetry loss · Generator · Discriminator

1 Introduction

Generative Adversarial Networks (GANs) [3] are generative models that learn the distribution of the data without any supervision. They can be used to generate data (images or text) that are similar to the original dataset which look real enough to be indistinguishable by a human. GANs use adversarial learning that puts two networks, a Generator network and a Discriminator network in competition to learn the distribution of the input dataset. A generator tries to produce data that can fool the discriminator wheres the discriminator tries to identify them correctly as fake. The convergence of a GAN is highly empirical and is decided when the generator and discriminator losses are stable and the decision boundary is equi-probable.

We attempt to train a GAN to generate new fashion designs. The idea here is to learn the distribution of the input designs and produce new ones that are inspired by them. Most of the fashion article types such as t-shirts, shirts, jeans

---

This work was performed when A. Patro was an intern with Myntra Designs Pvt. Ltd.

© Springer International Publishing AG 2017
M. Bramer and M. Petridis (Eds.): SGAI-AI 2017, LNAI 10630, pp. 405–410, 2017.
https://doi.org/10.1007/978-3-319-71078-5_34

and trousers are symmetric. Hence it is expected that the GAN learns the inherent symmetry in the input data used for training. However, we noticed that DCGAN [6], a widely used implementation of GAN using conv-nets does not necessarily produce symmetric images. Also we observed that there are distortions in the images generated using it. But the location of the distortions is not symmetric. We propose some enhancements to DCGAN to get rid of undesirable artifacts in the synthesized images.

We propose a trick to reduce the distortions in the generated images by exploiting symmetry. There are some recent attempts to invert the Generator in GAN [1,2,5]. These methods try to estimate the latent vector used to produce the generated image such that the reconstructed image is very close to the original. We reconstruct an image with minimal distortions by estimating the latent vector from the flipped version of the generated image.

2   Proposed Methods

We exploit the inherent symmetry in fashion designs to train the GAN. To satisfy the symmetry condition, the horizontally flipped image of the generated image should look similar to the original. But it's not necessary that it is exactly same at a pixel level owing to certain design elements that are typically placed only on one side of the article (e.g., pocket/crest of a t-shirt). We exploit symmetry in the images to produce aesthetically better looking designs and reduce distortions in the generated images. Our contributions are summarized in this section.

2.1   Enhancements to DCGAN to Generate Symmetric Images

We impose a new symmetry loss where the flipped version of a generated image is discriminated equivalently by the discriminator. We realize it using DCGAN, a popular implementation of a GAN. Training the traditional DCGAN consists of minimizing three losses (Fig. 1):

1. *d_loss_real:* error in identifying input training images as real
2. *d_loss_fake:* error in identifying GAN generated images as fake
3. *g_loss_orig:* error in identifying GAN generated images as real

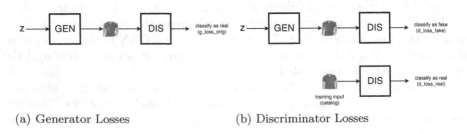

(a) Generator Losses   (b) Discriminator Losses

Fig. 1. Framework of DCGAN

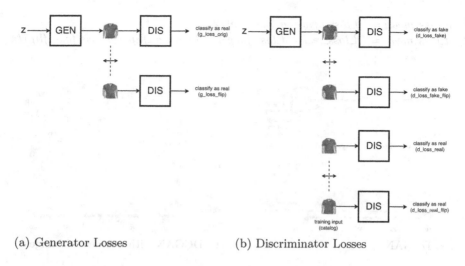

(a) Generator Losses   (b) Discriminator Losses

Fig. 2. Framework of proposed GAN

We trained a DCGAN and conducted experiments to check if it has learnt the symmetry of the images in the dataset. We flipped the generated images horizontally and passed them through the discriminator. If the distribution of the flipped images was also learnt, then the losses for the generated images and their flipped versions should be approximately equal. But we noticed that the losses for the flipped images are significantly higher (Fig. 3a). This proves that DCGAN has not learnt the inherent symmetry in the fashion designs.

We enhance DCGAN to learn symmetry in the input data by:

1. **Augmentation:** Training the GAN by augmenting the input images with their flipped versions.
2. **Classification Loss:** Introducing a new loss to check if the flipped version of the GAN generated image is equivalently classified by the discriminator (Fig. 2).

If the flipped augmented images are also used for training, the DCGAN should learn the distribution of them as well. But our experiments showed that it was not able to learn it (Fig. 3b). It can be seen that the generator loss for the flipped images is quite high though the discriminator learns well. We impose a symmetry loss and thus our GAN consists of evaluating six losses (Fig. 2):

1. *d_loss_real:* error in identifying input images as real
2. *d_loss_fake:* error in identifying GAN generated images as fake
3. *g_loss_orig:* error in identifying GAN generated images as real
4. *d_loss_real_flip:* error in identifying flipped input images as real
5. *d_loss_fake_flip:* error in identifying flipped GAN generated images as fake
6. *g_loss_flip:* error in identifying flipped GAN generated images as real

wherein the final losses that are minimized are:

1. $g\_loss\_mean = (g\_loss\_orig + g\_loss\_flip)/2$
2. $d\_loss\_mean = (d\_loss\_real + d\_loss\_fake + d\_loss\_real\_flip + d\_loss\_fake\_flip)/4.$

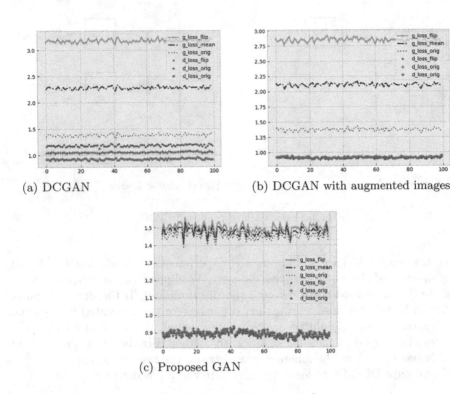

(a) DCGAN   (b) DCGAN with augmented images

(c) Proposed GAN

Fig. 3. Mean losses per epoch

We aid the discriminator by running the flipped images through it. Since the losses for the flipped images are used to train the discriminator, it will become better at identifying both the generated image and it's flipped version as fake. It can be found from Fig. 3c that the losses for the flipped images are just marginally higher than that for the original generated images. This proves that the generator trained using our method is able to produce images that are near symmetric.

2.2   Minimize the Distortions in Generated Images

When we visually observed the images produced by the generator, we found that they suffered from distortions (Fig. 4a). But the location of these distortions is asymmetric. We present a trick using symmetry to minimize them. We flip the generated images (Fig. 4b) and estimate the latent vector from which they are generated [1,5]. We run the estimated latent vector through the generator and reconstruct them (Fig. 4c).

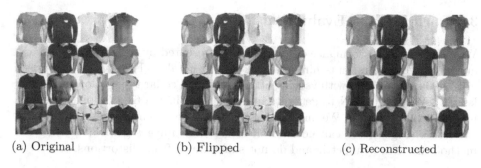

(a) Original   (b) Flipped   (c) Reconstructed

Fig. 4. Reconstruction of flipped images from GAN

We know that nearby latent vectors have close representations in the image space. Using this property, we try to reconstruct the generated images (X). An L2 loss between the generated image and its reconstructed version is minimized by using a regularizer on the magnitude of latent vector z [1].

$$L_{\text{recon}} = ||G(\hat{z}) - X||^2 + \lambda||\hat{z}||^2 \qquad (1)$$

We can notice from Fig. 4c that the distortions present in Fig. 4b are minimized. One possible explanation for this result is that the location of the distortion in the flipped image is different (flipped) from that produced by the generator. The generator, in general, does not produce the distortion at the same location as that in the flipped image. Hence in the process of estimating the latent vector and reconstructing the flipped image from it, the distortions are reduced.

For example the images in (Row 2, Column 3) and (Row 4, Column 1) have hands occluding the t-shirt (Fig. 4b). The corresponding images in Fig. 4c do not suffer from these artifacts. This is also true for the other asymmetric distortions in the rest of the images.

Fig. 5. Samples from proposed GAN at epoch 100

3 Performance Evaluation

We evaluate the performance of the methods presented by training DCGAN and our proposed variant on t-shirt images from our catalog. The dataset comprised of 45,000 solid t-shirts with varying attributes (e.g., collar type, color, and sleeve length). We train GAN to generate images of resolution 64×64 pixels using a modified version of [4]. We quantitatively assess the two methods by comparing the losses (Fig. 3). We can notice from Fig. 5 that images generated using our method are near symmetric and do not suffer much from distortions.

4 Conclusion

We introduce a symmetry loss to train GAN to produce better looking images. We evaluated the performance of the scheme and demonstrated that the proposed method converges faster. We also present a trick to reduce the distortions in the generated images by inverting the flipped versions of them. The visual results show that the reconstructed images do not suffer from artifacts that are generally produced by GAN.

References

1. Bora, A., Jalal, A., Price, E., Dimakis, A.G.: Compressed sensing using generative models. arXiv preprint arXiv:1703.03208 (2017)
2. Creswell, A., Bharath, A.A.: Inverting the generator of a generative adversarial network. arXiv preprint arXiv:1611.05644 (2016)
3. Goodfellow, I., Pouget-Abadie, J., Mirza, M., Xu, B., Warde-Farley, D., Ozair, S., Courville, A., Bengio, Y.: Generative adversarial nets. In: Advances in Neural Information Processing Systems, pp. 2672–2680 (2014)
4. Kim, T.: A tensorflow implementation of deep convolutional generative adversarial networks. https://github.com/carpedm20/DCGAN-tensorflow
5. Lipton, Z.C., Tripathi, S.: Precise recovery of latent vectors from generative adversarial networks. arXiv preprint arXiv:1702.04782 (2017)
6. Radford, A., Metz, L., Chintala, S.: Unsupervised representation learning with deep convolutional generative adversarial networks. arXiv preprint arXiv:1511.06434 (2015)

Predicting Service Levels Using Neural Networks

Russell Ainslie[1]([✉]) [iD], John McCall[1] [iD], Sid Shakya[2],
and Gilbert Owusu[3]

[1] Robert Gordon University, Aberdeen, UK
russell.ainslie@bt.com
[2] EBTIC, Khalifa University, Abu Dhabi, UAE
[3] British Telecom, Ipswich, UK

Abstract. In this paper we present a method to predict service levels in utility companies, giving them advanced visibility of expected service outcomes and helping them to ensure adherence to service level agreements made to their clients. Service level adherence is one of the key targets during the service chain planning process in service industries, such as telecoms or utility companies. These specify a time limit for successful completion of a certain percentage of tasks on that service level agreement. With the increasing use of automation within the planning process, the requirement for a method to evaluate the current plan decisions effects on service level outcomes has surfaced.

We build neural network models to predict using the current state of the capacity plan, investigating the accuracy when predicting both daily and weekly service level outcomes. It is shown that the models produce a high accuracy, particularly in the weekly view. This provides a solution that can be used to both improve the current planning process and also as an evaluator in an automated planning process.

Keywords: Neural network · NN · Prediction · Service levels · Early stopping strategy · Planning

1 Introduction

A key target during the service chain planning process [1] in service industries, such as telecoms or utility companies, is ensuring adherence to service level agreements [2]. These specify a time limit for successful completion of a certain percentage of tasks on that service level agreement. With the increasing use of automation within the planning process [3], the requirement for a method to evaluate the current planning decisions effect on service level outcomes has surfaced. Further to that, with the criticality of service levels to the company's performance, improvements to current techniques are also paramount.

For this purpose we present a neural network (NN) [4–6] model to predict the upcoming service levels based on the current status of the plan and investigate the accuracy this model achieves using some anonymized real world data. The model predicts the service levels daily, but does so in such a way that aggregate predictions can

© Springer International Publishing AG 2017
M. Bramer and M. Petridis (Eds.): SGAI-AI 2017, LNAI 10630, pp. 411–416, 2017.
https://doi.org/10.1007/978-3-319-71078-5_35

also be produced allowing a weekly prediction to assist the current planning process. As such the actual volume of tasks successfully completed are predicted and then used to calculate the service level percent, rather than predicting the percentage directly.

In this paper we first define this service level prediction problem in Sect. 2, describing the general problem and introduce our specific real world example. We then outline our NN model we used to solve the problem in Sect. 3. Section 4 contains the results achieved by this solution, looking at both the daily accuracy and the aggregated weekly prediction accuracy, before we conclude in Sect. 5.

2   The Service Level Prediction Problem

2.1   General Problem Definition

The service level prediction problem is that of accurately predicting the percentage of tasks, R_i, by service level agreement, i, which will be successfully completed on time given the current state of the plan. The time allowed varies depending on which service level agreement the task in question is covered by.

The current state of the plan is defined by the current planned completions, C_j by skill, j, the start of day workstack levels, S_j, by skill, j, the intakes I_j (the number of new tasks entering the plan) by skill, j, and the available capacity, V_k, by resource types, k.

$$R_i = f_i(C, S, I, V) \tag{1}$$

Here C, S, I and V define the input set of all completions, workstacks, intakes and capacities respectively, f_i is the function of these inputs to produce the service level of service level agreement i.

In addition, given that service level agreements are a commitment to complete tasks of that type successfully within a certain time frame, historic values of the inputs also need to be considered. For example, if the service level agreement for a particular task is to complete a certain number successfully within two days then the intake from two days ago would contain some tasks that required completion by today. We further define C_{jt} as the planned completions by skill j t days before the prediction date, similarly for S_{jt} and I_{jt} as the workstack and intake for skill j t days prior respectively and V_{kt} as the capacity for resource type k t days prior. For example the input C_{j2} would be the planned completion for skill j two days before the prediction date. Defining T as the maximum number of days and the sets C_T, S_T, I_T and V_T as the sets of all completions, workstacks, intakes and capacities respectively, where $0 \leq t \leq T$ gives the updated problem definition.

$$R_i = f_i(C_T, S_T, I_T, V_T) \tag{2}$$

2.2   Problem Example

The data used in this paper consisted of 203 data points, each data point representing a day. For each data point (or day) there was the plan state (C, S, I, V) and resulting service levels, R_i, for 56 separate areas. The plan state included the capacity levels for 3 resource types and the completions, intakes and workstacks for 6 skills giving 21 input values for each plan day. The service levels were for tasks on two different service level agreements.

To allow the outputs to be aggregated (e.g. to produce a weekly service level report or an aggregated value for multiple areas) then the number of tasks successfully completed, Y_i, and the number failed, F_i, require predicting separately for each service level i. This way they can be summed to calculate the percentage of tasks successfully completed at any reporting level required. The resulting service level for any aggregated level being calculated using the total success and failure predictions of the individual predictions as follows.

$$R_i = {Y_i}/{Y_i + F_i} \tag{3}$$

Here Y_i and F_i are still a function of the current plan state for the prediction date and the plan state for the past 4 days (chosen after correlation analysis) giving similar equations to 2.

$$Y_i = g_i(C_4, S_4, I_4, V_4) \tag{4}$$

$$F_i = h_i(C_4, S_4, I_4, V_4) \tag{5}$$

3   Neural Network Solution Method

3.1   Model Construction

A feedforward multi-layered perceptron [7] neural network was chosen as they are widely used for forecasting [8]. A single hidden layer, containing 12 nodes, was used to predict each of the outputs, Yi and Fi, individually, giving a single output node. The number of input nodes varied for each output as we dynamically selected the inputs to use from the plan state sets of C4, S4, I4 and V4. Each layer used the sigmoid activation function [9]. The network was implemented using the Encog [10] library in Java.

With such a large number of inputs there is a risk of noise impacting the accuracy of the trained models. As such we also employed a dynamic filtering technique previously used in [11] to use each input's non-linear correlation with the output that the current model is being built for to select which inputs to use. Some initial quick tests showed that choosing a value of 0.5 proved to be a good cutoff point. Thus, during the construction of the model to predict each output in each area only inputs with a correlation value of 0.5 or greater were used.

3.2   Training

The models were trained using the resilient backpropagation algorithm [12] with 25 random restarts. The training data was split into two sets, the training set and the validation set. The models being trained using the training set and having their final accuracies evaluated on the validation set.

Further, to avoid overfitting, the early stopping strategy [13] was used. In the early stopping strategy, after each training iteration, the current accuracy of the model is tested using the validation set. Once the accuracy on the validation set stops improving and starts to decrease then overfitting has started to occur so the training process is halted.

4 Results

4.1 Experimental Method

For each area we split the data into 178 training points and 21 for testing. This data was further clustered by day of the week giving 25 to 26 training points and 3 testing points per cluster. For the training process the training portion was split further, removing 5 points for validation leaving 20–21 points for training.

We then used this data to create and train a model for each of the 4 outputs (Y_1, Y_2, F_1 and F_2) for each of the 56 areas for each day of the week. Each model was trained using the training data points and then tested on the test data. The accuracies of the predictions against the testing data are presented for each experiment.

4.2 Daily Prediction Results

Table 1 shows the accuracy of the daily predictions grouped by day of the week. For example the Monday entry shows the average accuracies for predictions made using the Monday models created for each of the 56 areas. The accuracy is shown for the success prediction model, Y_i, and failure prediction model, F_i, for both of the service levels i, along with a column showing the resulting accuracy when the models are combined to give the service level prediction R_i.

The accuracy for the individual models (success or failure) are fairly low, being about 52.4% accurate on average for the two service levels at predicting failures. Failures are low volume however so this is to be expected.

Table 1. Average accuracy of predictions using early stopping strategy over all areas by day.

Day of week	Service level 1			Service level 2		
	Y_1 (%)	F_1 (%)	R_1 (%)	Y_2 (%)	F_2 (%)	R_2 (%)
Sat	80.3	56.4	89.7	87.1	59.4	92.9
Sun	61.0	4.2	86.1	52.3	−4.0	63.8
Mon	86.2	55.0	93.9	87.8	67.3	93.8
Tue	84.6	58.7	95.3	74.6	48.4	83.2
Wed	87.8	62.8	95.9	86.7	64.5	93.2
Thu	87.6	61.8	93.0	85.9	63.3	93.3
Fri	89.0	66.1	95.0	88.8	70.0	93.0
Average	**82.4**	**52.2**	**92.7**	**80.5**	**52.7**	**87.6**

This changes when we combine the success and failure model outputs to generate predictions of the resulting service level, R_i. The average accuracy across all days and both service levels in this case is about 90.2% even when including the lower accuracy produced by the reduced volumes on a Sunday. Considering the goal of the problem is to predict the service level this is a much better evaluator and as such we can see this model is useable in practice.

4.3 Weekly Prediction Results

To further evaluate the usefulness of this model to the current planning procedures, whereby senior planners take a weekly view of each areas workstacks to decide where might need additional resourcing, we also analyzed the accuracy of the predictions when aggregated to the weekly level. The success and failure models were summed for each of the three weeks and used to calculate the resulting service level for that week. We then counted the number of times the error was less than a certain percentage in each area and also calculated the average accuracy across all 56 areas for each week. Table 2 shows the weekly results achieved. The weekly level prediction showing an expected improvement over the daily accuracy, producing an average of 96.7% across all areas across all weeks. We can also see that around 78.6% of the time the error of the prediction in an individual area is less than 5% increasing to 92.9% when extending the range to 8%. This shows decisions can be taken using this model with reasonable certainty, particularly as some of the higher error values are caused by areas with lower volumes, something the senior planner would have knowledge of.

Table 2. Weekly accuracy across all areas using early stopping strategy.

Week	Service level 1				Service level 2			
	<8%	<5%	<2%	Avg Acc	<8%	<5%	<2%	Avg Acc
1	56	49	26	97.4%	46	41	22	96.4%
2	54	49	23	97.2%	52	42	21	96.4%
3	52	44	24	96.8%	52	39	18	96.3%

5 Conclusion

In this paper we identified the requirement for a service level predictor to assist the evaluation of plan solutions generated by automated planning methods as well as the opportunity to improve the current planning process. We defined this service level prediction problem, stating the general problem in Eq. 2 and introducing a specific real world example. Initial analysis of the data showed the requirement to include 4 days plan states as part of the inputs and we further split the problem into predicting the success (Eq. 4) and failure (Eq. 5) separately to allow their combination to produce a service level prediction at any level of aggregation. We then described the neural network model we used to solve these problems, including a method to dynamically filter the larger number of inputs created by the addition of the past plan states. The resulting model was then evaluated on the real world data, where we showed that we were producing good daily accuracy to give a reasonable evaluation of plan solutions as well as give current planners indication of days where problems are occurring. In addition we showed that the accuracy at the weekly level, where it would be used within the current planning process, was very good providing a good tool to assist decisions relating to release of additional resources to specific areas. With the current planners problem solved the next step is now to utilize this solution to evaluate solutions in an automated planning application. Additional work could also be followed in investigating other solution techniques, such as developing the model using support vector machines [14].

References

1. Voudouris, C.: Defining and understanding service chain management. In: Voudouris, C., Lesaint, D., Owusu, G. (eds.) Service Chain Management, pp. 1–17. Springer, Heidelberg (2008). https://doi.org/10.1007/978-3-540-75504-3_1
2. Verma, D.: Service level agreements on IP networks. Proc. IEEE **92**(9), 1382–1388 (2004)
3. Owusu, G., O'Brien, P., McCall, J., Doherty, N.F.: Transforming Field and Service Operations. Springer, Heidelberg (2013). https://doi.org/10.1007/978-3-642-44970-3_2
4. Anderson, J.: An Introduction to Neural Networks. MIT Press, Cambridge (1995)
5. Haga, M., Demuth, H., Beale, M., De Jesús, O.: Neural Network Design, vol. 20. PWS Publishing Company, Boston (1996)
6. Kourentzes, N., Crone, S.: Advances in forecasting with artificial neural networks. Lancaster University (2010)
7. Gardner, M.W., Dorling, S.R.: Artificial neural networks (the multilayer perceptron)—a review of applications in the atmospheric sciences. Atmos. Environ. **32**(14), 2627–2636 (1998)
8. Zhang, G., Eddy Patuwo, B., Hu, M.Y.: Forecasting with artificial neural networks: the state of the art. Int. J. Forecast. **14**(1), 35–62 (1998)
9. Sibi, P., Jones, S., Siddarth, P.: Analysis of different activation functions using back propagation neural networks. J. Theor. Appl. Inf. Technol. **47**(3), 1264–1268 (2013)
10. Heaton, J.: Encog: library of interchangeable machine learning models for Java and C#. J. Mach. Learn. Res. **16**, 1243–1247 (2015)
11. Ainslie, R., McCall, J., Shakya, S., Owusu, G.: Predictive planning with neural networks. In: Proceedings of the International Joint Conference on Neural Networks (2016). https://doi.org/10.1109/IJCNN.2016.7727460
12. Kisi, Ö., Uncuoglu, E.: Comparison of three back-propagation training algorithms for two case studies. Indian J. Eng. Mater. Sci. **12**(5), 434–442 (2005)
13. Prechelt, L.: PROBEN1 – a set of neural network benchmark problems and benchmarking rules, Karlsruhe (1994)
14. Tian, Y., Shi, Y., Liu, X.: Recent advances on support vector machines research. Technol. Econ. Devel. Econ. **18**, 5–33 (2012)

Using Machine Learning for Dynamic Multicast Capacity Planning

Vidhyalakshmi Karthikeyan[1], Detlef D. Nauck[1(✉)], and Miguel Rio[2]

[1] BT Research and Innovation, Ipswich, UK
{vidhylakshmi.karthikeyan,detlef.nauck}@bt.com
[2] University College London, London, UK
miguel.rio@ucl.ac.uk

Abstract. We are using service consumption data from BT's UK–wide IPTV service to identify main drivers of network capacity and to predict changes on the level of exchanges. We have used a decision tree to identify main drivers and find that provisioning data is sufficient to identify capacity requirements for cable links to exchanges. We have used cluster analysis to identify changes in service consumption and to construct an early warning system for potential capacity bottlenecks.

Keywords: IPTV · Network capacity · Decision tree · Cluster analysis

1 Introduction

We describe a method of using machine learning to assist IPTV service providers in planning cable link capacities. We use data from BT's IPTV service that uses multicast to deliver linear TV (MLTV) via broadband. Some channels are delivered by dynamic multicast meaning that there is only ever one copy of each TV stream being transmitted and only if at least one customer connected to that exchange is watching that channel. To save more bandwidth channels are also encoded with a variable bitrate (VBR). Cable links to an exchange have to provide sufficient capacity to meet the peak demand of concurrent TV channels being watched otherwise customers could experience denial of service when switching channels.

Planning the network capacity for an IPTV service—especially on the level of cable links to exchanges— is challenging and requires data about service consumption. In the literature we can find studies about general capacity planning considerations mainly focussing on server capacity [1] and studies on channel availability when switching or *surfing* between channels [7,8]. We used actual (anonymised) IPTV service consumption data from BT's UK-wide IPTV service to understand capacity requirements at the edge of the network. The data set from BT's two TV platforms YouView and Cardinal covers a three week period across more than 4,000 exchanges.

For the analysis we computed the peak concurrent bandwidth per second per exchange. BT's multicast delivery is user- and platform-agnostic. Time overlaps

© Springer International Publishing AG 2017
M. Bramer and M. Petridis (Eds.): SGAI-AI 2017, LNAI 10630, pp. 417–422, 2017.
https://doi.org/10.1007/978-3-319-71078-5_36

between joining and leaving customers on a channel are immaterial and a single channel-session is delivered to a geographical region for as long as there is at least one subscriber across any platform. Channel sessions were created from set-top box (STB) session activity per exchange, aggregating over multiple individual subscriptions over time. For the analysis the data was aggregated to concurrent user-agnostic, platform-agnostic channel-sessions. When a channel-session at an exchange sees a state change (start/stop), the concurrent bitrate delivered to the geography changes. In addition to active STBs per exchange per second, the number of TV- and broadband-enabled customers were also matched to an exchange to aid the modelling.

We also analysed the peak VBR for each channel across the 15 busiest exchanges for a single day (800 million rows of data, 32 GB compressed) to understand the bandwidth savings VBR gives over a channel's constant bitrate (CBR) before encoding. Doing this for the whole three week nationwide data set would have required two Petabytes of data and that was not feasible. We know that VBR gives us a comfortable safety margin and therefore we can run our analysis with global concurrent CBR maxima for each exchange at one-second granularity over the three-week trial period. Due to the commercially sensitive nature of the data we are unable to report exact values on capacities or service uptake. However, our methods described in this paper do not rely on specific values and apply to any IPTV service.

2   Modelling Exchange Capacity

Monitoring the actual peak concurrent TV traffic in an exchange is time consuming and costly because it requires either monitoring all TV sessions across all connected customers or live data monitoring in the exchange via probes which require hardware investments. Ideally, an IPTV provider would monitor capacity requirement indirectly via features that are easily obtainable and then give an early warning that more capacity might be required. Before an investment decision is made an exchange could then be analysed on a more detailed level using traffic data. We have used two machine learning approaches – decision trees and clustering – to identify drivers of capacity. The objective was to find out if such methods can provide sufficient information for capacity planning. After cleansing the available data we arrived at tens of millions of sessions across more than 4,000 exchanges across the UK (3.5 GB). For each exchange the daily peak conncurrent CBR values (PCV) were computed where sessions were available resulting in just under 14,000 rows with the following features:

- F_1–F_3: Proportions of PCV broken down by content resolution (SD, HD and UHD)
- F_4, F_5: Proportions of PCV broken down by BT's two TV platforms
- F_6: Number of concurrently active STBs at the time of PCV
- F_7–F_9: SD, HD and UHD Proportions of concurrently active STBs
- F_{10}: Ratio of number of concurrently active STBs at time of peak to total number of STBs seen on the day

- F_{11}: Ratio of total number of STBs seen on the day to the number of provisioned TV customers
- F_{12}: Number of TV provisioned customers
- F_{13}: Number of broadband provisioned customers
- L_{PCV}: PCV value discretised into *low, medium, high, very high.*

Features F_1–F_9 require knowing the time of the peak and information about the sessions contributing to the peak. F_{10} and F_{11} require keeping count of active STBs and F_{12} and F_{13} can be obtained without measuring any traffic.

3 Peak Concurrent Capacity Drivers

The purpose of this modelling activity was to understand key drivers for peak concurrent capacity and use this to identify which exchanges should be monitored over time for potential cable link capacity upgrade. We created four discretised classes of peak concurrent bitrates based on an assessment of their relation to cable link capacity. The classes were *low, medium, high, very high.* We used a decision tree as a classifier for the data because we are mainly interested in the feature selection capability of decision tree induction. Algorithms for decision trees are well understood and they use an information theoretic measure to select features and recursively partition the data space. Tree induction algorithms need to be stopped before they over-generalise and create partitions that potentially classify individual data records. This is typically done by restricting the height of the tree, the number of records required to create a new inner node (test node), and the number of records that have to arrive at a leaf node (classifying node). Most commonly, information gain ratio is used as a feature selection method and we have done so in our experiments. However, there is a large variety of measures that can be used [2,3] and it is typically not possible to say which single measure would perform best.

For our experiments we used the community edition of Rapid Miner Studio 6.5 (http://www.rapidminer.com). Using the Decision Tree operator which provides an implementation of Quinlan's C4.5 algorithm [6] we classified peak concurrent demand per exchange. Experiments began with the default model parameters (information gain ratio, minimal leaf size = 2, minimal size for split = 4, minimum gain for split = 0.1, maximal height = 20, using pruning with confidence level 0.25 and pre-pruning with 3 alternative nodes). We then varied leaf size and split size trading off tree complexity with classifier accuracy. The final configuration used a minimum split size of 20 items and a minimum leaf size of 10 items. Figure 1 shows the final decision tree. We cannot provide the actual split values because they reveal information about network capacity.

F_{12}, the number of provisioned TV customers for an exchange, was found to be the most influential feature to explain the size of the peak concurrent demand observed at that exchange. The tree only used one other feature (F_{11}) to distinguish between low and medium peaks for lower values of F_{12}. The higher the

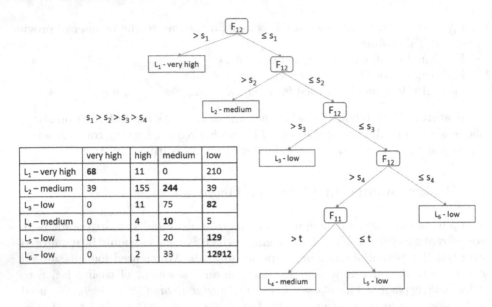

Fig. 1. Decision tree built to classify peak concurrent demand across all exchanges

value of F_{12}, the higher the concurrent bitrate to be expected. It is interesting, from a network design perspective, that none of the other time-dependent features were found to be as influential as both relatively static features.

Note that the tree contains only one leaf node L_1 for the *very high* peak category capturing 68 of those records and that there is no leaf node for the *high* category which contained only 184 records. These records have been mainly classified as *medium* by leaf node L_2. This node also contains the remaining 39 records with a *very high* peak. One method to drive a capacity upgrade programme is to flag and monitor all exchanges with $N > s_2$ TV provisioned customers (split value leading to L_2 – see Fig. 1), capturing all instances of *very high* peak occurrence. This captures also 90% of the *high* records and results overall in 10% of all exchanges being monitored. For exchanges monitored in this way detailed traffic data can be used in connection with the cluster analysis model described in the following section in order to detect changes in viewing behaviour that could lead to higher peaks.

4   Predicting Capacity Maxima

We used the K-means clustering [5] provided by the Clustering operator from RapidMiner to examine the predictability of peak concurrent CBR bitrates per exchange using its daily peak behaviour. The decision tree discussed above could become less accurate over time as customer behaviour changes and higher data rate streams such as HD channels grow in popularity. The method proposed in this section takes into account daily exchange-level behaviour to predict the band of global maximum concurrent bitrate that could be expected.

Features were normalised to range between 0 and 1 for equal bias but, after some trial runs to improve model accuracy, the peak concurrent bitrate value was weighted to be 20 times more influential in the model than other features. This was done to create clear divisions between the various concurrent bitrate bands. We iterated through up to 20 clusters using the Davies-Boudin measure [4] to find the optimal number of clusters with the most differentiation between the clusters. Five clusters were found to be optimal. Figure 2 shows the outcome of the learned clustering model (bitrates obscured for confidentiality reasons).

Exchanges with the highest concurrent bitrates are mapped to cluster c_1, followed by c_0. Clusters c_4, c_2 and c_3 show more overlap in concurrent bitrates. None of the iterations resulted in c_1 being split further to separate the highest concurrent bitrate values from those that are more moderate. This shows that there is little difference in features used between these values – an exchange that has a highest concurrent bitrate at the bottom of the range in c_1 could conceivably see a larger value in the absence of additional information.

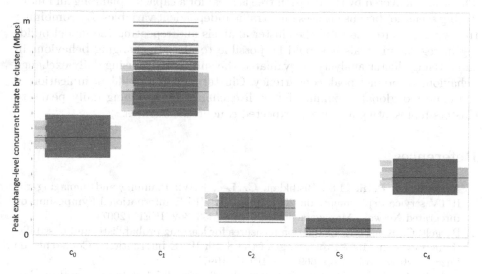

Fig. 2. Result of cluster analysis of daily peak concurrent bitrates per exchange

We label each exchange with the cluster id of its global peak in the training data. By mapping daily peaks to the clusters we can monitor if daily peaks are mapped to the same cluster as the daily peak or not. If they are, we use this a confirmation that the daily behaviour is consistent with the daily behaviour of the global peak. Exchanges mapped to c_1 can be monitored for further capacity upgrade. A mapping to a cluster different from the global peak of an exchange is most risky if it underestimates the expected peak concurrency, resulting in capacity under-provisioning and channel unavailability when capacity is exceeded during global peaks. This method underestimated only 8% of the exchanges where high global peaks were observed. The remaining 92% of exchanges were either correctly mapped to the same cluster as that of the global peak or mismapped between c_4, c_2 or c_3, all of which only contain exchanges with smaller concurrency values where existing cable link capacity is sufficient.

Exchanges whose global peaks were underestimated could behave differently when the global peak occurs compared to daily behaviour, i.e. the global peak is an outlier from daily trends. Adding further features to the clustering model datasets could improve prediction accuracy. For example, one estimates that customers tune away from a given channel at the start of an advertisement break, driving higher channel concurrency as each customer might hop to a different channel. A better understanding of customer journeys across content items at times of peak concurrency could improve the predictability of resulting content diversity and required network capacity to cater for this demand.

5   Conclusions

The result delivered by the decision tree is ideal for a capacity planning and monitoring scenario, because it uses only traffic independent variables. By combining this with the outcome from the cluster analysis and repeating the model building in regular intervals it should be possible to identify changing behaviour in time. Using cluster analysis we evaluated the suitability of using daily exchange behaviour to predict peak concurrency. Clustering can provide an indication of the expected global maximum for each exchange by assigning daily peaks to clusters representing a range of expected concurrent bitrates.

References

1. Agrawal, D., Beigi, M.S., Bisdikian, C., Lee, K.W.: Planning and managing the IPTV service deployment. In: 2007 10th IFIP/IEEE International Symposium on Integrated Network Management, IM'07, pp. 353–362. IEEE (2007)
2. Borgelt, C., Kruse, R.: Evaluation measures for learning probabilistic and possibilistic networks. In: 1997 Proceedings of the Sixth IEEE International Conference on Fuzzy Systems, vol. 2, pp. 669–676. IEEE (1997)
3. Borgelt, C., Kruse, R.: Attributauswahlmaße für die Induktion von Entscheidungsbäumen: Ein Überblick (Feature selection measures for the induction of decision trees: an overview (in German)). Data Mining-Theoretische Aspekte und Anwendungen (Data Min. Theor. Aspects Appl. (in German)), 77–98 (1998)
4. Davies, D.L., Bouldin, D.W.: A cluster separation measure. IEEE Trans. pattern Anal. Mach. Intell. **2**, 224–227 (1979)
5. Höppner, F., Klawonn, F., Kruse, R., Runkler, T.: Fuzzy Cluster Analysis. Wiley, Hoboken (1999)
6. Quinlan, J.R.: Induction of decision trees. Mach. Learn. **1**(1), 81–106 (1986)
7. Ramos, F., Song, F., Rodriguez, P., Gibbens, R., Crowcroft, J., White, I.H.: Constructing an IPTV workload model. In: Proceedings of ACM SICOMM Poster Session 2 (2009)
8. Ramos, F.M.: Mitigating IPTV zapping delay. IEEE Commun. Mag. **51**(8), 128–133 (2013)

Asynchronous Population-Based Hill Climbing Applied to SPICE Model Generation from EM Simulation Data

Lars Nolle[(⊠)] and Jens Werner

Jade University of Applied Sciences, Wilhelmshaven, Germany
{lars.nolle, jens.werner}@jade-hs.de

Abstract. In order to utilise the computing power offered by modern multi-core computer systems, APBHC, a new parallel search algorithm is proposed in this paper. This algorithm uses a number of parallel, asynchronous threads, each performing hill climbing independently of each other whilst sharing information about the best solution found so far amongst all threads. This information is used to adapt the maximum step size during the search. One advantage of this approach is that this new algorithm has no control parameters, which would require tuning. The other advantage is that it can make use of all processing cores available in a computer system. The new method was applied to the problem of Spice Model Generation. It was shown that it out-performs Genetic Algorithms (GA), which were applied to this problem in the past, without the need of time consuming parameter tuning.

Keywords: Electro-Magnetic simulation · Optimisation · Parallel processing · Hill climbing · Self-adaptation · APBHC

1 Introduction

In modern engineering, it is usually important to design systems that not only satisfy the functional requirements but also are as cheap as possible. Here, computational optimisation methods can help to find optimal designs automatically [1]. Various direct search methods have been proposed in the literature, for example Genetic Algorithms (GA) [2], Simulated Annealing (SA) [3], Particle Swarm Optimisation (PSO) [4], or Ant Colony Optimisation (ACO) [5]. All these algorithms start with initial solutions, which are stepwise refined according to a method-dependent strategy. A large number of these refinements are typically needed to arrive at a near-optimal solution. In this process, the bottleneck is often the evaluation of the quality, or fitness, of a new solution. A single evaluation might take anything from minutes to days. Since many modern computers have more than one computing core, parallel computing could offer a solution.

Parallel systems can be classified using Flynn's taxonomy [6]. Modern multi-core processors can run different programs simultaneously, processing different data. Hence they fall into the Multiple-Instruction Multiple-Data (MIMD) category of Flynn's taxonomy. Often, Random-Access Memory (RAM) is shared and equally accessible to

© Springer International Publishing AG 2017
M. Bramer and M. Petridis (Eds.): SGAI-AI 2017, LNAI 10630, pp. 423–428, 2017.
https://doi.org/10.1007/978-3-319-71078-5_37

all computing cores. This is called Uniform Memory Access (UMA) [7] or Parallel RAM (PRAM) [8] and allows for the exchange of information between the different parallel programs.

In order to use parallel computing, the problem at hand needs to be parallelised. One approach is to partition the problem and to let each computing core work on one partition in parallel. When all partitions have been processed one instance of the problem has been solved. The other approach, which was taken in this work, is to have each core to process one instance of the problem in parallel. The processing time of one fitness evaluation might depend on the input data. Also, sometimes, two or more instances of the fitness function have to share a computing core, which increases processing time for those instances. In both cases, it is clearly beneficial if instances do not need to wait for other instances to finish, because otherwise a fast process would waste computing time waiting for slower processes to catch up. This led to the development of Asynchronous Population-Based Hill Climbing (APBHC), which is introduced in the next section. Unlike other parallel search algorithms, such as parallel GRASP [9], APBHC can be used for mixed-integer function optimisation.

2   Asynchronous Population-Based Hill Climbing

Hill Climbing (HC) [10] is a well-established optimisation technique. Here, a trial solution from the neighbourhood of a current solution is evaluated. If the new solution is better than the current, the new solution becomes the current solution. This will be repeated until a stopping criterion holds.

Previously, it was shown that the performance of HC crucially depends on the definition of neighbourhood, i.e. the chosen step size [11]. If the step size is chosen to be too small, HC will eventually get trapped in the nearest local optimum, whereas using a larger step size increases the probability to overcome local optima but at the same time decreases the chance of reaching the global optimum. This led to the development of adaptation schemes like Self-Adaptive Step size Search (SASS) [12], which is a population based Hill-Climbing algorithm that uses sampling to adjust the step size dynamically. This can be seen as collaboration between search entities, which are often called particles. Another example of a population based search algorithm that uses collaboration is Differential Evolution (DE) [13].

In this work, the optimisation problem is solved by n parallel threads, each of which performs hill climbing (Fig. 1). The threads are non-blocking, i.e. asynchronous. Initially, a random solution is generated and evaluated. Since this is so far the only solution, it becomes the global best solution g. This global best solution is stored in shared memory, i.e. memory that can be read by any thread simultaneously. Subsequently the n threads are started. Here, n is the number of processing cores available on the computer system. If a thread has found a better solution than the global best during its search, it updates the global best solution. Figure 2 presents the UML activity diagram showing the strategy of a single thread. Once all the threads have finished their search, the global best solution g is returned as the overall solution. Each thread creates an initial solution randomly. This solution x is evaluated and the search is started. If the stopping criterion does not hold, the Euclidian distance d between x and the global best

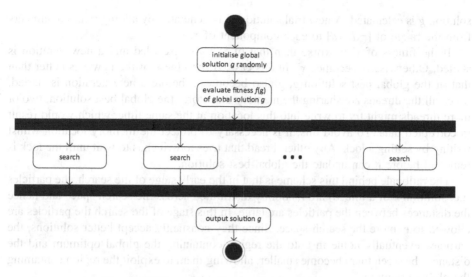

Fig. 1. UML activity diagram for the main program.

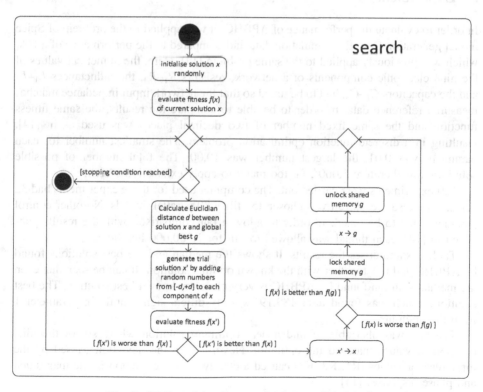

Fig. 2. UML activity diagram for one parallel thread.

solution g is calculated. A new trial solution x' is generated by adding random numbers from the range of $[-d, +d]$ to each component of x.

If the fitness of x' is worse than that of x, x' is discarded and a new iteration is started. Otherwise, x becomes x'. In this case, if the fitness of the new x is better than that of the global best solution g, g also becomes x before a new iteration is started. Since all the threads are sharing the memory that stores the global best solution, two or more threads might try to write into this location at the same time, which would result in corrupted data. To avoid this, it is necessary to protect the memory location whilst writing by setting a lock. Any other thread that tries to write has to wait until the lock is removed before it can update the global best solution.

The rationale behind this scheme is that in the early stage of the search, the particles (i.e. solution x of a thread) are randomly distributed across the search space and hence the distances between the particles are large. In this stage of the search the particles are allowed to explore the search space. Since they constantly accept better solutions, the particles eventually home in onto the region containing the global optimum and the distances between them become smaller, allowing them to exploit the region containing the global optimum.

3   Experiments

In order to evaluate the performance of APBHC, it was applied to the problem of Spice model generation from EM simulation data and compared to the performance of a GA, which was previously applied to the same problem [14]. Here, the numerical values of the nine electronic components of a network, resistors R_1–R_3, the inductances L_1–L_3 and the capacitors C_1–C_3, had to be tuned so that the network input impedance matches measured reference data. In order to be able to compare the results, the same fitness function and the same fixed number of two decimal places was used as in [14], resulting in a discrete function optimisation problem. The smallest number for each parameter was 0.01, the largest number was 10.00. The total number of possible solutions was therefore $1,000^9$, far too many to apply exhaustive search.

100 experiments were carried out. The computer used for these experiments had 32 cores. As a result, each run was chosen to utilise 30 parallel threads. No other control parameter had to be tuned. In order to allow a fair comparison with the results published in [14], each thread was allowed to run for 1,000,000 iterations.

Table 1 summarises the results. It shows the median and the best solutions found by APBHC and GA together with the known optimal solution. It can be seen that even the median solution found by APBHC is very close the known best solution. The best solution, which was found after 189.191 s, only differs significantly in parameter 1 from the optimum.

The GA was also able to find a near optimum solution where six of the nine component values matched the optimum. Nevertheless, the deviation caused by the three resistor values (R1, R2, R3) caused a clearly visible deviation in the magnitude and phase responses [14].

Table 1. Optimisation results found by APBHC algorithm.

Parameter	1	2	3	4	5	6	7	8	9
Name	R_1	R_2	R_3	L_1	L_2	L_3	C_1	C_2	C_3
Median APBHC	0.18	0.21	0.49	7.13	7.94	8.95	0.01	0.02	0.03
Best APBHC	**0.08**	**0.37**	**0.45**	**7.00**	**8.00**	**9.00**	**0.01**	**0.02**	**0.03**
Median GA [14]	0.27	0.26	0.32	8.91	8.22	8.94	0.01	0.03	0.03
Best GA [14]	**0.01**	**0.22**	**0.47**	**7.00**	**8.00**	**9.00**	**0.01**	**0.02**	**0.03**
Known solution	*0.20*	*0.30*	*0.40*	*7.00*	*8.00*	*9.00*	*0.01*	*0.02*	*0.03*

Based on the best solution and the median solution found by APBHC, the corresponding frequency responses have been calculated and plotted together with the response of the known optimum into the graph of Fig. 3.

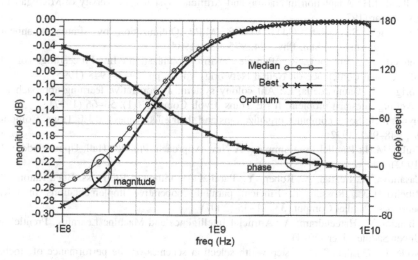

Fig. 3. Magnitude and phase response comparing best and median result from APBHC over 100 runs versus the known optimum solution.

Here, magnitude and phase of the complex valued data are shown separately. With the scale used the traces of the best solution (thin lines with crosses) seem to follow exactly the traces of the optimum solution (solid thick line). Also for the median solution the phase response (thin line with circles) follows the optimum, while the magnitude shows a certain deviation in particular at the lower frequency range (below 1 GHz). This clearly outperforms the best solution found by GA [14].

4 Conclusions

In this work, APBHC, a novel asynchronous, population-based variation of the hill climbing search strategy was introduced, which utilises multi-core hardware architectures of modern computer systems. The parallel threads share information about the best solution found so far, and use this information to escape local optima by adjusting their step sizes dynamically during the search. Not only does APBHC make use of all processing cores available on a computer system, it also has only one control parameter, which is the number of parallel threads. Since this number is set to the number of available processing units, it does not require time consuming control parameter tuning. It was shown that the new algorithm outperformed GA for the problem of Spice model tuning.

References

1. Nolle, L., Krause, R., Cant, R.J.: On practical automated engineering design. In: Al-Begain, K., Bargiela, A. (eds.) Seminal Contributions to Modelling and Simulation. SFMA, pp. 115–140. Springer, Cham (2016). https://doi.org/10.1007/978-3-319-33786-9_10
2. Holland, J.H.: Adaptation in Natural and Artificial Systems. University of Michigan Press, Ann Arbor (1975)
3. Kirkpatrick, S., Gelatt, C.D., Vecchi, M.P.: Optimization by simulated annealing: quantitative study. J. Stat. Phys. **34**, 975–986 (1984)
4. Kennedy, J., Eberhart, R.: Particle swarm optimization. In: Proceedings of IEEE International Conference on Neural Networks, vol. 4, pp. 1942–1948 (1995)
5. Dorigo, M., Gambardella, L.: Ant colony system: a cooperative learning approach to the travelling salesman problem. IEEE Trans. Evol. Comput. **1**(1), 53–66 (1997)
6. Flynn, M.J.: Some computer organizations and their effectiveness. IEEE Trans. Comput. **21**(9), 948–960 (1972)
7. Coffin, M.H.: Parallel Programming: A New Approach. Prentice Hall, Upper Saddle River (1992)
8. Casanova, H., Legrad, A., Robert, Y.: Parallel Algorithms. CRC Press, Boca Raton (2009)
9. Ribeiro, C.C., Rosseti, I.: Efficient parallel cooperative implementations of GRASP heuristics. Parallel Comput. **33**, 21–35 (2007)
10. Chandra, V., Hareendram, A.: Artificial Intelligence and Machine Learning. Prentice Hall, Upper Saddle River (2014)
11. Nolle, L.: On the effect of step width selection schemes on the performance of stochastic local search strategies. In: Proceedings of the 18th European Simulation Multiconference ESM 2004, Magdeburg, Germany, pp. 149–153, 13–14 June 2004
12. Nolle, L.: On a hill-climbing algorithm with adaptive step size: towards a control parameter-less black-box optimisation algorithm. Adv. Soft Comput. **38**, 587–595 (2006)
13. Storn, R., Price, K.: Differential evolution - a simple and efficient heuristic for global optimization over continuous spaces. J. Global Optim. **11**, 341–359 (1997)
14. Werner, J., Nolle, L.: Spice model generation from EM simulation data using integer coded genetic algorithms. In: Bramer, M., Petridis, M. (eds.) Research and Development in Intelligent Systems XXXIII, pp. 355–367. Springer, Cham (2016). https://doi.org/10.1007/978-3-319-47175-4_26

Author Index

Printed in the United States
By Bookmasters

Printed in the United States
By Bookmasters